No More Worlds To Conquer

No More Worlds
To Conquer

Sixteen People Who Defined Their Time –
And What They Did Next

Chris Wright

The Friday Project
An imprint of HarperCollins*Publishers*
1 London Bridge Street
London SE1 9GF

www.harpercollins.co.uk

First published in Great Britain by The Friday Project in 2015

1

A catalogue record for this book is available
from the British Library

ISBN 978-0-00-757542-8

Typeset in Garamond MT by Palimpsest Book Production Limited,
Falkirk, Stirlingshire

Printed and bound in the United States of America by RR Donnelley.

Find out more about HarperCollins and the environment at
www.harpercollins.co.uk/green

Contents

For Lovely Hanes

And in memory of my grandparents, Les and Mary Butler and Arthur and Monica Wright, with too late apologies for all the things I didn't ask them

Introduction

It was in the town of Dora, Oregon, in a room lined with bookshelves with a combined length equal to that of the *Bismarck* – and not by coincidence – that the question first arose.

I had been interviewing Don Walsh, who at the time was the only man alive to have been to the deepest point in the world's oceans, a feat he had accomplished fully fifty years earlier when he piloted a wonky steel-and-glue contraption called a bathyscaphe to Challenger Deep, on the floor of the Pacific Ocean's Mariana Trench. For an hour he had been patiently narrating the story of the voyage to the bottom – the very, very bottom, a place less frequently visited by man than the Moon. Though polite, he had told his story many times before, and his tone was automatic.

It was time to change the subject. What happened next, I asked? What was the next step in life after the voyage?

His face brightened and lightened. It lost five years in an instant. 'Well,' he said, 'a lot of people think I died.'

What Walsh *did* do next was anything but die. He commanded a submarine. He served in both the Korean and Vietnam wars. He gained three graduate degrees, worked in the Pentagon, founded the Institute for Marine and Coastal Studies at the

University of Southern California with the rank of dean, and built a successful marine consultancy. He visited the Arctic and Antarctic so often – over fifty times – and did so much there that there is an Antarctic ridge, the Walsh Spur, named after him. He has dived in Russian *Mir* submersibles on the *Titanic, Bismarck* and the North Atlantic Ridge. He told me about these things with bracing enthusiasm, an hour and a half of detail. And he did so with such radiance because, by and large, nobody ever asks him about any of those things. For the rest of his life, all anyone will ever want to know about is the time that he went to the bottom of the sea in that funny little submersible.

We do odd things with biography. We might occasionally immerse ourselves in the detail of a famous person's life but, ultimately, we reduce them to a line, a statement, based on the most pivotal thing they ever did. The former prime minister. The Olympic medallist. The first man to the bottom of the sea.

But what happens when that biographical kernel, that top line of the Wikipedia entry, is set so young in life? Walsh was twenty-eight in January 1960 when he climbed into the *Trieste*, an ungainly, thick-walled steel spherical cabin suspended under a thin metal float filled with gasoline ('it looked like an explosion in a boiler factory,' he said), and sank through more than 7 miles of the Pacific Ocean into the Mariana Trench. There was a lot of life left to fill after that, and so he filled it, to an exemplary degree, and still does. But all that living will never change the single-line distillation of his life: the man who went to the bottom.

And Walsh was not alone. The period from the end of the Second World War through to the early 1970s was one of extraordinary exploration, bravery, vision and innovation in America. From Chuck Yeager breaking the sound barrier for the first time in 1947, through to the Mercury, Gemini and Apollo programmes culminating in six lunar landings from 1969 to 1972, this was an era in which anything seemed possible. It was a time demanding unambiguous heroes, their profiles uncontaminated by the investigation of their personal lives that would be expected today, and instead slavishly venerated by *Life* magazine and its peers. Tall poppies aren't a problem in America, and they certainly weren't then; there was no need to chop a hero down, and instead they were celebrated, necessary, a catalyst for pride and hope as the Cold War and Vietnam ushered in an unfamiliar era of suspicion and cynicism. The crew of *Apollo 8*, the first to leave Earth orbit, the first three people to see our world as a whole out of their window and to perceive it as an orb hanging in space, would be told upon their return that they had saved 1968, a rare hopeful promise in a year of assassinations, war and unrest.

Yeager, Walsh, Armstrong, Aldrin: a vital vitality.

Like Walsh, all these heroic figures were young. Yeager broke the sound barrier over the Muroc airfield in Southern California aged just twenty-four. The Apollo men had spent much longer in training, patiently waiting for their Moonshot, but still most were in their early thirties when they walked on the Moon. The popular imagination keeps them in a form of suspended animation, preserved in their moment of heroic deed.

But that's just not how life is. So what did they all do next? How did they find meaning in the rest of their lives when the defining event of each life had so obviously already taken place?

*

I am fascinated by these American adventurers, and I suspect I'm not alone in that. I'm forty-three now, a long way from being young, and yet the last men to set foot on the Moon on *Apollo 17* did so before my first birthday. Like many of my generation, I look back on the achievements of that era, and in particular the Moon landings, with a sense of disbelief that so extraordinary a thing could have been achieved in a time when, to our modern eyes, everything – whirring and hissing computers the size of rooms, stocky tin cars with no seat belts, carpets and curtains in nuclear-blast orange – looked so utterly primitive. And that is part of the appeal: people using basic materials and technologies did extraordinary things, just to see if they could be done, and ideally tried to do them before some Russians did exactly the same thing. When Joe Kittinger skydived from 31 kilometres up in 1960 and set a record that would take fifty-two years to beat (and only then with his considerable assistance), he didn't do so in some extraordinary carbon-fibre spacecraft. He attached a gondola to a hot air balloon, waited until it cleared almost our entire atmosphere, and jumped out the side, hoping his hand wouldn't explode because there was a leak in his pressure suit.

Then there were the people themselves. There doesn't seem to be room for heroes today: we are just too cynical. No war is straightforwardly right and justified any more, if they ever were, so we will never again really celebrate an individual fighter pilot, a sniper or a warship commander. That post-war era in America seems to be cast in brighter, sharper colours, without shades and hues of complexity and doubt. That is wrong, of course; there was just as much moral ambiguity in that era as any other. Many of these things happened, after all, amid the Cold War, which was hardly the most noble spur to achievement and endeavour. But to dip back into that time, with its square-jawed heroes and its sense of possibility, is to take a holiday into the ribald technicolour of Space Race America.

Personally, I had other reasons to seek these people out. In the years before the Walsh interview, my grandparents had died within the space of a few years, and I was living overseas for

4

the passing of all four of them. I had come to realize, far too late, all the questions I had not asked them about their lives. One, my grandfather, had served on a tiny corvette called the HMS *Honeysuckle* in the British Navy during the Second World War, mostly escorting convoys over the top of Scandinavia through the Arctic Ocean to the Russian port of Murmansk, pitching and plunging in the freezing ocean while looking out for German U-boats. Then he served in the North African campaign. I know this not because of anything I ever asked him, but because the grandson of one of his crewmates researched the history of the ship and self-published a book about it, which he kindly sent to my family. If I look back now, the only thing I can ever remember my grandfather telling me about it himself was how terrifying the women were in Murmansk. This relatively sudden loss made me realize, belatedly, that once they're gone, they can't tell you anything, so you need to hear their stories while you still have them. And this, too, led me to seek out these fading Americans in their eighties while they were still there to be spoken to.

At first, I went to see them whilst working as a freelance journalist for magazines, chiefly *Discovery Channel Magazine,* publications which inevitably were more interested in visiting the moments that made them famous than their still-alive afterlife. But those interviews gave me the opportunity to put the same question I had asked Walsh – what happened next – to others, from Yeager to the Moonwalkers. After all, they had each had to wrestle with this feeling of standing on a summit and contemplating nothing but descent and decline. 'After *Apollo* I was standing on top of the mountain,' Charlie Duke, the tenth man on the Moon, said. 'There was nowhere else to go.'

*

But why stop there?

American explorers are a lot of fun, but when you think about it, the sense of being known for a single moment has a more widespread utility.

You can apply the same idea anywhere. What do you do if, despite a lifetime of effort in recorded music, you are still only known for one song? Ask Gloria Gaynor, whose 'I Will Survive' has such a remarkable resonance for so many people. What happens if you are an athlete or gymnast and your career peaks at fourteen? Nobody knows better than Nadia Comaneci, who scored the first perfect 10 in Olympic competition, then the second – and the third, fourth, fifth, sixth and seventh – in Montreal in 1976 before even reaching puberty. Ask Reinhold Messner what comes next when you have climbed all the really tall mountains, and forgotten England full-back Ray Wilson what you do after winning the World Cup in 1966 (in his case, turn your back on the game and become an undertaker in Huddersfield).

Not everyone is known for a positive moment, something that they have built towards. For others, the indelible single-line epitaph is something terrible that they have had to overcome. What did the captain and the chief flight attendant of a terrible air disaster, *United 232*, do to step forward from that ordeal? How about victims of lawless captivity, like Lebanon hostage John McCarthy and Sandakan prison-camp survivor Russ Ewin?

One of the great appeals of these people is that the answer to my central question – what next? – varies so much from one person to another. The chapters on the astronauts look at this in more detail, but if one just considers the twelve men who walked on the Moon, hardly any took what one could describe as a standard path. Armstrong retreated to academia, Aldrin to alcohol and depression before turning his life around, Bean to art, Irwin and Duke to religion, Mitchell to a lifelong study of consciousness and extraterrestrial life, Cernan to something like statesmanship, Conrad to commercial aviation, Scott to research and development (and a brief engagement to Anna Ford), Schmitt to climate change-denying Republican politics, Shepard to banking and big business, and Young to a lifelong devotion to NASA – probably the only instance in Apollo of someone doing what you would have expected them to do.

For some of my interviewees, the question was borderline ridiculous. By the 1980s, Nadia Comaneci was living a miserable life in Ceausescu's Romania, under constant surveillance from the Securitate following the defection of her coach to the USA, a step it would take her eight years to find the courage to repeat herself. It's not like she was sifting through sponsorship opportunities and wondering how to find meaning in later life. She was trying to find enough food to keep standing up.

At another extreme, some can put away their moment of fame as if in a box, compartmentalize it and move seamlessly on. Reinhold Messner speaks of six life stages, segmented with sturdy clarity, and considers his Himalayan peaks only the second of them. Done, dusted, finished; what next?

For some, the level of recognition afforded to their great moment grates with them, as if the wrong bit of their life is being venerated. The only reason I got an interview with Bill Anders, one of the *Apollo 8* crew and the man who took the famous *Earthrise* photo that is on the cover of this book, is because he realized he would finally get to talk about things that weren't *Apollo 8* or the famous *Earthrise* photo. Anders has led an extraordinarily successful life in business and considers it, for him, a greater achievement than Apollo was.

Others, for one reason or another, have not really moved on, whether by choice or inability. *United 232* captain Al Haynes has been delivering talks about his famous crash, many thousands of times by now, ever since. Some have tried to build an ordeal into an inspiration for later life: former Lebanon hostage John

McCarthy now speaks with considerable passion on behalf of the Palestinian people, despite having spent five and a half years in captivity without trial or even being *accused* of a crime, in an imprisonment imposed at least partly in the name of Palestinians.

They almost all recognize the challenge or oddity of being known for a moment, with some exceptions. Chuck Yeager, a magnificently blunt man for whom the phrase 'doesn't suffer fools gladly' was surely coined, resists any attempt to prompt introspection about the achievement he will always be known for. Life for him has been straightforward: he loves to fly, and keeps on doing it. He was eighty-nine when I interviewed him and had piloted an F-16 only the previous year. Still, while Yeager is far from an easy interviewee, you have to admire an eighty-nine-year-old still insistently living in the present.

Some have moved on by encouraging others to repeat their feats, even to beat them. Joe Kittinger's 31-kilometre skydive in 1960 was preposterous. No other word will do. For half a century nobody else did anything remotely like it. But when a high-tech team using the best of twenty-first-century technology allowed Felix Baumgartner to beat that record in 2012, the young pretender's mentor and guide was none other than Kittinger himself.

There are some obvious omissions. Where, you might ask, are all the women? Why is almost everyone white? Both of these things are partly a function of my starting point, with American adventurers who had come out of the post-war military. It's an unavoidable fact that they were almost all white men. Women weren't allowed to take part in the Apollo programme; the Soviet female space pioneers, notably Valentina Tereshkova, are not easily convinced to give interviews; and tragically the first two American women in space, Sally Ride and Judy Resnik, both died far too young. No African-American, male or female, went to space until the 1980s (and the first was, incidentally, not American but Cuban, going up on the Soviet Union's *Soyuz 38* in 1980). The parts of this book that deal with the space-race era — that is, about half of it — are unfortunately an accurate snapshot of opportunity at the time.

The achievements that made these people famous are well worth revisiting. They're famous for a good reason, after all, be it climbing all fourteen 8,000-metre peaks, leaving Earth orbit for the first time, or saving 185 lives on *United 232*. I was as captivated to hear them talk about these moments as anyone. But their attempts to move on, to define what happens when they wake up the next day and the next and the next after that, knowing that the moment their lives have been building towards has suddenly switched to the past tense: that's the great unknown in most of these remarkable lives.

*

Author's note: The use of metric and imperial measures varies from chapter to chapter according to what the interviewee used. American chapters, such as those about the astronauts, use feet and inches, pounds and ounces, because that's how Americans describe length and weight; Europeans like Reinhold Messner talk in metres so are quoted as such.

1

Don Walsh

Dora, Oregon, isn't much of a town. It is said to have an official population of ten – though residents reckon it might just have cracked three figures by now – and boasts not a single shop. There's a fire station that doubles as a library and a community centre, but it seems to be closed today. The town is less a conurbation than a loose affiliation of ranches, and in one of them, in a room surrounded by thousands of books, sipping tea from a mug emblazoned with the logo of the CIA, sits the only man alive to have been to the bottom of the ocean. The very, very bottom.

On 23 January 1960, Don Walsh, then a twenty-eight-year-old navy lieutenant, and a Swiss scientist called Jacques Piccard climbed into a top-heavy submersible called the *Trieste,* little more than a steel ball suspended beneath a gasoline-filled float. In it, they sank 7 miles to the bottom of the Mariana Trench, 250 miles off Guam in the Western Pacific Ocean. It is the deepest point in the world's seas and the lowest open point in the Earth's crust.

When I meet Walsh in Oregon in early 2010, fifty years have passed since he – or anyone else – went to Challenger Deep. Piccard died in 2008, and although the movie director James

Cameron has since repeated the feat, at the time of my meeting with Walsh he is the only man who can speak from experience about life on the floor of the world, 6,000 fathoms down. A friend suggests dubbing him 'The Hillary of the Ocean', but that's to do him a disservice: hundreds have followed Hillary and Tenzing's steps up Everest (and besides, if you dropped Everest into the Mariana Trench, there would still be about 2 miles of water above its peak). Even with Cameron, four times as many people have walked on the Moon as have ventured as deep as Walsh.

Walsh today, white-haired but utterly sharp, at first has a certain military cantankerousness rendered likeable by a dry wit. 'SubMARiner?' he interjects when I pronounce the word in what I think is the correct way. 'I'm not a subMARiner. A subMARiner is an inferior mariner. I'm a submarEENer. One who does submarEENing.'

Dora seems a curious place to find this pioneer of the sea, but that's the way Walsh likes it. 'I have bonded with my fellow man as much as I care to in this lifetime,' he says. 'My nearest neighbour is a mile away. If more than half a dozen cars go by the front of the house during the day my wife starts to complain about the traffic.' Is he a recluse? 'Not reclusive,' he says. 'Just selective.'

*

The *Trieste* was a remarkable endeavour, absolutely in the spirit of 1950s and 1960s exploration in America – the space race, the right stuff, Americans doing absurd things with technology and curiosity just to see what could be done. And the *Trieste* mission, though painstakingly planned through more than a year of research and testing, is a perfect adventure script: a capsule whose pieces were held together with glue; chucking dynamite into the ocean and timing the echoes in order to find the deepest point because there were no decent maps; fixing a weakness by jamming the craft against a timber battering ram with a forklift truck; ignoring an order from naval command in San Diego to abort the dive because of the sea state, replying only when the craft was 20,000 feet down. Then 5 miles into the dive, in a capsule too small for either man to stretch out completely, they heard a loud snapping sound that turned out to be an external window cracking. So what did they do? They carried on down regardless, confident in their research and their gear.

The journey really started for Walsh in 1958 when, as a submarine lieutenant, he volunteered to work on a programme leased by the US Navy from a family of Swiss scientists, the Piccards. The Piccards are a whole other story: pioneers of exploration so revered that *Star Trek: The Next Generation* named its captain, Jean-Luc Picard, after them. They had a submersible called the *Trieste*, an ungainly contraption known as a bathyscaphe comprising a thick-walled spherical cabin for crew suspended beneath a thin metal shell, called a float, filled with gasoline. Walsh recalls seeing it for the first time. 'I thought to myself: I will never get into that thing.'

The *Trieste*'s premise was simple: vent the ballast tanks to sink; slow or stop the descent by releasing solid weights filled with small steel pellets; and then, because the gasoline in the float is lighter than the water around it, return to the surface. The sphere itself, which would have to protect the crew from pressure 1,100 times greater than at the surface, was made of three rings, 5 to 7 inches thick and glued together with epoxy at the joints. When the admiral who ran the navy's Bureau of Ships came to see the *Trieste* and asked how it was fastened together, Walsh told him about the epoxy. 'Lieutenant Walsh,' he replied, 'the navy does not glue its ships together.'

Considering it was such a grand ambition, Challenger Deep

was little talked about at first. 'It wasn't until after I had reported to the navy laboratory to be assigned to the *Trieste* project that I knew something big was in the works,' Walsh says. 'It was never mentioned in the briefing to the commodore for good reason, because the top navy brass had not approved – had not even *heard* of this project.' Plus Walsh's experience of extreme depth was at this stage rather limited. 'You have to understand, I came to this job as a submarine officer; as a navigator I was only concerned about making sure you had enough water under the keel so you don't run into the side of a continent. I had no clue, really, how deep the ocean was, or how people dive in it. I wasn't a diver, I was a submariner.' He says it again for emphasis. 'A submarEEner.'

He learned fast, and so did the *Trieste* team, running test dives in San Diego before taking the bathyscaphe apart and putting it on a commercial cargo ship to Guam, the nearest major island to the Mariana Trench, in the late summer of 1959. In November that year, Jacques Piccard and navy chief scientist Andreas Rechnitzer broke the world depth record, reaching 18,150 feet. But there was deeper still to go – much, much deeper – and Walsh was keen to push further.

In the spirit of the time, Walsh and his Office of Naval Research colleagues – an interesting, pioneering civil science agency within the government, which he recalls as 'very free-wheeling: you placed your money on your bets' – dealt with difficult natural challenges with simple ingenuity. So when the *Trieste* came back from its record dive with failed glue joints because of the difference in sea temperatures during the dive, the team's machinist fixed the problem with a forklift truck and a timber battering ram to put the pieces in the right alignment, holding them together with a series of bands. 'It was a remarkable piece of shade-tree engineering and it saved the project,' Walsh says.

Against this spirit of experiment, Walsh still had to get approval from the navy, which he eventually sought face to face with Admiral Arleigh Burke, effectively the head of the navy, in Washington, DC. Burke was reluctant. 'The navy in its exuberance had claimed we were going to put the first Earth-orbiting satellite up. And they'd fire these rockets out of Cape Canaveral and they'd splash into the bay or they'd have to destruct them because they were heading for Kansas City. It was very embarrassing.' Consequently, Walsh was told to garner no publicity: it would be promoted only *after* it was successful. 'You tell [Lieutenant] Schumacher [who would be topside on Walsh's dive], if he doesn't come back up with Walsh, I'm going to have his balls,' Burke told Walsh.

In January 1960 Walsh dived in *Trieste* to 23,000 feet in the Nero Deep near Guam; the stage was set for the ultimate test. So, on 19 January, Walsh and most of his team set off in a corvette to the dive site and set about trying to find the deepest point by dropping dynamite into the ocean and timing the echoes. 'We didn't know exactly where the deepest place was: there were no maps or charts,' he says. 'We didn't care about exact depth measurement, only that fourteen seconds was deeper than twelve seconds.'

At the same time a navy tug pulled the bathyscaphe towards the dive site at 5 knots. It arrived on dive day, 23 January, in 'a pretty good sea state, 6 or 7 on the Beaufort scale'. For a craft like the *Trieste*, that was a challenge, but Walsh said they never considered aborting: 'If we'd towed it back in, our masters in San Diego would have said: that's it.' In fact, they did exactly that. But, fortunately, by the time the message reached them the *Trieste* had already dived. 'The chief scientist put it in his pocket, walked around for a while, then sent a message back to San Diego saying "*Trieste* passing 20,000 feet".'

Walsh and Piccard were together in the snug sphere for nine

hours. 'It was close. Jacques was 2 metres in altitude, and we had all our kit – equipment, instruments, cameras and stuff. We kind of coiled up inside it. But, shit, it's no more crowded than sitting back in peasant class on a trans-Pacific flight for fourteen hours. You want to know about discomfort, just fly from here to Singapore.' That's for my benefit: he knows it's the flight I have to take to get home.

The *Trieste* began descending at 8.30 a.m. and hit its first obstacle when it started bouncing along on the top of a thermocline, a thin invisible layer between two parts of the ocean with different temperatures, at about 300 feet under. Eventually Piccard and Walsh valved off enough gasoline to break through, and began sinking in earnest. It took five hours to get down.

It was dull in the main, but enlivened considerably at 31,000 feet. 'We heard and felt a giant bang.' All instruments looked fine – so they carried on.

From a distance this seems extraordinary: they were on a craft untested at this depth, deeper than anything had ever gone before, heard a bang clearly from the craft, yet they thought it was safe to proceed? 'We didn't *think* it was OK to carry on. We *knew* it was OK to carry on because our readings were normal.'

The *Trieste* sank further and further, deeper than they had expected, until finally the loom of the lights was visible, reflecting from the floor. Piccard ditched more shot to slow the descent and they made an easy landing; the gauge (wrongly, it would later turn out) read 37,800 feet. But this was to be no 'giant-leap-for-mankind' moment; the voice-modulated sonar system they used to communicate with the top had a slow data rate and wasn't built for sermons. 'We shook hands, congratulated each other and called topside on the underwater telephone. We told Larry Schumacher we had reached the bottom, 6,000 fathoms, and it was good.' What did he reply? 'He just acknowledged. You kept your messages pretty simple.'

There, it became clear what the bang was: a crack across the window in the entrance hatch. Bad as that sounds, it wasn't dangerous on the floor, since the entrance tube was always flooded during a dive, meaning the window was not a pressure boundary. It did, though, create a chance of being trapped at the surface. 'If we couldn't get out we'd be stuck in there for a few days, feasting on Hershey Bars.'

There is a sense of anticlimax about the bottom. No photos, since the landing had stirred up a cloud of sediment which didn't disperse; and only twenty minutes on the bottom since they needed to surface in daylight. 'It was like being in a bowl of milk. We didn't get any pictures.' The highlight, instead, was Piccard sighting a foot-long flatfish, 'like a sole or halibut', which confounded oceanographers given the intense pressure on the ocean floor.

The journey back to the surface was smooth. Once there Walsh fired off an emergency beacon transmitter common to the air force, and the support ships were quickly upon them. 'There was a sense of achievement. And some celebration: we worked like hell for almost a year to get to this place. And we did what we said we'd do, pretty much on time. We kept our word.' There was little celebration, though, 200 miles out at sea. 'After dinner I was ready to have a nap.'

A period of celebrity followed, a ticker-tape parade, and a meeting with President Eisenhower. Walsh didn't enjoy it at all, except as an opportunity to lobby for future exploration. 'I guess I'm genetically not programmed for celebrity stuff,' he says. 'But it was my duty, because we wanted to make sure the navy's programme – the deep-ocean exploration – got generous support. So I did Congressional hearings, Senate hearings, just talked about what we did. They were quite interested, so I told the story over and over again. But I also had a pitch in there, that we needed to support this kind of work, this capability, and we can't let it get away. I didn't enjoy the celebrity very much but it was the key to getting the marketing message out.'

It didn't pay: not long after the dive the navy decided it was not safe to dive below 20,000 feet, so the *Trieste* became, and remained until Cameron's 2012 return, a unique event.

For his part, Walsh says the motivation was not a record per se. 'I was never driven to go deeper and deeper,' he says. 'There was a singular goal out there and that was the deepest place in the ocean. Getting there required a systematic testing of the vehicle. Things broke, we fixed them. By the time we made the deepest dive we were pretty sure everything was going to work just fine.'

*

Don Walsh was my first attempt at interviewing an explorer, or finding one. I had been a financial journalist for the best part of twenty years and had reached the conclusion that I couldn't spend the rest of my life just interviewing bankers: Walsh was my bid to break out and write about something more interesting. Granted, I wasn't around when Walsh made his dive – wouldn't be born for another twelve years, in fact – but, for me, that only increased the appeal. The idea that one could go and find these people, anchored in exploratory history, was mesmerizing. When I pitched the idea of interviewing him on the fiftieth anniversary of his voyage, *Discovery Channel Magazine* jumped at it, which was a big moment for me, though I neglected to mention that I had not only not secured the interview yet, but had no idea where Walsh actually was.

How do you find an explorer, an adventurer, an astronaut? It's easiest to find the ones who have written books, and therefore have a publisher who can be contacted; or have something to sell, like Alan Bean, the fourth man on the Moon and now a professional artist. Walsh fits into neither of these camps, but I did hear that he sometimes served as an expert lecturer on tours of Antarctica, or on high-end tourism submersible visits to wrecks such as the *Titanic*. I reached Deep Ocean Expeditions, a diving group specializing in trips to the *Titanic* and *Bismarck* wrecks, hydrothermal vents and even the North Pole, beneath the ice. I asked its founder, Peter Batson, to forward an email request to Walsh, which he did, with some thoughts of his own. '*Trieste*'s Challenger Deep dive is one of the pivotal moments in oceanography and deep-sea exploration,' he said. 'What's really mind-boggling is they did it when deep-submergence technology was in its infancy. In 1960, knowledge of the deep oceans was sketchy at best. Piccard and Walsh really were diving into the unknown.'

The thrill of finding an iconic name, a Buzz Aldrin or a Chuck Yeager, in my inbox amid the analyst research notes and payroll queries and Viagra ads, has never become routine, and so it was with delight and trepidation that I checked my BlackBerry before going to bed in Singapore one January night in 2010 and saw the name 'Don Walsh' on the screen. At first he wasn't keen, wanting instead to send a written account of his voyage, but he seemed so astonished at my willingness to fly from Singapore to Oregon to see him that he agreed to an interview. There was just one thing, he said: he was off to Antarctica for a month the following week and it would have to wait until he got back. He was seventy-eight at the time, and this would be his twenty-seventh visit to Antarctica. This was something I would learn frequently in the course of researching these people: that adventurers don't tend to grow old gracefully and fade into the background.

I caught a flight from Singapore via Seoul to San Francisco one day in March 2010, with a car-hire reservation so I could drive up the California coast to Eureka for the night, before getting up early the next day and driving into Oregon for the interview. I had a sense of boyish excitement the like of which I couldn't recall since meeting Liverpool footballers in my youth. It wasn't just Walsh himself, but the realization of a dream so many British people have of hitting the open American road. I had plotted the route carefully: over the Golden Gate Bridge; a pause at the Marin Highlands to take some pictures and try out the new Canon I had bought for the trip; the coast road past the Mendocino Headlands through Fort Bragg; the giant trees of the Humboldt Redwoods State Park. My Lonely Planet *California* was snug beside me in the aircraft seat. I simply could not believe that anything this fun could ever be considered work.

But then, as the plane lined up for descent into San Francisco, the California coast clearly visible through the window, a sudden shiver gripped me. I have two driving licences, British and Australian, and tended to use the Australian one overseas since it has a photo ID, which my old paper-based British licence did not have. That's what I had done this time, leaving the British one behind. But, unlike British licences, Australian ones expire fairly frequently and need to be renewed. As I pulled my wallet out of my pocket with tepid dread, something in me knew what I was going to find: the licence had expired the previous week.

It's hard to imagine anywhere in the continental United States less accessible by public transport than Walsh's Oregon ranch, and the situation took some resolving. After fruitlessly begging a few car rental agencies to contact Britain's DVLA to confirm my British licence, I found a United flight leaving later that day to the Oregon town of North Bend, and got on it. There, I found some taxi numbers and managed to book one for the entire following day, first to take me 40 miles into the Oregon forests up the East Fork Coquille River, along the old Coos Bay Wagon Road pioneer route, then to wait at Walsh's ranch for a few hours, and then take me another 120 miles to Eugene, from where I was due to fly out that night. The company quoted me US$300 which, on top of the unexpected flight cost to North Bend, pretty much erased the agreed fee for the whole article. I swallowed hard and agreed to it, and checked into the Quality Inn, Coos Bay.

Thanks to the international date line, it had been Thursday for about two days by now, one great big endless relentless arse of a Thursday, and I needed a drink. Although I had just turned thirty-eight, they asked for ID at the local liquor store. I gave them my Australian driver's licence.

The clerk looked hard at it. 'Sir,' he said, 'this licence has expired.'

*

Be honest: had you heard of Don Walsh? If not, it's probably at least partly because he has never sought publicity for what he did. He has worked hard not to be defined by what he achieved in his twenties, leading an extraordinary subsequent life in academia, adventure, exploration and private business. He's been to the North Pole five times, commanded a submarine, founded and run a whole new school of the University of Southern California, had a ridge named after him in Antarctica. But it's no good: when you do something so remarkable at the age of twenty-eight, your obituary is only ever going to focus on one thing.

While Walsh is generous with his time, one senses he is sick of talking about the *Trieste* despite his evident pride in the practical success of the mission and equipment. 'It was fifty years ago,' he says. 'You do a certain thing, and that was it.' Perhaps it's the military way, but after half a century, he talks about the adventure with a tone and vocabulary of absolute understatement.

Instead, Walsh is most dynamic when talking about the sea itself, the science of exploration – the question of *what's down there*. For this reason, when asked about the swashbuckling exploratory spirit of the 1950s and 1960s, Walsh doesn't mention the space race once, instead recalling the achievements of sub-marEEners of the time: the *Nautilus* going across the Arctic Ocean under the ice cap by way of the North Pole; the *Triton* circumnavigating the world totally submerged. 'When I met President Eisenhower I realized that he had only given personal decorations to three military persons in eight years,' Walsh says: himself, Bill Anderson of the *Nautilus* and Ned Beach of the *Triton*. 'They were all submariners.'

One senses a disappointment about the US's failure to keep pace with manned submersible technology, and with dispropor-tionate spending on space exploration. 'Few of us are going into space. It's entertaining, and certainly the son et lumière of a space launch is formidable,' he says. 'What we do, one minute it's there, the next minute it's a cloud of bubbles. It's not very exciting. But it's very important.' These days, America is nowhere in deep-sea exploration capability: the technology resides with Russia, Japan and China. 'But we don't live in space,' he protests. 'We live here, on this planet called Earth.'

Besides the ocean, there is another subject that gets Walsh off the autopilot that he himself admits comes on when he talks about the *Trieste* ('I flick the switch') – the rest of his life after the dive. Get him on to that subject and two hours fly by.

After *Trieste*, he first went back to submarines, serving on two, and in wars in both Vietnam and Korea. 'I think two wars per customer is sufficient for a lifetime.' While he is only technically a Korea veteran, having been in service during the conflict but not in the field in Korea, he was among the very first Americans to be involved in Vietnam, serving on the first submarine to do a war patrol in the Gulf of Tonkin in 1964, spending sixty days submerged.

Along the way, there was a period during which he had to wait a few years to be due a submarine command, and so took to study, to an extraordinary extent: he ended up with three separate graduate degrees, a Master's in political science from San Diego State, and both a Master's and a PhD in physical oceanography from Texas A&M University, focusing on remote-sensing oceanography. 'I'm not terribly proud of that,' he says, 'because I didn't plan it very well.' From there, he went straight from finishing his dissertation to taking command of a submarine, the *USS Bashaw*, a Gato-class hunter-killer that had seen service in the Second World War.

By the end of the 1960s, he had finished his command tour and was sent to Washington, DC, to something called the Office of the Chief of Naval Development, where he was put in charge of swimmers, salvage and diving, 'only one of which I had a background in. But I was like the cocktail-lounge pianist who says: I don't know it, but if you hum a few bars, I'll play it. Fortunately, before I'd been there long enough to commit too much damage, a job possibility came up in the secretariat of the navy.'

This took him into the Pentagon to work for the assistant secretary for the navy for research and development, and he became the special assistant on submarines. 'It was the second-best job I ever had,' he says. I assume he means the first was the *Trieste* programme, but at this he looks affronted. 'The best, of course, was command.'

After three and a half years at the Pentagon, he went to Woodrow Wilson International Center for Scholars, then housed in the Smithsonian Institution's first building, the Castle. He was sent on a fellowship among a flock of high-flyers (though perhaps this is entirely the wrong term to use for Walsh; for submariners, surely the accolade for achievement should be deep divers). He believes, though can't confirm, that two of the thirty-one-strong group were nominated for Nobel Prizes during his fourteen months there, though the nomination process is too confidential to be sure. 'It was not your usual bunch of guys.' And this would prove transformative, ultimately putting paid to his next job as deputy director of naval laboratories. 'After I'd had that intellectual high at the Woodrow Wilson Center it was really hard for me to go back to tedium, even if it was good tedium.'

And so he shifted to academia, and was recruited to the University of Southern California to set up the new Institute for Marine Studies. He recalls being flown out to Los Angeles for an initial interview with no expectations in being appointed, and so decided to give it to the president of the university straight, pointing out flaws, hammering home just how much work there was to do. 'I fly back and get home that night from Dulles Airport and Joan's asking me over the table, how did it go? And I said: I don't think I'll hear from them again. She said: well, good, we don't want to live in LA anyway, it's a really crummy place. Honest to God, the phone rang right then, and they said: come back, we want you.'

Walsh speaks about his ability to move from military to academia with greater pride than anything bar commanding a submarine, and certainly more than about the *Trieste* trip. Perhaps there were more similarities between the two than he had expected. 'Universities are more rank-conscious than the military,' he says. 'I told them: for me to do this job effectively within the university, I've got to have a portfolio. And that portfolio has to say tenured full professor, and it has to say dean, otherwise I'm just going to be peeing into the wind. And they said yes.' Suitably galvanized, he pressed on. 'They said: what do you want to be paid? I pulled a number out of my ear, really high compared to what I was making in the navy as a captain, and they said: we can do that.' And then he pushed it too far. 'I said: I also want a parking space. They said: that's a bit harder to do.'

Nevertheless, he made a move from near the top of one profession to another, built an institute from scratch, and spent almost nine years on it before being riled enough by a change of management to move on. Of particular irritation were two incidents – one when he had procured a tuna clipper to convert into a new research ship but found funds raised from the sale of its predecessor diverted elsewhere in the university, and the other when he persuaded California Governor Jerry Brown to let him use a National Guard armoury as his department building, only to find it nicked by another bit of the university for use as a library. Tuna clippers and armoury buildings don't seem the usual political minutiae of academia, but then, Walsh's hasn't been an ordinary life.

Next came the launch of a consultancy, which still exists as an Oregon corporation today and has worked in twenty countries, but by now Walsh was being drawn to a fascinating new life: working on expedition ships, in particular around the Arctic and Antarctic.

This phase of his life had its roots in a navy project called Deep Freeze, through which the navy would inhabit Antarctic stations and run them on behalf of students and scientists. He first visited in 1971, spending two months on the ice after being handed a project by the Pentagon to provide support to the National Science Foundation's operations there. 'I didn't think I'd go back,' he says. But the NSF appreciated his efforts sufficiently to name a small mountain ridge after him: the Walsh Spur. You can still find it, if you know your Antarctic geography, near Cape Hallet, a few miles east of Mount Northampton in Victoria Land. 'I have never been there and it's unlikely that I will,' he says. 'Too remote.'

By the 1990s, expedition cruising was beginning to gather

pace, with groups of up to 100 people on ice-strengthened ships, and Walsh found himself in demand as a lecturer. On one ship, the Russian ice-breaker *Kapitan Khlebnikov*, he was part of only the eleventh ever full circumnavigation of Antarctica – Captain James Cook having accomplished the first – a trip he was able to take his wife, Joan, along on. They have been married since 1962. 'That trip was our time in the sun,' he says. 'Or the snow.'

*

Put him on these subjects and he is an articulate raconteur, his intonation and body language transformed from the repetition of the *Trieste* narrative, and full of great stories. Like the one where the Russians stole his project to go to the North Pole – the *real* North Pole, on the ground 15,000 feet below the ice cap and the water.

In 1997, Walsh was on a North Pole trip on a Russian ice-breaker with Mike McDowell, the Australian who had founded Quark Expeditions, a pioneering top-end adventure travel group. 'Most of the engineering staff on this nuclear ice-breaker had come from the Soviet sub service,' he says. 'So we would sit in the bowels of the ship and drink lots of vodka and talk about our adventures in submarines. They showed me periscope photographs of the US aircraft carrier *Kitty Hawk* they had taken from their Soviet sub.' Or maybe it was the *Ranger*, either way, they made their point.

One day, over the vodka and 'a lot of meaningless toasts', someone remarked that nobody had ever been to the real North Pole. Between them on the ship they had the contacts and ability to do it: all they needed was an ice-breaker like the one they were on, the Russian *Mir* submersibles – at that time the most advanced deep submersibles in the world – and some money, which could be gained through the sale of tickets to high-paying tourists. It was while waiting for everything to come together that McDowell and Walsh started running dives to the *Titanic*, including taking James Cameron down for his film work, and the *Bismarck*. 'They were just placeholders, bookmarks. The real goal was the North Pole.'

Finally, in 2006, everything converged: charters, *Mir*, and money, with twenty tourists putting in US$50,000 apiece. 'And just two months before we were to go out, the Russian government said: *nyet*.' So they tried again the next year, and got a shock. 'The Russian government said: "We're going, but it's going to be an all-Russian expedition, no foreigners". The Russians came in and took all our planning and hijacked the whole thing.' Walsh was invited to watch the record take place from the ice-breaker but couldn't bring himself to do it. 'They trumpeted this thing like it was going to the Moon, this great Russian triumph. It was pretty hard to hold our noses through all that. The real story has never come out that it was planned and financed in the West and the Russians just hijacked it.'

It's worth noting that, had Walsh done the North Pole dive in 2007, he would have been seventy-six at the time. And there is, finally, a dawning sense that it might be time to slow down.

'Now that I'm seventy-eight, it's probably time to act my age,' he says. He and his wife talk about a ritual burning of the parkas to symbolize the last trip. His immediate schedule – a host of engagements around Europe – doesn't sound much like slowing down. 'But in the polar regions you're working out of the zodiac boats, helping passengers who've never been to these places before,' he says. 'You don't want this geriatric old fart stumbling around tripping over penguins.' He's even selling his experimental bi-plane.

And there are salmon to be caught in the river at the back of the ranch. 'It's nice here. There's all these books to read,' he says, gesturing at an extraordinary collection of tomes on the shelves that surround his office, designed by his wife. 'She says if you put all the shelves together, it's exactly the same as the length as the *Bismarck*,' he remarks.

One of the many achievements of Walsh's life has been finding a wife who not only tolerates his adventuring but knows how long the *Bismarck* is.

It's the most extraordinary office, a second-floor addition to the house, more of a library than a workplace. The books, filling every bit of space, are organized carefully into categories: naval, philosophy, history. The aviation ones have had to be moved downstairs for lack of space. Even the *Bismarck* is not a sufficient model for the shelving his books require. He's going to need a bigger boat.

As he shows me out it's striking that in this house filled with paraphernalia, with a range of clocks showing the time in various world locations, with a deep-sea diving helmet and paintings from around the world and more and more books, there is hardly any memorabilia related to the *Trieste*. There's a painting of the vessel in the choppy surface seas, but he has to dig that out from somewhere, and, in any case, he's not in it. You wouldn't quite say he's burying the memory. But he's certainly not focusing on it either.

One thing he does plan to do is produce a memoir, in which we may well hear more of the oddity of only being remembered for one thing, half a century ago, and the injustice of a society that recognizes achievements when you go up, but not when you go down. 'It's an unauthorized autobiography,' he dead-pans. 'The Right Stuff, The Wrong Direction.'

2

The Moonwalkers

In a dimly lit corner of an Arizona ballroom, a handful of elderly gentlemen sit at two lines of booths. Some of the men have walking sticks, others hearing aids; perched on stackable conference-room chairs behind folding tables, they chat genially with people passing by. They look a lot like the rest of America's sprightly and vibrant eighty-something generation, but they are crucially different: because unlike the other 7 billion of us, these are six of the eight surviving men who have set foot on the Moon.

It is a monstrously hot Tucson day in June, and although the vast cacti surrounding the JW Marriott Tucson Starr Pass Resort & Spa look like they've been planted for some contrived theme, they probably pre-date the building, and are a whole lot better suited to the climate than anyone actually attending. Not much else can grow in the grounds in this parched and heavy heat; crop out the roads and the buildings and you could be on Mars. Perhaps that's why they've chosen to hold Spacefest IV here, the biggest example of an increasingly popular field: the space conference.

Events like these bring together a curious mix of scientists and astronauts, artists and scholars, conspiracy theorists and space groupies. It's this eclectic combination that gives them their appeal. There is real, important science here: panels collect some of the world's foremost voices on asteroid assessment, spacesuit design, propulsion technology and the feasibility of visits to Mars. They gather in panels and talk about the cutting edge of space exploration to small gatherings of earnest attendees. The questions come thick and fast: some scientific ('What do you think about the properties of Asteroid DA-14?'), some opportunist ('How much can we make from mining helium-3?'), and some out there ('Should we get asteroid insurance?').

But for many people, and certainly for me, it's the astronauts of the 1960s and 1970s who are the main draw.

There has been a revival of interest in Apollo, and the Gemini and Mercury programmes that preceded it. With every passing year, it seems more and more astounding that we went to the Moon six times from 1969 to 1972. The astronauts are in decent nick for men in their eighties, but still, with every clutch of thinning white hair, every fading faculty, it becomes glaringly obvious how long ago it all was. And space exploration appears to have regressed – at least in terms of people leaving our planet rather than just orbiting round it – in the intervening four decades. Gene Cernan, crag-jawed and steely of rhetoric, the statesman-like Last Man on the Moon, bounced along the Taurus-Littrow Valley more than forty years ago, in 1972. Ask anyone among the diverse cast of delegates, from professional auctioneers to curious beauty-salon entrepreneurs, and they'll tell you the same thing: these guys aren't going to be around for long, so let's hear what they've got to say while they're still here.

*

My route to Tucson had begun the previous November when *Discovery Channel Magazine* had asked me to produce a cover story called: 'How To Be an Astronaut' – and added that, since there had been a problem with the planned cover story for the next edition, it would be great if I could turn it round in ten days.

I contacted NASA in Houston – just those few words were enough to bring a grin to my face, as if I was in a movie, or going back in time – and had a very helpful interview with Duane Ross, the head of the astronaut selection board at NASA. But underscoring the conversation, a spectre in the wings, was a problematic fact: America no longer had a vehicle capable of taking the astronauts he trained into space. There was no Space Shuttle, nor any programme in any meaningful stage to replace it. When you apply to be part of a NASA intake today, you need to be between 1.57 and 1.9 metres in height, with require-ments on arm and leg length too, not because of the size of any American craft but in order to comply with the requirements of the Russian Soyuz capsules that Americans have to book passage on in order to get to the International Space Station. These days, Russian-language skills are more important than the test-pilot stripes that dominated selection in the 1950s and 1960s.

Clearly, to get the more interesting perspective on space – some-thing to appeal to the young kids in the magazine's readership, to get them dreaming – I needed to go a lot further back in time, and so I thought about the Moonwalkers. It seemed, on the face of it, outrageously ambitious: nothing in the history of human endeavour has ever quite compared with the feat of leaving our Earth and walking on another world. These people must be ethereal, unreachable.

Well, some of them are, but actually, tracking down Moonwalkers proved to be easier than you might think.

At the time, Neil Armstrong was still alive, but it was widely acknowledged that there was no point in contacting him for an interview if you wanted to talk about the Moon. Armstrong is sometimes painted as a recluse, but that's not true; he just turned to academia at the University of Cincinnati and devoted the rest of his life to his great love, aviation. Armstrong was not impossible to reach, and if one asked a detailed technical question about, say, the Bell X-1B's landing gear, or the self-adjusting control system on the North American X-15, one would likely receive a clinically precise answer. It's just that he was heartily sick of talking about the Moon within a year of having walked on it, which rather defeated the point of approaching him at all.

Aldrin, too, can be reached, since he has conquered the alcoholism and depression that blighted his post-Apollo life, and today is a major fixture in the debate about the future of commercial space flight.

But everyone knows Armstrong and Aldrin; what happened to the rest, I wondered? As we'll discuss, the diversity of answers is part of the joy of Apollo's aftermath.

To my surprise, I found two Moonwalkers within a day or two.

The first was Alan Bean, the lunar module pilot on *Apollo 12*, and therefore the fourth man to set foot on the Moon in November 1969. There is a reason that Bean is relatively easy to reach: because, after leaving NASA a few years after his second and final flight into space on the *Skylab 3* mission in 1973, he became a full-time painter in 1981. More or less everything he has ever painted since – and he continues to paint, prolifically – has been a variation on the same theme: astronauts on the surface of the Moon. These paintings are highly prized, and truly unique, because he uses small pieces of his original spacesuit mission patches, which are covered in Moondust, in the paintings themselves. He uses a bronze-embossed cast of his Moon boot, and the hammer he used to pound the United States flagpole into the lunar surface, to add texture to his paintings. These paintings are for sale (and then some: one of his paintings, *The Spirit of Apollo*, is currently on sale for $344,700, and the cheapest I have seen went for $25,450), and he has a website as a gallery, so therefore he can be contacted.

Then, on 23 November, the name 'Alan Bean' popped into my email inbox, agreeing to a call. I was living in Singapore at the time, and his suggested time of 10 a.m. CST (he lives in Houston) was exactly midnight for me. So it was that I found myself nervously sitting in the dark, trying not to wake the kids while I spoke to the fourth man on the Moon.

I have interviewed a lot of senior people in my life – several prime ministers and presidents, and the chief executives of some of the biggest banks in the world – but I don't think I've ever been quite so starstruck and apprehensive as when I picked up the phone to call Houston that night.

'Hello.'

'Hello. Captain Bean?' Two advantages to this appellation. One, all these guys are ex-military: it shows respect to know what rank they retired at. Two, it gets round the otherwise inevitable: Mr Bean?

'Chris! This is Alan.' He was in his studio in Houston, he told me, working on a painting of Neil Armstrong piloting the *Eagle* over a crater towards its landing site. He had made a model of the lunar module, he said, and was struggling to work out how to represent it accurately.

Still somewhat overwhelmed at the oddity of chatting to someone who has crossed the void and glimpsed infinity and felt the tread of his boots sink into the dust of another celestial body, I asked him what it was that the Apollo astronauts had that was so different from the rest of us. What was in their character for them to succeed?

'First of all,' he said, Texas loud and clear in his accent, 'you had to want to do it. Quite a number of pilots had no interest in it. My opinion is that you need to be a certain IQ so you can learn things quickly. But you don't have to be the smartest guy in the class.'

He talked about the importance of being able to get along with all sorts of other people, and the need for good health and vision, and, back then, the ability to fly aircraft well.

'You don't necessarily end up with the smartest people, but people smart enough to learn, who can get along with people enough and have demonstrated that they can. It's not just hiring a valedictorian and hoping they work out.

'That's the way I imagine I was selected, because I never was the smartest guy in the class, two or three usually. I wasn't the best pilot on the squadron, I was two, three or four. But add all those numbers up and they must have been enough for them to say: I think I'll take Al Bean.'

In fact, Bean had to work uncommonly hard to get his Moon shot – which was the very first time he ever flew in space. He was rejected the first time he applied for the Apollo programme, getting in the second time in 1963 in a group of fourteen that also included Buzz Aldrin, Gene Cernan and David Scott, all of whom would go on to walk on the Moon. Having got in, Bean watched from the sidelines as others got their turn in space for six full years before he made a flight. If you wade your way through the many volumes of autobiography that have come out from Apollo veterans, both in the air and on the ground, and through the vast accompanying literature led by Andrew Chaikin's definitive *A Man on the Moon,* you find more than one opinion that Bean was overlooked by the most powerful men in the astronaut office, Al Shepard and Deke Slayton, for having a more intellectual outlook on life than was the norm among his peers.

In fact, much later, when I had come to know a great deal more about Apollo and spoken with many of its membership, I interviewed one of his friends and contemporaries Bill Anders, whose story is told in the chapter on *Apollo 8*. 'I could never understand why I got a flight before Alan,' Anders told me. 'He was a very good pilot, a very thoughtful guy. I wouldn't want to say naïve. He just wasn't quite as Machiavellian as I was.'

Bean recalls the period well. 'It was very frustrating because other people in my group were flying and I wasn't,' he said. 'You know that if you're not flying, they're picking the ones they think are the best to fly first because that's how things are done. I was aware that I wasn't stacking up in Deke Slayton's mind and Al Shepard's; they were the two bosses that had everything to say about who was selected and the like. I said: I don't know what's wrong here, but I'm not able to show Deke and Al my good qualities.'

At this stage Al Bean had known me for about four minutes, never met or seen me, nor read any of my work. And yet the trust and introspection he showed in what came next is something I have since marvelled at.

'Looking back on it now, I am an introvert, and that's an extroverted world,' he said. 'Everybody else is an extrovert, except me and Neil.' Neil. He means Neil Armstrong. First-name terms. Well, of course he is: they worked closely for many years and are bonded by something truly unique. 'It's much easier to be an extrovert in an extroverted world, to be the guy that's going to parties, and speaks up in meetings more than I did. One thing against me, though I didn't realize it so much, was I didn't want to go hunting with Deke, for example, and he's a big hunter. Politics is in everything. It's not bad, it's just the way it is. People had favourites.'

I could hear him warming to his theme, on the other side

of the world, and pictured him in his Houston studio. I liked to think he was gesturing expressively. 'Another thing that made it frustrating to me is I'm the kind of guy – I see that now – who has a lot of ideas. They pop into my head the whole time. That's how come I'm an artist. I'd go in to Al or Deke with an idea, and sometimes they would say it's great, and other times they'd look at me like: where the hell did that come from?' At this point he was helped by his deep friendship with one of the astronaut group's true elite, Pete Conrad, who by now was already a veteran of two Gemini missions. But for a flip of two Apollo missions because of delays in the development of the lunar module, Conrad might well have been the first man to step on the Moon, rather than Armstrong. But that was for the future: at this point, he was a loyal ally to Bean.

'Pete helped me understand: don't go in to those guys before you tell me what that idea is. There is a difference between a left-brain guy and a right-brain guy. The ideas I went in to talk about from the left side of my brain, they liked, because they were left-brain guys, like most astronauts. I am left and right. I knew I was different, because I cared about things other guys didn't, but I didn't know how to conceal it. Some of these ideas, I'd say, it's the best idea I've had in six months, but it's a right-brain attitude, it ain't going to fly.'

I had not spoken in about ten minutes at this stage, but Bean was just getting into his stride.

'One of the best ideas I've had as an artist is the texture I use with a Moon boot and a hammer. I've never heard of an artist doing it – never.' This is perhaps not so surprising, since very few artists have access to used Moon boots, but still. 'In my opinion, it's a right-brain great idea. If Al and Deke had been on my committee as a painter, let's say, and if I said I want to do some texture on these paintings with a Moon boot and a hammer from the Moon, they'd say: what you do that for? It's a crazy idea, Bean. They'd be looking at me like: that is *really* stupid.'

And so he would use Conrad as a filter between his mad ideas and them actually leaving his mouth in the direction of a senior decision-maker. 'I'd say: Pete, what do you think? He'd say: don't do it, Bean, it marks you down as a guy that's unpredictable, and you can't assign people to space missions that are unpredictable.'

He paused briefly. 'I learned to shut the fuck up.'

He might have gone on like this indefinitely – 'It was frustrating at first. I didn't know why. People would say: why is Al Shepard mad at you? I don't know, but I can tell he's pissed off . . .' But I was conscious that I had negotiated forty minutes and did have to fulfil *Discovery*'s brief about astronaut selection, and so remorsefully interrupted him to bring him on to more mundane matters, about the changing nature of what is expected for an astronaut. He ran through the practical side dutifully, and then I asked him about *Apollo 12*.

History doesn't remember this follow-up to *Apollo 11* with anything like the same reverence, but those who know their Apollo history recall it as a wonderful mission that combined technical achievement – it landed with astonishing precision at its expected location, the site of a Surveyor 3 unmanned probe which had been sent to the Moon on 1967 – with a sense of absolute unbridled joy. But for a time it appeared to be a doomed mission. *Apollo 12* launched during a rainstorm (conjecture continues to this day that the launch went ahead in poor conditions because President Richard Nixon had flown to Florida to attend it) and the vast craft was hit by lightning after just thirty-six seconds, and then again after fifty-two. All three fuel cells were knocked offline, along with a great deal of instrumentation, and there was talk of abandoning the mission until one of the legions of experts on the ground in Houston, John Aaron, remembered a similar telemetry failure from a test and suggested an obscure switch to put the cells back online. Neither Conrad nor the flight director had ever heard of the switch, but Bean had, and it worked.

Still: strapped on top of a Saturn V, to this day the tallest, heaviest and most powerful rocket ever made operational, with the best part of 3,000 tonnes of fuel burning beneath it, and then struck twice by lightning; was fear part of his job?

'We knew that before we joined up,' he says. 'We were doing things like that in airplanes for our whole career. Some who weren't so good at it got killed. You have to have luck.'

He turns to the Space Shuttle disasters. '*Challenger* [the Space Shuttle that blew up after launch in 1985], no matter how good an astronaut you are, you're going to get killed. Neil Armstrong said he thought he had a 90 per cent chance of getting back alive, a 50 per cent chance of making a landing. You have in your head these thoughts, you think: is it worth it? Obviously to us it was worth it. For others it wasn't and they didn't want to be astronauts.

'As Bill Anders used to say, if you are crossing the desert and really thirsty, you pay a lot for that first drink of water. After that, you might want to negotiate the price.'

What did he think his own odds were on *Apollo 12*?

'Strangely, about the same, 90 per cent of getting back. But no one knew. In our opinion, losing two crews on the Shuttle –' a second, *Columbia*, disintegrated when returning to Earth in 2003 – 'was better than we thought. We thought we'd lose more. If you back up to Magellan's trip around the Earth, he left Spain with five ships, 236 men. Three years later one ship gets back and something like fifteen men get back, with Magellan killed in the Philippines.'

'When you want to explore, it's not like the American public thinks it is. You are on the cutting edge of what you can do. We were on the cutting edge of what a spaceship could do. We got lucky. Thirteen had bad luck, but the best possible bad luck, let's call it that. Like lightning. We were hit twice, but they weren't maximum amperage hits. It tripped one of our three guidance systems. If it had been bigger, with more amperage, it could have tripped two or three. You need luck.'

Apollo 12 did make it to the Moon, with Conrad and Bean landing in the Ocean of Storms on 19 November 1969, while Dick Gordon remained in lunar orbit. As he stepped on to the surface of the Moon, Conrad – who had made a bet with a newspaper reporter that he could say what he wanted on the Moon, rather than being scripted – said: 'Whoopee! Man, that may have been a small one for Neil, but that's a long one for me.' (Conrad was one of the shortest men in the space programme.)

I asked Bean what details stuck in his mind about the Ocean of Storms, and I found it telling that, in answer, he immediately retreated to the medium of painting.

'I don't know . . . when I do a painting, I think of a story I want to tell. The one I'm working on now is when Neil overflew that boulder field and landed further along than we planned on landing. I worked on the boulder field this morning, and the module this afternoon. I've got a month or three weeks to go; it's not like it's quick. I can think about these things. I tend to be usually thinking about the painting I'm working on, the edge treatment of the craters, are they sharp, the density . . . that sort of thing that wasn't as important as an astronaut.'

Eventually he came back to his memory of the real Moon, rather than a painting of it.

'What I remember in my feeling about it is the Moon is far, far from Earth. And it's funny, when we were training in the simulator, it didn't seem that far away. When I would go out and look at the night it didn't seem that far away. The Romans thought it was a shield, not up that high.

'As the years passed, and looking up there and seeing the Moon, it seems almost impossible that we could go there. It's an impossible dream. Going to the Moon and back is an impossible dream. It still is. When we go back to the Moon again, it will be in fifty years, would be my guess.' Uncharacteristically, he paused. 'Maybe I'm wrong about that. I'm wrong about a lot of stuff. I said thirty years ago that we're not going back for fifty and everybody made fun of me.'

He talked through the costs of getting back to the Moon today – he reckoned $300 billion, in addition to the $20 billion he said NASA was getting at the time, 'which lets us send unmanned spacecraft to Mars and lets us pay the rent at Johnson.' We talked about the possibility that the next person on the Moon could be Chinese – 'no, it won't' – and about the decline in American standing in space exploration. We discussed commercial spaceflight and space tourism, which Apollo astronauts (Aldrin being a particular example) are more positive about than one might think. 'It is the big hope, in my opinion, for the future of space.' And we discussed the remarkable accuracy of his own mission, landing about 300 feet from the Surveyor probe, which required a major redevelopment of the software MIT had provided for the mission. 'Humans can do a lot of things with good leadership and dedication. That was an impossible task to do in four months. We did it in three and a half.'

After Apollo, Bean set what was then an endurance record in space on *Skylab 3*, on which he spent fifty-nine days and covered more than 24 million miles from July to September 1973, this time as commander. The main thing he took from this mission was an improved understanding of human fitness in space, which he likes to think will be applied if space tourism ever really takes hold. 'Some day, when taking passengers up in space, like on a ship, we're going to say to every passenger they must spend one hour a day with a physical trainer. If a passenger says: I feel sick today, the captain's going to say: you've got a choice. Exercise one hour a day, or you're going in this brig, because when you get back you're going to die and blame it on me.'

And then, a total change of life.

'For some, maybe a majority, they have difficulty finding a dream,' Bean said. 'Many young people don't have a dream, so the work it takes to be good is not really worth anything because they don't care. They don't want to be the best pilot or astronaut. It's not something they dream about or want to do.

'I was very lucky, and so was Pete and I think some others, in that on the way home when we talked about it, Dick wanted to fly commander and walk on the Moon [sadly, the mission in which he would have done so, *Apollo 18*, was cancelled through budget cuts], Pete and I wanted to fly *Skylab*, so we wanted to do something else. After *Skylab*, I wanted to back up ASTP [the Apollo-Soyuz Test Project, a joint venture with the Soviet Union partly designed to thaw Cold War attitudes], and did. I wanted to fly the Shuttle.'

But then, something changed. 'When I was training to fly, I began to say: wait a minute. There's young men and women here who can do this, but I'm the only guy who's interested in art, who cares about art, who can celebrate this great human achievement in paintings. It won't replace movies . . . it's just another way to celebrate something that's equivalent to, or maybe even better than, Magellan or Columbus. We need to celebrate these amazing, huge achievements.

'I said: if I can learn to paint better, that's what I need to do. They're not going to miss me at NASA. The other astronauts are as good, or better. But if I don't do this other job, it isn't going to be done. That's how it looks to me now. When I'm dead and gone these paintings will remain and tell stories that will be lost any other way. When people do go back to the Moon, the crewmembers will look at them and read the stories, and maybe read the one about me throwing a football to Pete, though we didn't really do it.'

He was referring to a painting again: it's called *If we could do it all over again – are you ready for some football?* When it was sold in 2004 for $182,369.60, it earned a place in the Guinness Book of Records for the 'most expensive Moonscape painting ever sold'. But it depicts a completely fictional scenario: Bean chasing a football thrown by Conrad, across the lunar surface. Again, when talking about the Moon, Bean was doing so through the prism of art, and fiction.

'And maybe they'll say: we're going to go back and take a football and do some of this other stuff Bean wrote about. That's how the painting seems to me.'

Interestingly, Bean has a very clear equivalent in the Soviet space corps: Alexey Leonov, one of the most gifted of the cosmonauts, and the man who conducted the world's first space walk in March 1965. But for a few moments of fate beyond his control, he might well have become the first man to walk on the Moon. Like Bean, Leonov is an accomplished artist who has drawn and painted numerous images of space, both recalled and imagined, and has published many volumes of them. He took coloured pencils and paper into space when he flew on the Apollo-Soyuz Test Project in 1975 – which Bean had been a backup for on the American side.

Talking about painting took Bean off on another tangent. 'Right now what I'm doing, with this painting of Neil and the Eagle overflying the boulder field, I have learned so much more about him doing that.'

I asked him: did you call Armstrong about it? Do you guys all still talk?

'First, I read everything he said about it. I don't want to bother those guys; when I get it nearly finished I'll call him up. I did a couple of paintings, one called *First Man*, and it's a painting I did from studying training videos of Neil as he took a photo of Buzz. I painted that and, during training, Neil had a watch on his right wrist, so I painted that in. Then when I was looking at it in the Air and Space Museum [in Washington], someone told me he left his watch inside because it had lost one of its timers, so he didn't wear a watch out there. So I asked him, and he could see I had painted it in – he said, "Whatever way you painted, that's the way it was." That shows the kind of guy he is.' And, to show what kind of guy *Bean* is, he didn't settle for that, did more research, found that Armstrong had not been wearing the watch, and so took the painting off the wall and overpainted it. 'I try to do things right.'

One senses Armstrong probably would not have been overly bothered by the detail. 'I'll call Neil when I get this done, and say I did this. Because if you just ask him something in general he won't tell you; he doesn't think that way, he's very much a left-brain guy, way out on the bell curve. I ask him what his memory of it is, he'll tell me: not much. He might say something. But he's not a guy that is going to chat with you about it. Pete would. Gene Cernan would chat a bit. John Young doesn't want to hear from me. I don't call him.'

Armstrong died about a year after the conversation; Conrad, for his part, is long dead by now, having died in a motorbike crash in Ojai, California, in July 1999. By then Shepard, the first American in space during the Mercury programme, and, after being the scourge of Bean's existence in the astronaut office, the fifth man on the Moon on *Apollo 15*, had died of leukaemia

43

in 1998, and Jim Irwin, the eighth man, of a heart attack in 1991. Eight left.

Our conversation ended. It was after 1 a.m. and I was in no mood for sleep. I jumped on Facebook and tried to be blasé. 'I keep being kept up all night by bloody astronauts. You know how it is.' But in fact I had found the conversation thrilling, the more so for its oddity. And I thought: how curious to make a major change in your life to move away from the Moon, and then to anchor yourself back to it with everything you ever paint.

*

By now, another wonderful name had appeared in my inbox: Charlie Duke. You might think you don't know Charlie Duke, even though he was the tenth man to set foot on the Moon, on *Apollo 16*. But you probably do. If you find that footage of Armstrong and Aldrin piloting *Apollo 11* down to the lunar surface as the fuel falls to the dregs of the tank, when they finally touch down, and when Armstrong reports: 'Houston, Tranquillity Base here, the Eagle has landed', a musical Southern accent is heard from Houston: 'Roger, Twanq – Tranquillity, we copy you on the ground. You got a bunch of guys about to turn blue. We are breathing again.' That person is the CapCom, or capsule communicator, always an astronaut, entrusted to be the point of contact from Houston for the astronauts in space, relaying messages between the two. And on that famous night in 1969, it was Charlie Duke in the chair.

Duke has a biographical website with videos about his time at NASA (and his subsequent religious conversion, of which more later) – and a link to paintings of him by Alan Bean, including one portrait saluting in his spacesuit from the Descartes Highlands of the Moon, entitled *Small Town South Carolina Boy* (that's where the accent comes from). It has a contact section, as these things tend to, which is no guarantee of a response, but a couple of days after sending my request I received a message: 'Give me a call,' and a number in New Braunfels, Texas.

Once again, we settled on a time in the middle of the night in Singapore and mid-morning in Texas, and once more I checked the kids were asleep and shut myself in my home office in our apartment, closing the windows to drown out the noise of the ten-lane East Coast Parkway outside the window, and jumped on the phone to call a man on the other side of this world, who had walked on the near side of another world.

Duke is a genial, friendly, impeccably polite man, much loved by his peers. I didn't realize until later that I couldn't possibly have picked two more accommodating members of the Moonwalker fraternity to approach. Conscious of my what-does-it-take assignment from *Discovery*, I started by asking him about the character required to be an astronaut.

'The personality I would describe as one of adventure and curiosity,' he said. 'As a fighter pilot, a test pilot, the dream was: higher, faster, and let's see what it's like out there. That would describe my personality.' He paused. 'As far as character, how would you define that?'

I said I imagined it would require a combination of the adventurousness he had described and a lot of focus and patience.

'Yes, I think those words are quite descriptive of the character of a test pilot. There is I think a false image of test-piloting as being seat-of-the-pants, fling your body into the air without any preparation and take what comes. Even in the early days, there was a lot of planning and a lot of thorough preparation that went into a flight, so it wasn't just: let's go strap it on.

'Certainly you had to have daring, because even with the planning you never knew what was going to happen, especially in the early days. So I think also patience was a good character trait because you needed to wait your turn.' He talked about the responsibilities he had at Apollo, about training, about self-confidence, about trust, about faith in the equipment.

We talked about how the requirements of astronauts had changed from the days when he joined in 1966 out of test-pilot school – he had studied, among other places, under the legendary Chuck Yeager, who is interviewed in the final chapter of this book. Duke was around long enough to see the increasing role of science, particularly among payload specialists, that came with the Space Shuttle programme. 'Of course, 50 per cent of the competition was cut out in our generation, because no women were allowed.'

Like Bean, Duke's was a long wait. He joined NASA in 1966 and walked on the Moon in 1972 – with no spaceflights in between. He flew precisely once in space, and went all the way to the Descartes Highlands. Unlike Bean, the waiting didn't feel so much of an affront to Duke. 'I don't remember much about the waiting part. What I remember is the engineering duties that we were given.' In his case, his job was monitoring the develop-ment of the monstrous Saturn V boosters, and the propulsion systems for the lunar module. Like all the others, he studied geology, in the hope of more fully understanding (and being able to describe) the rocks they would find on the Moon; and more than anything, he spent time in simulators. 'I probably landed on the Moon 2,000 times over the time I was there – crashed a lot, too. There were certain failures the sim instructors could put in 20 feet off the ground you just couldn't recover from, and it resulted in a crash. On the one that counted, we pulled it off.'

By the time he sat in the CapCom chair in 1969 Duke was still three years from his own mission, but he was a trusted man to be the voice in the ear of the pioneers descending towards the Moon. It was he who had to relay instructions after Armstrong and Aldrin twice encountered an unfamiliar error message, a 1202 programme alarm, which flummoxed both the people in the lunar module and those on the ground. 'You are go for landing,' Duke told Armstrong, belying a whirlwind of information, debate, conjecture and simulator-honed experience among the myriad boffins behind the scenes in Houston.

'The actual moment of landing was one of intense relief,' Duke told me. 'I remember the tension in Mission Control was the highest I have ever seen it and felt it. I had been there for a couple of early Apollos and the last couple of Gemini flights, and while we had problems in all of those missions that required a lot of focus, the tension in Mission Control getting down to the final minute or so was extremely high, and the anxiety.

'I remember dead silence in Mission Control, which was extremely rare, as people focused on their consoles. Look at the old films and photographs that were taken, during the final minutes, you can see the tension on our faces. It was a great relief. When Buzz said, "Contact light, engine stop," it meant they were on the ground and we knew they were in good shape. But it seemed to me an eternity – in fact just a few seconds – before Neil came back and said, "Houston, Tranquillity base here, the Eagle has landed." It was like a balloon popping in Mission Control. I was so excited, I couldn't even pronounce "Tranquillity". I corrected myself. It was true: we were holding our breath waiting for that landing.'

Less than a year later, in April 1970, Duke was again intrinsic- ally involved in an episode of Apollo lore when *Apollo 13* suffered an explosion in space. Duke had been on the backup crew for the flight, specifically as lunar module pilot, backing up Fred Haise. Thanks to Ken Mattingly, the assigned command module pilot, being exposed to German measles (by Duke himself, via one of his kids) shortly before the flight, one member of that backup crew – Jack Swigert – *was* bumped up to the main crew.

Where was he when things went wrong?

'When I first got there it was about a half-hour after the accident. The first focus was to get them back on a free return, with the lunar module powered up, then would we have enough stuff to make it?' Duke was referring to two things here: first, the decision to keep the astronauts going all the way to the Moon, before using its gravity as a slingshot to send it home again – a so-called free-return trajectory – rather than trying to turn round in space immediately after the accident. Second, the damage to the service module, the heart of the spacecraft heading to the Moon, was so severe that the astronauts instead had to use the attached lunar module, which they otherwise would not have ventured into until the landing itself, as a lifeboat in order to keep themselves alive. Every step of the process of getting home was fraught with difficulty and untested challenges, and the actions of those on the ground were every bit as important as Lovell (who was also on *Apollo 8*, which is the subject of chapter 9, within which Lovell is interviewed) and his crew in space.

'If I recall, John Young and I went to the simulator, with Gene Cernan and a couple of others, and figured out this procedure if we got it powered up,' Duke told me. 'We had a sort of a checklist, we got that developed and called it up to them. When we had at least got them headed home there was a little relief. But we looked at the consumables, the oxygen, the lithium hydroxide canisters, all the electrical power; everything was running out. Twenty hours before landing, I just thought: we ain't going to make it.

'But we got smarter. Nobody gave up. We kept twisting the power configurations and verifying them. After we had shot around the Moon and started heading back, we had arrived at a configuration where they were not going to run out. My attitude changed from half pessimistic to relatively optimistic with the thought that if we don't make a mistake in Mission Control, and the crew don't make a mistake, we're gonna have enough stuff to get back. There were a lot of unknowns.'

And then his turn came in April 1972: *Apollo 16* with John Young and, ironically, command module pilot Ken Mattingly, the one whose exposure to Duke's measles had seen him booted off *Apollo 13*.

By then, having seen what he had on *13*, there must have been a sense of fear that he might not come back?

'No, it really wasn't. We were really just excited about getting a chance to go. We had faith; we made the spacecraft as best we could, with a lot of confidence. The Saturn had never failed us. Our focus was: let's go, let's launch.'

By the time of *Apollo 16*, NASA had become ambitious in its lunar landings. Whereas Armstrong and Aldrin had spent twenty-one and a half hours on the lunar surface, and two and a half hours outside their spacecraft, Young and Duke spent seventy-one hours on the lunar surface and conducted three Moonwalks totalling twenty hours and fourteen minutes. Whereas earlier missions had focused on simply getting there, by now the priority (indeed, the only justification for keeping the programme going at all) was to find the most interesting bits of the Moon from which to harvest rocks. The landing in the lunar highlands was intended to gather geologically older material from the Descartes Formation and the Cayley Formation – though in fact what they found was nothing like what was expected, and served chiefly to disprove a theory that the formations were volcanic.

Apollo 16 was the second of the J missions, which meant that they stayed for longer than the first three landings, and used a lunar roving vehicle – to most of us, the Moon buggy.

The landing almost didn't happen after a malfunction in the lunar module engine's backup system, delaying the descent by six hours. But having made it, the mission achieved plenty, and did so, like Bean's *Apollo 12*, with a sense of enormous joy from the astronauts themselves. The euphoria of mission commander John Young was a surprise to some: he is remembered by many who served in the Space Shuttle programme, for which Young was not only the maiden pilot but the head of the astronaut office, as being anything but joyful.

You looked like you were having fun. 'We did, we trained that way. John has a great sense of humour,' Duke said. 'He kept me in stitches the whole time. That carried over into our real life: we just continued in the same vein and manner and character we've done in training. We decided we were going to have fun, to do our job, to get everything accomplished but enjoy ourselves. And I'm glad it came across because that's the way we felt. Enjoy this beautiful, exciting adventure.'

The only time the enjoyment caused problems came during a spot of Olympian competition.

'The only time in the mission I had fear was when I screwed up right before we parked the rover,' he said. 'We were going to do the Moon Olympics – high-jump records. If you watch that on TV, we're standing behind the rover, John starts to jump, I start bouncing, and then I really gave a big jump and fell over backwards. That was scary. That backpack was not designed for that kind of impact. I scrambled around and was turning to my right, which fortunately broke my fall. My heart was pounding. If my spacesuit splits, I'm dead.'

Instead, the mission is better remembered for footage of Duke falling forward and attempting to bounce his way back on to his feet. 'That's not scary. Falling forward you can break your fall, with your arms as shock absorbers, but falling directly on your back is a different matter. Falling right on the backpack – it's a fragile system. Mission Control was very upset. If you listen to the tapes . . . it was the end of the Moon Olympics.'

You've still got the record, though. 'Yes. I got the record for the high jump.'

The mission had sufficient time to allow the astronauts to appreciate the stark beauty of the lunar surface – what Buzz Aldrin had spontaneously described as 'magnificent desolation.'

Duke told me: 'On our second EVA, we drove the rover to the south and up the side of Stone Mountain. When we got up two, three hundred feet off the valley floor and turned the rover around on a little bench on a hill, and looked across the valley of the Cayley Plains, it was awesome, a very dramatic sight. There was a distinct gap between the lunar surface and the blackness of space, and the lunar module sitting in the middle of the valley. It was a dramatic moment. The emotion, the beauty of the Moon.'

Still, for all Duke's radiance, there was a darkness to the Moon too, and it fell a long distance away. Duke, like many others, wrote an autobiography of his time on the Moon but, unusually, he co-wrote his with his wife, Dotty. She wrote movingly about the depression she felt in being neglected during Duke's career, saying it almost led her to suicide.

Never having met the man in person, and speaking to him over a crackly phone line, I raised this subject carefully, asking about the darker side behind the glamour of being an astronaut.

'I don't think people see the hard work that goes into getting ready to go,' he said. 'You see in Apollo three guys walk out and climb aboard that Saturn rocket, and there they are, going to be launched to an exciting adventure. But in our case, counting the backup for *Apollo 13*, it was almost three years of intense training. There's a lot of separation from your family. A lot of anxiety.

Is the mission really going to go? What's the political climate? Things were changing.'

And then, the question of what next.

*

'After Apollo was over, I was standing on top of the mountain,' Duke said. 'There was nowhere else to go.'

I asked him how he began to move on, and where faith came in.

'After Apollo was over, that drive that took me to the Moon was inside, that focus that we had, that energy that we had. It was still there, and it was: now what are you going to do? Some guys decided they could fulfil their dreams and desires by staying in the space programme. My two colleagues did. Others of us left. I tried the Space Shuttle for about three years but realized it was not as dynamic as Apollo. I found this business opportunity, a new challenge.' There would be several. He formed, and was president of, Orbit Corporation, a beverage distributorship for Coors in San Antonio, which was successful but frustrating and which he sold out of in 1978; he became a partner in real-estate shopping-centre development, Campbell-Duke Investments; was president and investor of several companies; and is the owner of Charlie Duke Enterprises, which produces videos, and president of Duke Investments, his private investment company, though he says it's no longer really active.

'Throughout all of this was this searching for peace, and that's where my faith came in about 1978, so I found a peace and a purpose through my faith. The spiritual side didn't take over so much I lost my desire for adventure: I still fly airplanes, but I see life as more a one-time adventure, one accomplishment. I'm pleased that what happened to me was so significant and

I'm delighted that God has been able to use that in my life, to bring me a peace and a purpose in life.'

Duke's website hosts a wealth of interesting footage of the mission, and an explanation of some of the practical minutiae of space travel, from going to the bathroom to the parachutes that deploy on the returning capsule after re-entry ('Without those chutes, we would have hit the water at a great rate of speed that would spoil your whole day'). But also there is a three-part video called *Walk with the Son*, with an opening shot of a blood-red holy Bible next to a model of the Moon, in which he explains his faith, and its appearance in his life after the Moon, in more detail.

'When I was on the Moon, I didn't feel close to God,' he says in this video, standing dwarfed by a Saturn booster in the background. 'I wasn't searching for God. It wasn't a spiritual experience for me. It wasn't even a philosophical experience. I just had a real technical experience. I didn't think I needed any more God than what I had.' A classic small-town boy from South Carolina, he had been raised with the church, baptized at twelve, and was a faithful Sunday church attender, but did so more to please his parents than out of faith. He didn't have much use for religion during his training days – 'I guess if I had to look back on it now, what was really my god was my career' – and didn't much need it immediately afterwards in business.

But there had been a certain emptiness. 'It's pretty tough to top a walk on the Moon, even in the space programme,' he says. 'So I was concerned about what I was going to do with the rest of my life. And that was really exciting for about a year after the flight was over: the thrill of the training was still there, the thrill of the flight, the thrill of all the parades and the speeches and all the accolades that we were receiving. Then after a year, in 1973, I began to think: is that all there is to this? What was I going to do with the rest of my life? I was thirty-seven years old and I really didn't have any challenges left in my life.'

It was his wife, and her struggles, that caused a change. 'If you looked at my family and me we were pretty average,' Duke says in his video. 'We looked like a successful family, we had a nice home, a couple of cars, went to church every Sunday, involved in all the things Americans got involved in. But if you had been a fly on the wall of the Duke household for a couple of days you'd have seen that everything wasn't peaches and cream in my family.'

In fact, by 1974, Dotty 'was really on the verge of suicide and deep depression and just didn't see any meaning in life', he says. Then, in 1975, some people visited their church on what was called a Faith Alive weekend, and Dotty found herself transformed, and gave herself up completely to her faith. Charlie at the time didn't really notice much except that his wife appeared to be feeling better, 'and wasn't nagging me'; she did invite him to pray when he started losing interest in the beer business he was building, and prayed for it to get so bad that he would sell out (it did, and he did, which is perhaps not what everybody would see as a sign from God, but it worked well enough for the Dukes). But, for his part, it wasn't until the month after he'd sold his business in March 1978 that religion caught up with Charlie too. He went to a Bible study at a tennis ranch in New Braunfels, intending to learn a bit about the Middle East, but came away utterly converted.

'There was no blast-off into eternity, no angelic music, or heavenly visitation by angels, or any blinding flash of light,' he says. 'But there was a sure knowledge and a sure peace in my heart that Jesus really was the Son of God.' From that day on he took to the Bible in earnest and accepted a few home truths. 'The problem with your marriage is you. The problem with your relationship with your son is you.' He was able to rebuild his marriage. 'We are not steaming towards the rocks of divorce any more. Praise God.'

The idea of turning to religion after seeing the stars in such proximity makes a lot of sense to some, less to others. Does getting out there into the blackness and seeing the unspeakable beauty and wonder of the Earth and the stars strike one as evidence of a supreme being? Or does it instead do the reverse, and show that our faiths are based on limited understanding, and that all instead is a function of stardust and science? In any case, Duke was certainly not alone. Well before Duke's own conversion, Jim Irwin, the eighth man on the Moon on *Apollo 15*, had styled himself a 'Goodwill Ambassador for the Prince of Peace' and had been travelling the world repeating: 'Jesus walking on the Earth is more important than man walking on the Moon.' By 1973, Irwin had started leading expeditions to Mount Ararat in Turkey, looking for the remains of Noah's Ark, and he would continue to do so for a decade thereafter.

It's certainly easy to understand how one would gain a different perspective on the significance of things from space. 'When I was on the Moon, I could hold up my hand at arm's length, and underneath my hand was the Earth,' Duke says. 'And the thought occurred to me that underneath my hand is 4 billion people, plus or minus. And from the Moon, you looked up at the Earth and you didn't see America or South America or Asia or Israel or Russia. You just saw Earth. And we're all one down on spaceship Earth. I thought if man could just learn to love one another, we'll be all right.'

Duke's video concludes: 'That walk with Jesus is a lot more fun than that walk on the Moon.'

*

I ended my call with Duke fascinated by the differences in him and Bean, and in particular in the outlet they had found in order to create a meaningful life after walking on another world. I wrote my article for *Discovery Channel Magazine*, and then resolved to write a book tracking down all the Moonwalkers, only to find that this had already been done, and done brilliantly, by another Brit, Andrew Smith, whose book *Moondust* I promptly ordered and devoured in a single day, ending it both exhilarated and depressed.

Still, I'm sure Smith would be the last person to suggest there was any kind of monopoly on interviewing Moonwalkers, and by now I was addicted, buying every autobiography and account I could find. It was fascinating to immerse myself in that half-century-old yet science-fiction world, to cross-reference what Deke Slayton had to say about this or John Young had to say about that, to learn all the little subplots at play as this outrageous ambition was realized. One of those subplots was that plenty of the astronauts didn't actually like one another, which shouldn't be a surprise considering they were mainly alpha male test-pilot jocks (albeit generally very smart ones), but it grates somewhat with the popular impression of an immeasurable teamwork at play. In particular, Aldrin and Gene Cernan clearly couldn't stand one another.

I found that there was an annual space festival, Spacefest, run by a pair called Kim and Sally Poor. The next one, its fourth incarnation, was coming up in Tucson, Arizona. Among the astronauts in attendance would be both Bean and Duke, as well as Aldrin, Cernan, David Scott – and Ed Mitchell. I pitched a piece on the conference to Qantas's excellent in-flight magazine, *The Australian Way*, and then hit upon another idea – for which I would need Mitchell, perhaps the most remarkable and different of all the Moonwalkers.

*

And so to Tucson.

For the astronauts, Spacefest is a little industry, a fund-raiser – because, after all, nobody got rich being paid by NASA, and even in retirement many of them could probably use the money. The norm is that they charge for autographs and pictures.

One of the fascinating asides of a conference like this is just what a clear hierarchy exists among the astronauts, based upon what they did and when they did it. Top of the tree by an absolute mile in terms of his charges is Buzz Aldrin: $400 for an autograph, $1,000 if it completes a set with Neil Armstrong and Mike Collins (his colleagues on *Apollo 11*, the first to land on the Moon), and, inexplicably, $1,500 if it's on a baseball. Other mission commanders of Apollo landings like Gene Cernan and Dave Scott, from *Apollo 17* and *15* respectively, charge $200 as a base fee, with an arcane methodology of extra charges for 'difficult to sign' items; Moonwalkers, but not commanders, like Alan Bean, Charlie Duke and Ed Mitchell charge $100–150. Those who flew to the Moon and orbited it but didn't land on it, like Al Worden and Dick Gordon, are in the $80–90 bracket, and those who flew the Space Shuttle less again.

And then, in a corner, there's Richard Hatch from *Battlestar Galactica*. He charges $30 a pop.

One of the most memorable scenes of Smith's *Moondust* comes when he goes to a *Star Trek* convention attended by Dick Gordon from *Apollo 12*, who is largely ignored while people queue long and deep to meet actors. 'A roomful of people who are famous to one degree or another for pretending to be death-mocking space adventurers and here, tucked away in a corner, is a real one, and no one knows who he is. Or wants to know. The fakes look more convincing.' Today, though Hatch from *Battlestar Galactica* is drawing a reasonable crowd, the single most photo-graphed person or object by far is Buzz Aldrin's fee card.

Still, a look at a nearby auction helps to explain why the

astronauts have started seeking a piece of the financial action. A fast-talking auctioneer is fronting a combined internet and ballroom sale of some quite fabulously obscure items. A flown SRB APU exhaust duct goes for $325 to an internet bidder. A steal at $75, a flown SRB nose cap combined detonating fuse is inexplicably passed without a bid. And then a moment of excitement: a man in a cowboy hat successfully bids $75 for a 'remove before flight' streamer from the Space Shuttle – meaning, presumably, that it was *removed before flight*. The man in the cowboy hat breathes deeply with relief; a bystander gives him a high five.

And this is nothing. Alan Lipkin runs Regency Superior, a Los Angeles-based collector and auctioneer of collectibles in space and aviation, among other things. His business – one of four or five established houses – conducts three auctions a year for space memorabilia, typically turning over between half and three-quarters of a million dollars a time. He once sold a Gemini spacesuit for US$180,000, and a Mercury suit for well over $100,000 over fifteen years ago.

Seeing the scale of the memorabilia business, he doesn't begrudge astronauts charging for autographs, but notes opinions among the astronauts themselves 'vary quite strongly. Some astronauts rarely, if ever, sign autographs: Neil Armstrong is famous for quitting signing in 1996.' Armstrong did so because he had come to resent the commercialization of his signature (none of which, of course, benefited him), but the result of his decision was to push up the value of existing signatures enormously: Lipkin says his signature ranges from $300 to $500 on a blank piece of card to up to $4,000 on a photo or letter, and up to $10,000 on unusual items. 'Others, such as Bill Anders [who flew on *Apollo 8* and took the legendary *Earthrise* photo – see chapter 8] have never been free with their autographs. Others have been so free with their autographs they have become almost worthless in the auction market.' An example here, perhaps surprisingly, is John Glenn, the first American to orbit the Earth. Why? 'He's a politician, so he signs a lot of signatures! It's supply and demand.'

What's the appeal of memorabilia? 'It's history. A new age of exploration,' says Lipkin. 'Would somebody want a signature of a Columbus or Vasco de Gama or Magellan? A piece of the *Santa Maria* would be a museum piece of incalculable value, but you can get a piece of the *Apollo 11* capsule that has been on the Moon and purchase it. It is a true piece of world history.'

But back to the astronauts. I introduce myself to Bean and Duke, both of whom genially at least pretend to remember speaking with me; they pose for photographs with the magazine, and my pic with Bean – me grinning like a loon, festooned in a vest bulging so full of camera lenses I appear as a wannabe Marine in a flak jacket – remains my Twitter picture to this day.

I spend a little time with Cernan and Scott, the two mission commanders here, but since they're not formal interviews I won't dwell on their asides. Gene Cernan, the last man on the Moon on *Apollo 17*, I catch up with just as a woman called Suzanne whose business card says 'age reductionist' is planting a kiss on his cheek. He's still got it, clearly, all these years after he met his wife-to-be on a flight (she was a stewardess) and tracked her down through a friend who worked at Continental. It's hard to interrupt him because he is signing his way through a huge stack of what look like maps, a lucrative way to spend an afternoon. A schoolgirl near his desk talks about her plans to study the Middle East, while her father admonishes her for not studying her Bible with sufficient rigour.

What are you doing here? I ask age-reductionist Suzanne. 'It's part of history, and honour,' she says. 'These guys were heroes and when the space programme ended they were dishonoured, in a way.'

Dave Scott, commander of *Apollo 15*, a brilliant astronaut and flyer whose reputation after a perfect mission suffered because of a scandal around auctioning postage stamps they had smuggled to the Moon – and who was later engaged to Anna Ford – is low key and unassuming when I meet him, at odds with his sometimes high-handed reputation during the Apollo era. Do the astronauts meet up any other times apart from this conference? 'Nah,' he says. 'It was forty years ago. Everyone's doing other things now.' Mainly, I talk to him about Chuck Yeager, who I'm about to go and meet in Edwards Air Force Base in California after the conference. 'Just ask him about hunting,' Scott says.

And Buzz? Well, Buzz has a syntax and manner all of his own, looking askance as he talks to you, answering questions you haven't asked in a curious, mangled style. The way to get Buzz talking, it is widely understood, is to ask him about orbital mechanics. In the Apollo days, his peers used to call him Dr Rendezvous, such was his obsession with the science of bringing two craft together in space, which would be essential for the success of the Apollo programme. He knew his stuff, no question: with a PhD, he was, quite literally, a rocket scientist, but his fixation with the subject would sometimes amuse colleagues like Al Bean, who might be trying to chat up a girl at a party while simultaneously trying to get Buzz off the subject of in-flight orbital trajectories. Anyway, not much has changed, and if you lob him a question on either that or the possibilities of commercial spaceflight – ideally involving a freight route to Mars – then he's happy as Larry, hands moving in mid-air, a vast intellect shining through. Short and stocky with barrelling broad shoulders, he also looks, by a distance, the fittest and healthiest of the Moonwalkers.

But the one I'm really here to see is Edgar Mitchell.

*

Mitchell is quite unlike any other astronaut. He started out on a familiar path to the rest of them, except perhaps for the fact that his mother – 'an artist by temperament and a farm wife by necessity' – wanted him to be either a preacher or a musician. He was born in the West Texas dust bowl in the middle of the Great Depression to a Southern Baptist family in a tough but happy existence, and then moved to Roswell, New Mexico – yes, *that* Roswell – as a boy, where his grandfather put together a cattle herd.

At thirteen, Mitchell took a job at the local airport washing small and fragile aircraft, and was just fourteen when he soloed in one of these planes, 'made of light framing and lacquered cloth, and experienced for the first time the sense of freedom found only in the seat of an airplane; release from the Earth'. Quite apart from a love of the air, this engendered in him a love of both engineering and nature. Life on the farm had given him a strong understanding of farm machinery – this is also true of Chuck Yeager, who credits his own success to an impoverished background in West Virginia, where he learned a great deal about mechanics at the most rustic level of the farm.

An oddball from the outset, he was an unusual but successful figure at Carnegie Mellon. 'At times I would see myself as I believed others might see me: a cowboy with jug-handled ears and straw in his teeth: simple, but earnest. And every now and then I played to their expectations.' Industrious and hard-working, he took a full-time job cleaning slag from burned-out blast furnaces at a steel mill, often finishing a midnight shift before getting a little sleep and heading straight into class. Rather than delay or extend his studies to cope with this sleepless toil, he instead accelerated them, finishing early and marrying his girlfriend Louise whom he had somehow found time to acquire along the way.

He moved back to the ranch in New Mexico but enlisted for the Korean War with some misgivings, reasoning two things: one, that if he didn't, he'd be drafted anyway so conflict was unavoidable; and two, enlisting with the navy was the only way for a married man to get to fly, given the arcane military rules of the time. He moved to San Diego for boot camp, then Newport, Rhode Island, for Officer Candidate School, and next Pensacola, Florida, with Louise now pregnant, and then Whidby Island in Washington State, by now with a daughter in tow. He saw conflict in the Pacific for three years, spent a year in San Diego again on carrier duty and then ended up, as so many Apollo veterans did at one time or another, in the Mojave Desert, where he designed a new delivery system for atomic weaponry. In his time in the Pacific he had seen the detonation of atomic bomb tests in the Kwajalein Atoll, and recognized with some alarm the same extraordinary glows he had seen from the White Sands Proving Grounds near his Roswell home as a boy. He could see the murderous, terrifying power of his duties in weapons technology and was distressed by it, wishing to use his skills for exploration instead, and when the Soviets launched the Sputnik satellite in 1957, he had a first sense of how it could be done.

But first, more of the peripatetic life so common to the Apollo veterans: a move to postgraduate school in Monterey to study aeronautical engineering; and then the Massachusetts Institute of Technology, which would also be an alma mater to Aldrin, Scott and Duke, to take a revolutionary new course in aeronautics and astronautics. He changed his status with the navy to aeronautical engineer, moved to Massachusetts and immersed himself in the course.

This was the pathway that would take him to the Moon, but it did plenty else besides: it first taught him about quantum mechanics and the theory of relativity, subjects that continue to guide him today.

Having qualified, he moved to Los Angeles to join the military's own space programme, but realized that he was going to be kept out of astronaut selection by lack of flying time, and so moved to the test-pilot school at Edwards, where a new space curriculum had been added under Chuck Yeager's guidance. Then it was a question of waiting, as all the Apollo men did, for the legendarily curt call of acceptance to the space programme by Deke Slayton – 'never one to use a paragraph where a phrase would do,' as Mike Collins put it in the finest of the astronaut autobiographies, *Carrying the Fire*. Mitchell's call came in the late spring of 1966, when he was thirty-six.

Just like Duke, Mitchell flew in space but once, and went all the way to the Moon. His route there was filled with chance. He and his commander, Alan Shepard, along with command module pilot (the one who doesn't land on the Moon but orbits it) Stuart Roosa, had been the original crew for *Apollo 13*. But Shepard had been banished from flight for several years with Ménière's disease, a disorder of the inner ear which affects both hearing and balance, and was still recovering from an experimental procedure to cure it. NASA's top management – in the only example of Deke Slayton being overruled on anything, as far as anyone knows – insisted that Shepard be given more time to train. So Shepard, Mitchell and Roosa were pushed back to *Apollo 14*; and Lovell, Haise and Mattingly (later replaced by Swigert) pulled forward to *13*. Had that not happened, it would have been Mitchell trying to deal with an explosion on a spacecraft as far from home as it is possible to be.

Mitchell was considered capable and an expert on the lunar module, but he was undeniably different from the crowd, and this manifested itself particularly through his interest in the philosophical side of his reasons for going to the Moon, and, in particular, supernatural or paranormal phenomena. One day, a couple of months before launch, he was taking a brief holiday diving in the Bahamas and met with two medical doctors, Edward Boyle and Edward Maxey. Mitchell describes them as 'interested in the full spectrum of consciousness'. Mitchell felt a bond with them, calling them 'well-read, experienced and competent men of science', and they proposed a test: whether extra-sensory perception could be conducted over 200,000 miles from Earth, twenty times as far as any two human beings had ever been from each other before Apollo. They planned to use Zenner symbols – a square, a circle, a star, a cross and a wavy line. Mitchell, in space, would concentrate on a symbol and a random number, and at the same time his colleagues on Earth would see if they could visualize what he had chosen.

Mitchell says he kept his plans confidential, and Slayton makes no mention of them in his own autobiography until after the mission, but Gene Cernan's autobiography claims Slayton brought him and Shepard together one month before the launch to discuss Mitchell's interest in ESP. 'Deke held up two fingers of his right hand, about an inch apart. "I'm about that close to pulling Ed off the flight and replacing him with Joe Engle," he told us. "What do you guys think?"' Cernan says Shepard was bothered by the ESP stuff 'but rated Ed a crackerjack LM systems man who was qualified for the flight on every other point'. Slayton stuck with Mitchell.

When *Apollo 14* took to the Florida skies on 31 January 1971, Mitchell found its sense of perspective instantly transforming. 'Within only a few minutes, we were there,' he wrote. 'We were in outer space, that vast domain where I had once been taught the kingdom of heaven lay. Though space is only a vacuum, it is just as beautiful and strange as anything possibly conjured by a child's potent imagination. There is a sense of unreality here, with the absence of gravity and the tapestry of blackness broken only by an overwhelming glitter of stars that surrounded our craft. It occurred to me that the sky is not simply above the Earth – it is below and all around us, invisibly shrouding the home planet twenty-four hours a day out to the edges of the universe.'

Apollo 14 was the last of the H missions, those that were primarily just to get there, before the later J missions which had greater scientific scope. It was smooth, a return to form after the near disaster of *Apollo 13*, although it achieved rather less than the scientific community would have hoped; Smith's book quotes a respected Apollo figure, whom he doesn't name, saying that sending science-and geology-phobic Shepard to the Moon 'was a complete waste of time – we might as well have sent that jerk to Dallas'. If the mission is remembered for anything, it is Shepard playing golf on the Moon.

But the point I am interested to speak to Mitchell about came on the way back.

*

In person, Ed Mitchell is tall but stooped, in a sand-coloured polo shirt with brown braces. He uses a walking stick, wears a hearing aid, and looks a little older and wearier than his mainly tanned and toned space corps peers. But in speech, his intellect is razor sharp.

We sit down at one of the modest booths and talk. Behind him, held up against a red, white and blue striped curtain, is his *Apollo 14* mission patch, reproduced a couple of feet across: a golden star shooting through the heavens from the Earth in the background to a bigger Moon in the foreground. Around its perimeter are three names: Shepard. Roosa. Mitchell. Of whom Mitchell is the only survivor.

I had heard, and read, about a moment of epiphany he had encountered on the way back from the Moon. I ask him to explain it to me.

'Coming back,' he says, 'my tasks on the mission were roughly completed on the Moon, so I could be a little bit more relaxed about coming home.' I have already noticed, in my brief acquaintance, that astronauts tend to lift their hands in speech, in order to try to illustrate to those of us who have always been bound by gravity just how trajectory and direction work in space. This he does. 'It was our orientation. We were perpendicular to the plane of the ecliptic, and rotating. So we were flying this way –' he moves one hand – 'but rotating that way.' He moves the other. 'So every two minutes you had a picture of the Earth, Moon and Sun coming through the porthole, and a 360-degree panorama of the heavens. And that's pretty wild, particularly since outside the atmosphere the stars are ten times as bright and numerous as we can see on Earth.'

At this point, he remembers, his studies at MIT and Harvard kicked in. 'I knew that the star systems were what manufactured the molecules that make up our bodies,' he says. 'So all matter is made of star systems. We're all stardust. We're all the same stuff. And that was a big *Wow*.'

It's evocative enough in person, but tough to discuss these ideas off the cuff with a stranger. It's clearer still in print, in his book, *The Way of the Explorer: An Apollo Astronaut's Journey through the Material and Mystical Worlds*. (You can tell by the title that this isn't a typical astronaut memoir.) Here, he recalls: 'What I saw out the window was all I had ever known, all I had ever loved and hated, all that I had longed for, all that I once thought had ever been and ever would be. It was all there suspended in the cosmos on that fragile little sphere. What I experienced was a grand epiphany accompanied by exhilaration, an event I would later refer to in terms that could not be more foreign to my upbringing in West Texas, and later, New Mexico. From then on, my life would take a radically different course.

'What I experienced during that three-day trip home was

nothing short of an overwhelming sense of universal connect-edness. I actually felt what has been described as an ecstasy of unity. It occurred to me that the molecules of my body and the molecules of the spacecraft itself were manufactured long ago in the furnace of one of the ancient stars that burned in the heavens about me. And there was the sense that our presence as space travellers, and the existence of the universe itself, was not accidental, but that there was an intelligent process at work. I perceived the universe as in some way conscious. The thought was so large it seemed at the same time inexpressible, and to a large degree it still is.'

His life was changed forever.

He tells me now: 'After I got back, while in the mission still, I realized that the story of ourselves as told by science was possibly flawed, because we didn't have all the answers, and the story of ourselves as told by our religious cosmologies were archaic, and probably flawed. So now that we were having this whole new picture of the heavens – and the Hubble has increased that over the years – the enormity of the universe of which we know so little . . . it was a Wow, an A-ha.' That word again: wow. It comes up frequently with Mitchell, and it's a relief that it does, as a conversation can drift into the complex world of quantum mechanics and consciousness pretty quickly and pretty deeply. But really, what better word for what happened to him? How else to describe the interconnectedness of all of matter revealed to him as he tumbled across the void, the bright heavens displayed in revolution around him. Add to that the increased understanding since the discoveries with the Hubble space tele-scope, launched in 1990 and still in operation at the time of writing. Wow.

'We're just basically starting to get acquainted with what we are all about. So that was the epiphany. But I didn't understand it immediately.'

An orange-tanned woman in her sixties with bright blonde hair, so immovable it looks like it could support a suspension bridge, asks for his autograph. He grants it.

When he got home, he started reading up on religion and science, but couldn't find anything that matched his experience. He went to professors at Rice University, he tells me, to experts in palaeontology and anthropology. 'I said to them: I've had this experience, what can you tell me from ancient literature?' They brought him descriptions from Sanskrit, of a sense of unity and oneness, followed by a feeling of ecstasy. 'I said: that's the experience. What's it called?' In Sanskrit 500 years ago, they told him, it was called *savikalpa samadhi*; in Greek, *metanoia*, or change of mind; in Zen Buddhism, enlightenment. 'I have always tended to be critical of our war-like behaviour and killing each other over who's got the best gods. And this has made me realize we do that because we are unenlightened. We are too motivated by ego, and we need to learn to do better than that.'

Again, his autobiography clarifies just what happened to him when he got home. 'What lay in store was an entirely different kind of journey, one that would occupy more than forty years of my life. I have often likened that experience to a game of pickup sticks: within a few days my beliefs about life were thrown into the air and scattered about. It took me twenty years to pick up those sticks and make some kind of sense of it all.'

I ask him about the different reactions of people who went to the Moon, and how many of them seemed to come back changed but express it in different ways: Duke and Irwin through religion, Bean through art, Al Worden – command module pilot on *Apollo 15* – through poetry. Would you feel this way, I ask him, without having gone to the Moon?

'I don't know. The fact is that all of us that went to the Moon and looked back at the Earth all agreed that if we could get our political leaders to have summits in space, we would have different political systems. Because it is a life-changer. And so the answer is yes: all of us, we might not have had exactly the same experiences, or describe it in the same way, but it would amount to the same thing – the powerful experience of reshaping Earth and the way you look at our whole place in the cosmos.'

The idea of a different political perspective as a result of viewing the Earth from above is something he's raised before in writing; again, it came from the window of *Apollo 14*. He wrote:

The planet in the window harboured much strife and discord beneath the blue and white atmosphere, a peaceful and inviting appearance. On a small peninsula of southeast Asia, a brutal civil war was being waged within the thin canopy of foliage. This was a war that commanded the attention of another country defined by invisible borders on the other side of the planet.

The sense was particularly acute because his younger brother was down there at the time in Vietnam, flying missions for the air force. It all seemed absurd, the more so in light of his sudden attuning to a greater, ancient purpose.

Billions of years ago, the molecules of my body, of Stu's and Al's body, of this spacecraft, of the world I had come from and was now returning to, were manufactured in the furnace of an ancient generation of stars like those surrounding us . . . And what I felt was an extraordinary personal connectedness with it. I was overwhelmed with the sensation of physically and mentally extending out into the cosmos.

69

Of the twelve men who set foot on the Moon, Mitchell's subsequent beliefs are probably the furthest from the mainstream. I wonder what the reaction of NASA, and the state, has been.

'If you're talking about NASA as an organization, I couldn't care less,' he says – not firmly, not stridently, but as an observation. 'They're just people, and the political system. The people who count are the ones who say: yes, I understand that experience and I want more of that, and are interested in my Noetic Foundation and my new Quantrek Organization that's digging deeper into the quantum world and the biological world, because we see things coming out of this we didn't know before. It's more discovery, which is what science is all about, how our universe is put together. These are subtle things. It was 400 years without the quantum world, and without consciousness as a scientific subject. And late in the twentieth century we've started to look at these issues. The message is, we've got a lot to learn and we're just getting started.'

At this stage, some context is necessary about what Mitchell did next after Apollo. With his first marriage having failed as his interests changed and moved to ethereal ideas of consciousness, he then quit NASA in 1972, and founded the Institute of Noetic Sciences in California. I must confess I had to look up 'noetics'. Originally, the term referred to metaphysical philosophy around the mind and intellect; today, noetic sciences are considered to be around consciousness and spirituality, and in particular how beliefs affect the physical world. Mitchell says his aim at that time was to study 'the totality of consciousness', and his institute – a non-profit foundation that would allow him to function as an independent scholar – he envisaged as 'an organization that wasn't so much a place as a state of mind'. Launched with a $600,000 donation from a philanthropic couple in California, which they pledged to repeat annually, Mitchell set about building a detailed programme, only for the funding to disappear when the couple went broke; then, one day, a young woman turned up in a VW van and gave him a cheque for $25,000, then promptly left again. Funding would always prove somewhat unpredictable for the Institute of Noetic Sciences.

Quantrek is a newer venture, billed as 'engendering the best possible future through frontier science', and focuses in particular on quantum holography, something I'm not even going to begin to attempt to explain except that it is believed (by Mitchell anyway) to be the basis of consciousness and 'elevates information to the same fundamental status as matter and energy'.

I have read that the Noetic Foundation, despite its secular and even anti-religious ideals, started to become something of a church; even that people tried to draw a connection between the fact that there were twelve Moonwalkers and twelve disciples of Jesus. Mitchell himself has written: 'On many occasions it has seemed as though I was expected to become a high priest in some kind of new religion.'

I ask him about this.

'I think what you're alluding to is the fact that we do create a structure around our beliefs,' he says. 'If you've read my book you know I tell the story of my mother's healing by Norbu Chen, the Tibetan healer, the initial blush of being healed of her glaucoma, until she realized he was not a Christian.' Indeed, the story is remarkable: Norbu put Mitchell's near-blind mother into a relaxed state, put himself into a trance, floated his hands over her head, and sent her to bed. The next morning, Mitchell's mother rushed in to him, shouting: 'Son, I can see, I can see!' More than that, her vision was perfect: no contacts, no glasses.

But then one day his mother called him to ask if Norbu was a Christian. Mitchell said he was not. She convinced herself that her newfound eyesight was the work of the devil – and within a few hours it had disappeared, requiring thick new glasses again.

'According to her belief system,' Mitchell says to me now, 'she considered she had been healed by Satan. Those are the types of structures we erect in our mind to account for a lot of things in our own way.' Yet that wasn't the end of the story. 'My mother was a very bright woman, so by the time she passed away, even though she had rejected her healing, she had decided: if I got rid of the healing, I can get it back. And she did. By the time she passed her eyesight was down to normal reading glasses.'

Through belief?

'Through her changing her mind. She came to the enlightened view that: I got rid of this through my lack of belief, certainly I can get it back. We have seen that type of healing going on forever. Jesus was a healer, from that tradition.'

He turns to me. 'You may or may not know I have been healed of both prostrate and kidney cancer by alternative means. By mind means.' He nods for a few seconds. 'So we can do that. That's the way of the future. I'm not knocking the medical model, but what is coming out of this is that we can do an awful lot with our belief system.'

He then starts to lose me, talking about the impossibility of creating an equation for an intention, and the arrangement of incoming information into belief systems, and when he says: 'Those are the ideas on the frontier of what we're talking about,' my first impression is to think: no shit. But then, unprompted, he says this:

'One would suspect, and we can't prove this at the moment, that our ET visitors, if they have the ability to get here, and we don't have the ability to get there, they have a better handle on this than we do.'

Ah. I was hoping he'd bring this up.

*

It so happens that immediately before coming to Tucson, I visited Roswell, New Mexico, surely the world capital of alien conspiracy theory – and Mitchell's home town.

In July 1947, something crashed on ranch land north-east of Roswell, and was discovered by a ranch hand called W. W. Brazel. He'd never seen anything like the debris before. He put the wreckage in his pickup truck, and later drove it to the local sheriff's office. The sheriff called the Roswell Army Air Field – Roswell was, at the time, a far bigger military hotbed than it is today, with much of the nation's nuclear testing taking place not far away – and the base commander sent over an intelligence officer, together with a press officer called Walter Haut.

Later, Haut called a local radio station, KGFL, with an important press release to be read on air. It was no ordinary release and it was swiftly picked up elsewhere, including a front-page story in the *San Francisco Chronicle*. The release referred, unequivocally, to the crash of a flying saucer.

But just three hours later, Haut was back at KGFL with a new press release, saying that the first had been a silly mistake, and what had crashed was just a weather balloon. A photo was taken, purportedly with some weather-balloon wreckage – jetsam that those who saw the original debris say had absolutely nothing in common with it – and people were told, with a firmness that would not become clear until much later, to stick to this revised truth.

In the years since, numerous witnesses said they had been intimidated into silence with threats of prison and worse. Others, with the passage of time, said that a request had been made from the military for child-sized coffins that could be hermetically sealed, and some claimed that not only had the crash definitely involved a round disk, with an unfamiliar metal that would regain its shape instantly after being crumpled, but that there were child-size humanoid bodies with large heads, large oval eyes and no noses amid the wreckage. On his deathbed in 2005, Haut, the man who had put out the original story and then retracted it, left a sworn affidavit saying that the first version of events had been the true one, that he had seen bodies, and, to quote: 'I am convinced that what I personally observed was some kind of craft and its crew from space.'

Rumour about what really crashed – alien spacecraft, experimental American warplane, Russian spies – has raged ever since.

Roswell today is something of a circus, it must be said. It would be an unexceptional American town, a long way from anywhere in south-east New Mexico, but for the little things that set it apart: the little green aliens all over the front of the local Walmart, for example, and the flying saucer protruding from the roof of the McDonald's. The theme of alien visitation is the bedrock of the local economy, particularly now most of the military has gone, and at its heart is a UFO museum.

I had spent most of the day in Roswell being driven out to the crash site, three hours' drive from Roswell itself, by a man called Frank Kimbler. It is a peaceful place: the scrubby, barren emptiness of the windswept high desert. There is a plaque here, though deliberately it is in slightly the wrong place, but little else.

Kimbler is, on first glance, weird: he believes he may have found parts of an alien spacecraft, though he's prepared to concede they could also be bits of a beer can. But here's the thing: he's actually not weird at all. Indeed, an awful lot of the true believers in aliens are *not that odd*. Kimbler is a respected teacher at the New Mexico Military Institute. He calls himself an educated sceptic, a scientist. He wants to get independent verification of the isotope ratios for the metals he found, which would demonstrate whether they have come from beyond the Earth; he wants to do it publicly, in front of an audience for verification, using an analysis machine called a Niton. He has no problem with being wrong because of the useful science involved in being so.

Similarly, when I return to the UFO Museum and Research Center later in the day, and when I've finished looking around the awkward combination of academic rigour in the library and alien toilet paper in the gift shop ('Designed for hard to reach areas like Area 51. Also good for areas 1 or 2. Use generously for an out-of-this-world wipe'), I sit down with Mark Briscoe, who is the centre's librarian. He approaches his job with sufficient professionalism and rigour that the library he manages is now linked to the Library of Congress and the Smithsonian, and receives contributions to exhibit from NASA. I do not find myself sitting with a crackpot raging about Them. I find a conservative, practising Southern Baptist who worries about the declining standards of punctuation and the throwaway mentality of today's children (the first several minutes of our interview are spent bemoaning the fact that nobody bothers mending toasters any more). He has three degrees, one of them in psychology, and has been a successful college professor. He is a practical man who tolerates the presence of the gift shop because it brings in 85 to 90 percent of the money for the museum, and so funds his own efforts in the library, which include logging all of the UFO sightings that are reported around the world.

This is all another story, but I mention it for two reasons. One is that, after a while with people like this, I do not automatically jump to a conclusion that people talking about aliens are mad or ridiculous. And the other is that, within this community, Ed Mitchell is considered an absolute rock star. The museum has a section quoting his views on Roswell on the wall, because what a gift he is to them: a local boy, a great American hero, a Moonwalker – and a believer.

So it is no surprise, and in fact the next question I had been intending to ask, when Mitchell brings them up himself.

Have we had ET visitors? I ask him.

Mitchell, generously, has written that there are no stupid questions, only stupid answers. But this is the only time he looks at me as if I have asked something like: is the Earth round?

'I have no question about that,' he says, frowning. 'They have probably been coming here for centuries. The evidence may be a little sketchy, but in the biblical realm there are accounts of chariots of fire in the sky. Michelangelo's paintings contain UFOs. We had the so-called Phoenix Lights event in 1997,' a series of sightings of light formations reportedly seen by thousands of people, mainly in Arizona. 'I don't think there's any question we have had ET visitors, and to a greater or lesser extent, they have had effects on us.

'I'm not saying it's all good,' he says, and already we have moved beyond any conjecture about *whether* we have had alien visitors, on to a justification of their behaviour. 'There are some accounts of abductions that don't sound so pleasant. But maybe it's a misinterpretation. It could be that some of our visitors are not as enlightened as others, and since we have enlightened and unenlightened people here on Earth, I wouldn't be surprised if it's true there too.'

Dick Gordon, the command module pilot from *Apollo 12*, walks over as if to ask something, hears what Mitchell's talking about, looks at each of us in turn, and decides to retreat back to his booth without a word.

I tell Mitchell that I was in Roswell, and that his views are popular there. What's his view on the Roswell incident?

'I grew up in Roswell, I have lectured there, and I do know the people who helped set up the museum. Without delving into specifics, yes, I do have a firm belief that we have been visited. The Roswell incident was a real live ET presence, and what more can I say?'

Well, the other side of it is not just the visitation, I say, but the governmental . . .

'Cover-up? Yes.' He pauses to consider his answer. 'At that point of time, I suspect the reaction was that people aren't ready for this: that people will panic at the idea of alien visitation. I think it has been supplanted in recent years by the fact that there is enormous profit potential in having the keys to that technology. I'm fairly confident that has been the rationale behind the secrecy in recent years. President Eisenhower said in his retirement speech from the presidency, beware the military-industrial complex, and I have a suspicion this is exactly what he was talking about.'

Again, there is no effort to convince me that a spacecraft crashed in Roswell, nor that the government continues to keep the crash materials in order to reverse engineer it. These things are assumed, obvious.

Views like this are the reason I had asked earlier what NASA makes of him today. In 2009, he addressed the National Press Club and called upon the government to open up about Roswell and alien visitation, saying that he had raised the issue of evidence from local Roswell residents with the Pentagon a decade earlier. He spoke quite specifically about a cover-up, and included NASA in his remarks. It all prompted a polite but firm denial from NASA that it was involved in cover-ups regarding alien visits.

'We'll have to see in future where this goes: open it up, make it public, and have people recognize that we have been visited,' Mitchell says. 'We are going to need the type of technology that the extraterrestrials possess if we are going to go off this planet and continue to survive, because we can't survive on this planet the way we're doing it. We're on a non-sustainable course.'

When many people talk about UFOs, they are mocked, I begin to say, but he asks me to repeat it, looking concerned and offended. Softening the question, I say: you're probably one of the most respected people who think this way, a scientist, a Moonwalker, an American hero. Is it helpful when a voice like yours is saying this?

It's the most relaxed he has looked in the interview. Proud, even. 'Well,' he says, 'somebody's got to lead. And since we're dealing with a real phenomenon, that's how I try to talk about it: how do you use it, how do you benefit from it. I'm convinced we're working with a real phenomenon.'

Time is up. He poses uncomfortably for a few photos in front of his mission patch, frowning into the lens, then shakes my hand and leaves. As I check my recorder has picked everything up OK, I can see some of the other astronauts looking at me. None of them judge or criticize Mitchell for his views, but I do have the feeling they don't want to see him as representative of the way the rest of them see the world – and beyond. 'I like Ed, I respect him,' an Apollo veteran will later tell me. 'But he scares me a bit.'

For my part, though, I come away from the interview delighted that someone with such capacity for unusual thought was granted the chance to have stepped on another world, and to express just how much he was altered by it. It seems to me to be to the world's benefit that Mitchell went out there and had his mind blown by cosmic epiphany. It enriches our shared knowledge of experience. I can't subscribe to everything he talks about; I try, later, to read some of his academic writing, with titles like *A Dyadic Model of Consciousness,* or *Nature's Mind: The Quantum Hologram,* and can make no sense of it. But maybe he's decades ahead of all of us, and we're the ones with the limited view.

Oh, and that ESP experiment? He tried it four times on the way to and from the Moon. He took out a kneeboard with a table of random numbers and the Zenner symbols, and concentrated on pairs of them for fifteen seconds at a time. On the ground in

Florida, his collaborators tried to write them down in the same sequence. He called his findings 'statistically significant'.

*

Saturday night at the Tucson conference brings a banquet, with anniversary presentations and tributes to long-lost friends. Charlie Duke reprises his famous line, and obligingly stumbles over the word 'tranquillity' to widespread delight. And Gene Cernan, the statesman, wobbling a little now in both knee and voice, makes a familiar call for 'kids to dream about doing things they didn't think they were capable of doing, to reach out and once again do the impossible'.

By the end of the evening I have spent at least a little time with six of the then-nine surviving Moonwalkers. Aside from Armstrong, there are only two absentees. One is John Young, a NASA careerist who went on to become the first commander of a Space Shuttle, and who by the end of his career had flown six times across four different classes of spacecraft from the first manned Gemini mission in 1965 to the ninth shuttle flight in 1983, having travelled to the Moon twice. He went on to be chief of the astronaut office, although to rather less acclaim from fellow astronauts, and was devastated by the *Challenger* tragedy in 1985, but stayed the course in less public roles at NASA for many years, not retiring until 2004 after forty-two years of service.

The last is Harrison Schmitt, the first true civilian on the Moon (Armstrong technically was too in 1969, but came up through the military). His appointment on to Cernan's flight in 1972 was controversial and involved him being bumped up a flight in the roster to ensure that the last Moon landing, as *Apollo 17* would prove to be, contained a geologist. He left NASA in 1975, and ran successfully as a Republican for a Senate seat for

New Mexico. He was later defeated in 1982 by a competitor who ran on the slogan: *What on Earth has he done for you lately?* Years of consultancy followed, combining his uniquely diverse skill set of geology, space travel and public policy. He still lives in Silver City, New Mexico, and remains an adjunct professor of engineering physics at the University of Wisconsin-Madison; one of his passions has been the idea of using the helium-3 that can be found on the Moon as a fuel for nuclear fusion. But these days he's also somewhat well known for being a climate-change denier, and as recently as May 2013 wrote a passionate defence in the *Wall Street Journal* of rising carbon dioxide levels, bemoaning 'the single-minded demonization of this natural and essential atmospheric gas'. Which, if nothing else, confirms Mitchell's view that people who have been to space come back with a unique perspective on politics.

I find it strangely pleasing that the twelve men who walked on the Moon took such markedly different routes to finding meaning in their lives after the Moon. The diversity of their responses to life after Apollo is like the scattershot debris field of asteroid craters on the Moon itself: one defining event for impact, a host of unpredictable outcomes blown out in every direction. But always anchored by the fact that those footprints are still up there, eternal in the dust, no wind to erase them. Armstrong actually said, later in life, he wished somebody would go up to the Moon and smooth his prints out.

Finally, on the Sunday morning, after a $180-a-head break-fast panel where I find myself arguing with Space Shuttle veteran and excellent astronaut writer Mike Mullane about Palestine, comes the Apollo panel, moderated by writer Andy Chaikin. Five veterans, Moonwalkers and Moon-orbiters, household names one and all, shoot the breeze for an enrap-tured audience. They weep for dying friends from the Apollo

80

years, of whom there are many; they reiterate, again and again, how it took 400,000 people to get them to the Moon; they bemoan, angrily, America's sliding status in space exploration; and they bicker as close friends do about the minutiae of spaceflight and the pranks they played on one another. There is an acute sense of an increasingly distant and thrilling past, a fading out of heroic explorers, galvanized by a crowd of far younger people whose fascination with Apollo has never been greater.

3

Nadia Comaneci

I don't want to be mean about a place I hardly know – and when you're from Birkenhead, you don't really have much right to be mean about anywhere – but Norman, Oklahoma, is not the sort of place you expect to find one of the most revered of all Olympic athletes, least of all a woman who had all the varied glories of the United States to choose from when she defected from Ceausescu's Romania.

Interstate 35 thrusts through here on its way from Dallas to Oklahoma City, and a rumble of trucks and cars rolls off it across the car dealerships and garages to the western side. In sight of the highway is a building named the Bart Conner Gymnastics Academy, and across the other side of a windblown parking lot from it, where tall brown grasses are buffeted in the dust, is a neat and functional single-storey office block. Everything's single-storey here: no need to go higher than a ground floor, with all this Oklahoma flatness and space.

It is late December and a staff Christmas lunch is taking place inside the building's hall, with a friendly and multinational group of people gathered round a few tables. And sitting in the middle of them all, with just a little bit more glamour in the hair and the jacket and the make-up and the shoes than those around her, is perhaps the most famous Olympian of the 1970s: Nadia Comaneci.

At the 1976 Montreal Olympics, Nadia – she's always been Nadia, someone a generation of people could refer to by her first name without any ambiguity who they were talking about – scored the first perfect 10 ever awarded in Olympic competition. Then she got the second. Then the third. Over the course of the next few days, she logged seven unbeatable scores, a feat considered so inconceivable that the scoreboards had not been designed to accommodate it and at first, lacking sufficient digits, flashed up 1.0. She won three gold medals along the way, plus a silver and a bronze. And she did it all at the age of fourteen.

And at fourteen, at that moment in Montreal, her career peaked before she'd even reached puberty. Her medals were for women's gymnastics, but go back and watch her beam and bar and floor routines from 1976: she wasn't a woman at all; she was a girl. She was catapulted from the supervised and deliberately impeded outlook of an Eastern Bloc child to international celebrity in an instant. She was on the cover of *Time, Newsweek* and *Sports Illustrated* in the same week. And then she went home, knowing that professionally her life would simply never be this good again.

So what next? Where does life take you when its defining moment has already taken place before your first kiss, your first drink, your first drive? Well, it turns out you end up in Norman, Oklahoma. But the getting there is quite a story.

*

We are a long way from the Romanian town of Onesti, in the foothills of Romania's Carpathian mountains, where Nadia was born on 12 November 1961, the daughter of a car mechanic who never owned a car. He walked 12 miles a day to and from work instead, reasoning, from the experience of his labours, that cars always broke down.

Many people assume that Nadia, who was recruited into a gymnastics academy at the age of six, never had time for a childhood, but when I ask her about it she paints a very different picture.

'I had a childhood,' she says, sitting in an office surrounded by the plunder of a lifetime of recognition: pictures of her with presidents, a trophy with a Canadian flag built into it, Orthodox religious imagery, photos of her wedding. 'I experienced my own grandmother's backyard. I used to climb the trees, swing from bridges, fun stuff. I did a lot of things that a lot of kids today don't do.

'Being a child was for many years simple, but beautiful and rich, I think.' It was basic but ample, in a way that Romania would not always be: there was enough food, warm clothing, and if there was no concept of brand names or gourmet choices then nobody was any the worse for it, simply eating and wearing the same things as everyone else. There was no TV that would keep a child inside, just a tiny black-and-white set receiving three state-approved stations. She describes an idyllic early existence of outdoor play on her grandmother's farm, digging up carrots and eating tomatoes straight off the vine.

More than anything, she was a tomboy, playing football with the boys on the rare occasions when she wasn't swinging off something, and this perhaps is what led her mother not just to allow her to follow gymnastics, but to actively encourage her to do so in order to save the furniture. 'I used to jump on the couches and the beds. I would do things in the house, destroying the pictures on the wall, and I don't think my mum was very happy about that.' Fearing none of her possessions were going to survive Nadia's childhood intact, her mother took her to a gym, where she joined her first gymnastics team, called The

Flame, while still in kindergarten. 'I don't know if she was familiar with the term "gymnastics", but that's what it was, and that's how I ended up there.'

One day when she was six, a man came into her school and asked a question that probably didn't sound like a life-changing interrogation at the time: 'Who can do a cartwheel?' This was Bela Karolyi, who would go on to become perhaps the most famous ever gymnastics coach, first in Romania and then in the US, revered and reviled in roughly equal measure depending upon whom one talks to. He and his wife, Marta, were creating an experimental gymnastics school in Onesti. Nadia and Bela's accounts of their early days differ – in fact, their accounts of pretty much everything differ – but the story goes that he saw Nadia and another girl doing cartwheels in the playground and almost despaired of finding them again, going from classroom to classroom until he eventually tracked them down at the end of the day.

Even today Onesti still has a population of less than 40,000, and I am struck by the extraordinary coincidence of one of the world's greatest gymnasts and one of the world's greatest gymnastic coaches happening to find each other in this way in a remote town almost 300 kilometres from Bucharest. 'Yeah. It was a happy coincidence, I can say.' She looks thoughtful. 'I don't know how he ended up there because he's not from there either. He used to coach a handball team. I think his wife got a job and that's how they ended up coaching in Onesti. And the story all starts from there.' Do you remember your first impressions of him? 'A big, tall guy, massive. Bushy moustache. Something like that.'

Nadia was still extremely young, but it's clear that as a child she didn't see the rigour of the gymnastics academy as any sort of theft from childhood, and, if anything, equated it with freedom to do things she couldn't do at home. I can't help but look stunned when she says: 'I was almost six and a half when I started, so I had been playing as a child for all those years until I signed up for gymnastics.' But then I realize she doesn't mean that one replaced the other because she doesn't see one stopping as the other starts, but instead a childhood that happened to involve a hell of a lot of time swinging around on bars. At the school they worked six days a week, with four hours a day in class and four in the gym; she lived at home and walked to school each day. She was monitored and disciplined to a degree that might seem restrictive and damaging today, with strict specific portions of meat, vegetables and milk, and instruction on precisely when to turn out the light each night, but then again, what children don't have routine forced upon them? And it was considerably better than not eating at all, as would be the case in a bitter alternative Romania she would discover in later life. So, knowing no different, she loved it all. When she got her first leotard, upon which she made her mum sew a big red 'N' on the nametag, she abandoned her little doll, Petrutra, and slept with the leotard on her pillow instead.

The school provided focus for a useful confluence of her attributes: a clear innate ability, of course, but also an intensely strong work ethic and sense of competition. If she was asked to do twenty-five push-ups, she'd do fifty. Karolyi, who has developed a reputation for sometimes unnecessary toughness and even cruelty towards his gymnasts (something Nadia never, not once, has said about her own experience with him, though she can see how others would feel differently), was not about to tell her to slow down, and the result of it all was that she was deemed ready for the National Championships in 1969. She was eight.

We tend to picture Nadia as arriving, fully formed, as if from nowhere at the 1976 Olympics, a flawless and miraculous ascent to perfection. But naturally the truth was nothing like it, and the most valuable lesson she learned in her first championships was failure. She fell off the beam. Then she fell off it again.

'Not always I had success,' she remembers. 'I made mistakes. I fell from the beams three times. I got 7s. I tell kids: I wasn't 10, 10, 10 all the time.'

Nevertheless, it was clear early on that she was special. When did it become apparent to her?

'Nobody told me that I am great and have such a talent directly, but there was some talk around – I don't know if I overheard it – but people telling that we have a girl who potentially is going to be pretty good. But, you know, you say this to kids to make them feel good.' She laughs, a big, friendly laugh, which is not at all her reputation: she is considered cold and distant, and it's true that she doesn't smile and looks somewhat distrustful upon first meeting, but it's surprising how she opens up after a short time in conversation.

'I didn't lean on that feeling, though, like I'm going to be great some time in the future. I liked the competition. I like to challenge myself. I like to learn new things. It was a discovery for me, the sport, and I wanted to be better at it. There were others,' she says, 'who had more talent than I did. But my success had a lot to do with always doing more than I was asked to, and in time that built up.'

Karolyi, among his other skills, was considered an outstanding spotter – the person entrusted with catching a gymnast if something goes wrong, as it inevitably will when learning a new routine – and this helped her gain confidence to try steadily more challenging things. She calls it 'filling up your bag with knowledge, so when you need it, it is there'.

She won her first Romanian Nationals in 1970, won her first international all-around title in a meet between Romania and Yugoslavia in 1971, and won the all-around gold, vault and uneven bars titles at the Junior Friendship Tournament in 1973, aged eleven. Up against gymnasts in their late teens and twenties, she remembers walking in with her colleagues from the school, tiny little girls in pigtails. Then, in the Eastern Bloc, her name was made a year before Montreal, at the 1975 European Championships in Skien, Norway, winning gold in every event except the floor. In gymnastics, this was every bit as important as the Olympics, since at that time every serious competitor in the sport was from Eastern Europe anyway. 'The US came later,' she says, adding pointedly, 'After Bela moved to the States.' In her view, clearly, one led to the other.

In many ways, for her, the pivotal tournament had been the European Championships. 'I was young at that one too,' she recalls. 'It was the first big competition for me and I was nervous about it. Would I be able to compete in an arena that so many great names would compete in? I had that on one side, and my great fear was not to make a mistake.' She knew what she could do in training, so had tried to discipline herself to *pretend* she was in training, 'so there's nobody around. You just try to block everything. That's a tool of an athlete: to be able to cut out everything around you and to deliver what you know how to deliver.'

That's something you're known for, your ability to focus.

'Yeah. But I've been criticized for that too, because people say I didn't smile.' She puts out her hands in opposite directions. 'It's either like that, or like that.'

But surely that didn't bother you?

'No. I didn't know about that. And I didn't quite care. I tell people: why don't *you* go on that 4-inch beam and you laugh and smile. See how it is.' She laughs. 'You have to concentrate, and this is how I grew up. This was me.'

She was very rarely injured, and in fact did not break anything until well after her professional career was complete – in an exhibition event, when she was distracted by having heard that the tennis star Monica Seles had been stabbed on-court that day. Did her concentration, and her ability to block things out, contribute to the extraordinary lack of injury through her top-flight career? 'I didn't get injured because we did a lot of physical preparation,' she says. 'Which I didn't like. Nobody likes it, because it's boring to do running and abdominal push-ups. Also, children like to try things because they're fun.'

Was a childlike lack of fear part of the reason for her success? 'Oh, I was going for things I wouldn't go for now,' she says. 'Daring things, that kids like to do. And also your coach says: I dare you, you can't do that. I'm like: oh yeah? I can do that! You don't think about it when you're a kid. Now,' she adds, 'I think three times before I do anything. I don't want to do extreme things now, like bungee. All the things people dare to do now, I have done them all when I was a kid.'

But if being a fearless child was part of the recipe for her success, then this raises a troubling argument because, under today's rules, she wouldn't even have been able to compete in Montreal: now the minimum age for Olympic gymnastic competition is sixteen rather than fifteen (she was able to compete at fourteen because it was the year of her fifteenth birthday). Does she think that is a mistake?

'Yeah,' she says. 'Gymnasts are not ready to compete very early because you need years to learn those tricks and put them together and be competitive. One year doesn't make a difference. It's not like they raised it from fifteen to nineteen, that's a gap. But raising from fifteen to sixteen? A lot of kids will be fifteen and will miss an entire Olympic cycle by one or two days, and then have to compete at nineteen with the young ones, and that will be their first attempt. A first attempt at nineteen compared with a first at sixteen? That's quite a big difference in gymnastics.'

I ask her what Romania was like during her childhood: if she had a sense that the nutrition and balanced meals she was enjoying at the school were not something everyone enjoyed. 'Not too much because the conditions in the time when I was growing up, the 1960s and 1970s, were good,' she says. 'Probably the end of the 1970s and the 1980s was [when it deteriorated]. But you don't know other ways. You don't know what you have unless you go out and see what other people don't have or have. We had a doctor, we had maybe better nutrition than poor people had, but it's not like they were throwing richness at us.'

This was the Nadia Comaneci that prepared to go to Montreal in 1976: confident and focused, a success in her discipline already but without media intrusion, and still a girl, with a view of the world necessarily limited in its scope. Neither she, nor the Olympics, had any idea what was coming.

*

On 18 July 1976, a little girl with stern eyebrows, a brown pony-tail and scarcely a visible pelvis walked up to the uneven bars in a snow-white leotard with red, yellow and blue piping down the side. About thirty seconds later, she was world-famous.

I'm a long way from being any sort of expert on gymnastics; when the commentator exclaims, with nothing short of joy, 'oh, look at that amplitude!' I sort of understand, but I couldn't tell you precisely what made her routine so technically magnificent. But what anyone can see, looking at the slightly faded 1976 footage with its mustard block-capital captions, is the extraordinary combination of youth, confidence, beauty, poise, precision and flat-out audacious talent. It was a brilliant athlete arriving without fear at exactly the right moment, and it was just the sort of achievement and performance that the Olympics exist to celebrate.

Small wonder, looking back, that she became the face of the Games, of the whole modern history of gymnastics; she was simply remarkable, and the ponytailed guileless innocence of it all only added to the popular appeal.

But the world didn't stop watching when she dismounted, in an effortless stomach-launched spring, from the uneven bars. From that moment on, everyone wanted to know her.

I ask her whether that attention, if not the strain of competition itself, is an argument for protecting a child from the Olympics, as is now the case?

'No.' She's authoritative on this. 'I think it's better to be thrown into that when you are fourteen. If you put a nine-year-old in to sing on *American Idol*, they are going to go for it, they don't have that nervous thing you have when you're nineteen or twenty. For me, it was easier at fourteen than at nineteen; it was the other way round to what people think. Kids do what they like! They just go in there. They don't have that understanding of what people are expecting from them.'

I ask what she made of the whole carnival of the Olympics. 'I knew it was something bigger than the Europeans, but I kind of experienced that the year before. I knew the *idea* of the Olympics was much bigger, with more people watching it, more coverage on TV. But that doesn't change your performance, because this is what I know, this is what I do. The other teams cannot do anything to incapacitate you.'

Besides, as she patiently tries to stress to me several times through the interview, the whole point is not the number of people watching, but competition with yourself and your own standards. 'You belong to yourself. You perform. Everyone else can compete on their own. It's not like I prepare a routine for the Olympics and then I see someone from the Russian team and think: oh, I'll try that instead. You can't try it because you need three years to learn it.'

And you were competing with largely the same people as in the European championships?

She looks at me patiently once more. 'It's mostly competing with yourself.' I leave a pause but she doesn't fill it: there's nothing else to say on the matter.

The Karolyis, sensing the importance of focus, had kept the Romanian team largely sheltered from the rigmarole of the Olympics. The gymnasts were not allowed to walk in the opening ceremony because Karolyi didn't want them standing for six hours before the competition. No matter what else was available in the Olympic village – and she saw pizza, cottage cheese, peanut butter and breakfast cereal for the first time in her life – the doctors would only let them eat things they were already familiar with. Her lasting impression of the Olympic village was that everything seemed to be free: badges, movies, soft drinks, clothing, bags, hats, pins.

As to the routine itself, I have heard that she has since said that her first routine was not perfect and did not warrant a 10. 'Well, the first time I got it was at the compulsory routine where everyone does the same thing,' she says. 'But the way I did it, I added more amplitude on every trick. We created something that was different and much better.' The problem was, she said, the person before her had been given a 9.95; since Nadia's routine was demonstrably better in every respect, the judges had painted themselves into a corner. 'When I landed the dismount I did a tiny little hop,' which is an imperfection and should normally have been marked down. 'But it didn't matter because the routine was so much better than the person before, and there was nowhere to go, so they had to go to 10. It wasn't a 10. There was a tiny little bobble.'

In this view, she is aligned with Olga Korbut, who was in many ways her equivalent figure from the previous Olympics, Munich in 1972, where she won three gold medals for the Soviet Union (she is Belarusian). They have more in common than just being the young new face of women's gymnastics at consecutive events; they were both, one way or another, intrinsically linked to the Cold War too, and both ended up in the States, in Korbut's case in Scottsdale, Arizona. But they have never been close and Korbut, somewhat churlishly, has dismissed Comaneci's 10s in 1976 as propaganda.

Still, what a moment: that scoreboard, her competition number 073 in clunking great 1970s LED lights, and the 10 beneath it, Olympic history so brazen it was beyond the capacity of the screen. After a moment of stricken confusion at the number, Nadia, already on her way to the next apparatus, gave a rare smile, a girl's smile, an incongruous rictus grin. And then she went off and did it again.

And so the routines went on over three days, with impossible grace and technique, on the beam – the excited commentator, 'free cartwheel into flick-flack!'; then the uneven bars again, with that signature move, a somersault with legs almost in the splits to grasp the same bar. Three 10s by now. 'It makes one wonder,' the British commentator said, 'where do the judges go from here?' Then the uneven bars once more, and the beam again. 'Have you ever seen anyone so confident on a 4-inch beam?' Uneven bars, a fourth time, and the beam, a third, the cameras clicking in symphony with every backward somersault. Seven perfect 10s in one competition; history made, sevenfold. The commentators, having cleaned out their store of adulatory adjectives, were stricken. 'The score that we said made history only days ago, now becoming commonplace for Nadia Comaneci.'

Was she aware, as all this was happening, that she was being elevated to a global household name? 'I was aware a little bit, but not to the extent of what was happening. I realized it was big but didn't realize it was huge, let's put it this way.' Later, she would write – or someone would write on her behalf: 'No one knows when he or she is about to make history. There is no warning and no instruction manual on how to handle the moment.'

Karolyi kept Nadia and her colleagues away from the media to the greatest extent possible, and wanted to get them straight home to escape the attention after the Olympics; finding no aircraft available, they all went to a youth camp in Canada instead, much to Nadia's delight.

But if she had been insulated from global attention, there was no escaping her changed relationship with Romania itself. When she landed back in Bucharest thousands of people were waiting. Nicolae Ceausescu, the despot leader of Romania, had ordered a national celebration for the team's arrival, and personally presented her with a government award. She was a hero, but still just a girl; she would later recall that she had been crying before disembarking the aircraft, because she had been carrying a doll but had lost it after somebody pulled on its leg.

But once the celebrations had passed, life returned to a crushing normality. No Romanian got rich from the Olympics; there were no TV chat-show appearances, no agents, no endorsements. She returned and went back to school in Onesti. Her dad still didn't own a car.

What's it like, I ask, to go back to normality, so young, after achieving all of that? 'Waking up, having breakfast, going to school, going to gym. That's how I see it,' she says. There was no suggestion of changing anything or forging in any new direction. 'I couldn't see anything else I could do that would be meaningful. Plus, the career doesn't end with an Olympics. I wasn't twenty-one.' She says the number as if it represents venerable old age: the deeply compressed lifespan of a female gymnast.

Still, she was growing up, and after 1976 she began to struggle under the strict routines of Karolyi and the school; where once she found guidance and discipline, she began to feel overbearing intrusion. As she saw girls her age dating, she began to want the same things for herself as other teenagers, and started to clash with her coach. Her love for gymnastics began to fade, and in 1977 she parted company with her mentor. She moved to Bucharest to take classes and consider what to do next – she was, after all, still too young to work – while the Karolyis moved to build a new training centre in the village of Deva. She remained active in gymnastics, but with a far more mellow coach who let her do what she wanted. So she watched TV, slept, ate ice cream. She gained weight and changed shape as her body entered puberty. Her parents divorced, something she took badly.

'I don't know exactly what I was thinking, or maybe I wasn't thinking,' she says, when I ask her about this time. 'I was growing up. I just grew up. I thought probably I wanted to do something else in 1978 but I wasn't sure exactly what.' It was a dark time. One of the prevailing rumours about Comaneci – and there are many – is that in 1978 she attempted to commit suicide by drinking bleach, though her own version of events is that she was so sick and tired of being monitored by female officials, perhaps Romania's feared Securitate secret police agency, outside the door of her apartment that, on one occasion when they showed an absurd level of interest in her doing her laundry, she simply *threatened* to drink the bleach she was holding in her hand.

In any event, her separation from gymnastics didn't last. 'After a while,' she says, 'just a few months after that, I actually wanted to go back. That's what I knew. I felt bad watching the competition and sitting on a bench. I thought: I should be there, so I decided to go back.'

Needless to say, Karolyi was the engine of her return. When he first saw her after her spell in Bucharest, he was horrified at the shape she was in, relating his impressions of her weight gain in characteristically abrupt terms, and told her that coming back would be the hardest thing she would ever do. This description appeared to be exactly the sort of challenge that appealed to her, and galvanized her into her return. Was it as hard as he had said, I ask?

'It was, but if you want to do something so bad, then you get over it.'

But it wasn't just a question of getting fit again. She was dramatically taller, so a lot of older routines had to be not just relearned but reinvented. 'We had to change some moves, to adapt some skills. But if you can go this way –' she demonstrates by twisting her body – 'you adapt. That's how tall gymnasts do it: you twist more, you go flipping backwards, you take the code of points and see what are the tricks that can still give you points.' She returned to Karolyi's tuition in his new academy in Deva, sharing a temporary house nearby with her mum and brother, with the two siblings sharing a room. She was entered for the 1978 World Championships before her recovery was complete, and hated the experience of failing; but when others said that she was over the hill at just sixteen, she was once again using a setback as a spur to improve. By the 1979 European Championships, she was tall, lean, powerful – and back.

Is the achievement more impressive for having done it twice – gained the ability and form, lost it, and regained it? 'I think people realize now, when they see it, that it is really hard to do it twice,' she says, and this seems to amuse her wryly. 'I'm talking about the all-around, not one event. Now you can specialize and do two events or even one every four years, because you know you're the best at it.'

Still, she was battling between professional excellence and being a teenager wanting freedom, and after returning from the World Championships in Fort Worth in 1979 – not a great time, as she had contracted food poisoning in Mexico beforehand and then suffered an infection from the buckle on one of her hand-guards, eventually needing surgery – she resolved not to live under Karolyi's thumb any more and moved back to

Bucharest, enrolling at the Polytechnic Institute to study for a degree in sports education. Suffering from sciatica and sometimes unable to feel one of her toes, she could sense that her time at the top was coming to an end, but nonetheless was determined to stick with it through the 1980 Olympics in Moscow.

It is tempting to picture a cosseted star at this time, with everything she could possibly need, but her salary at the time was worth about US$100 a month. She had used the money she won in competition in order to make a down payment on a house in Bucharest. Only through gymnastics had she gained the wealth to do even that, but this was no glamorous existence: she once again lived with her mum and brother, but couldn't afford to heat the house even with her mother taking a job as a cashier, and so in the winter they lived and slept in the kitchen.

*

And so to 1980: the Games that the US boycotted because of the Soviet involvement in Afghanistan, not that it made much difference to Nadia, since all her competitors were Russian or East German anyway. It was, as she said, walking into the lion's den, the Russian home turf, but as ever she considered that irrelevant, since her main concern was competing against her own standards and expectations.

It has become commonplace to present the 1980 Olympics as a corrupt institution in which Comaneci was cheated of a gold medal in the all-around category. By the time it came to the final exercises, the competition had come down to her and the brilliant Russian Yelena Davydova. Comaneci was due to compete on the beam, then Davydova on the bars. Contrary to the planned order of competition, Comaneci's turn on the beam was repeatedly delayed until after Davydova had completed her bar routine, upon which she scored 9.95. This meant Comaneci needed to score 9.925 to tie, or more to win gold outright.

After Comaneci completed her routine – good, but not, by her own standards, great – no score appeared on the scoreboard. Half an hour passed without the score appearing. When it eventually came, it was 9.85, giving Davydova gold and Comaneci silver. Karolyi, furious, immediately accused the Soviets of cheating, first in delaying her routine until after Davydova's performance so that the judges would know exactly what score was needed to keep the Russian with the gold, and second in marking down Comaneci's routine.

To her considerable credit, the one person who has never believed there was foul play at work is Comaneci herself. She has repeatedly reminded people that the single biggest reason she never won gold was because in an earlier round, she had fallen on the bars, a score that was then carried through to the final day of competition. I remind her of this.

'I did! I know!'

So did you think you were cheated?

'Everyone has their own thinking,' she says. She notes that if the preliminary rounds were not carried through to final competition, as is the case today, she would probably have won gold, but that's not a question of cheating, just of process. 'From fourth place in the preliminary, I ended in second, which I felt was still pretty good because I could have sat down with nothing,' she says. It was good for the competition: 'It opened the gate for everybody to reach for the medals. It's not always what you think on paper. Before every Olympics I can give you, on paper, who I think are the best technically, but they may not have the day of their life, they may make a mistake. So that's what happened with me. I didn't get cheated, I made a mistake, and I ended up where I was supposed to.' People tend to forget she still came away from Moscow with two golds and two silvers.

Still, to Western eyes, the Moscow Olympics seemed to epit-omize a period of suspicion about the independence and motives of judges. Did she have a sense of corruption or unfairness there?

'Well, there's always favouritism. The judge from Romania is going to give a higher score to the gymnast from Romania.' But she then explains the range of differences this can possibly lead to: if a judge is too high or too low, they will likely be called back together with the other judges. 'They get them together and say: you gotta go down, or you gotta go up. Cheating's, let's say, she deserved 9.5 but because she's from my country I'm going to give her a 9.6. This is what this means. At the end of the day, the numbers kind of end up where they are supposed to be.'

And then it was over. Her last competition was in 1981, and although she continued to take part in gymnastics shows for a while afterwards, her time at the top had come to an end. 'I retired when I was twenty,' she says.

And then things started to go wrong.

*

It's not as if she expected to be a top gymnast forever. 'I was prepared that this was going to end at some particular time,' she says. Not that, in Romania, life had been all that different because of her success anyway. 'Today, if you are an athlete, you are also a celebrity. When I was growing up, I was an athlete and that's it. You need a job. Nobody is going to give you a job because you are an Olympic champion. This is how we lived at that time: celebrities were only in Hollywood.' She says she had always worked hard at school, and then in university in Bucharest, 'because I didn't know what I was going to be. I was going to be a doctor, a surgeon, something that makes you an income, because you have to work somewhere.'

After 1980, she struggled with two simultaneous challenges: anonymity – with its attendant impact on income – and the growing poverty of a Romania that was under profound and cruel mismanagement by Ceausescu. While studying, she was also trying to support her brother and mother, and had nothing, struggling through the second half of each month like everybody else. The medals, awards, achievements on the world stage meant nothing.

Like everyone else in Romania, she slipped back into an ancient model of barter. A friend who worked in a clothing factory would bring her clothes; another friend in a bakery would supply bread. She would trade fruit and vegetables with other people, then decide what the family would eat that day based on what she got. Maybe she had some cheese and could trade it for some fish. She is apparently still a great improvisational cook today, a consequence of this time, ignoring recipes and just using what is to hand.

In interview, she tends to talk little about this time in Romania, and presents its challenges a little dismissively, as though they no longer interest her. 'You live in the sixties and seventies and see how it's getting harder, then harder, and it doesn't . . .' She pauses. 'You don't see that it's a place to improve. Everyone was trying to get by, by their own way, by their friends, by whatever they could do. Then you just adapt to that too. You live with what you have, because what are you going to do? Not too much.'

There is a book, *Notes to a Young Gymnast*, ostensibly written by Nadia Comaneci, which covers this period in considerably more detail and with utter bleakness. I have read accounts that have distanced her from this book, noting that it was ghostwritten by Nancy Richardson Fisher, who also wrote Bela Karolyi's autobiography; there have also been articles in which Nadia appears to disown it a little. It's a curious approach, too, written as if addressing a response to a young (fictional) gymnast who has asked her questions about her life, though personally I like it. Clearly, understanding her time in Romania rests partly on the accuracy of this account, so I ask her first about it. 'It was not even intended to be an autobiography, it was intended to be something else,' she says. 'It just . . .' She moves her hands apart, looking for a word. Evolved? 'Yes.' But it wasn't written by her? 'I worked with a lady for maybe a couple of days and hours, and she just wrote it the way I said it.'

And this is what she said.

'I was twenty and felt the weight of my life as well as my family's, and at times it was overwhelming.' She writes about a seventy-year-old neighbour who would get up at 4 a.m., to stand in line in freezing winter at the grocery store, just to see if there was anything on the shelves; usually, there was just mayonnaise, mustard and beans. 'Not a day went by that we didn't share something with our neighbours. We used to joke that we'd borrow each other's old meat bones to make soup. It was a tragic and difficult life for everyone. People would have been happy if they could just have put something on the table for their kids to eat.'

That, though, was impossible: all the good food was being exported to pay off Ceausescu's debt. She came to realize just how lucky she had been during her gymnastics career, where her diet was considered an important matter of national pride. 'I was so much better off than most everyone else. But when my gymnastics days were over, I was left in the same unhappy position as the rest of the people of my country.'

Learning about this period of her life, I realize how frivolous the central conceit of my book and this interview – deciding what to do with the rest of one's life after an immense and defining achievement – must seem. Because in her case, what came next was a bitter, constant, day-by-day battle to stay afloat.

How naïve to picture this iconic woman sifting through a mass of opportunities and offers, agonizing over something as trivial as meaning and direction.

But things did appear to improve when she got a job as a choreographer in a dance team. This gave her a little money, made her feel like an adult for the first time in her life – she could invite people over for a drink, a small but intense moment of independence – and in 1981 she was called by the Gymnastics Federation, who told her a group of gymnasts would go and do an exhibition tour in the USA. She was offered $1,000 to take part, which, considering she was earning $3 a day in her job, was a lot of money, so she agreed. Bela and Marta went with her, along with the director of the federation and several undercover policemen who would be introduced to people as journalists. They called the tour Nadia 81.

She could have no idea just how this trip would come to change her life immensely in both positive and negative directions. The high point, she recalls, was sharing a bus ride with a group of American gymnasts; one of them was Bart Conner, who would go on to win two gold medals at the 1984 Olympics and, later, improve Nadia's existence dramatically. But the low point, by far, was the decision by Bela, Marta and a choreographer called Gez Pozsar to defect. They were never going home.

'I never asked him or got into the details,' she says now, 'but he was maybe prepared to do this move. He wasn't sure that it was going to happen. But he just decided to not come back, and he told me about that, in a nice way.'

This, too, is something she expands upon in the book, marvelling at the bravery and sacrifice that was involved: Bela and Marta left a daughter in Romania without being sure if they would ever see her again. 'To decide the course of your life and that of your family in one night, with no assurance of success, is unfathomable. I sometimes wonder, to this day, if courage is just another word for desperation.' She talks about the famous Edvard Munch painting, *The Scream*. 'The first time I saw that painting, I knew it. Really knew it. The man is a prisoner, and he will never escape the cell Munch painted him in; he will never be free. I imagine that is how Bela, Marta and Geza felt when they realized that they were trapped by a lie, when they accepted that they had no choice but to defect from their country.' They had a couple of suitcases and their clothes, and barely spoke English. They didn't know anybody in America. But this still felt like their only choice.

Though she didn't immediately take it seriously, or even understand what she was being asked, Bela did ask her if she wanted to remain in America.

'I wasn't prepared to do any of these things,' she tells me now. Why, you weren't ready? 'No, I was still too young. I have a family. What am I going to do, where am I going to stay? I wasn't mentally prepared. The glass wasn't full enough for me [to justify defection]. It was hard for everybody, but not like: I've gotta get out of here.'

Had she known how life was going to deteriorate from that point, she might have thought differently.

Upon her return, she was no longer allowed to travel outside Romania, even to friendly Eastern Bloc nations like Russia. Often her name would be put on a list for a Gymnastics Federation trip; it would come back with her name crossed out by some anonymous but high-ranking official. She felt as if she was being treated as a traitor, an unutterably unjust situation for someone who had devoted her youth to bringing pride to her country. This had a financial impact too: no extra money from foreign trips, which was a life-changing, though small, amount of income. In her book, she wrote: 'When my gymnastics career was over, there was no longer any need to keep me happy. I was to do as I was instructed, just as I'd done my entire life. I was expected to keep sacrificing.' Of Bela, 'his defection brought a spotlight on my life, and it was blinding. I started to feel like a prisoner. In reality, I had always been one.'

Here, too, she dilutes these emotions in person. After Bela's defection, she tells me, 'I went back and I did basically whatever I did before. The only thing that was different was I understood that I was followed, and bugged in the house.' She speaks of 'a little bit of fear' but goes no further into her surveillance and control, saying, 'I don't know because I never ask and I'm not curious to know because it doesn't make any difference.'

Like it or not, she was still somewhat part of the orbit of the Ceausescu family because, in her choreography job, she found herself working in the same building as the family's son, Nicu. This is one of several oblique areas of Nadia's life. Some rumours say she had an affair with him; others that she was abused by him. Her book states the matter carefully: 'I can say that Nicu and I were acquaintances and that he seemed to be a nice guy. It has been written that he was a wild drinker and a womanizer. I don't know if any of that was true. What I heard is that he helped a lot of people. Many mysteries surround him, but it is not my place to judge.' Then she addresses the big question. 'I have never talked in detail about Nicu because there isn't much to say. I'm not interested in the speculations about our so-called relationship . . . So, let me make this very clear – Nicu and I were never boyfriend and girlfriend.' Those are, clearly, carefully chosen words.

When I tentatively raise the three rumour-filled areas of her life – the supposed bleach suicide attempt, Nicu Ceausescu, and her relationship with the man who helped her to defect in 1989, which we'll return to – she says the book is her final word on it. 'Every time people ask me, I'm like: why you ask me all over the same thing, because I don't have something to tell you that's going to shock anybody, it's already out.' She laughs. 'It is what it is.'

One reason people do repeatedly raise these things is because the story has a tendency to change. An article in *Life* magazine in 1990 quoted her as saying she *had* drunk bleach to kill herself and was hospitalized for two days. And her mother has been quoted as saying that Nadia was abused by Nicu Ceausescu and even had her fingernails pulled out by him, something Nadia herself has denied.

Still, her past is her past, and it is entirely her choice what she reveals of it and how; if indeed her suffering was even worse than her book portrays, then perhaps it is natural she would not want to revisit it.

Meanwhile, years passed in struggling mundanity, leavened only by the still-unexplained surprise decision to let her attend the 1984 Los Angeles Olympic games, at which Romania was the only communist nation not to observe the Soviet boycott. That apart, she graduated with her diploma, got a job in the Gymnastics Federation, and survived.

But petty torments continued. On her twenty-fifth birthday the government started taking a large portion of her meagre salary because she had no children. This decision has its roots in Ceausescu Senior's vision that the Romanian population should increase from 23 million in the mid-1970s to 30 million by 2000, to create more followers, more tax dollars and a more powerful country. Under this policy, a foetus was the property of society, and anyone who failed to create one was nothing less than a deserter, abandoning the laws of national continuity. Abortion was banned, and anyone who didn't have children by twenty-five was fined for their lack of patriotism. The policy was ludicrous – there was not enough money or food to feed the people who were already there, never mind an expanded population, nor to support pregnant women – yet the arrival of the so-called menstrual police was a fact of life for Romanian women. By the early 1980s, food rations were one to two pounds of meat per month for an entire family. The country was starving, and worked to death. Factories moved to seven-day weeks, and pay was cut. Religion was banned. Electricity became increasingly rare in the cities.

I talk to her about her decision to defect. 'As I was growing up, some friends would tell me they sent an invitation to come to this, to attend this, and none of those came to me,' she says. 'Then I realized I don't have access to anything that people are giving me from outside.' Initially, it wasn't that she wanted to leave, 'but there was a frustration: I want to know, and let me make the decision where I want to live and what I want to do.' Her friends could do that, she says, even her Romanian ones, yet she could not. 'Of all of the people we had been together, I am the only one, and I wonder why, because I haven't done anything different. It's not like I spy or call somebody. I don't even have information. What will they get from me? I don't know things that I can say to people.' She realized that where she was in life, was where she was going to die. She would later write: 'I realized that I could either be like all of those people silently screaming around me or give myself permission to have a voice, to decide how my life should go.

'I finally heard myself scream, and I listened.'

*

Before I started researching Comaneci's life, I knew she had defected, but had no idea what this involved. I think I had pictured her calmly walking into a Bucharest embassy, or simply refusing to go home after a foreign trip. The truth was immeasurably more difficult and dangerous.

One day in the late 1980s she went to a birthday party attended by several Romanians who had defected and become US citizens; with American passports, they could now come and go as they pleased. One told stories of living in Florida, of palm trees and endless sunshine and water one could swim in all year round. He had helped a cousin get out by swimming across the Danube. This was Constantin Panait, who would become the latest in a long sequence of questionable male influences in her life.

An idea had been planted in her head. She talked about it with her brother, also her closest friend, and he advised her to go. But it was not straightforward: she was monitored constantly by the security services.

To get round this monitoring, she was told to make regular visits to a home near the Hungarian border, so that the government and security staff who tailed her would be used to seeing her go there to socialize. Over these visits she met six other people with whom she would defect. She settled her affairs in Romania, transferring her home into her brother's name, knowing it would otherwise be seized by the state, and hoping the transfer did not attract suspicion.

Every time she went to the house near the border, she would have to sign in and out at a security gate. And then, one day in November 1989, she signed in, but never out.

Defecting involved walking across frozen woodland until they reached Hungary, where Constantin had arranged to collect them. The guide was one of the six fellow defectors who had already made the trip three times, each time being returned to Romania by the Hungarian state. But he wasn't much of a guide: they could use no light, in case they attracted the attention of border guards, and no communication, with each simply putting their hand on the shoulders of the person in front. They slipped frequently in cold and ice. At one point they walked across a frozen lake; the ice cracked, and they all fell into knee-deep water.

She estimates they spent six hours in temperatures well below freezing, scrambling about in the dark, and they never did make it to the place they were meant to get to. The first indication that they had made it into Hungary was when they saw a plaque with a place name on it, and found it full of the letters z and s – a sure-fire sign of a Hungarian, not a Romanian place. Eventually they ran into two guards, and said the only word of Hungarian they knew: hello. They were taken to the police station.

I ask her how this dangerous, terrifying experience was. 'It's like that kid thing that I talked about: I bet you can't do that, I bet I can,' she says. 'My intuition was pretty good all the time. If you build up to something, if you want to accomplish it, and this is the only thing you are thinking about, and your intuition tells you you have to do that – it's like testing a skill in gymnastics. I'm ready to do it now, and then you just go for it. If I have to think of all the bad things that can happen . . . I knew that it would be dangerous, but I knew that I may be able to make it. So why shouldn't I go? Plus, I didn't go by myself.'

When they got to the police station, all seven were questioned individually. The Hungarians were thrilled to find Nadia Comaneci in their country and immediately offered her asylum, along with two others, but the other four were told they would be returned to Romania.

I have heard that Nadia then said she would decline asylum and go home again if the others were not allowed to remain: that it was all of them or nobody. I ask her if this is true.

'I did, yeah. Because I didn't want to be alone. I wanted to be with my friends.'

This strikes me as an amazingly brave thing to do: the consequences for her, if returned to Romania, are almost unimaginable.

'Yeah.' There is a long pause: nothing else to say.

The police agreed to her request.

Constantin Panait, having tracked them down, took them all to a hotel where they slept fitfully in a single room. Getting up the next day, she saw her picture on the front page of a newspaper: news was out. But Hungary was not the final destination they had in mind, and so they split into two carloads and drove for six hours to the Austrian border, and then spent another night out in the cold risking their lives. Again, Panait drove across to wait at the other side while the defectors fended for themselves. Nadia believes they scaled seven barbed-wire fences, a far more tightly controlled border than that of Romania and Hungary: Hungary to Austria was, after all, the crossing point from the Eastern Bloc to the West. This was the Iron Curtain.

They emerged, covered in blood, and hid by a roadside. Panait had said he would knock out one of the headlights on each car so they would know when to run out and make themselves known, and they did. Once more they slept in a single hotel room, but this time they were celebrating: they had made it.

The next day the defectors went their separate ways, while she and Panait went to the American Embassy in Vienna. It created quite a reaction. She was told there was a Pan Am flight to New York leaving in two hours, and that she would be on it.

She wrote in her book:

I thought I'd died and gone to heaven. Everything was going to be easy now, a veritable piece of cake. I'd fly to the United States and get a great job and make tons of money. The public would admire me for my past accomplishments and I'd be rewarded in terms of my shining future goals. But if you believe that is how it happened, I have a bridge in Romania to sell you.

*

Here is a profile of Nadia Comaneci from *People* magazine, in November 1990. 'There are precious few who think of Nadia Comaneci with fondness these days. And she knows it.' Those are the opening lines. And this was supposed to be a supportive, her-side-of-the-story piece.

The story of America's falling out of love with Nadia starts with her landing at JFK in November 1989. Straight off the plane, she was ushered into a Kennedy conference room for a news conference. She did not come across well. She gave short answers and appeared indifferent, even arrogant. She was asked about what Romania's response to her defection would be. 'It's not my business,' she said, according to an Associated Press account from 1 December 1989. 'I know it will be different. I was nine times in the States, I know the life here.'

Then, over the next few days, it emerged that Constantin Panait was married with four children, and she appeared to confirm that she was in a relationship with him. When she was asked about his family, she said: 'So what?' Regularly dressing in garish, plastered make-up, in miniskirts and heels and fishnets, it took no time at all for America to forget the refreshing fourteen-year-old they had remembered from Montreal and to see her instead as a homewrecking harlot. A policy of charging heavily for interviews – and, to be clear, she doesn't charge me a cent for mine, nor ever suggests it – didn't endear her to the media.

It is surely impossible not to have some sympathy with the way Nadia presented when she arrived in New York, and in the hurried following days. I had known roughly the process of her defection, but not until I talk it through with her am I quite aware of the extraordinarily truncated chronology: leaving home and family forever, spending a night trudging through frozen fields and water with the constant threat of death, interrogation by the Hungarian authorities, a few hours in a hotel, a drive across Hungary, another night spent scaling barbed-wire fences, a little sleep, an arrival at an embassy, then a flight two hours later, lasting ten hours – and straight into a press conference, all shouted questions and flashing camera bulbs. How could anyone appear remotely together after that?

She smiles. 'Bela used to say I am a scorpion,' she says. 'And I *am* a scorpion. He said if you throw a scorpion in with all those bugs, a scorpion figures out a way to . . .' She raises her hands in what I think is meant to be a gesture of fighting, of resilience or defiance. 'I've been trying to do that, all the time.'

In that *People* profile, a year on from her arrival, she claimed that she was effectively a hostage to Panait, who, having organized her defection, then took it upon himself to be her manager. In that interview, she said: 'I want to clarify this nightmare that happened to me. This was not me. I was not in love with this man. He helped me to escape, but beyond that I wanted nothing to do with him. I wanted to find somebody and explain the situation, but I couldn't. I was closed in the hotel room. I couldn't answer the phone. I couldn't speak with nobody. He would not let me. All the time I thought somebody was watching me and I was not safe. I was afraid.'

In this version of events, her supposed romance with Constantin was invented by him and his wife, Maria, with Maria's consent, in order to rouse the media. The article quotes John Florescu, who was co-executive producer of a (deadeningly lamentable) Disney TV movie on her life, as saying that Panait demanded all cheques be made out to him, not her. Nadia claims Panait then kept all the money, and threatened her with a return to Romania, and violence, if she did not do what she was told.

Her book, written fourteen years after that interview in *People* magazine, presents the situation differently and places more blame on herself. In this account, she says she accepted his involvement in her life as fair payment for the risks he'd taken in helping her to defect. 'People died every day trying to defect. They drowned attempting to swim the Danube, got bullets in their backs for trying to cross the border, or risked suffocation in containers buried in the holds of ships bound for America. Some people believe Constantin kept me in a virtual prison, but I look at the situation in a different way because he helped me to come to the United States.'

Instead, she focuses on the errors of her early appearance. 'I wish I could take back the way I spoke, acted and dressed . . . I thought that was how I was supposed to look. The funny thing is, I thought I looked good.'

Having seen this conflict in accounts I ask her: is it fair to say that when you went to the States, you were being controlled once again?

'No, I think I was unprepared,' she says. 'With everything. With language. Plus, I was shocked, I thought I was just going to immigrate like Joe Nobody. It would have been easier. It's just that . . . I didn't know what to do, and you just try to float, you try to exist, to survive in some way, until you've figured it out.'

She points at my tape recorder. 'I didn't know if even this was going to be the right thing. You just, like . . .' And she starts to move her hands in a waving, darting motion, as if demonstrating a snake's motion through grass, or a fish navigating its way upstream. 'You just go from one place to get to another place, and you figure out which is the person you feel more comfortable with, and lean towards those people. From here to there to here.' She makes the motion with her hands again: finding a way.

Several people who had known Nadia before became worried by what they were seeing. One was Bela Karolyi. Another was Bart Conner, who was invited to join her on an ill-fated appearance on *The Pat Sajak Show*, which she now sees as something of a nadir of her public image in the US. A third was another Romanian, a rugby coach called Alexandru Stefu, who lived with his wife in Montreal. Again, there are differences in accounts here; in her tell-all *People* interview she says Stefu invited her and Panait to Montreal under the pretext of a lucrative endorsement contract, managed to separate the two of them, and was told by Nadia: 'Alex, I have a problem. This is a bad guy. Please help me.' In this narrative, Panait was gone the following day, with $150,000, leaving $1,000 for Nadia. Her book mentions nothing of her asking for help, instead saying: 'When I woke up the next morning and went downstairs, Alexandru told me that Constantin was gone. I never heard from him again, but I hope he is well and thank him for his help.'

One way or another, she was finally free. And while she had been undergoing that painful transition, so too had her country, which overthrew the Ceausescus in December 1989; he and his wife were tried and convicted on Christmas Day, then executed. (Ironically, Nadia therefore needn't have fled the country when she did, as it was about three weeks short of revolution anyway.) Romania, like Nadia, found the change difficult, and was in a chaotic power vacuum, cruelly illustrated when CNN announced they had managed to contact her family and wanted to arrange a live conversation with them. Her mother, having absolutely no idea what CNN was, believed the journalists and producers were really from the Securitate; when they were taken to a hotel room and given snacks and champagne, she believed it was their last meal; and when they were taken to the hotel roof in order to secure a signal for the satellite, she was certain they were to be thrown off the edge of the building. When they finally spoke, her mother cried; she had been told that Nadia had been shot.

*

After Panait went wherever he went, Nadia stayed with Alexandru Stefu and his wife in Montreal, a city she came to love so much she gave up her US refugee status and became a resident of Canada. But bad luck was to strike again when Alexandru died in a diving accident by the walls of a dam. Knowing she could not stay and be a burden on his wife and son, it was time to move again.

By this stage Bart Conner had been making appearances in her life since 1976, when he had given her a peck on the cheek for the cameras at an event in Madison Square Garden. They had met again on the Nadia Tour in 1981, the one on which Bela Karolyi defected. Then he had met her again on one of her Panait-arranged TV appearances. Next, Conner had been commissioned to interview her in Montreal for the ABC. He found her fascinating, and very different from his own open, ebullient nature. 'I'm the kind of guy, I have like a thousand friends, and she only wants three,' he said. In the early 1990s he invited her to come to Oklahoma to train – teaching her, along the way, that gymnastics could be recreational rather than purely competitive – and they performed together in a show called *The Magic and Mystery of Nadia* in Reno, Nevada. After Alexandru Stefu died, Conner invited her to move to Oklahoma, and she did.

When she arrived, she was given a room in the house of Paul Ziert, Bart Conner's manager. Ziert is the person with whom one must negotiate to get an interview with Nadia, and I must confess that after my twentieth unsuccessful attempt to reach the man, I was getting frustrated with him. But meeting Ziert and understanding the role he has played in the lives of Conner and Comaneci quickly disarms any of that. He is courteous and generous in person, with a resonant deep voice that inspires trust; Nadia would eventually give her son the middle name Paul after Ziert. When she arrived in Oklahoma, he treated her with kindness and eventually became her manager too, and they began to do gymnastics tours, spokesperson work and public appearances together. Like everything else in her life, she worked hard and studied for it: she worked on public speaking, diction, eye contact.

She was delighted to find that gymnastics could still provide her a life so long after she had ceased to compete. 'Before, we used to say: you spent so many years in learning something that not too many people can do and has a value of zero,' she tells me. 'What are you going to do? Tricks at a party? Somebody is going to hire you to do handstands on a bar? What are you going to do?'

She speaks again of 'hard work, vocation, and a passion for what you do. The key of success in anything is the same.' Her work ethic now guided her again.

And along the way, she and Conner got engaged.

I meet Conner only briefly but he is big-hearted and broad-smiled, instantly disarming. He asks where I'm from and about my family. We both have seven-year-old boys, and I marvel at what the energy and boisterousness of one born to two Olympic gold-medal-winning gymnasts must be (and not just any old Olympic gold-medal-winning gymnast: Conner, too, won one of his with a perfect 10, on parallel bars in 1984). They warn me there's a time limit on the interview because they have to get to their son's school for a Christmas show of some description, and the whole thing just seems so normal, so centred, that it is impossible to think that Conner has been anything other than a positive influence on her life.

Then again, he is responsible for her living in Norman, Oklahoma. And the question can no longer be avoided.

How do you like Oklahoma?

It is the biggest smile of the interview. 'I like it! Because it's a quiet place, and people are very nice.' She gives an example of going to the store and forgetting her wallet. They don't mind: pay next time, they say. 'A lot of people ask me why Oklahoma. They think I would live in Monaco. But it's easy to live here. When you have a child, family-wise it is much more relaxed and settled here. I can go to the grocery store, do things like regular normal people, and when you go out and you become the celebrity, it's different.'

I have, in any case, been deeply ignorant to judge the town by the ugly strip along the Interstate; Ziert will later explain to me the rich culture linked to the nearby University of Oklahoma, which is also how he came to be here in the first place, setting up academies and scholarships around gymnastics linked to the university.

I ask her if, after her difficult start in the US, Americans now accept her.

'Yeah, I think people like me; I do good things for the community.' This is true: she is involved with a host of charities both in America and Romania, particularly around the Special Olympics and muscular dystrophy. 'I don't know everything. I'm still learning. But I feel comfortable with what I know, and if I don't know, I go and ask.'

She is back in Romania every two or three months, but has never forgotten her first return five years after her defection, with Bart alongside her, planning to ask her father for her hand in marriage. She was welcomed by thousands of people tossing flowers, was met by the new prime minister, and took nine hours to complete a normally four-hour drive to Onesti through village after village filled with crowds.

They decided, on that trip, to hold their wedding in Romania, in the Orthodox two-day style, and when they came back for it in 1996, it pretty much shut down the country. It was as close as the country has come to a royal wedding since its royal family was disestablished in 1947. People stayed off work, half of

Bucharest closed, and 10,000 people waited outside the hotel plaza before the couple went to the church. Conner, attempting a speech in Romanian read out phonetically, won people over with his effort. Photos of the day fill both of their offices, and when I ask her about it, she doesn't say a lot, mainly smiles.

*

She and Bart prepare to head off to the school Christmas show, and Paul Ziert shows me the diverse business empire he has built around gymnastics: manufacturing leotards, putting together decals to go on T-shirts, making shoes, publishing the biggest gymnastics magazine in the country. He gives me a bottle of Perfect 10 wine, with an image of Bart and Nadia embossed upon its label in svelte silhouette; he has the good grace to have a sense of humour about it.

Nadia Comaneci is the youngest person to be interviewed in this book, even though her moment of achievement pre-dates that of many others. She is fifty-two when I meet her, and could pass for much younger; partly, as she has freely admitted, this is because of her cheerfully plentiful use of Botox. She is still glamorous but with nothing like the plastered make-up of earlier days. She wears towering heels, but otherwise a sober if smart look: a black jacket, white top, earrings, two gold crosses around her neck. Having met most of my interviewees towards the end of their lives, it occurs to me there is scope for plenty more living in Comaneci's.

Before she leaves, I ask her: what ambitions are left?

'My ambition is to be a good parent.' She left this late, after all, becoming a mother in 2006, aged forty-four. 'I'm not sure I know how to do that, because I'm learning from other parents. What happens if your son doesn't want to take a bath?' She laughs.

'All these things are important today. And to try to get enough time to go and see my mum and my family back in Romania, because I think time goes faster now than it used to when I was a child.

'That's how I feel.'

4

Reinhold Messner

If you're going to meet Reinhold Messner, it might as well be in a castle.

He looks like he should live in a castle. He *does* live in a castle, some of the year, and once broke his heel scaling its walls after locking himself out of it one night. And his has been a life so elemental, so committed to pitting himself against the wilderness, that it seems only appropriate to find him amid battlements, flanked by rugged stone that has stood for many centuries.

But mostly it's the look of the man that makes the setting appropriate: a stocky, ursine might, a vast bouffant of silvery-grey hair and a beard, as Tom Baker would have it, you could lose a badger in. These are the whiskers of a man who should live in a fortress, glaring at barbarians at the gates – although when he smiles to reveal surprisingly perfect white teeth, I am struck by the idea that he would make a fitting replacement for a deceased Bee Gee.

When I first catch sight of Messner, it is in the café in the courtyard of Sigmundskron Castle near Bolzano in the Italian South Tyrol, a fortress whose recorded history goes back to AD 945 and which has a millennium of rich and bitter political history behind it, but which now houses part of Messner's

119

burgeoning collection of mountain museums. His size and hair make him easy to spot, but it's the herd of captivated people round him that really give it away, for in this world he is a hero, the greatest of them all. People from teenagers to octogenarians queue excitedly to be pictured with the great man, a task he accepts with cheerful and grinning equanimity.

They do so because Reinhold Messner has the strongest claim to be called the finest mountaineer who has ever lived. A claim like that is fraught with difficulty, in the arcane and often bitchy world of elite mountaineering, but no serious discussion of the best could take place without his name being in the mix. It's not just what he's done. It's not just how he's done it. It's the fact that, implausibly, and damn near uniquely in this peer group, he's still alive.

*

Ask what Messner is famous for, and most people with a passing acquaintance with mountaineering will mention two things: he was the first to climb all fourteen peaks over 8,000 metres in height; and he was the first, with friend and colleague Peter Habeler, to climb Everest without supplemental oxygen in 1978.

Ask an avid student of mountaineering and they're more likely to name his second ascent of Everest, solo, again without oxygen (they've all been without oxygen) and on a new route up the Tibetan side; or the first ascent of Nanga Parbat by the south face; or the first climb of Gasherbrum I, which brought a minimalist Alpine style of climbing to the Himalayas for the first time; or the traverse of both Gasherbrum mountains, I and II, in one climb; or the hat-trick of three Himalayan peaks in a single brief season in 1982. You get the point: there are a lot of highlights.

The challenge is in explaining the aggregate of the achievement. Messner was not the first to climb any of the 8,000-ers, which are concentrated in Pakistan, Nepal and China; they had variously been bagged between 1950 and 1964. But in today's era of somewhat commoditized mountaineering, where one can pay to be pretty much dragged up Everest with scarcely any experience, it is easy to forget just how remote the Himalayan peaks remained when Messner turned his attention to them from the Alps in the 1970s. Messner was the first person to climb three 8,000-ers, and four, and every other increment to fourteen.

The figure of 8,000 metres is, as he says himself, an arbitrary one: if Europeans spoke in terms of feet, like Americans and Brits do, instead of metres, then there would hardly be much kudos attached to topping all the mountains over 26,246 feet, 8 and $^5/_8$ ths inches. And, while Messner clearly did want to be the first to climb them all, that's not really the point. 'For me, personally, the 8,000-metre peaks have no importance,' he tells me, though it won't convince everyone. 'It is true that, in the end, I wasn't sitting there and saying: let somebody else do it first. But the single approaches are much more important to me.'

By this he means that he cares far more about the *way* that he climbed them, and this is clearly what he would prefer to be remembered for.

Messner grew up not far from the castle in which we meet, in a collection of villages now known as Villnoss in the South Tyrol, the Italian sweep of the Alps. His father, Josef, a teacher, was a tough man, and not one who showed much warmth to his nine children; but he did introduce Reinhold to the infinite pleasures of mountains, taking him up his first peak at the age of five. Hooked, the boy had found his life passion at an early age, perhaps discovering release from the pressures of a large and tightly confined family, and maybe seeing the rugged Dolomite peaks as a way to prove himself to his father.

By his early teens he was a regular climber, and by his early twenties, with his brother Gunther, among the finest mountaineers in Europe. And, along the way, an ethos formed in his mind. Cutting his teeth in the Dolomites and then the broader Alps in his youth, Messner believed strongly in the Alpine style of mountaineering, eschewing the siege mentality typical of earlier mountain expeditions, and instead carrying the absolute minimum of gear. He never, for example, used an expansion bolt. (These are self-anchoring bolts that create an anchor into a rock face, and are therefore considered not just a safety measure but a climbing aid.) 'Expansion bolts make it theoretically possible to eliminate uncertainty, the very element that gives climbing its excitement,' he once wrote. 'I would have felt cheated if, from the outset, I had cancelled that out with some technical device.'

Transferred to the Himalayas, where the big-team, multi-base, fixed-rope siege approach had long been considered the only feasible method of assaulting a mountain, Messner's attitude manifested itself not just in a minimum of equipment – many summit pushes were undertaken without so much as a tent, instead relying on high-altitude bivouacs dug into the snow – but in refusing to use bottled oxygen. Messner was not the first to climb an 8,000-metre peak without oxygen (the French mountaineers Lachenal and Herzog climbed Annapurna in 1950 without it). But it was very rare at the time, and to this day remains dangerous.

Above 8,000 metres, you are in what is known in mountaineering as the death zone, and there's not a hint of melodrama about it: at that height you are, quite simply, dying all the time. At this point, biology tells us that the amount of oxygen in the air is not sufficient to sustain human life. The longer you stay here, the greater the deterioration of bodily functions. You are decaying. You will, eventually, lose consciousness and die. It's just a question of whether you get up and down again before it happens. Particularly when it came to climbing Everest, which at 8,848 metres is pretty much a kilometre into the death zone, climbing it without oxygen was widely believed in the 1970s to be impossible.

This is the context: trying to do something new in an environment that is going out of its way to kill you all the time. As if that's not enough, he climbed four of them twice, each by different routes.

By 1986, the race to be the first to climb all fourteen had become quite a story, albeit one that Messner goes out of his way to distance himself from, apparently embarrassed. And when he summited the fourteenth, Lhotse, in 1986 at the age of forty-two, his feeling was not what the world might have expected of him.

Upon making it back to Lhotse's base camp with Hans Kammerlander on 17 October, he wrote:

> There was no pride. I didn't feel especially heroic to have climbed all fourteen of the eight-thousanders. Not exceptional in any way as a climber. I had seen something through, that was all, a task I had set myself four years before. I was pleased to have done with it. If it meant I had won the 'race', then I was pleased to be done with that, too, and all the people who were making such capital out of it. It was all behind me at last. This was the morning I could start living the rest of my life. I felt light and free. The whole world lay before me.

It was this last remark, rather than the dazzling mountain accomplishments that preceded it, that made me want to interview Messner for this book. How remarkable to come to the end of a defining success and to greet it with relief and freedom, as if it was a tedium to be swept away – as if it was not the finish line, but the start. Asking how one moves on from such a triumph is almost redundant when he appeared bored with the triumph in the first place. So it is here that I intend to start the interview, starting at the end, or at least at the next beginning. I start to quote that line back to him: 'This was the morning I could start living the rest of my life . . .' But that's as far as I get.

'No,' he says firmly. 'Not the rest of my life. The next period. The next stage.'

I had been half-expecting this after reading a colossal, comprehensive interview he once gave to *National Geographic*, in which he segmented his life into six stages: from one, as an elite rock climber in the Alps, through two, as the high-altitude mountaineer in the Himalayas, to several subsequent ambitions and reincarnations. I had wondered if this had been an affectation of the writer or the man, but now I have my answer.

'It was one of my goals, and it was not the most important one, because I was much more interested in how I do the single climbs,' he says. 'I found always new challenges. They were not there. Challenges are never there. They are invented.' He has a taste for metaphysical lines like this and is capable of articulating them clearly in a minimum of three languages.

'After the fourteen 8,000-metre peaks, if I went further in this direction, I would repeat and repeat and repeat myself. So I decided I would do something else. I would go and cross the huge ice fields and deserts. And that was only the third period of my life: I did afterwards a few more.'

This one-liner – 'I would go and cross the huge ice fields and deserts' – not only offers the most immediate answer to the question of what one does when one has conquered each of the mightiest mountains on Earth, when there are no higher peaks to climb, but also gives some hint of the scale of the man's life. 'Crossing the ice fields' refers to his 2,800-kilometre trek across Antarctica via the South Pole with Arved Fuchs from 1989 to 1990, and the longitudinal crossing of 2,200 kilometres of Greenland in 1993, and the attempted Arctic crossing from Siberia to Canada in 1995, and just maybe the crossing of South Georgia in 2000 following Ernest Shackleton's route. Any one of these would be the crowning achievement of many an explorer's life, but next to the mountain achievements, few people have any idea he did any of this. 'Crossing the deserts', meanwhile, refers to his 2,000-kilometre trek on foot across the Gobi Desert in 2004, or maybe the Taklamakan Desert in China's Xinjiang Province in 1992, or possibly the Atacama in the Andes in 1998, or even the Thar Desert in India in 1999.

You get the picture. Only you don't, still. In the very same year that Messner summited Makalu and Lhotse to complete his fourteen peaks, he also scaled Mount Vinson in Antarctica to complete the so-called seven summits – the highest point on each of the seven continents, with a Messnerian twist of replacing Australia's Mt Kosciuszko, which you can pretty much walk up with your grandma, depending on the condition of your grandma, with the Carstesz Pyramid on Indonesia's Irian Jaya. (Somewhat irksomely, he was not the first to do this, but he was the first to do so without supplemental oxygen on Everest.) And this doesn't include the east-west crossing of Bhutan, or the many expeditions to Tibet, Kailash, Uganda, Mongolia, Tanzania, and so many others.

So how did these expeditions stack up in comparison to the mountains? Did he feel the same fulfilment?

'The same fulfilment, yes, but a totally different approach. In the mountains you need certain abilities; in the deserts, the exposure is much bigger,' he says. Exposure is a key metric for Messner, a vital peril. 'The exposure on mountains is not so high – there's an exposure to cold, there's an exposure that you are days in high altitude, but only for days. In Antarctica, you are exposed for months. In Antarctica, you have no chance to escape in case of emergency.'

He settles into an account which he will deliver twice during our truncated discussion, and I sense I am not the first to hear it. 'You have three facts which are making an activity into an adventure: *difficulties*, which you have to be able to overcome; *danger*, which is there in the wilderness, and which you have to avoid; and *exposure*. And the most important thing is exposure.' He plots his various adventures on a matrix with these three axes. Mountains bring danger but, in his view, comparatively little exposure (to most mere mortals, they offer about as much exposure as one could possibly imagine, but Messner has a frame of reference on these things rather different from the rest of us). Antarctica brought limited danger in terms of falling, but vast exposure, 'because if you have a small accident in Antarctica, you don't escape. There's no chance of escape.'

I ask if his Alpine-style approach to mountains was reflected in these later, horizontal, one-foot-in-front-of-the-other trudges. 'Yes. In all my activities.' He turns back to his early days in the mountains to explain why. 'My economical base was too low to do like the Americans did in '63.' He is talking about an American assault on Everest led by the climbers Unsoeld and Hornbein. The first ever traverse of Everest, going up the West Ridge and down the South-east, it is actually an expedition Messner clearly admires, though he does tend to use it as an exemplar of siege-tactic largesse. 'They spent more money than I will spend for my whole life. They did one expedition, I did more than 100.'

This is an important point because, while Messner is an apparently loaded chateau-dwelling mountain aristocrat now, which seems to piss an awful lot of people off, it wasn't always this way, and in fact a paucity of cash had a lot to do with the mountain-climbing style he pioneered in both the Alps and the Himalayas. Ethically disposed against the siege approach he may have been, but really it was never an option. When Messner and Peter Habeler transformed Himalayan climbing with their low-budget, two-man ascent of Gasherbrum I in 1975, there's no doubt they did so partly with an eye on the glorious Alpine-style aesthetic; but they also did so because Messner was skint. There was just no way he could have funded anything bigger at the time. Those who pillory him for the dashing sweep of his personal brand – and there are many – forget that he started down this path as a method of funding expeditions and repaying their debts, not to make a ton of money.

I am keen to ask him about something else he did after his fourteen peaks. I have read that he became an avid scholar of the yeti, and spent years trying to get to the bottom of this ancient Himalayan legend. It seems unlikely: a folly in this most driven and structured of lives.

But, unembarrassed, he nods enthusiastically. 'I was many times in the Himalayas and I heard many stories and listened to many ideas, but I never saw anything similar in my hikes and my climbs,' he says. 'In the end I was the first to say that the yeti story is pure imagination. There is nothing real behind it.'

That changed quite dramatically when he met one.

It was Eastern Tibet in 1986 – *another* thing he did that year – when one evening 'I had an encounter with a being which was very near to what the legend was telling about the yeti. And from this moment on I said: there is something real behind it.'

He stretches his arms out. 'Here is the legend told by the local people –' he raises his left arm – 'and here is reality.' He raises his right, divergent from the left. 'And I found out that legend and reality are meeting. It's the same story.' He brings his wrists together to demonstrate. 'But it's a legend. And the legend was built on a real animal. It's the Tibetan bear, no doubt. A special bear: the local people call it the snow bear, or the bear man. And if you put it together and take out the bear, it is coming out "snowman". It's logical. It's clear.'

Logic. Clarity. Is that what we want, with a yeti? There is a sense of disproving Santa Claus in this conclusion; it's almost disappointing to think, as Messner firmly believes, that a bear standing on its hind legs is the source of thousands of years of whispered stories and wide-eyed children. There are some who won't accept Messner's rather prosaic solution, but the man himself has no doubt – indeed, he doesn't have much doubt about many things.

So the attraction was what, to prove what it was?

'Yes. When I understood my view was wrong: that there is more than a legend. The legend is a legend. But the bear was a base to the legend, maybe thousands of years back.

'You are American –' I am not American, but I decide to let that go awhile, since if he thinks I've flown from America rather than Gatwick North Terminal he might give me longer for the interview – 'and I am sure Bigfoot is based on the brown bear, but I cannot prove it because I have never studied it. On the yeti, there is no doubt.'

So, if crossing Arctic wildernesses was stage three, and the yeti was stage four, stage five took a most unlikely turn: politics. From 1999 to 2004, he held office as a Member of the European Parliament. What attracted him to parliament?

'I was an invalid. I broke my heel.'

It is an unusual source of a calling to public service, but then again, it's a great story. Is it true, I ask him, that your injury happened because you were climbing into your own castle?

'Yes, yes.'

Because you were locked out?

'Yes, yes, yes.'

He looks so improbably sheepish at this, ducking his head into the protective fold of his vast head of hair, like a rebuked yak, that I cannot help sniggering. I'm sorry, I say: I shouldn't laugh.

'No, it's OK. I was ashamed, but it happened. And I was an invalid, and somebody asked me. I ran without approaching a party: I was a freelance, I won my seat, it was not easy because I was a solo runner, and I did five years in parliament.'

His assessment is not a great surprise. 'I was not happy there. But I learned a lot. I am happy that I did it. When I was perfectly OK with my heel again, I did not run for a second term. I am not a person sitting at a table to discuss what the others have to do. I like to decide for myself and do what is important.'

This seems an opportunity to talk of his politics, which is an important point. But one treads carefully here, for several reasons.

We are speaking in a place of great political symbolism for the South Tyrol, and, indeed, one whole tower of the castle is devoted to a presentation on its role in regional history and as a focus for dissent and rebellion. The largest protest rally in the history of South Tyrol was held here, when a leader, Silvius Magnago, addressed 30,000 people in demanding freedom for the province.

South Tyrol is, and long has been, between two stools: part of Italy, but largely German-speaking, far more culturally connected to neighbouring Austria and further Germany than to the rest of Italy. (I had discovered this for myself three years earlier when I brought my family to the region for a holiday, staying near Bolzano in a place called Volser Aicher. Paying insufficient heed to the Teutonic name, I had learned Italian especially for the trip, only to arrive and find that nobody actually spoke it.) This feeling of not fitting in anywhere has consistently had practical impacts on Messner himself, firstly in trying to attach himself to any national expedition to the big mountains in his youth, since he was neither Italian enough,

German enough, nor Austrian enough to get on those expeditions; and also, latterly, in making it difficult to attract any sense of national pride.

In 1948 South Tyrol was incorporated with Italian-speaking Trentino, south of Bolzano, into a single autonomous province called Alto Adige; the combination of the two appeared to have been done in order to make German-speakers a minority. The museum, which rather wears its heart on its sleeve in documenting all of this, includes one caption saying: 'What is important today is that equality and access be afforded to all three minorities in the region: the Ladins [an ethnic group in the Tyrol] and Italians in South Tyrol, and the German-speaking South Tyrolians as a minority in Italy.'

But the other reason one treads carefully in bringing this up is an ugly moment earlier on, in 1939, when the population of South Tyrol was asked to decide whether to remain in the province of Bolzano and accept full Italian legislation, or to accept German nationality and move to Germany. This was, in essence, a choice between Mussolini's fascism and Hitler's national socialism, a horrible choice. As many as 85 per cent of those entitled to vote decided to become German citizens – effectively, Nazis. And one of them was Messner's father.

Still, Messner has served in office and has never been short of an opinion of his own, nor particularly close to his father, for that matter, so this seems fair game. I raise it by asking about whether he wanted, in office, to represent South Tyrol. 'No, no, no,' he says firmly. 'I am a very critical citizen. I like this country, I am living in this country, I am part of this country, my children are living in future in this country. But I am describing what I see. I am not a criticizing man, but I say: this is this, this is this, and this is this.' This, he says, is why he ran as a freelance: not to represent a party, or a province, or a country, or anything really, except to express his own views on particular issues with his unusual unwavering sense of right and wrong.

As for his father, Messner appears to have been determined to escape the man's influence from the outset, most obviously by proving Messner Senior wrong in saying there was no life to be had in climbing. 'In the family, there was only one chance,' Reinhold says. 'To break, to be broken, or to be stronger than the father.'

*

Messner's hard-faced attitude towards politics is one reason that his next life phase – the sixth, I think, but these things get a bit blurry after a while – involved a lot of challenges. The Messner Mountain Museum now spreads across five locations in the South Tyrol, with a sixth under way, dedicated to various aspects of the mountains: mountain people, mountain exploration, ice. This, for Messner, is giving something back: museums to explain the mountains that have given him his life and his livelihood.

The idea of the museums, Messner says, 'is to tell what is happening when mountains and people meet. This is my goal.' One senses that he did so with something he learned from climbing, an Alpine style: using what was there, minimal outlay, guerrilla style. 'If I had done this kind of museum in a different way, my money, my economic power, would not have lasted.' And where does he find the danger that used to be so essential to his life? 'The danger here is to die, or not . . . what's the famous British line?' To be or not to be? 'Yes, to be or not to be. It was to survive economically, or to fail economically and be out of the play. If I had failed here I would be begging. I risked everything for doing it, especially here.'

At first glance, one can't help but find a certain ridiculous boastfulness in having five, soon to be six, museums named after yourself. And in the day and a half before the interview I have been pinballing around the South Tyrol seeking out the various far-flung museums, expecting to find this cult of personality everywhere. But what I find is not what I expect: there is barely any reference to Messner in any of them, bar the name. Outside the most remote museum of the five, on the side of Mount Ortler, there is a large poster of the great man frowning and looking down with ice in his beard, saying: 'Great things are done when men and mountain meet,' but that's about it. Oh, and the museum bookshops: Messner has written such a staggering number of tomes now that he seems to have lost count. I ask him how many and he says 'about fifty', but I can identify at least sixty-three, across numerous languages.

What the museums do show is a great devotion to the mountains and their people. Arriving at Verona Airport I drive straight to the newest one, called Ripa, housed in Bruneck Castle not far from the Austrian border. It is, like all of them, staggeringly appointed, and is dedicated to the lives of mountain people, with sections on Alpine farmers, Sherpas, and various Andean ways of life, among others. Frustratingly, I have arrived too late in the season to see the next one, the Dolomite museum – in fact, I have arrived exactly one hour too late, only to find it closed for the year – but I make the drive anyway past the resort of Cortina along many vertiginous climbs and descents among the grass of the hillside meadows, still verdant green in October, and the toothy jags of the Dolomite spires. This museum is in any case really about the view, and that is resplendent – the greatest advertisement for the reverence of mountains one could find.

Next morning, it takes an hour and a half from Bolzano to reach the Ortles museum in Sulden, 1,900 metres up the side of a mountain, and quite different in scope from the others: accessed down a side road that is being slowly repaved when I visit, it first appears to be housed in a barn, next to a café called the Yak & Yeti, although the bulk of the museum – a tribute to the exploration of ice – turns out to be underground. A yak (but no yeti) munches stoically in a nearby field, while chickens and geese wander around in pens. There is an ancient water cistern with a brassy model of a bear on it – and, inscribed on a heavily battered orange bivouac, fortified and now looking like a sort of rusted metal shed, there is a tribute to his brother Gunther.

On the way back to Bolzano, I pull in and hike half an hour up the valley side to see Juval, Messner's home, where he lives in the summer. (This is the place where he broke his heel after forgetting his keys and assaulting the walls that time.) It is imperiously placed, with a combination of Alpine ruggedness and Asian touches: Tibetan chortens and prayer flags, and a brilliant gold plate with twelve handprints round the perimeter, signifying the Sun, over the west gate. As a museum, it is devoted to mountains as places of mystery and spirituality. But what a place to live! A proper buttressed castle, with battlements and a great blocky-square tower. It is the kind of place that looks like it has had people imprisoned in it in some distant wintery past. There is, oddly, a peacock outside.

Finally, Sigmundskron Castle, where we meet, which houses the Firmian campus of the museum, is its anchor and centrepiece, a striking combination of tributes to mountaineers through the ages, and recognition of Asian cultures and religions. Dispersed oddly around these Middle Ages fortifications are statues of Buddha, Ganesh and various other gods and icons; a whole turret of the castle is given over to a huge Tibetan chorten, and our interview in the café takes place a few feet away from a reclining Buddha in the Thai or Burmese style.

It took eleven years between Juval, the first, and this Firmian centrepiece opening, partly because it took three years of work to restore the castle, but mainly because of a heated battle between Messner and various arms of local government about whether he should be allowed to in the first place. 'They tried to cut my possibilities, especially the local part, and did everything to keep me out of this museum,' he says. 'I had a huge fight for ten years.'

Why? 'Because the castle, this one, has a historical background. And they don't like me because I tell openly what I think about local politics.' He then launches into his longest single answer of the interview: about how Italy is controlled and run by media, not by politicians, how they have used their power against him, how they fought to scratch a signed contract he had in place to run the museum, how he was the only one who fulfilled the conditions of a tender to run the museum for thirty years without subsidies. 'They were hoping they could force me to leave the country,' he says. 'I didn't. They made a mistake.'

Having seen the five museums, I am inclined to give Messner a lot more credit than I had expected to. They are not a tribute to himself. They are a tribute to everything about his beloved mountains. They do him credit. And they give him evident pride. 'It is not easy, and it was a long fight to do it. And after I do the last museum –' taking shape in Corones, not far from Bruneck, and dedicated to traditional Alpinism – 'it is finished for sure. And then I do something else.'

Another of his life stages involves farming. He has three, he says: one a very small winery, one a small yak farm at 2,000 metres, and another a biofarm, 'where we produce everything you need for surviving. In the case of emergency, the world is quite fragile, I will go with my family and we will live. Many people can live there.'

Characteristically, not content with exploring or enjoying rural agriculture, Messner thinks he has reinvented it, or at least preserved a model of self-sufficiency that was prevalent 100 years ago. Messner's model is not only to be self-sufficient but to sell produce directly on the market to tourists passing by. 'So the whole chain of success is in one hand.' Removing inter-mediaries from the process, all of the profit stays with the farm. 'I think in the globalized world this is one answer to very small economies, especially on mountain farms.'

'All these three farms were empty, nobody was there any more. I got them for quite nothing. The people were gone, and they said: we cannot survive. But now three families are surviving.' Also characteristically, he narrates this as a him-versus-the-establishment ruck. 'Hundreds of farmers are coming and saying: how is this functioning, this system? They say: I do not believe in Messner, because he is making money outside of his farming world, but the farmers can say: this is working, it's functioning. Families are doing it.'

So which of your life phases is this? Six? 'No, this is part of the cultural one. Saving a culture that was forgotten, to show that the know-how of this time is helpful for surviving in the future.'

*

Messner's capacity for reinvention, to look forward and find fascination in new and disparate fields, is impressive, and inspiring. But there has, inevitably, been a lot of looking back-wards, too, and not all of it positive.

It has been noted that Messner's extraordinary force of personality and willpower has a side-effect that manifests itself in falling out with his expedition partners. I mention that he has frequently written that success brings enemies as well as friends, and ask whether he has made peace with that now.

'I think that Americans don't have this problem . . .' It is time to front up as the Brit I really am. 'OK, British and Americans.

You are not so full of . . .' He grapples with a word. Envy? Jealousy? 'Yes, jealousy. Like the Germans and Italians. In Italy and Germany, especially in the last decades, jealousy was growing enormously, and not only against me.

'You have to see, the most famous German climbers for ten years tried the Rupal face on Nanga Parbat, for two generations before me, and they had no chance. Along came a twenty-five-year-old boy from South Tyrol, not even known in the climbing community, and he did it. They said: this is impossible. And in the end, they said: maybe he killed his brother for being successful. It was envy. Pure envy.'

And this takes us to the darkest of all subjects: where the quest for the 8,000-ers began, and where Messner was changed forever.

*

There is absolutely no question that there is one mountain, and one climb, that defines Messner, and that changed everything that was to follow. That climb was Nanga Parbat, 1970.

Nanga Parbat is the most imposing of mountains. Unlike those in Nepal and elsewhere in Pakistan it has no immediate neighbours of comparable size: instead it rises, mighty and forbidding, at the western extreme of the Himalayas. The Indus skirts it on its journey to Pakistan's flatter plains to the south-west. It is the sort of mountain you might find in a Disney cartoon, or at the end of some Tolkien quest; it would be no surprise at all to find a dragon living in the thing.

It is this anchoring role on the far extreme of the world's highest mountain range, and the starkness of its relief relative to what surrounds it, that gives Nanga Parbat the steepest, tallest, harshest mountain face in the world: a 4,600-metre ice cliff called the Rupal Face, twice the height of the Eiger's legendary north

face. It had been notorious since the first successful climb of
Nanga Parbat, by the Austrian climber Hermann Buhl in 1953,
who in reaching the top from the north side had a unique
perspective on the south. 'The highest mountain wall in the
world,' he called it, 'plunging 17,000 feet in one sheer sweep
from the summit into the unplumbed depths.'

In 1970, this wall had never been climbed. A German expedition had recently failed trying in 1968. Messner, at this time,
was out-growing the Alps: in 1969 he had completed the most
difficult route in the Eastern Alps, the Philipp/Flamm on the
Civetta, and had done so alone, during a storm. Then he'd
conquered the hardest face in the Western Alps, the North Wall
of the Droites – solo, again, and free-climbing. The Himalayas
were the natural next step.

Being South Tyrolean, he had little expectation of being invited
on to any national Himalayan expedition, Italian or German;
instead he fell between the two nationalities, and at the time –
he was twenty-six in 1970 – certainly had no money behind him,
having spent every cent, lire or deutschmark he ever earned on
Alpine climbing. To his surprise, in the autumn of 1969 he was
invited by a German, Karl Herrligkoffer, to join his expedition
to Nanga Parbat the following year. Better still, following a later
drop-out, his brother Gunther, two years his junior, was invited
too: for although Reinhold would make his name as a loner, at
this stage the brothers were very much a double act, renowned
across the Alps.

This was an expedition in the classic style of the time: big,
big, bigger. Teams of Germans and Austrians battered at the
mountain through May and June 1970, and Reinhold and
Gunther, the kids from the South Tyrol, were generally out in
front on the south, Rupal Face.

It was relentless, and tedious. The brothers spent more than
a week snowed into the middle of the face on one occasion.

And then, in July, with the expedition looking doomed, one final attempt was made. Reinhold, Gunther, and three other climbers met up at their top camp at 7,400 metres.

There is so very much confusion about what happened on 27 July 1970 and the days immediately afterwards, and it all starts with a mistake. The previous evening, Reinhold, Gunther and a third climber, Gerhard Baur, were in their tent at the foot of the Merkl Couloir, a long and extremely steep gully – vertical, really – that they hoped to follow to the summit. The idea was that base camp, upon receiving the weather report for the next day, would fire a rocket for the men at the top camp to see. If a red rocket was fired, that indicated bad weather, and Reinhold would make a solo bid for the summit with the absolute minimum of gear. If the rocket was blue, then the forecast was good, and all three would ascend as a team, with two more climbers to follow from a lower camp. At eight o'clock in the evening, a red rocket was sent up. Bad weather ahead; time only for a quick and daring solo raid by Reinhold.

It would be a long time before either brother would realize that the wrong rocket had been fired.

In the early hours of the 27th, still in darkness, Reinhold set out alone with just his crampons and an ice axe. Gunther and Baur set about fixing rope to help him get back down again. But Gunther, the younger brother, upset at being left behind, and once again eclipsed by the status and shadow of Reinhold, couldn't stand it. After a while, he dropped his ropes, chased his brother – and, incredibly, caught up with him. Gunther had climbed 600 metres, 600 *vertical* metres, of utterly exposed high-altitude thin-air rock and ice up the Rupal Face in just four hours.

Together, they made it to the summit, the first men to climb the entire face. But it was late, too late. 'In our youthful enthusiasm we were prepared to push things further than ever I would now,' he says. They summited at five, and didn't leave for another hour, itself a very unusual amount of time to spend on an exposed summit. But Gunther, in particular, was exhausted, and apparently suffering altitude sickness. One cannot help but wonder how different things might have been had the correct rocket been sent up: the two brothers would have gone up together at a natural pace, and Gunther may have been less drained by the effort.

But that is not what happened.

Reinhold Messner has always maintained that, at this point, it was clear that his brother could not get back down the Rupal Face. 'It would have been irresponsible, not to say impossible, to try and shepherd him back down,' he later wrote, 'especially as we did not have a rope with us.' He decided, instead, to retreat down the mountain's West Face in order to lose some height – the single most vital remedy to altitude sickness. 'It was a short-term measure,' he says. He believed they could then get on the Rupal Face the next morning, and that by then help would be at hand. The two exhausted men were able to descend as far as 8,000 metres before darkness fell, and then 'waited out the long and dreadful night. We were at a height of 8,000 metres and had no bivouac equipment: no down jackets, no oxygen, nothing to eat or drink. It was a night that undermined us totally, physically and psychologically.' They had a single space blanket between them, and the temperature dropped to minus 40 degrees.

By the morning both men were in a desperate condition, and Gunther critical, and then came the next moment of confusion. Two other climbers, Peter Scholtz and Felix Kuen, appeared from below, climbing up the route the brothers had taken the previous day. The Messners and the other climbers were about a football field apart, and shouted to one another. But Scholtz and Kuen were not on their way to mount a rescue, having not realized that anything was wrong. Instead, they were going for the summit themselves. The Messners, still not knowing that the wrong rocket had been fired, did not understand this. Scholtz and Kuen have since died and cannot be asked, but during their lives they claimed that Reinhold had shouted that they were OK. Whoever was to blame, the message of the Messners' desperation was not understood.

By 10 a.m., Reinhold had accepted that help was not coming. He decided his brother could still not make it down the Rupal Face, and that it would be safer to descend on the Diamir Face, on the opposite side of the mountain, which describes more of a slope. They would traverse the entire mountain in order to get down.

'I was nearly out of my mind, and it was at this point that I fell down and felt my spirit leave my body,' Reinhold would later write. 'I watched myself roll down the mountain. Then, summoning up one last surge of effort, I forced myself back into my body.'

They carried on until midnight, then struck another bivouac, now at 6,500 metres. The next day, Gunther appeared to be improving and, seeing this, Reinhold began to forge ahead – too far. He stopped at a stream to drink for the first time in days, and waited for Gunther to catch up. He did not. He was never seen again.

Retracing his steps, Reinhold saw an avalanche and realized that Gunther must be beneath it. He lost his mind. 'A whole day and night I looked for him,' he wrote. 'In the frozen rubble of this glacier world, parched, with frostbitten hands and feet, I made my first acquaintance with madness. I no longer knew nor cared where I was, nor what I did. I could barely walk.' Finally he staggered into the Diamir Valley, still hallucinating, and eventually met some woodcutters who carried him out. He was passed to the police, who were driving him to hospital when they caught up with the departing expedition. His colleagues had given the brothers up for dead.

Physically, the effect of the climb was debilitating: he lost seven toes and three fingertips, which, among other things, meant he could no longer rock climb with the same ability, precipitating a shift to ice-climbing from then on. But the physical effects were nothing compared to the mental ones. Messner says it took years to get over it; 'I never believed I would be able to go back to the mountains. Nor did I want to.' When he did go back, it was straight to Nanga Parbat, to try to find his brother's remains. Reinhold's father, a difficult man, quite openly blamed Reinhold for failing to bring his brother home.

Nanga Parbat would become something of an obsession for Messner in the years ahead. After going back in 1971, looking for Gunther, he was back again in 1973 to climb it solo, and failed. He tried again in 1977, and failed again. 'Only in 1978, after I'd learned that life can be borne alone and that man is an individual, after I had given up thinking in terms of pairs, only then did I have the courage,' he wrote. He climbed the Diamir Face, alone, on a new route, with no technical aids bar his crampons, axe, tent and a sleeping bag. Never quite content, he then descended by a different new route.

Conquering Nanga Parbat solo was a vitally important moment for him and his career; from that point on, he says, he didn't pursue mountaineering with the same animal earnestness as before. From then on, he said, the mountains would be 'a natural theatre where I can express all my skill, my craft, and my instincts'.

But the conquering of the physical mountain has been only part of the problem. For years after the disaster on the mountain, Messner blamed his expedition colleagues for not helping, while those on the expedition – and plenty who were not – blamed Messner himself for his brother's death. (Messner would also be blamed for two deaths on his second 8,000-metre summit, Manaslu, in 1972, a tragedy which convinced him to go solo wherever possible thereafter in order to avoid being responsible for other people again.)

For many years, there was something of a silent truce, until shortly after Reinhold and another brother, Hubert, went back to Nanga Parbat on the thirtieth anniversary of Gunther's death in 2000. The following year, in 2001, Messner spoke at a press conference hosted by the German Alpine Club for the publication of a biography of Karl Herrligkoffer, the man who had put together the expedition. Speaking at the press conference, he lashed out once again at the expedition members who, he said, 'wouldn't have minded if the two Messners hadn't returned'.

In the aftermath of that, two expedition members broke their silence. More than that, they wrote books about the event. One claimed that Messner had always intended to traverse Nanga Parbat – that is, going up one way, down another – and that he had left Gunther to die on the Rupal Face in order to do so.

In 2005, an unusually warm summer caused a significant melting of ice. Three climbers from Pakistan were walking in the Diamir Valley when they came across the remains of a climber. It was Gunther. The position of his body appears to confirm Reinhold's account: it is where one would expect it to be if it were swept away by an avalanche on the Diamir, not the Rupal, Face.

*

Today, when I ask him about moving on from what others have said, there is a distinction to be drawn. I ask him first about Peter Habeler, a brilliant Austrian mountaineer who was Messner's closest climbing companion after Gunther's death. He was with

Messner on two of his most significant climbs: Gasherbrum I in 1975, the climb that proved Alpine-style climbing could work in the Himalayas; and the first ascent of Everest without supplemental oxygen in 1978. But then they fell out, over a book.

'We never had a problem,' Messner says today, which is not the popular view. 'When he did his first book after Everest he had a ghostwriter doing it. And the ghostwriter knew exactly how this envy, this jealousy, was functioning. He wrote in his book: "Messner did not give me credit, I was the first man climbing Gasherbrum I." But I wrote two pages in my book about how Peter is climbing in front of me on Gasherbrum I! He did not read it, or the ghostwriter was not interested in it, but this was the key. It was exactly the opposite, and for this I was really angry.' He says he spoke to Habeler about it, who acknowledged Messner was right, and said he would correct it, 'but he never corrected it because the editor knew that the jealousy story sells much better'.

It's clear that the issue rankled for some time. Messner's handsome 1999 tome, *All 14 Eight-Thousanders,* contains a photo of Habeler on the summit of Hidden Peak (Gasherbrum I) with the caption: 'These pictures prove only that Messner was "working hard" up there, not that Habeler got to the top first.' Nevertheless, the two are now believed to be reconciled.

Asking the same question about anyone who was involved in the Nanga Parbat expedition, though, elicits a quite different response.

'If somebody tells stories like this, telling that . . .' He shakes his head and looks down. 'They never say that I killed my brother. But between the lines they say that I killed my brother. For becoming famous.'

After a pause he looks up again. 'To such people, I would never like to speak.'

I have provoked him with this question, and he takes off on an attack on the German Alpine Club – it was in a press conference for this group that he made his renewed attacks on his colleagues in 2001 – and in particular its provenance. 'The German Alpine Club has a problem with me because I became too successful or too famous, I don't know what. I was the only one telling them it's time you spoke out about the fact that from [19]24 you kicked all of the Jewish out of the Alpine Club. I was the first one to tell it openly, and they said: we were forced. The Nazis forced us. In '24? The Nazis were not in power in '24. They came to power in '33.'

He turns back to the Nanga Parbat colleagues. 'I don't like to see them. Hopefully they are not coming into any public discussions with me, otherwise I don't know what I do with them.' He then has a go at the expedition leader, Herrligkoffer. 'He was a fascist. He did a contract with us – and mea culpa, we signed it – saying you should not tell even one sentence of this, so he could change the whole story. And he made out it was his success on Nanga Parbat! He did not even know where the mountain is.'

*

It would be quite wrong, though, to suggest that Messner has no respect for his mountaineering peers. In fact, the reverse is true. Perhaps because of my now-revealed British background, Messner praises the great British mountaineer Chris Bonington on three separate occasions during our interview – and praises him in detail, admiring his 'beautiful leadership' and talking at length about specific expeditions. Also, the museum in the castle in which we sit has reverent presentations on a host of mountaineers, from Hilary and Tensing to earlier Alpine pioneers, without, as far as I can see, any presentation on Messner himself.

When you go out of the castle doors to leave, you go past a list attached to the wall, called 'rock and ice stars'. It is a list of great mountaineers, and although it includes Walter Bonatti, Joe Brown, Bonington, Habeler, and Doug Scott, it doesn't include Messner.

There may be a reason for this. Next to the list is an explanation of the conditions one must meet in order to appear on 'this exclusive list of mountaineering greats'. One, they must give their consent to be on it; two, they must have made a significant contribution to the development of mountaineering through the deeds or art of technical or medical findings or innovation; and third – here's the clincher – they must have survived the experience and reached seventy.

Messner, when we meet, is sixty-nine, and I'm half inclined to come back next year and see if he's added himself to the list, which is where he surely deserves to be. (Instead, I write to him in early 2014 and ask whether he will be added to the list when he turns seventy. I receive a scanned printout of my email by reply, annotated in red biro: *yes*.) Surviving, after all, is a somewhat underrated virtue in the annals of mountaineering: it is, perhaps, the hardest thing to do.

Consider this: during the supposed 'race for the fourteen', there was only really Messner in the frame, but two other competitors were talked about. One was Jerzy Kukuczka, a fine Polish climber, who did eventually climb all fourteen (and climbed three in winter, a first). But then, in 1989, he took on the unclimbed South Face of Lhotse in Nepal in October 1989. Leading a pitch one day at an altitude of 8,200 metres, his rope snapped, and he died.

Then there was the Swiss climber Marcel Ruedi, who was amid a quest to summit all fourteen when he topped Makalu in 1986 – his tenth of the fourteen summits. Messner, by chance, was in base camp preparing his own expedition to climb it and had become aware that Ruedi's climbing partner was desperately worried about him. Then Messner saw Ruedi coming down; he and his team got tea and food ready for the clearly exhausted Swiss climber. But Ruedi disappeared from view and never reappeared. Eventually Messner and his team climbed up towards where they had seen Ruedi, and found him sitting in the snow, dead.

And there were the eight outstanding mountaineers who died on big mountains between 1982 and 1984 alone, among them Peter Boardman, Joe Tasker and Yasuo Kato on Everest, and Reinhard Karl on Cho Oyu.

It is important to note that Messner failed on almost as many 8,000-metre attempts as he succeeded, on Makalu, Lhotse, Dhaulagiri and – several times – Nanga Parbat, among others. In its own way, that is as impressive as the ascents.

When you read what others have said about Messner, more often than not they mention the oddity of his survival, and the shrewd judgement of knowing when to stop, as much as they mention the skill of conquest. 'On those expeditions where Messner has met with no climbing success, I have been amazed by his clear and humble attitude,' wrote the great Japanese climber Takashi Ozaki. 'If the danger is incalculable, he turns his back on it, time and time again.'

Ozaki died on Everest in 2011.

Kurt Diemberger, who made the first ascents of both Broad Peak and Dhaulagiri a generation ahead of Messner, wrote: 'I can only marvel that someone who has climbed all fourteen eight-thousanders, some by their most difficult routes, has survived to tell the tale.' Diemberger is still alive, but is one of only two survivors of the 1986 K2 disaster which killed five fellow mountaineers during a single storm, including his partner Julie Tullis; those deaths followed eight more on the same mountain in the previous six weeks.

And so my final question to Messner has to be this: how is it you are still alive?

'I was also lucky,' he says.

*

We are out of time, and he stands, a mounting crescendo of height and hair, grins warmly, shakes my hand and wishes me luck. As I leave I turn back and see him pausing for a moment, chatting with the waiter and looking around. What must he see: a castle he has bent to his will and his image, filled with people who mostly want to visit it because of his name.

There is time for one more diversion before driving back to Verona for the flight back to Gatwick. I decide to drive out to his home town, in Villnoss, which is a commune of a number of small mountain towns with names like St Peter, St Valentin, St Jakob and St Magdalena. It can be found about half an hour north-east of Bolzano, if you come off the motorway before the Brenner Pass that links Italy to Austria, and head out among the farmhouses and meadows that look more Swiss or Bavarian than Italian.

Today, it is a place of exquisitely manicured houses, well-kept hedges, wooden garage doors carved with the care a craftsman might apply to a child's crib. There are floods of bright pink, red and white flowers on the balconies and window boxes, shaped with continued attention. It speaks of wealth and pride now, and there are a handful of cafés, restaurants and hotels dotted about. The houses have names like Bergheim, Florian, Elizabeth, Glatscheum, Tenenberg, Rosenheim, Weidenhaus, Burgmullerhof. A modest creek bubbles between the houses; the smells in the air are woodsmoke and cows.

Behind the towns, that vivid carpeted green one finds only in the Alps sweeps up the gradients to trees and, behind them, a cluster of Dolomite granite. From St Peter, in the valley, there are mountains in every direction: nothing too imposing, not for a Himalaya-conquering Messner, but one can begin to imagine what it must have done to a young kid growing up without much else in the way of other interests, one of nine kids, looking for something to define himself and keep him clear of a tough father. That toothiness again, the distinctive way the Dolomites rise in angular pillars: they just beg to be climbed. And so, for the world's greatest climber, this is where it all started.

5

Joe Kittinger

When the Austrian skydiver Felix Baumgartner captured the world's imagination by jumping out of a balloon capsule 39 kilometres above the Earth in October 2012, he broke a record that had stood for fifty-two years. As he slid his boots tentatively towards a modest step outside the capsule and prepared to lean out into the hostile void, so high that the curvature of the Earth was clear all around him, he heard a reassuring voice in his ear from his capsule communicator on the ground. 'Our guardian angel will take care of you,' the voice said.

It was a voice with some authority. It was the only voice in the world, in fact, that could possibly speak to Baumgartner with that authority. It belonged to the man who had set that record back in 1960, and had spent much of the previous twenty years trying to help others to break it: Joe Kittinger.

What was it about 1960? This was the year that Don Walsh and Jacques Piccard sank 7 miles to the bottom of the Mariana Trench in the *Trieste,* the year before Yuri Gagarin became the first human in space, the beginning of the decade that would see men walking on the Moon. And in this environment, powered by the twin engines of exploratory zest and Cold War politics, in this era in which anything could be done if you tried hard enough and should be attempted anyway just to see what happened, Joe Kittinger put himself in an open gondola beneath a cavernous helium balloon, drifted more than 31 kilometres into the sky – so high, in fact, that one can't really talk of a sky, more a stratosphere – and stepped off the side with an experimental parachute.

The will and the ability to do such a thing is one of the interesting things about Kittinger. The rest of his life – which included a year as a prisoner of war in the notorious Hanoi Hilton camp in Vietnam, a solo transatlantic balloon flight and a post-retirement career as a skywriting stunt pilot – is another. But perhaps what's most remarkable of all is the idea that, having made your mark in history, you then spend decades trying to subjugate it to somebody else's achievement, urging them to do better.

This is a new take on what to do next after your moment of triumphant inspiration: erasing yourself from the record books.

*

Joe Kittinger today lives in the pleasant Orlando suburb of Altamonte Springs, in a house surrounded by immaculate green lawns not far from Lake Orienta, one of the countless little basins that dot the limestone of central Florida. A mighty Stars and Stripes flag hangs from a pole by the front door. He's not at all far from where he grew up, a little further north on the St Johns River, and that's not such a surprise, because his childhood here made him the man he became.

It's a long time ago now – he's eighty-five years old, a big man, white-haired – but he hasn't forgotten what childhood gave him. 'I was very fortunate,' he says, settling into a deep sofa, dressed head to toe in leisure-comfy white. 'My father loved to fish and hunt. We had a houseboat out on the river and I spent a great deal of time out on the water. Just a wonderful upbringing.

'And it gave me a feeling of self-confidence, that I could take care of myself in any environment, that I wasn't afraid of nature or living out on the land.'

The slow-moving waterways of his youth sound idyllic, a childhood of turtle stews and steel guitars and the sounds of clinking beer bottles from a riverside juke joint, but with a daring sense of unsupervised bravado that kids just wouldn't be allowed today. He would navigate the hidden channels at night in a duck boat, ferrying beer to fishermen or shining spotlights to attract and catch alligators, revelling in the joy of local knowledge, of secret ways and places, that so appeals to a child.

But it would be the air, not the water, that proved to be his calling. 'Right off the bat as a young boy I wanted to be an aviator,' he says. 'I had no Plan B. There was only Plan A.' A teenager during the Second World War, he was not old enough for combat, but it was a returning veteran, hired by his father to work in the family business, who gave young Joe inspiration; the airman would take the boy up in his Piper Cub and land it on the lake on floats. Converted and driven, Kittinger joined the newly established air force in 1949, stuffing all his worldly goods into a barracks bag and catching a five-day train ride from Orlando to Goodfellow AB in San Angelo, Texas.

His first flight as an aviation cadet was in a single-engine trainer called a T-6 Texan, just after dawn one day in 1949. 'I climbed up through a hole in the cumulus, and as I looked down at the feathery cloud tops and up at the great dome of the sky all around us, I realized that I was in love. It was the most beautiful thing I'd ever seen. Nothing compared.'

He was lucky to get a role at all: after the war, he says, 90 per cent of the people who had been in the air corps were discharged, so there was very little demand for new pilots. 'I was lucky: I was there at the right place at the right time.'

That could be the story of his life, because the pivotal moments of his life have been defined by being in the right place, and then grabbing an opportunity before it passed by. He spent time in Germany, Italy, Libya and Denmark, becoming a skilled test pilot along the way, but the assignment that would change his life came when he was sent back to the US in 1953 and joined the Fighter Test Section at Holloman AFB in Alamogordo, New Mexico. Here, he heard about a place called the Aerospace Medical Laboratory and in partic- ular its colourful colonel and medical doctor, John Paul Stapp, whom Kittinger would later describe as 'not only one of the smartest, but quite possibly the bravest man in the United States Air Force'.

One day Stapp called for a volunteer for a project on zero gravity, and Kittinger put up his hand. Only after being accepted did he realize that absolutely nobody else in the room had put their hand up.

He grins. 'Many a time they would ask for volunteers and I'd put my hand up and look around and I was the only one,' he says. 'I just was always looking for a different challenge, some- thing new, and I made a career out of volunteering for special assignments.'

Stapp was considered something of a maverick mad genius, and was, Kittinger says, an early evangelist for the idea of space travel. Stapp's focus was how humans would be able to perform in a weightless, zero-gravity environment. Early tests were simple: putting a plane into a huge parabolic arc, the top of which would allow up to twenty seconds of effective weight- lessness, the ancestor of what later came to be known as the Vomit Comet. Kittinger, as a pilot, would monitor the moment of weightlessness using a golf ball tied to a piece of string hung in the plane's cockpit: when the ball floated, he knew they had achieved zero gravity.

Then Stapp announced a plan to send a sled down a track powered by nine rockets, at the end of which it would go from roughly Mach 1 to a full stop in about a second. He asked Kittinger to provide aerial photographic documentation, which meant flying over the start line at exactly 350 miles per hour at exactly the right moment. It took him weeks of practice to get the timing right, but only on the day of the sled run did he become aware that Stapp intended to be on the sled at the time.

The logic of doing so was to determine whether pilot bailout at supersonic speed was survivable. There was, he recalls, 'an honest difference of opinion among the medical staff of Holloman about whether it would kill him or not'. Stapp survived 41 negative Gs; the air force had previously insisted that 18 Gs was the limit of human tolerance. When Kittinger saw Stapp, all the blood vessels in his eyes had burst, but he was otherwise in reasonable condition, and Kittinger gained enormous respect for a man who wouldn't ask anyone to do something he wasn't willing to do himself.

*

Stapp's next project was called Manhigh, and this time Kittinger would be the test pilot. The idea was simple: to raise a human being above 99 per cent of the Earth's atmosphere in order to create an environment that largely represented space, and then leave him up there for a day to see what it did to the body. They would achieve this through a pressurized capsule under a helium balloon. In order to get funding, Stapp pitched it as a test of a proposed manned space vehicle, and so today Kittinger considers it the world's first manned space programme, an unheralded predecessor of NASA's Project Mercury, and indeed of the Soviet Vostok programme.

Although the project officer and brainchild behind the system was a man called Dr David Simons, Kittinger was assigned to take the capsule up first on a test run. In preparation, Kittinger first had to become a rated parachutist and a licensed balloon pilot, both of which captivated him. He tested out pioneering pressure suits – 'it felt as if I was wearing an octopus' – and the capsule was developed with a mixture of cutting-edge technology and simple intuition, using a 30-pound chunk of dry ice as a cooling system under the biggest balloon ever made, manufactured by a crew of young women who worked in stockinged feet and had to have fingernail checks each morning in case they punctured it. An early test flight took up a load of guinea pigs in little frame helmets.

As with all testing, there were mishaps, and on one routine balloon training flight from Holloman the gondola flipped upon landing, with the lip ending up on the head of a colleague, Don Fulgham. He was wearing a helmet, which saved him, but all the blood vessels in his scalp were ruptured and his head swelled up like a basketball. 'It was grotesque. You could barely see his nose.' This would have been bad enough at the best of times, but it happened near Roswell, New Mexico. Kittinger believes that the sight of Fulgham with his alien-sized head, along with the wreckage of a high-altitude balloon, got wrapped up in the legend of the 1947 alien incident and grew from there over the years.

The first Manhigh flight, on 2 June 1957, looked like it was doomed. First, the VHF radio failed; he could hear his ground crew but they couldn't hear him. He resorted to Morse code: NO SWEAT. At 40,000 feet, he noticed half his oxygen had already gone, far more than should have been the case. He didn't abort, and headed up, hitting the jet stream, which knocked the capsule over almost 90 degrees.

The balloon survived. At 96,000 feet, Kittinger enjoyed the exceptional rarity of a view 'that no living creature had ever enjoyed.' He wrote: 'A handful of rocket-plane pilots had arced up this high, but only for an instant.' He could still see blue sky in a band along the horizon, but if he let his eyes drift up, the blue darkened to indigo and 'an almost indescribable black. It was the darkest thing I'd ever seen. Blacker than ink.' Yet the sun was shining. 'I was able to sit there, run my eyes along the horizon, and see the curvature of the Earth. It occurred to me that I was the first man to leave Earth's atmosphere for any significant duration.' He realized 'that I was in a very different realm. Space. I had become the first astronaut.'

That's not a claim you'll find backed up in any textbook; received wisdom has it that Yuri Gagarin became the first man in space four years later, when his *Vostok 1* flight took him to a peak altitude of 327 kilometres, more than ten times as high as Kittinger that day. Today, convention has it that space begins at an altitude of 100 kilometres above sea level, known as the Kármán line, while NASA (and other US agencies) award astronaut wings at an altitude of 50 miles (80 kilometres). Under these rules, Kittinger never made it into space.

Are they wrong, I ask? Should you be recognized as the first in space? 'I should be,' he says. 'But NASA were very profound in their publicity and their media, and they didn't want to recognize anything anybody else had done. They weren't about to recognize Kittinger being there, the air force. They wanted people to think everything to do with the space programme originated with NASA. And that's not so.'

Kittinger has no doubt that Manhigh made a major contribution to NASA's Project Mercury, which put the first American into space (Alan Shepard) and the first to orbit the Earth (John Glenn). Indeed, NASA might have learned more from Manhigh. Kittinger and his team had done pioneering work on a multigas cabin atmosphere mixing helium with oxygen, whereas NASA, in the Apollo capsules, insisted on highly flammable pure oxygen. Kittinger says he specifically recommended that NASA use Manhigh's research, but that it refused; the pure oxygen environment was one of the main contributors to the *Apollo 1* launchpad fire that killed three astronauts, two of them friends of Kittinger.

But that was all for the future. Meanwhile, as Kittinger was making history on the edge of space, David Simons, whose craft it was, was growing increasingly agitated that Kittinger was going to skydive out of the capsule and abandon it. Simons started sending orders to descend. Kittinger, in fact, was already valving helium in order to do exactly that, but decided to annoy Simons anyway, just for the hell of it. He tapped out in Morse: 'Come up and get me.' Half a century later, it would become the title of his autobiography.

With Kittinger's test flight complete, a modified craft, *Manhigh II*, would take Simons up for thirty-two hours to a peak of 101,500 feet two months later, though by then Kittinger had been ousted from the project for winding up Simons. No matter: there were other adventures to have.

*

One day in September 1957, three months after his Manhigh flight, Kittinger was flying an F-100 Super Sabre from Holloman and suffered a series of catastrophic failures, forcing him to eject, but far too low for the canopy to have time to inflate and slow his fall. He had no chance. But by fluke, he didn't die, the parachute inflating and swinging just once before he hit the ground.

He had this moment very much in mind a month later when Stapp called again and asked him to help work on an emergency escape system in Ohio. Having just had his life saved by such a system, Kittinger thought it was fate, and accepted.

The essence of the challenge was designing an ejection and parachute system that would keep an aviator properly aligned no matter how badly they were spinning and even if they were unconscious, falling from very high altitude or at very high speed.

Kittinger put a team together. For various reasons, they wouldn't be able to use powered aircraft for their testing, and so in order to access high altitudes, they would use balloons. He picked a target altitude of 100,000 feet. Stapp called the project Excelsior, which has its roots in a Latin word meaning 'ever higher'.

Relishing the challenge of a small team trying out untested things, this was a hard-working, no-bullshit crew, working early and working late and working Sundays and working over beers, throwing problems at one another to solve them, and overcoming budget problems by making life as simple as it could be. One consequence of this approach was that, rather than a pressurized capsule, Kittinger would go up in an ordinary balloon gondola, jumping in a pressurized suit. 'We would essentially make the trip to the edge of space in an open basket,' he says.

The first test flight, on 15 November 1959, was almost a disaster. The faceplate fogged up for much of the ascent so he could not see his instruments, and the helmet appeared to be trying to work itself free; if it had, and the pressure seal had broken, Kittinger would have died almost instantly. Next, by the time Kittinger's faceplate cleared sufficiently to read his instruments, he had already passed his planned jump altitude. Then – and, in hindsight, this is darkly funny – he prepared to jump and found his backside was wedged in his Styrofoam seat. It took him so long to pull his arse free that he'd passed 76,000 feet by the time he was ready to jump, a good 16,000 feet higher than intended.

He jumped, and even though everything about this experience was new – no atmosphere, so no wind, so no sensation of speed – he could tell something was wrong. His stabilization chute had not deployed properly and he was spinning out of control, eventually about 120 times a minute.

He passed out.

The next thing he knew, he was underneath his reserve chute about 3,000 feet above the desert floor. It would take a while to work out what had happened: in wiggling his way out of his Styrofoam seat he had accidentally activated a jump timer, which in turn meant that his stabilization chute had deployed much earlier than it was meant to, and curled around his neck. He was unconscious by the time his main chute deployed, and when it did, it got wrapped around the first one, and neither would work. A third chute had been designed to deploy if the jumper did not override it and, since Kittinger was unconscious, it did deploy, again tangling with the other chutes. But a genius on Kittinger's team called Francis Dupre had somehow foreseen exactly this possibility and designed the chutes with different-weighted lines so that if the parachute was fouled, some lines would snap and the reserve chute would be freed to open properly. It did, and it saved his life.

'I'm only here,' he says today, 'because Francis Dupre anticipated everything.' But even in near death he could see a silver lining. 'Even though we hadn't intended it, Excelsior had proved exactly why we needed a stabilization chute system.' It is a classic test-pilot mentality: that when something goes wrong, even almost fatally wrong, it's still worthwhile because you learn from it.

By the time I sit down with Kittinger I have interviewed several people like him – Walsh, Yeager, five Apollo astronauts – and one thing they all have in common is that they hate to be described as daredevils. Instead, they take enormous pride in the rigorous due diligence they conduct and the scrupulous testing of their equipment.

'Absolutely,' he says enthusiastically when I put this to him. 'I did not want to give the impression I was a daredevil, because I wasn't. Everything I did, I had confidence I was going to live through it or I wouldn't have done it. I love life.'

He tells me, 'It takes three things to do a project like that.' This is another test-pilot characteristic: the methodical division of a description into segments, the insistence on turning the most daring and abstract of adventures into measurement. 'It takes confidence in your equipment, confidence in your team, and confidence in yourself. And that's a common denominator for any new exciting adventure or experiment. Walsh had it. Yeager had it. Armstrong had it. They went prepared, mentally and physically, or they wouldn't have done it.

'We used to do a test, then go and have a beer and talk about "what if",' he says. 'What if this happens? What if? And in one of those what-if sessions, Dupre came up with this emergency parachute system that saved my life. Everything that could go wrong did go wrong, but I was saved because we anticipated it.'

A month later, from the wonderfully named New Mexico town of Truth or Consequences, they tried again, flawlessly. It was time for the big day: the 100,000 foot jump.

*

On 16 August 1960, Kittinger climbed into the gondola on the bed of a truck from which the balloon would launch. On the base of the gondola, somebody had attached a sign: *This is the highest step in the world.*

Just as Walsh's record-breaking ocean dive would never have taken place had the navy got a message to him in time, Kittinger's flight should never have taken off; their air force meteorologist had detected a changing weather pattern and was on his way to the launch site to scratch the flight when Kittinger left the ground. And, once it did get aloft, there was another problem: one of the gloves on Kittinger's pressure suit had not inflated.

This was an enormously dangerous development. The target altitude for the flight, 100,000 feet, was almost entirely out of the Earth's atmosphere, just shy of the vacuum of space. Without pressurization, an exposed limb or extremity would expand to . . . well, no one knew how much. How could they? Everything about this was new.

But he did not abort, and I can't help but put this to him in the face of what he has just said about not being a daredevil. You made a conscious decision to press on, I say, yet you risked permanent damage to your hand.

'There was a risk,' he acknowledges. 'Because no one had ever gone up as high or in an altitude chamber with pressures down to what I was going to be looking at with an unprotected hand or foot. I had no idea if I was going to survive with that hand unpressurized.' But he made a choice. He knew if he radioed the ground, they would abort the flight; he also knew that the air force, tight on budget and deeply concerned about the near-disaster of the earlier test run, would be unlikely to approve another flight. Also, beneath the pressure-suit glove he was wearing a tight silk glove, and he reasoned that these two gloves in combination would limit how much his hand could possibly swell. 'If it had been completely exposed to the environment, that would not be very good because blood boils,' he says, matter-of-factly. And so, although he could no longer use his hand at all, and would need it for several moments of procedure during the flight, he made his choice. 'I really felt it was import-ant that I do the job and I took a calculated risk that I would survive with my hand unpressurized.'

By 7 a.m. he had reached the balloon's equilibrium: 102,800

feet. While there, in order to get as close as possible to the planned landing target, he was required to drift for eleven minutes, which meant, at last, he could enjoy the view.

'Those eleven minutes,' he says, 'were the only time I had in the whole flight that I could look out and enjoy the environment and watch it. Eleven minutes just sitting there with the panorama right in front of me, because the door was open.' He looked to the horizon and saw not the edge of Planet Earth but the transition from the stratosphere to the familiar robin's egg blue of the troposphere. He could see the Sun, brighter than it had ever appeared, against the ebony backdrop of deep space. 'Nothing is familiar where I am,' he thought. 'Nothing seems real.'

For years afterwards, people will ask if he was scared to jump. He will tell them: no, it was the quickest way down.

'I suddenly had a powerful and unfamiliar sense of my own remoteness from everything I cherished in life,' he says. He knew that 99 per cent of the atmosphere was below him. Stapp had once told him to think of it as being enveloped in cyanide: 'swimming in an invisible poison that would kill you in seconds'.

His ground crew urged him to say something for posterity. He looked for words and found only one appropriate: hostile. So he told them: 'Looking out over a very beautiful, beautiful world. A hostile sky. As you sit here, you realize man will never conquer space. He will learn to live with it, but never conquer it.'

He was 80,000 feet above the clouds, and the New Mexico desert floor was another 20,000 feet below that. He could see whole cities in the distance, and it occurred to him that from that height what he was seeing was a map. Over there was Flagstaff, Arizona, more than 300 miles to the west. Looking east, he could make out Guadalupe Pass in Texas. There is an entire state, New Mexico, and not a small one, between the two.

He worked his way through a forty-six-item checklist without his useless right hand, unplugged the various monitoring systems connected to his suit and helmet, stood up – this time without getting wedged in Styrofoam – and turned on the cameras. With ninety seconds to go, he confessed to his ground crew the problem with his hand, knowing they couldn't urge him to abort now. He cut loose a 200-foot antenna, his last connection with the ground, so he wouldn't tangle with it while falling. He was truly alone.

He inched to the brink of the gondola and put his toes over the edge. A little platform, then 100,000 feet of nothing, then the ground. He said: 'Lord, take care of me now.'

He stepped off the platform.

If you watch the video of his jump, as he plunges downwards, legs kicking listlessly, drifting to one side, his height above the Earth is apparent but is also meaningless, incalculable. You can see his justification in believing himself to be an astronaut, to have visited space. Because the void he jumped into doesn't look like a sky, but a nothing, an emptiness. There is audio enabled on the video, but nothing to hear: no wind to offer roaring resistance, nothing to indicate speed. There is a camera on his helmet too and, as he spins, different views come in and out of shot: distant clouds, the curve of the Earth, the infinite black-ness above him, the blinding starburst of the Sun.

Accelerating fast, gaining 22 miles per hour of speed each second, he rolled and looked up at the brilliant white balloon, dazzling him. He free-fell for sixteen seconds before a 5-foot stabilization chute opened, allowing him to arrest spins and giving him control, but scarcely arresting his pace: at 90,000 feet he was moving at more than 600 miles per hour, the cusp of supersonic flight. But he could feel nothing, no ripple of fabric or tension on the pressure suit, no visual reference. He felt like he was just spinning in space, not falling.

Then, a problem: he couldn't breathe. His throat tightened as if constricted. He imagined fingers digging into his windpipe. He became light-headed. But then, within a minute, the pressure released. To this day, they don't know why it happened.

He continued falling: 70,000 feet, 60,000. It was minus 94 degrees; 50,000 feet. And here, at the inexact boundary of the stratosphere and troposphere, he finally began to feel density in the atmosphere, and to get some sense of resistance and speed. On the video, the roar of air rushing past him is deafening, frightening, but to Kittinger it meant reassurance. 'The sensation was wonderfully welcome.' He could feel himself slowing, to 250 miles per hour.

At 20,000 feet he hit the clouds. He pulled up his knees reflexively, as if to brace for impact, though what he felt instead was darkness.

Then, at 17,000 feet, after four minutes and thirty-six seconds of free fall, the main chute opened. He was through the cloud, into the light, and heading home. On the tape, he shouts: 'Ahhhh, boy! Lord, thank you for protecting me during that long fall.'

The flight plan had required him to cut away his instrument kit from beneath him at this point, but with his hand so swollen, there was no way to do it, and he hit the ground hard, thirteen minutes and forty-five seconds after leaving the gondola. His crew landed nearby in a helicopter. There is footage of them tending to him, a man in a red cap giving him a good-natured couple of slaps on the cheek, Kittinger grinning with what look like swollen eyes while a doctor examines his hand; in the next shot, he's bare-chested and lighting a cigarette. His hand, after some early alarm, was back to normal within hours.

Talking about it today, Kittinger isn't particularly poetic on the jump itself, having been asked about it relentlessly for fifty years, but he does have strong feelings about its legacy, and in particular in justifying it as a scientific achievement rather than just a record-breaking stunt.

'The work we did on Excelsior was directed toward escape from high altitude, and we developed a small 5-foot-diameter drogue chute that we used to get down. That system is still being used today,' he says. 'Every ejection system in the world uses a small drogue chute for stabilization. What we developed in 1959 and 1960 is still saving lives.'

He acknowledges he was part of a remarkable era. 'It was such an exciting time in aviation. Pre-space age, there were so many great things happening, and mine was just one of hundreds of interesting things that were going on.' And, while NASA still doesn't consider him an astronaut, nobody can argue with this. 'I was the first to be outside of a craft at that altitude, the first person to be in space. I was actually out there, up in an open basket, in a space environment.'

And if you're wondering what happened to the gondola, it came down and was requested by the Smithsonian for its museum. The team cleaned and painted it, and put it on a C-123 – which crashed. The gondola survived that, and was patched up again. It was then put in a warehouse awaiting transport to Washington, when the building burned down. 'I guess we'd exhausted all the gondola's good luck on the project. The Smithsonian never received its exhibit.'

*

With Excelsior, the defining event of Kittinger's biography was written. But the rest of his life has been vividly active too. After Excelsior, he was involved in a project to put a telescope up in a balloon in order to get through the haze of the atmosphere – a forerunner of the Hubble space telescope. This was Project Stargazer, but it didn't last long; by now it was clear that space research would be done by NASA, in rockets.

Kittinger turned instead to combat, serving three tours in

Vietnam. I mention that many of the Apollo veterans I have interviewed feel guilty for having missed combat despite almost all of them being members of the armed forces; Ed Mitchell, for example, had told me about drifting over Indochina and being aware that his brother was down there fighting. Kittinger, engaged in visionary projects, could presumably have missed out too, yet he actively sought deployment. Why?

'It was a sense of duty,' he says. 'I'd been trained as a fighter pilot, and I felt I should volunteer for Vietnam, which I did. I never regretted it.' He addresses the Apollo men with a tone that sounds halfway between a rebuke and self-deprecation. 'The Apollo pilots? All of them could have gone if they had volunteered but none of them, not one, volunteered to leave NASA to go to combat. So they were smarter than I was. But I felt I owed it to the air force to do my bit in Vietnam.'

His first deployment came in September 1963; he came back with a Purple Heart after being hit in the left leg by a bullet while flying in a B-26 bomber. He approached combat apparently without regret, even finding ways to bring his characteristic sense of unorthodox rebellion to the job, on one occasion during his second tour dropping 10,000 empty beer bottles on the Ho Chi Minh trail in order to get rid of them.

A third tour put him in command of the 555th Tactical Fighter Squadron, the famed Triple Nickel, tasked with shooting down MiG fighter jets. Gallows humour again: the squadron's unofficial motto was 'World's largest distributor of MiG parts.' Kittinger himself shot down one MiG, clearly still a point of pride today.

But on 11 May 1972, seventeen days before the end of this third and final tour of duty, and on his 483rd combat mission, his plane was hit by a missile and he ejected at more than Mach 1. He survived the wrenching torsion of ejection; the man in the back seat, Tiny Reich, did not, though Kittinger did not learn this for a year. Landing in a rice field 30 miles outside Hanoi, he was captured and taken to the notorious Hoa Lo, the Hanoi Hilton, where he would spend almost a year.

Torture of POWs had more or less stopped by this point in the war, but they knew who Kittinger was and made an exception for him. Kittinger was and is tough, but anyone who has been through this acknowledges there is a breaking point, and it is just a question of when it is reached. Winched and bent on ropes and bars, he believed his spine was splintering, and prayed for a bone to break so he would lose consciousness. Wounded too, with a leg injury that was dangerously infected, it couldn't last. 'I was in such agony that I couldn't even think straight,' he later wrote. 'Before I knew what I was saying, I told them I'd answer their questions.' Hating himself, he told them things he believed they already knew.

After torture and solitary, things did improve, though it was three months before he was confident he would not need to have the leg amputated. The camp was divided between newer inmates like Kittinger, and others who had been there as long as seven years; they came to call the two camps the FNGs and FOGs, for Fucking New Guys and Fucking Old Guys. As the most senior officer among the FNGs – the second most senior officer ever to be captured in Vietnam – he was therefore the commander of the prisoners, the Americans believing very strongly in preserving a military structure during incarceration. 'I had never desired any command position less, but I kept this feeling to myself. It was an awesome responsibility, and it weighed on me from the first moment.' On one occasion he put everyone under his command on hunger strike in order to get medical attention for a badly burned aviator. He started a church service – impeded by the fact that no soldier in the entire complement could remember the second verse of any hymn in the history of musical composition – and imposed morning workouts.

Kittinger makes no apology for Vietnam, arguing in his book that 'the US mission in South East Asia was a noble effort – at least initially. The objective, to help a small country repel communist invasion, was one we all believed in. I personally couldn't wait.' But he did take the view that the US was approaching the mission all wrong by trying to run it from the White House: he thought they should either withdraw completely, or declare war on North Vietnam and hand the whole thing over to the military. He was part of a subcommittee recommending exactly this. Suffice to say, too, he is no friend of Jane Fonda, who visited Hanoi during the war and denounced American involvement. 'Fonda was a traitor to our country and in my estimation should have been formally charged with treason.'

He was released in March 1973. Until almost the end, his family had no idea whether or not he was alive, and had in most cases assumed not.

Prison had caused him to make some resolutions. 'I'd made a solemn oath to myself that when I got out, I was going to take advantage of everything life offered me. I'd learned just how precious our time on Earth is and how lucky I was to have the opportunities I'd had. I'd also resolved that I was going to spend the rest of my life trying to be happy.'

Asked about it today, he is brief, focusing instead on the plans for the future he made while in solitary. When I ask how it affected him and the person he became, he says: 'It was a challenging experience. I was a person of interest to the North Vietnamese. They were hoping to break me, they were hoping to use me for propaganda, and I wasn't about to let them do it. The experience made me love my country even more because of what we have.' He seems not to want to paint himself as having suffered particularly, because there were people in the same camp who had been there seven years, compared to the eleven months he spent imprisoned.

But he says: 'The happiest day of my life was the day I was released as a POW.'

*

There was a bright side to incarceration – with Kittinger, there is always a bright side to some crushing misfortune – and it came with the ability to dream. 'While I was in solitary confinement, which while I was there was quite a bit, I planned how to fly around the world solo in a balloon,' he says. 'I designed the capsule, the balloon, the communications, the team; that's how I kept my mind engaged.'

He had resolved while in prison to spend the rest of his life trying to be happy, and the balloon vision was very much a part of that, but as anyone trying to recover from trauma will tell you, resolving to be happy is only part of the problem. The minutiae of real life tends to get in the way, and it would take many years before his dream would be realized.

Having been freed in 1973, by 1978 Kittinger was suffering considerable anti-climax, and he quit the military, joining a company called Martin-Marietta as an engineer on the Pershing missile project. Around this time, his marriage ended; his first wife is mentioned maybe four times in his entire 250-page autobiography, and is never named. It doesn't look to have been happy.

After five years of Martin-Marietta, doing something he didn't love, it was time to be impetuous again, so he did something ridiculous: quit, and took charge of Rosie O'Grady's Flying Circus, linked to an Orlando restaurant. In the mornings he would fly paying passengers in a hot air balloon, and in the afternoons, would tow an advertising banner behind a light aircraft. 'I had been flying for Rosie O'Grady's on the weekends when I was working for Martin Marietta,' he says.

He realized that it was this, rather than the money from being an engineer, that made him happy. So he took up the weekend job full time.

'I was flying every day, and I'd never been happier. I wasn't making much money, but what I found was that didn't really matter.' Helping his newfound spirit of bonhomie was a woman called Sherry Reed, now his wife. He learned to skywrite – 'it's trickier than it looks' – and took to the considerable challenge of writing 'Rosie O'Grady's' in the sky. (His boss called him after his first flight. 'Listen, Kittinger. I can teach you how to skywrite, but I can't teach you how to spell.') I imagine the apostrophes would be maddening – correct grammar is hard enough at the best of times, never mind when upside down in a light aircraft – but it turns out the real problem is getting a perfectly rounded 'O'.

'You know, Sherry would frequently go out with a radio and say: your A's aren't quite right, to help me. Because I was trying to fly the perfect mission. And I never did fly the perfect mission.' I love his use of stoic military terminology and discipline to apply to a skywriting job, and behind him, sitting at a table fielding calls on a cellphone with a Harry Potter ringtone, Sherry smiles too. She's been a vital part of the happiness of his later life, it's clear.

Around this time, Kittinger began entering an annual gas balloon race called the Gordon Bennett, winning it at the fourth attempt after crash-landing in Cody, Wyoming, dislocating his shoulder and breaking his arm. Undeterred, he went on to win it twice more. And, by now a highly accomplished balloonist, in 1984 he set off on an ambition to become the first man to fly solo across the Atlantic in a balloon. Today, he paints this as a method of gaining attention and sponsorship for a round-the-world flight, a mere stepping stone, but this flight was still an exceptionally daring attempt. His flight plan, requested by the Canadian authorities who would be in charge of any rescue mission that might be required, looked like this:

Point of Departure: Caribou, Maine
Destination: Unknown
Route of flight: Unknown
Duration of flight: Unknown
Altitude: Unknown
Fuel on board: zero

'Having the paperwork,' Kittinger says, 'seemed to make the Canadians happy.'

Characteristically, it wasn't all smooth; his stove caught fire on the first full day and had to be thrown overboard; the gondola was rattled by Concorde's sonic boom, leading Kittinger to believe his balloon had exploded; it was constantly freezing, touching minus 20 at one point; and he broke his foot falling out of the gondola upon landing. But he made it, all the way from Maine to Italy after four days aloft. If anything, the celebrity from this moment was greater than on Excelsior: he was honoured in Italy and France, was flown to Washington to meet Reagan, went on Letterman. He never gave up on the Hanoi idea of a solo round-the-world flight – the last great ballooning prize – but, on that one, his friend Steve Fossett beat him to it. 'All I could do,' Kittinger says, 'was salute him.' He knows Fossett well, and Richard Branson; there is something of a community of these ballooning adventurers.

Then, from 1993, he and Sherry spent several years doing something called barnstorming. This is a tradition of flying around from town to town in old Jenny bi-planes offering people flights. They bought a plane, called it Stanley, and barnstormed their way across the USA, Sherry acting as the roustabout, collecting money and loading passengers in and out of the aircraft. Kittinger clearly had found his soulmate, and appreciated it. I ask Sherry how she liked it. 'I loved it, I really did.'

They were busy: in one eight-day period in 1995 they flew 955 passengers in a total of forty-three hours, making 240 landings. 'I had a blast. I always had a blast if I was flying.' All told, they would fly about 10,000 people, ending in 2002.

He has not visibly calmed. In his eightieth year, having been given a hunting permit to control Florida's alligator population, he and a friend caught and wrestled a 12-foot alligator from the St Johns River. 'I was back where I'd started.'

*

But one other thing happened along the way.

Every year from 1960 onwards, somebody would contact Kittinger saying they intended to break his record. 'Most of these people,' he says, 'were just glory-seekers or daredevils, but there have been a few serious projects.'

Some he was not keen to be associated with, and they ended in disaster. The skydiver and adventurer Nicholas Piantanida was one example. 'That guy called me and it was very obvious he was a wise ass,' Kittinger recalls. 'He calls me and says: I'm Nick Piantanida, I'm going to break your record. I said: well, good luck. He said: no, you don't understand. I want you to help me.'

Kittinger, busy with other things, did not have time to help, and in any case could see problems. 'I said: what do you know about pressure suits? He said: nothing, but if you can wear one, I can wear one. What do you know about how hostile it is? He said: I don't care, if you did it, I can do it.'

Piantanida then leaned on his union, who in turn leaned on a senator, who leaned on a general, who called Kittinger ordering him to get involved in the project; Kittinger advised him the air force should stay away, which it did. Piantanida went on to fly a manned balloon to 123,500 feet, a record, in February 1966, but three months later he tried to do the same thing and then jump, only for his face mask to depressurize halfway up. Piantanida landed in a coma from which he never awoke, dying four months later.

Kittinger went to a medical conference the year after Piantanida died and met the general who had tried to order him to help with the project. 'The general walked up to me and he said: Captain, I owe you a bottle of Scotch, you saved the air force a lot of embarrassment. I said: sir, you owe me a *case* of Scotch.'

Clearly realizing how insensitive this sounds, Kittinger then looks troubled. 'The poor guy had a crappy team, a crappy attitude, he was a smart-ass, and he ended up dying and leaving a wife and five kids,' he says. 'It was a tragedy, a horrible tragedy. But he represented the types of people that tried to get me involved, and he demonstrated what happens if you don't have the right team, the right approach and the right safety.'

He was, though, willing to help others who did appear to have the right approach. In the early 1990s he worked for almost a year with 'Nish' Bruce, a high-altitude military parachutist who had been the first special forces soldier to parachute into the South Atlantic at the start of the Falklands War, in a project backed by the philanthropist Loel Guinness to jump from 130,000 feet. Kittinger agreed to help and began working on costings and logistics, visiting Russia to look at pressure suits. But doubts about Bruce's persistent failure to take a physical led Guinness to axe the project after a year of work in 1992, and Kittinger agreed. 'I always felt very uncomfortable with Nish, because he wouldn't take a physical and he smoked so bad,' he says. 'But it could have been done, and I would have worked on it.' It turned out later that there were bigger problems than the smoking; Bruce suffered several years of mental illness in the years after the project was abandoned, and in 2002, aged just forty-five, jumped out of a Cessna 5,000 feet above Oxfordshire – without a parachute. 'It ended in tragedy. A real tragedy.'

These two sorry events might have convinced Kittinger that it was better not to put anyone into harm's way by assisting them with a record attempt; after all, the fact that the record stood for fifty-two years shows just how exceptionally difficult it was to break. 'If it was easy to break, it would have been broken a long time ago,' he says. But a couple of years after Kittinger had pulled the plug on the barnstorming and settled into proper retirement, he heard of someone new: the Austrian skydiver and base jumper Felix Baumgartner.

Kittinger entered this project in 2008 when he was contacted by a man called Jack Bassick who worked for the David Clark Company, which makes some of the world's finest pressure suits, and invited to attend a briefing on a new Red Bull-sponsored project called Stratos. The idea was to take a man higher than ever before and have him jump, not only beating Kittinger's record but also putting a man through the speed of sound in free-fall, something Kittinger had been just slightly short of doing on his own jump.

Kittinger had been deeply cynical of most ideas like this in the past: '99 per cent of them had not got any idea of the hostile environment that they were going to,' he says. They didn't share the discipline of the military test pilot: small incremental steps, learning from every one. 'When you test fly an airplane, you don't up to max altitude and speed on the first flight. You take off, you do a certain airspeed and altitude, you learn from that, you do another step, and another step, and eventually you show the whole capacity of the aircraft.' Similarly, nobody attempting a balloon skydiving record should try to achieve it on the first flight, but instead in increments, and very few people who contacted Kittinger seemed to think that way. But when he heard the Red Bull technical project director Art Thompson speak, he was impressed. 'It was obvious to me they were interested in the safety of the jumper. That was paramount: I was not going to get associated with anything that was going to get somebody killed.'

Red Bull asked if he was interested in joining, and Kittinger set a number of conditions, each of which he expected to be deal-breakers. First, he said there had to be three jumps. 'I thought they would say goodbye, Kittinger, because it increases the cost.' He said there had to be two balloons at every jump, 'because if the balloon gets destroyed, I don't want to have 200 people waiting six months to build another one'. And the third concerned Felix Baumgartner himself. 'Felix was a base-jumper. I said my third condition is Felix can no longer do any base jumps.' They agreed with all three.

After that, with characteristic zeal, Kittinger immersed himself in everything to do with the project. 'I worked on all aspects of the mission, because I had knowledge of it,' he says. 'No one on the team had ever made a stratospheric balloon flight, or had ever seen one.' He helped the team make decisions on the balloons that were selected and the techniques that were used, and all told was extremely busy for five years. 'I designed the life-support systems, the balloons, I worked on the parachutes, the pressure suits.' He brought the sense of test-pilot method-ical rigour from his old days. 'I had a whole book on Felix's project with every contingency that could happen. It was three inches thick.' The book's title: *What If*.

Why, though? Why devote so much time and effort to removing your own mark in history?

'The reason was because we were going to make a contribution,' he says. It was to help prove the next generation of pressure suits, to make measurements of physiology that had never been attempted, and of course to set a record; Kittinger's first jump in 1960 had done so as an afterthought, a side-effect, but this time it was a target in its own right. 'To be a part of that was a great opportunity for me.' That still doesn't sound like the whole answer. 'It gave me an opportunity to really get involved in an interesting project. And records are made to be broken: I was amazed it took fifty-two years.' And then: 'It was helping a young man achieve his dream.'

I'm still not convinced, but we move on.

There were challenges along the way. 'Most everything Felix had done was a one-man show. That was a disadvantage because you have to work as a team, and Felix had never worked on a team.' One big problem – the biggest, really – came when Baumgartner developed a fear of his pressure suit and, despite having jumped in it fifty times, suddenly abandoned the project days before a decompression-chamber test. 'Well, this was devastating, because we had worked for two and a half years. He said he couldn't do it, and he got in the airplane and went home. There went the whole programme.'

They got past that, finding someone else to test the capsule and in the meantime finding performance psychologists to help Baumgartner to get over his fears. Red Bull, a loyal and patient sponsor apparently, gave them the time to get it right. Another challenge came when the final jump was soon to take place: a dust storm blew up and destroyed the balloon. Kittinger, of course, had insisted on there being a second balloon, and his prescience saved the day.

Kittinger is amusingly blunt about the role Baumgartner actually played. 'Felix never made a decision on the whole thing,' he says. 'First, he wasn't an engineer. Second, he wasn't a pilot.

Third, he had never been on a team, and fourth, he spent most of his time in Austria anyway.' The team would make decisions and expect Baumgartner to accept them, which he did.

Still, Baumgartner had the biggest thing to do: jump. And jump he did, Kittinger in his ear the whole time, reassuring, cajoling, directing. The video of Baumgartner's jump has been watched many millions of times, but the moment when Kittinger says: 'Start the cameras . . . and our guardian angel will take care of you' still sends shivers down the spine. Baumgartner makes a muffled announcement in reply, salutes, and then drops like a stone, as applause can be heard in Mission Control in the background. Four tense minutes follow, as Baumgartner enters a dizzying spin and eventually corrects it, until a parachute opens. Kittinger, sitting in Mission Control with a big black headset on, dead-pans: 'Couldn't have done it better myself.'

'The happiest moment of all was when he landed on the ground and was safe,' says Kittinger today. 'We were just so elated, because we had accomplished what we had set out to do.' In the video, at the moment Baumgartner lands, Kittinger has his hands high above his head in applause and is beaming from ear to ear.

If Kittinger sounds dismissive of Baumgartner's role, that's not the case; he is enormously complimentary about the jump itself, and says Baumgartner had requested Kittinger be the CapCom because they were comfortable together. But after hearing this account, I think I understand better what appealed to Kittinger about involving himself in a project to push himself out of the record books. No doubt helping Baumgartner achieve his dream was rewarding, but I think it was more about being at the heart of a project, making decisions, making things happen, and doing it successfully. Mission accomplished.

It's interesting, though, just how much pride it clearly gives him. On several occasions during our interview I ask a question about Kittinger's Excelsior jump, and in his answer he turns to an account of Baumgartner's jump instead. At one point I ask him which of the three major achievements of his life as I see it – Manhigh, the Excelsior jump, and the transatlantic balloon crossing – he is most proud of. He puts his jump at number one, but, at number two, instead chooses helping Baumgartner. 'It allowed me to be an engineer and go back and do what I'd done fifty-two years before.' And maybe, in the end, that's the real answer: Baumgartner made him feel young again.

6

Gloria Gaynor

It is an E major 7th that kicks it all off: a hammered E bass with the left hand and then a dextrous trill up and down the keyboard with the right, all delicate and foreboding and a little bit flirty.

More than that, it's a signal. At a wedding, it's a signal to fill the floor and throw reservation to the wind, to adopt a pained expression and throw your arms in the air and holler in a stricken falsetto. In your own home, maybe it's a signal to remind yourself about self-belief and resilience, no matter what has gone wrong in your day or your week or your life. To some, it's a signal to celebrate faith. But however you interpret it, you certainly know it: it's the introduction to 'I Will Survive'.

I had been determined to include a musical star in this book but agonized for the longest time about whom to approach. A one-hit wonder would have diminished the book, I decided. But most true stars are known for a range of songs rather than a particular moment. What I wanted was someone who built a successful and lasting career covering a range of styles and eras, yet who would always, like it or not, be known first and foremost for a single song.

Gloria Gaynor has been recording music for forty years. She

has had multiple hits all over the world and has performed in seventy-five countries, from Buckingham Palace to the Pyramids. She has recorded disco, gospel, rhythm and blues and plenty else besides. But mention her name to anybody and we all know what the first thing that comes to mind will be: 'I Will Survive'. So I'm interested to know how a hit like that changes somebody's life. Clearly it would bring vast recognition, and probably wealth, but is it a millstone around the neck too, a frustration that prevents any more of a person's output from ever being properly acknowledged?

Ever since the song's appearance in 1978, people have been finding a resonant source of encouragement within its back-to-the-wall, irrepressible lyric. The obvious interpretation is to read the song as a stubborn rebound from lost or unrequited love, but it's remarkable just what a range of people have found inspiration in this disco anthem. In 2013, a book based on that song was produced by Gloria Gaynor and Sue Carswell. Titled *We Will Survive: True Stories of Encouragement, Inspiration and the Power of Song*, it compiled the accounts of forty different people, from the mother of an autistic son to an Auschwitz survivor, as they explained what the song meant to them.

What's interesting about Gaynor is how the song has evolved for her, as it has for other people. What the song meant to her when she first sang it, at a time of injury and fading success, is not the same as what it means to her now. Having gained faith in a big, big way over the years, she has since tried to recast the song as a Christian modern hymn, applying new words to her biggest ever hit and continuing to perform it around the world in the spirit of salvation and rebirth.

It's been a hell of a ride for a record that started out as a B-side.

*

Gloria Gaynor is the only person in this book who I don't meet in person. She has just had knee surgery, and her agent, Stephanie Gold, tells me she therefore wants to do the interview by phone. It's not ideal: you get so much more out of people in person, and can develop a better sense of trust, upon which a foundation is built for much more to be said. You get to see how they look, their body language, what they wear. But there is an advantage in doing it by phone: all you can focus on is the voice.

And it is quite a voice, deep and velvety and rounded and assertive. It is a slow melt of a voice, and a precious commodity: although Gaynor has written many songs, it's through performing them that she's made her life.

She is apologetic for being late, having had car trouble, and there is something pleasing about a multi-platinum-selling star grumbling about the mundane things in life that afflict the rest of us too. Bad day? Oh, I will survive.

What is it about 'I Will Survive', I ask her, that so connects with people? 'I think that the problem of having a difficult time in your life, that you think is insurmountable and that you hope you will survive, is universal,' she says. 'When a song addresses that and brings hope and encouragement to help you through that, as this song seems to do for everybody, it's going to be universal as well.'

More universal than she had expected. 'I really thought it was only going to be a woman's song,' she continues, 'because men really aren't great at expressing their feelings and letting anybody know. And I thought it was going to be more about unrequited love and issues of the heart than it has turned out to be. But instead it's been, you know, people with all kinds of illnesses, the Holocaust, child molestation victims, somebody whose husband was trying to murder her.' It's quite a list, and a dark one too. 'That,' she concludes after a pause, 'did surprise me.'

*

Gloria Fowles, to give her the name she started out with, grew up with modest means. She was the fifth of seven children born to her mother through three men, none of whom stuck around for long. She described her mum as having had more relationships with men than any woman would wish to have in a lifetime, and not all of them were wise choices. One molested Gloria when she was twelve, which was the second time, and not the last, that she would be abused by a man during childhood.

She was, naturally, scarred by all these experiences: not just the abuse but the abandonments. Her mother was five months pregnant with her when her father left, causing her mother to stop eating. 'So much of what I have done has been motivated by my lifelong insecurity,' Gaynor later wrote. She believed she suffered trauma while still in the womb, and attributed a lifelong fear of hunger to this betrayal four months before she was even born.

Her childhood home was known as 150 and a half Howard Street in Newark, New Jersey, a Harry Potterish address that stems from the fact that her house sat behind number 150, and could only be accessed by walking through the middle of it past the people who lived there. She lived on the ground floor of 150 and a half, with other families on the next floor, and in the attic; in her apartment, intended for a family of two, lived eight people, with no bath or shower and no heating. Bathing took place in a tin tub on the kitchen floor. The kitchen was also where she slept, along with her brother Arthur. She lived here for ten years – ten years to the day, in fact – before moving into a government development called the Stella Wright Housing Project in New Jersey in her teens. It was hardly a childhood of abundant riches but, as she says, 'children never mind or even know that they are poor, as long as they are loved, which we certainly were'.

That said, she was lonely, with few friends – there is a telling moment in her 1995 autobiography when she ranks the four women she considers her 'very best friends' – and understood that she was in a rough area that limited her horizons. Her mother was a great role model but there were no positive male influences, and this would affect her for her whole life. From twelve years old, she battled with her weight too; by the time of her graduation she had started a diet so ridiculous it caused her to hallucinate fried chicken walking around in the yard. Drifting through childhood, she felt bored, and boring. 'I felt that if all the interesting things that had happened to me were written on the head of a pin, there would still be room left for the Gettysburg Address.'

Like many people before and since, her life was transformed by music. Holding down jobs at Bambergers Department Store and Brown's Beauty World Shop, she got her start in a more vibrant life through a combination of luck and ability. She used to sing in a friend's house where she would babysit, and noticed that footsteps above her head would stop when she did so. It became a game for four or five days: stop the footsteps by song. Then, a few nights later, she and her brother went to a Newark nightclub called the Cadillac, to watch Eddie McClendon and the Pacesetters. To her surprise, during the set, the bandleader called her from the audience to sing, which she did – 'Save Your Love For Me', by Nancy Wilson – to great applause, and sufficient acclaim that she was asked to join the band. The man whose footsteps she'd been stopping with song? He was the manager of the club and had spotted her in the crowd.

Making your way on the music circuit is not easy, and the next few years were a procession of tours, 10 p.m. to 4 a.m. sets, unpredictable money, disreputable agents, drummer boyfriends, changing line-ups and guitarists who are also the van drivers. She called it the Chitterlings Circuit. 'It means that you've made so little money and been so poor, that all you could afford to eat is hog guts.' The names of the bands have the sound of a bygone era of smoke-filled lounges and session musicians in suits, of keyboard players who give themselves the middle name 'Hammond', of saxophonists called Sport and Grover and Junior. After Eddie McClendon and the Pacesetters came Cleave Nickerson and the Soul Satisfiers, then Unsilent Majority featuring Miss GG, then City Life with GG.

If it sounds a romantic, picaresque existence, it wasn't. One day, at Fudgy's in Scarsdale, New York, a man was shot in front of her while she was onstage. Another time, in rural Maryland, in a scene straight out of *The Blues Brothers*, they turned up with all their disco finery to find that the clientele only liked country music, and the argument over pay escalated until they were given twenty minutes to leave town by the police.

When I ask her about this time, she seems to remember it fondly. 'I really feel that it is something that is missed by young artists,' she says, 'because they make a record today and tomorrow they are a huge star on stage in front of hundreds and thousands of people.' She clearly sees this instant fame not as an asset or achievement, but a disability. 'I had a chance to hone my craft before I got to that position,' she says. 'I got to learn how to actually sing, how to form words so that people understand what I'm singing, how to stretch my range, how to work an audience, how to work the stage, how to appear. All of these things I learned before anybody could ever call me a star.'

Along the way she changed her name from Gloria Fowles to Gloria Gaynor, a name suggested by record executive Johnny Nash for no other reason than the pleasing alliteration of the double G. Nash's record company, Josida, recorded her first song, 'She'll Be Sorry', though the label folded not long afterwards. Plenty more would come and go over the years, often accompanied by vicious negotiations: Columbia, MGM, Polydor, Ecstasy, Chrysalis, Stylus, and a host more since. There were plenty of managers and agents, too, one of whom, Jay Ellis Leberman, she would end up in multimillion-dollar lawsuits with.

But success did come, starting with 'Honey Bee' in 1974, considered one of the early standards of disco, followed later that year by 'Never Can Say Goodbye', a Clifton Davis-penned song first performed by The Jackson Five. The album that featured the two hits went gold and was the first ever to be made of non-stop programmed dance music. 'I guess it was a milestone in the story of the new kind of disco music everyone was going for.' The years of graft paid off: in 1975 she was elected Queen of the Discos by the International Association of Discotheques Disc Jockeys, an event which might sound twee today but led to such crowds when she was crowned at New York's Club Les Jardins in March 1975 that the police had to rope off the streets.

*

About disco: there is a tendency to look back upon it and mock it, and a look at the photos and record covers of the time makes it easy to see why, with the clothes and the heels and the make-up. Any era that can produce the Village People has only itself to blame for a little lampoonery. It was a style so brazen that it was asking to be mocked, but it also encouraged the dancer and the listener to forget about taking themselves too seriously and just let go, and that ethos seems to tap into something universal no matter how the fashions might have changed over the years.

Also, as with any musical movement, there is a social side to it that first prompts the style's emergence, then is reflected within it. Disco might be seen today as vacuous and absurd, but in fact it was born out of the utter misery of 1970s New York. 'In the early seventies,' writes Peter Shapiro in his passionate defence of disco, *Turn the Beat Around: The Secret History of Disco*, 'the words

"New York City" became a shorthand code for everything that was wrong with America.' The *New York Times* writer Vincent Canby went further. 'New York City,' he wrote in 1974, 'has become a metaphor for what looks like the last days of American civilization. It's run by fools. Its citizens are at the mercy of its criminals. The air is foul. The traffic is impossible.'

It had come to this because of a confluence of demographic, political, social and cultural trends. The Vietnam War had escalated terribly, and along the way the apparent civility of flower power protest had been replaced by race riots. Recession had kicked in, exacerbated later by the OPEC/US stand-off that quadrupled the cost of fuel in America. A huge number of poor rural African-Americans, both US citizens and immigrants from the Caribbean and elsewhere, were converging on cities like New York at exactly the same time that the manufacturing industries that might have supported them started to decline. White people fled to the suburbs, and took their tax contributions with them. New York, nearing bankruptcy, fired more than 63,000 municipal employees in 1975. Strikes started: sanitation, firemen, police. Murder rates soared, climbing 173 per cent between 1966 and 1973.

But this apocalyptic decline was the birth of disco, and without the misery you would never have had the music. 'Disco is all shiny, glittery surfaces; high heels and luscious lipstick; jampacked jeans and cut pecs; lush, soaring, swooping strings and Latin razzamatazz; cocaine rush and Quaalude wobble,' writes Shapiro. 'Disco was the height of glamour and decadence and indulgence. But whatever its veneer of elegance and sophistication, disco was born, maggot-like, from the rotten remains of the Big Apple.' And it had to be that way, he argues. Disco 'could only have emerged from the dark underground of a society teetering on the brink of collapse.'

There's a fabulous book called *Disco* that chronicles the era in great big slabs of garish 1970s colour, and its foreword has this to say. 'Music is always indicative of the social climate. So what could the social climate have been that acted as a catalyst for disco music and the clothing that no designer had previously imagined?' Disco music, the foreword continues, came about as a form of relief from the drudgery of life during the global economic decline of the 1970s.

The writer then recalls the 'brilliant idea' of taking a music entertainment venue, putting in a dance floor, and then adding a booth, 'which was more than occasionally made from a storage closet, converted by cutting off the top half of the door'. This was the birth of the DJ booth, in a club within which the cover charge would be modest if it existed at all. 'I always felt that nothing could be more gratifying for an entertainer than to know that you are the reason that people are out on the floor not just to dance, but to shake off the worries and tensions of their day.' The author of this foreword? Gloria Gaynor.

I ask her what disco means to her now. 'Disco, I thought, was great music in its purest form,' she says. 'And by that I mean clean lyrics and great beat and just good music. I thought that it was great because I recognized – which most people don't seem to recognize – that it is the first and only music in history ever to be embraced by people of every race, creed, colour, nationality and age group.'

Why is that? The simplicity of it, the beat?

'Yeah. Just fun music. Everybody has a time in their life, probably every week, when they want to just have fun, to release the tension of the day and the week and just loosen up and enjoy themselves until they have to go back to work on Monday. That's what the music did.'

Along the way she feels disco got a bad press. 'The subject matter generally was fun, till people started bringing in all this sex stuff and started associating drugs with it,' she says. 'They sang jazz in opium dens, but nobody associates opium with jazz. For some reason, disco music got associated with half-naked clothing and over-indulgence and drugs and alcohol.'

That's her view today. But she was perhaps not so distant from disco's reputation while living the moment. Life on the road, and later stardom, led to its fair share of disreputable living: she got pregnant twice and had two abortions, in one case not being at all sure whose the baby was. She would become deeply regretful about the abortions in later, Christian life. She found love along the way, marrying Linwood Simon, the brother of her backing singers, and although that brought her stability it also brought her into a lifestyle in which cocaine was all but unavoidable. 'I hated cocaine,' she wrote. 'But the terrible thing about cocaine is that cocaine doesn't care if you hate it. You must have more.'

*

One of Gaynor's onstage tricks involved her snapping the microphone cable like a whip. One of her backing singers would grab it and the two would feign a sort of tug of war through which Gaynor would be pulled back towards the centre of the stage.

One day in March 1978, she was onstage at the Beacon Theatre in New York. She tried the trick but the other singer didn't grab hold of the cable; instead, Gaynor fell, crashing backwards over a monitor. Ever the pro, she carried on with the show, but woke up the next morning unable to move. She spent two weeks in traction in hospital, came out for two weeks, and was then admitted again in even worse shape, spending three months there recovering from spinal surgery.

This incident had two considerable impacts on Gaynor. One was that it rekindled a present but dormant interest in Christianity within her, as she read the Bible closely when she had nothing else to do. She wasn't instantly transformed from her previous hedonism – the day she got out of hospital in a back brace, she ignored instructions to go home to bed and instead went to the International Disco Convention in New York to watch Donna Summer – but this would prove to be the start of a transition from a sort of half-observed faith to one that would absolutely dominate her life.

The other was that it was in this frame of mind, wounded and listening to people tell her she was finished, that a writer called Dino Fekaris came to her with a song written by him and producer Freddy Perren called 'I Will Survive'.

It is scarcely believable, given what the song became, that it started life as a B-side. It entered the recorded world as the flip side of a song called 'Substitute', which wasn't even a new song: a South African all-woman group called Clout had just had a hit with it in Britain and Polydor wanted to try it again with Gaynor's vocals in the States.

When Fekaris came to the studio for the first time, he'd forgotten to bring the song with him; Gaynor's first sight of 'I Will Survive' was when he scrawled the lyrics on a brown paper bag that happened to be at the studio. It was an ignominious beginning to a life-changing moment.

'When I first heard the song I believed, and I do believe, that it was an answer to prayer,' she says now. 'At the time, the record company had said they were not going to renew my contract. I had fallen onstage and woken up the next morning paralysed from the waist down, and I was in hospital praying and asking God: what's going to happen to me? Where do I go from here? I was asking for guidance, strategy, instruction.

'And when I left the hospital I was pretty sure God was going to fix my situation, I just didn't know how.' When she was called by the record company, with a new president, she saw it as a sign. 'I thought the assignment was the answer to prayer.'

The feeling grew when she flew to Los Angeles to record the

song. 'When I began to speak to the producers, they talked to me about what sort of songs I liked, what kind of subject matter. And they said: we believe you are the one we have been waiting for to record this song we wrote a couple of years ago.'

Whether God-sent or not, Gaynor says she was immediately clear on the song's potential. 'Absolutely. Because I was standing here relating to the song because of what I was going through, and I thought other people would do the same. My situation had nothing to do with unrequited love, so I just really thought that people would do the same thing,' that is, relate to it whether they were lovelorn or had some other reason to identify with it. 'I really believed the song was going to be a huge hit and it would be popular for as long as the radio would play it.' Indeed, radio airplay and constant live performance eventually gave the song such a following that Polydor re-published it as a single in its own right in 1979.

Such is her connection with the song, it is sometimes easy to forget that she didn't actually write it. It's also interesting to wonder what had happened in Dino Fekaris's life to prompt him to write words that have proven so sonorous for thirty-five years. 'I Will Survive' was just one of a number of hits he wrote or co-wrote for more or less everyone who mattered in the Motown era: The Supremes ('You Gotta Have Love in Your Heart'), The Temptations ('Mother Nature'), Diana Ross ('Love Me'), Curtis Mayfield ('She Don't Let Nobody'). Still, Gaynor herself seems to know little of the song's genesis. 'All I know is it was written by Dino and Freddy, but I don't know which one wrote what.' Fekaris is usually the one linked with the lyrics; does she know what in his own experience had prompted him to write it? 'I have always thought that Dino had a situation with unrequited love, and him and Freddy wrote the song together, but I honestly don't know. I have no idea really.'

'I Will Survive' went number one everywhere. It was simultaneously the number one in five countries at one stage, including the USA and the UK. It and the *Love Tracks* album it appeared on have sold 14 million copies and won a Grammy. The song has been certified multi-platinum in the US and recorded in at least twenty languages.

But those numbers don't really mean anything. What is extraordinary about 'I Will Survive' is the sheer range of people it connects with. You don't need to like disco to have danced to 'I Will Survive'. You can actively hate disco and still have danced to 'I Will Survive'. In fact, if you've ever been to any wedding in the Western world, you've probably danced to 'I Will Survive'. But it's more than a boozed-up floor-filler that we holler with a hint of irony when we can rarely stand. The odd thing about it is that it is simultaneously a karaoke standard – the number one karaoke selection, I have read, though I'm not sure quite how one quantifies such a thing – and a source of enormous spiritual strength.

That book of individual accounts of the song I mentioned at the start of this chapter, called *We Will Survive*, is quite something. The first story is from a woman whose son had autism and was unable to go on with the emotional drain of her situation; 'I Will Survive' came on the radio, and she found the strength to continue. The second is from a ninety-three-year-old survivor of Auschwitz who lost almost all of her family to the Nazis, then her husband to cancer. She heard the song and found it spoke to her life. 'I have all my life to live and I have so much love to give and I will survive,' she says. And so they go on: a breast cancer survivor who fought her way through chemo with the mantra 'Oh no, not I, I will survive'; the woman who awoke from a car crash-caused coma paralysed and who used the song as a motivation every day when trying to recover; a traumatized first responder to the Oklahoma City bombing who found it 'my rock, my strength, and a subtle yet constant promise of better days to come'; a woman whose daughter was killed in a hit-and-run, who took the song as her motto, the inspiration 'to live every day to the fullest after experiencing the worst thing that could ever happen to a parent'.

But has it all been too much?

*

Gaynor has been making a living from singing for half a century. Is it frustrating to be so closely connected with just one song?

'It has been a frustration in that there are so many people who like my music, but they don't know I recorded sixteen albums,' she says. 'A lot of people have no idea that I do pop music, rhythm and blues, I do contemporary Christian music, I do jazz music. They don't know that unless they are a real fan who comes to my concerts. The general people who like the song haven't experienced all this other music that I've done.'

But she realizes that is a small price to pay for the benefits the song has brought her. 'I've come to understand that that is my ego speaking. And God has been gracious enough to give me a song that has lived for so many years, and has had a positive impact on so many lives of every nationality, race, creed, colour and age group' – that line again. 'I'm happy with that.'

But did it bring a pressure to achieve success on that scale again and again?

'I consciously, purposely refused to bow to that pressure. I always thought that whenever I've recorded, whenever I've gone into the studio, I have taken the best of every element necessary that is available to me, and brought forth the best recording that I could do at that time,' she says. 'I may have had a *better* best the next day, but the day I was recording I did the very best that I could, and my mother used to say: even an angel can't be expected to do better than its best. So I did my best, and hoped for the best, and that's it.'

Is it even her favourite one of her songs? 'Well, I'm not going anywhere looking for it on the radio,' she laughs, 'but it is definitely my favourite song to perform in the show because I know that the audience is going to love it. I know the audience is going to be uplifted by it and be 100 per cent with me when I sing that song.' There are other songs, though, 'that I love just as much, in a different way.' Ironically, one of them was also once called 'I Will Survive', a Christian song which Gaynor recorded and changed the title to 'He Gave Me Life'. 'It really ministers to people, and I love doing that.' Her favourite of her own compositions is another Christian song, called 'Please Let Me Show You'.

I ask how the song's success changed her life. 'Well, it took me to a lot more countries,' she says. 'Before "I Will Survive" I had probably been to thirty countries, but now I've been to nearly eighty countries to perform. The song broadened my scope and changed my world view and helped me mature. It gave me access to experiencing so many different cultures and fans around the world. And it put a few more dollars in the bank, I have to say.'

I'm curious as to whether the success of the song, or her injury, led to her increasingly religious focus from this time.

'Well, actually, it was after the record,' she says. 'At the time of the record, well, you know how when we get in trouble, we always call on God? Whether you're religious or not, it's what you do: "Oh God, help me!" And I was doing the same thing.

'A couple of years later I was going through my mother's things and I found a baptismal certificate that I had from when I was sixteen years old. And all my memories came flooding back how I had seriously and earnestly given my heart to the Lord at that time. But unfortunately the church that I went to then did not teach me anything. After a year or so I just kind of went my own way and never came back to it.

'But thank God, he's not as unfaithful as I am, and he never gave up on me. He kept me. So it was at that time, a couple of years after "I Will Survive", that I really re-dedicated myself to God and determined that I was going to purposely live in the way that he would have me, through a personal relationship with Christ.'

One has to ask how she reconciles this view with the free-wheeling approach to life that was characterized by the disco era. She has, after all, written that at the height of her success she 'could feel myself sinking into the depth of degradation', through the time-honoured expedients of sex, drugs and rock'n'roll (or disco, anyway). I ask her how she squares her faith with her past.

'What I propose to do is share the love and knowledge of Christ through my music,' she says. 'So I began to put a couple of Christian songs in my show, knowing that people came to hear me sing "I Will Survive" and other disco songs.' Some of her biggest disco hits are now performed with different, Christian lyrics; does this represent a rejection of her disco life, and a sense of regret, or is this just a new interpretation for a new phase in her life? 'Just that. A new interpretation, taking the opportunity to let people know: here's where I'm coming from right now.'

Gaynor's disco career lasted for some years after 'I Will Survive', and in order for it to do so, disco had to do some surviving too. The backlash against disco that began towards the end of 1979 was among the most venomous that has ever been lobbied against a particular style of music, something Gaynor tells me she attributes to 'Middle America saying I don't want my children associated with this stuff, so let's kill it.' It is also argued that new movements such as punk thrived as an alternative to the political apathy inherent in disco, since disco's lyrics were hardly associated with social complaint, or pretty much anything other than a sense of freedom and fun. *Lost in Music,* as the song had it. It was in this environment that a stunt to blow up a load of disco records at a Chicago White Sox baseball game in July 1979 attracted more than 50,000 people, who approached their destructive task with such bracing enthusiasm that they eventually had to be dispersed by riot police. An unlikely but illustrative document of the time is the 1980 classic movie *Airplane!* There is a scene where a city skyline is shown with a radio tower and a neon-lit call sign. A DJ voiceover is heard: 'WZAZ in Chicago, where disco lives forever!' Then the plane cuts the tower in half with its wing and the voiceover goes silent.

In this environment, Gaynor's disco albums released in 1980 and 1981 sank without trace. But she had one major hit to come, with 'I Am What I Am' in 1983. It was arguably disco's last rallying call until revivals decades later, but it had been good while it lasted, and Gaynor has been adamant that disco never died, nor ever deserved its bad press. 'Music is like money,' she says. 'It takes on the character of the person who's using it. You can't blame money for murder, just because somebody, for love of money, wants to kill somebody. And you can't blame any of that drugs and alcohol stuff on disco.'

And how did it feel, for those few great years, to be – as they used to call her – the Queen of Disco? 'It felt great to me, because I'm only thinking of the purity of the music, and how it helps people to have fun and release tension. That's all I was ever thinking about, and the fact that it was embraced by such a variety of people.'

She tells me a story to illustrate.

'When they had the reunification dinner in Europe for . . . I can't even remember what country it was in, for when the wall came down.' She is talking about German reunification in Berlin in 1989. 'Yeah! They called me. They called for disco music at that event.'

This is a revelation so surprising I am reduced to this response: wow.

'Yeah! They didn't call for jazz. They didn't call for rhythm and blues. They called for disco music.' Did you go? 'Yes, I did. I sang.' And how was it? 'Awesome! It was awesome. Because there were people there from all the different countries, and all the dignitaries . . . it was great.'

By then, though, she had decided on a change in direction. Since the 1980s the vast majority of her output has been Christian music of one form or another. In this respect, 'I Will Survive' has been something of a problem, because it is so indelibly part of her that it is hard for her to forge a following as a gospel singer even though she's now been doing that much longer than the disco part of her career.

'Well, you know, people tend to brand you,' she says. 'My brand now is "I Will Survive". It has nothing to do with Christianity or gospel music. So that makes it very difficult for me to be accepted either by the Christian community or the secular community in that area. But I'm of the belief that if God wants this to happen it will happen, and no one will be able to stop it. I'm just looking to do what I believe he would have me do and let him do what he does.'

An atheist myself, I find this attitude interesting but difficult to understand. I can understand somebody of faith believing they have been granted a gift and being grateful for that gift, but the sense of taking one's hands off the wheel and assuming somebody else is going to be in charge of all the decisions seems at odds with a creative talent – particularly a songwriter – whose whole life and success has been created by drive and seizing the moment rather than leaving decisions to anybody else.

Though Gaynor in person is perfectly reasonable and not at

all judgemental about faith, there are points in her book when her belief in divine leadership is beyond me. There's the conversation with God, recounted verbatim and with some frustration, during which she believes he tells her to stop singing anything but gospel. And, chiefly, there's the moment when she believes she has been called to double-park outside a music store and go inside to find a tape in the gospel section that God has intended her to re-record. 'I bought the book, bought the tape, got back outside, and thanked the Lord for letting his angels stand by my car, which was still there.' Still, that said, the tape she found was the other 'I Will Survive', the one she re-recorded as 'He Gave Me Life' and which became probably the most successful recording of her post-dance career, so maybe she's on to something.

In any event, her religious calling didn't just influence her view of her future, but her past. And in the spirit of this change of direction, she did something that is either divinity or heresy, depending on where you stand: she changed the words to 'I Will Survive'.

*

Today, when you go and hear Gloria Gaynor sing, you don't hear:

> At first I was afraid
> I was petrified
> Kept thinkin' I could never live without you by my side.

Instead, you'll hear this:

> Only the Lord could give me strength
> Not to fall apart
> Though I tried hard to mend the pieces of my broken
> heart.

When I tell people this, they look aghast, but she insists she's never had any negative feedback about her decision. 'I also re-recorded "Never Can Say Goodbye" and "I Am What I Am", which were my two biggest songs [besides the obvious], and changed a couple of the lyrics to reflect my faith. And I began to sing them that way in my shows so people would know where my support lies, where I believe my blessings come from, and to share that knowledge and that resource with them. I was just sharing what were the optimum words. I wasn't beating anyone over the head with the Bible or shovin' my faith down anybody's throat. I was just saying: here's what I believe, and if you'd like to believe it too, it's available to you.'

And the response? 'Fine. It was a response that I wanted. People who wanted to know more about God would write me letters and ask me different things, and people who didn't just enjoyed the show. I'm sure there are people on both sides of that who never contacted me and I'll never know until some day I'm in heaven.'

Still, while Gaynor has been reinterpreting her flagship song as a hymn, the rest of society has been taking it through a quite different evolution. When it turned up on *Priscilla, Queen of the Desert* in 1994, it gained the song another lease of life as a gay anthem (which, incidentally, is also what has happened to 'I Am What I Am'). It gained a young new following when Robbie Williams adapted it for his 2000 song 'Supreme'. Williams had been in Switzerland and noticed that the tourists around him, though speaking no language in common, were all humming the string solo to 'I Will Survive'. In 1999, a young animator called Victor Navone was looking for music to set an animated dancing alien to and settled on 'I Will Survive', in a clip that went viral (and landed Navone a job at Pixar along the way). Many millions of people have since watched the sassy little one-eyed green alien who is flattened in full flow by a falling discoball; Gaynor's representatives, knowing a good thing when they saw it, opted not to sue for the unlicensed use of the music but instead put a link to it on her website, for a while at least. Navone got the idea after hearing a DJ put the song on at his wife's office Christmas party; that's another institution that is surely never complete without 'I Will Survive'.

When I ask her about *Priscilla*, I get the bluntest answer of the interview. 'I don't think it had any impact on my music and my career at all.' I clarify that I meant to ask whether it had brought new fans to her music. 'The people who frequented that show already knew me.' Puzzled at the uncharacteristically terse response, it's not until later that it occurs to me that I should have asked how she reconciles a gay fan base with her particularly literal and scripture-based interpretation of the Bible.

*

We talk a bit about her views on modern music. She talks about her love of Beyonce, 'who is a really great performer', but she can't quite leave it at that: 'And then she goes and throws it away with all the crap that she's done. God help her.' She loves Alicia Keys, she says, and if she's not listening to gospel music she'll put on Whitney Houston, or even Justin Timberlake or Bruno Mars.

What do you make of Lady Gaga?

'Oh,' she says, with a groan of something like agony. 'I try not to even think about her.'

I ask if she still has ambitions.

'Oh, yes,' she says. 'My greatest ambition at this point is to be somewhat instrumental in making people understand the importance of fatherhood. Specifically, trying to bring fathers to understand how important it is for them to be active in the lives of their children, even if they are not with the mother.'

She gives lectures on the subject, and is in touch with government agencies to spread the word.

This must surely be an enthusiasm driven by the challenges of her own childhood. 'Absolutely, my own childhood,' she says, then backtracks slightly to familiar ground. 'Well, at first, I thought it was something that God had just dropped into my life and told me to do, but I've come to understand that even if that's so, it's because of my experience that I can stick to that. I believe that what God calls you to do, he equips you to do. And what he equips you to do is what he calls you to do. And I am equipped to speak about the plight of young children being raised without fathers, because I was one of them.'

'In Christianity,' she concludes, 'your mess becomes your message.'

How about musically? 'Yeah, I continue to write, because I have always been a writer. I would either sing the songs myself or make them available to other people. I am getting up there in age, and soon it will be time to stop bouncing around the disco stage. But I can see myself performing for at least the next five years.' At the time of our interview in early 2014, she is sixty-four.

She's still performing now, despite a brief lay-off for the knee surgery. She's just played a casino in Madeira, and her bookings list for the rest of the year after our interview covers Quebec, Marbella, Malta and Fort Lauderdale. Her next booking after we speak, though, seems the most unlikely: Bahrain. 'I've done quite a bit in the Middle East,' she says. 'Dubai, Sharjah, Abu Dhabi.'

This reminds me of a story I heard about her dutifully learning the Arabic for 'I love you, Lebanon!' and saying it, with perfect pronunciation, in Syria. She laughs. 'Yeah,' she says. 'I got out of that one.'

How? By winning the audience over again by shouting out another Arabic word she'd learned: *Anabadaish! Anabadaish!*

Many years on, she might be slightly misremembering this; *ana badaish* means 'I don't want,' which seems unlikely to turn a crowd onside. More likely, she shouted: '*Anaa Ba Eieesh*'.

Which means, as you might have guessed, 'I Will Survive'.

7

United 232

What is it about air crashes that fascinate us even as they appal us? Is it that all of us can picture ourselves in that situation, in a troubled descent, with time to think hard about the end? Is it the dice roll of their destruction, the bitter democracy that it can happen to anyone? Is it their scale, hundreds of lives ended or saved in an instant, a blink, a breath of air?

Whatever it is, we are clearly drawn to their postscripts, the *Air Crash Investigations* and the *Air Crash Confidentials* and the *Maydays*: the first of those series has run to ninety-eight episodes at the time of writing and there have frankly not been enough disasters to meet its viewers' appetite. I remember once staring in disbelief at a TV at the departure gate in a Malaysian airport showing an episode. There was a reasonable crowd sitting round watching it, rapt. And then they boarded their planes.

The twin Malaysian Airlines disasters of 2014 were a case in point, particularly the first of them; at the time of writing, its wreckage could not be found but was presumed to be 3 miles down in the remote Indian Ocean. Not only is everyone a fascinated voyeur but everyone's an expert too, and every online news story is followed by a thousand strident comments under pseudonyms and nom de plumes, each with their own theory about what happened: the fire in the cockpit, the loss of cabin pressure, the suicide plunge, the secret landing in Diego Garcia. We can't stand the not knowing, the lack of resolution. Because we can all imagine the interior of an aircraft cabin, we just have to know what happened.

While it probably says something unpleasant about us that we relish these mass-death accounts, it is easier to understand our love of heroics in the air. Think of Chesley Sullenberger putting his plane into the Hudson, his gravel-voiced staccato instructions to LaGuardia's air-traffic controllers warning brusquely that he was heading for a river, without losing a single soul. Or the British Airways jet which lost all four engines in an Indonesian volcanic cloud and still made a landing ('like negotiating one's way up a badger's arse', as Captain Eric Moody later said). 'Ladies and gentlemen, this is your captain speaking. We have a small problem. All four engines have stopped. We are doing our damnedest to get them going again. I trust you are not in too much distress.' That, we can get behind.

United 232 fits between the two extremes. It is at once one of the greatest achievements in the history of aviation, and a desperate tragedy that cost 112 people their lives.

On 19 July 1989, a United Airlines DC-10 took off from Denver for Chicago O'Hare with 296 people on board. You don't see DC-10s any more, nor their configuration, but in their time they were the leading wide-bodied aircraft in the skies, driven by three engines, one on each wing and a third mounted in the tail. An hour or so after take-off, that tail engine exploded; worse – far worse – the shrapnel from the failed engine severed all three hydraulic systems for the plane, a combination of circumstances formerly believed impossible. No rudder. No flaps. No control, in short, of the systems that are supposed to help a plane turn left or right, or go up or down, or to be in any condition or trim to fly at all, let alone land.

At that point, it's over. The possibility of all three systems failing was so remote it had never been trained for. It was not survivable, so why bother? This wasn't like Joe Kittinger and his endless what-ifs. It was beyond a what-if. There is no way to land a jet aircraft with no hydraulic controls. But through a combination of extraordinary ability and a considerable amount of luck, the crew brought the jet down in Sioux City, Iowa, and, though it crashed, almost two thirds of those on board survived when everything in aviation said that they should have died.

The crew – and four of them were involved, including one who started the flight as a passenger – are unquestionably heroes; the same was clearly true of the flight attendants, marshalling the fearful in the back. But also they felt, and were sometimes described as, failures. I am curious to know how one moves on from this nasty dichotomy, and precisely what one does with a second chance.

*

The fog is dense when I land in Seattle and it is late into the night, though at least I have had an empty seat next to me: if ever you want to prompt a fellow passenger to change seats, simply get out an air-crash investigation transcript, a gutted fuselage on its front cover, and begin to read.

The fog is still there the next morning as I drive to a modest address just a few minutes from SeaTac Airport, the screams of the jets clear in the wet morning air, though the aircraft themselves are invisible in the dense fug above.

I am here to meet Captain Alfred C. Haynes, the captain of *United 232*. He's eighty-one and long retired now, and one might expect declining health in a man whose body has been tested by unspeakable violence, but in fact he has been working out on a treadmill downstairs, and conducts the interview in his gym gear.

The living-room walls are filled with paintings and photos of mountains, Mount Rainier in pride of place, and a pitching sailboat. On the shelves and mantelpieces there are numerous model aircraft, including, I note, a United DC-10. There could be many more: he later tells me there are four boxes full of plaques, awards and so forth beneath the house, and there's not nearly enough room upstairs to accommodate them all, nor, presumably, any sense that it would be healthy to have them up here anyway. Not that Haynes has ever tried to hide from the accident: in fact, I will learn, he is a passionate advocate of the view that the way to recovering from a trauma is to talk, and talk, and talk about it again.

'I have dry mouth,' he tells me as he sits down. 'If I start to slur, tell me to drink some water.' That's as much of an ailment as one can perceive in the man. He leans back into a beige armchair and we begin.

By the time Haynes flew on *United 232*, he was fifty-seven and had amassed 29,967 hours of total flight time with United Airlines, having joined them more than thirty-three years earlier in 1956. He'd spent a few years as a Marine Corps aviator before that: basically, a professional lifetime in the air. In all of that time, had any experience or training prepared him for a hydraulic failure on this scale?

'No.' His voice is deep and firm. He's a baseball announcer of many years' repute, and one can hear the steady authority. 'A full hydraulic failure was considered to be something that could never happen. It was foolproof. I think a billion to one were the odds.' In fact, it had happened once before, in a Boeing 747-400 owned by Japan Airlines, just four years before the United crash; but the pilots could not control the plane and it flew into a mountain, killing 520 people in the deadliest single-aircraft accident in history. That accident only reinforced the view that if the hydraulics go completely, nothing can be done;

hence the lack of training for it. 'Since it can't be done, they figured it couldn't be flown, and if it did lose it all there's no procedure for it. So we didn't practise in the simulator. We didn't drill for it. We didn't train with it. It's completely foreign to us.'

Had he experienced emergencies before in all those years of flying? 'I had some. I don't think we had anything that a company would call an emergency. I did once, in the military, get into an inverted spin practising dropping A-bombs. I couldn't get out of that and was about to bail out. But when I let go of my stick, as I started tightening my straps, the plane righted itself. That's the closest I got.' He never experienced an engine failure in either the military or at United, barring a piston failure. 'Nothing really critical. All just irregular procedures, as they're called, which you can handle through the checklist. I don't remember diverting but once, and that was because of a death on the airplane.'

United 232 – he pronounces it 'two thirty-two' – was a routine flight from Denver to Chicago, he says. Bill Records, the co-pilot, was the one actually flying the plane. In those days there was a second officer, or flight engineer, and on that day it was Dudley Dvorak, sitting at his instrument panel, which in a DC-10 was sideways relative to the rest of the cockpit controls, mounted on a bulkhead.

'Bill's flying it, I'm working the radios. And we had just finished our lunch, and all of a sudden there was this big bang. The airplane was shaking. I thought it was a bomb, it was so loud, and I can't imagine what it was like for the people back there in the tail.' He saw Bill Records grab the flight controls – 'that's normal procedure, it's his leg so he's gonna fly the airplane' – and Haynes and Dvorak set about shutting the engine down. The plane was shaking so badly it took a moment to be clear which engine had failed, but they quickly established it was number two: the one mounted in the tail. Because the throttle had jammed they couldn't reduce the power to idle, so they shut it down by cutting off the fuel flow to the engine.

'And then Dudley called my attention to his hydraulic panel. And I looked, and we had no hydraulic pressure. No fluid. Which can't be. And then Bill said: I can't control the airplane.'

That was no surprise. A total hydraulic failure means a pilot can't use the rudder, to turn the plane left or right; or the elevators or ailerons, which orientate it to go up or down. Worse, the plane was banking hard to the right, and could not be corrected using the flight controls.

Here, Haynes refers to the cockpit voice recorder, part of the so-called black box that aids investigations of accidents. 'Now, I don't know how long this was, because the cockpit recorder is only thirty minutes long, and we took forty-five to get down, so we recorded over the first fifteen. But we realized we didn't have anything. And we were starting to roll over on our back. I turned round and Bill was calling for a maximum climb: the yoke was all the way back and all the way left.' That is, Records had the flight-control column in a position that should lead to a roll to the left with the nose rising – a pair of inputs that would never normally be used simultaneously in flight – and was receiving no response. 'It didn't make any sense.'

With no options left, and needing to stop the plane from rolling on to its back, they turned to the throttles. On big commercial aircraft, the throttles for all the engines are next to one another so that they can be operated in concert, and with one hand. On a DC-10, there were three of these throttles. Since the centre one that controlled the broken engine had jammed, two hands were needed to control the others, and, in any case, each throttle had to be operated to do different things. By giving the right-hand engine more power than the left, they could at least start to cancel out the rolling motion of the plane, and to level off. 'By experimenting with the throttles, we got the thing back level again. But now the problem is: what are we going to do to get the plane on the ground? And we didn't know.'

Dvorak called United's maintenance team in San Francisco for advice, 'because there was nothing in the book on how to do this'. Records and Haynes grappled futilely with the yokes, and with an additional problem that the plane was pitching up and down very slowly, a motion known as porpoising, or more formally as a phugoid. 'If you close the throttle on an airplane and leave it alone, it will porpoise until it finds the speed to fly. But because our plane was rolling, we had to keep changing the power,' and this stopped the plane from naturally finding its own equilibrium.

At this point, having experienced the absolute extreme of bad luck, a slow tide of better fortune began to ebb their way. A flight attendant came to the front and told them a passenger had approached her and said he was a training check airman who had taught the DC-10. Would the crew like him to help? Haynes said: bring him up.

This was Dennis Fitch, known to all as Denny. Fitch was himself a DC-10 captain, albeit one only very recently qualified, but, more importantly, he was a trainer. A training check airman is someone who guides pilots through their mandatory annual check rides, a large part of which takes place in a simulator. In Fitch's case, he supervised these training rides at the United facility in Denver. 'We get into a simulator,' Fitch said in a later interview with the US series *First Person* (he is, sadly, no longer around to interview). 'The flaps won't come down, the gear gets stuck, you have engine failures, hydraulic failures, electrical failures, explosions, fire; things are going to happen and you don't know what they're going to be. You just have to deal with them. This is how we train pilots so they're ready for it whatever happens.'

The fact that a passenger at the back of the plane happened

to be a man who spent his life in simulators re-creating exactly these sorts of emergencies was one thing. But that would have been useless without the willingness of the captain to accept his help. And this is not the given you might think.

*

In the 1980s – and sometimes this is still the case today – the captain of a jet was viewed with such reverence that it could occasionally become problematic. Whether for reasons of seniority, ego or a hangover of military norms, challenging the captain, or even offering him (and it was always a him) advice, was just not done in most cultures and airlines.

In fact, until not long beforehand, this had been the case in the US as well, in one instance leading to a crash on a United Airlines jet.

In December 1978, *United 173* had been a scheduled flight from New York's John F. Kennedy Airport to Portland International in Oregon, with a stop in Denver. When the plane approached Portland and lowered its landing gear, the crew heard a loud noise, felt vibration and yawing, and saw there was no green light to show that the gear was down and locked. The captain aborted the landing and set about diagnosing the problem, but spent so long doing so that the plane ran out of fuel and crashed, killing ten people. On the transcript, the first officer and the flight engineer can be heard stating the level of fuel remaining on the jet, but the captain does not hurry up his approach – and his colleagues don't urge him to do so. The National Transportation Safety Board (NTSB), which investigates all crashes, said in its report that there were two principal causes: the failure of the captain to monitor properly the aircraft's fuel state, and 'the failure of the other two flight crewmembers either to fully comprehend the criticality of the fuel state or to successfully communicate their concern to the captain'.

After the crash, everything changed in North American commercial aviation – and particularly at United. It was the catalyst for a change in the way airline crew were trained. The new approach was called Crew Resource Management. 'That crash on United is what caused us to get CRM,' says Haynes. 'The captain just wasn't listening, or wasn't hearing what he was being told, and he ran out of fuel and crashed. And that's what started CRM.'

'What that programme taught me,' he says, 'is: if you don't know how to do this, swallow your pride, swallow your ego, and find help anywhere you can. When you have a problem, let everybody there take part. One of the biggest, most successful things about CRM is that it taught the other two members of the crew: don't be afraid to speak up.'

By the time of *United 232*, CRM had been in practice at United for eight years, and Haynes was well versed in it. And it was this training that allowed him to invite a stranger into the cockpit and hand over the throttles without even having had a chance to look him in the face. 'After a minute, I reached around and introduced myself to him, but I was so busy I never even turned round,' says Haynes. 'You know, after the accident, I went into a hospital room to visit him. And as they brought me into the room I said: I hope he's the only one in there, because I have no idea what the man looks like.'

Fitch, for his part, was impressed by the gesture. 'These three men were not known to me,' he said in his *First Person* interview. 'They were all Seattle-based, and I'm out of Chicago. At the time I think we had 7,500 pilots in the airline and we didn't know each other by name, face or reputation. The only thing that was controlling his aircraft was his throttles.

'He transferred to a perfect stranger the control of his aircraft.

Now that is an amazing thing if you take into consideration that pilots don't give up control very easily.'

Fitch had no magic answers from his many days in the simulators, but he was another pair of hands, which was proving to be vital, particularly since the throttles needed two hands instead of the usual one in order to operate them independently.

There was no spare seat, so Fitch stood between Haynes and Records, both of whom were battling other controls, and operated the throttles from there. 'He smoothed out the phugoids,' says Haynes, referring to the repeating upward and downward motions of the plane, somewhat like a sine wave, that were taking it up and down 2,500 feet per minute as it tried to regain its natural equilibrium. 'He never stopped them, but he had a slightly better control of heading. His full concentration was on giving us whatever we thought we needed. It was the three of us working together – I'm not excluding Dudley, he was very busy with other things [briefing flight attendants, dumping fuel, preparing checklists and manning radios, among other things] – and as Denny began to fall in synch with us he began to anticipate what we needed. That way, we got the airplane back.'

At this point, a few more elements of good luck began to redress the balance, just a little, in the crew's favour. The explosion had taken place over the flat Midwest, in daylight, and without any of the storms that typically blight the region.

There was talk of two airports in Nebraska: at first Omaha was discussed, and then Lincoln, which was United's preference since that city was believed to have a bigger and better emergency recovery and National Guard unit. But the airline's wishes never got through because there were only two radios on the plane. 'Dudley was on with the maintenance base, and we weren't about to turn off with them because they were giving us advice. And the other was for air-traffic control, and we weren't about to turn off with them either. We never even knew they wanted us to go to Lincoln.'

Instead, when the pilots eventually regained sufficient control over the jet to turn it round and keep it steady after a dizzying slew of right-hand turns, they found themselves lined up with Sioux City, Iowa. When I ask Haynes what took him to Sioux City, he says: 'The airplane.' I laugh, slightly nervously, fearing it was a stupid question. 'No, really. People say: why did you go to Sioux City? Because the airplane went to Sioux City. We were just keeping it flying. We didn't aim for anything.' If that's the case, it would turn out to be an excellent decision on the part of the plane, since Sioux City's airport could take a DC-10, and the strength of emergency assistance on the ground there would soon become extraordinarily clear.

The transcripts from the plane's cockpit voice recorder make sobering reading as the men battled to bring the plane down to the runway. Through it all, they kept gallows humour. At one point, Fitch says, 'I'll tell you what, we'll have a beer when this is all done.'

Haynes replies, 'Well, I don't drink, but I'll sure as shit have one.'

And as they get closer to the airport, Sioux City Approach radios to give guidance on wind conditions and says: 'You're cleared to land on any runway.'

There is laughter in the cockpit. 'Roger,' says Haynes. 'You want to be particular and make it a runway, huh?'

But then: 'Whatever you do, keep us away from the city.'

*

Behind them, the flight attendants, marshalled by Jan Brown, had done an exceptional job of keeping almost 300 people calm despite the very clear realization that they might soon die. It was, in many respects, worse for the passengers; they were helpless, with nothing in their own hands to influence their salvation or demise.

Jan Brown was twelve years into a second stint as a flight attendant when *United 232* happened. Finding herself a single mother of three, she had returned to the skies in 1977. By the time of *232*, she was the lead flight attendant, and ultimately responsible for the rest of the cabin crew and all passenger safety. She was the most senior figure on the aircraft behind the cockpit. I reach her in Chicago and she gets back to me quickly, signing off her emails: 'Smiles, Jan.' She agrees to a call.

When the engine blew, she says, they were in the middle of a meal service. She had set up first class to do their service, and was in economy picking up trays, about three-quarters of the way through serving. She was in B zone, which in a DC-10 was the forward part of economy class; she was about five rows from an over-wing door.

'I instinctively sat on the floor and held on to an armrest,' she tells me. 'I didn't know if it was a decompression, and I didn't want to be sucked out.' She laughs, as she often does, disarmingly. 'I always used to read about accidents to pick up whatever tips I could, and I knew that in an Aloha incident [*Aloha Airlines 243*, involving a Boeing 737 between two Hawaiian islands in 1988, a year before the United crash] the top of the roof came off. And I heard a flight attendant went to make an announcement and was sucked out. That,' she says with another slight chuckle, 'had made a very strong impression on me.'

After a few seconds the plane stabilized and, with the instincts of her profession, she immediately looked for passenger reactions. The first person she clapped eyes on was a mother holding her twenty-two-month-old son. 'She looked like she was going into panic,' says Brown. 'And I don't have panic on my airplanes.

I immediately went back to stop it before it spread. I spoke to her very quietly.' The woman was Sylvia Tsao; the boy, Evan. The two were to have a profound impact on Brown's life that continues to pervade it today.

While she was talking to Tsao, the first announcement – Dudley Dvorak's – was made. 'I remember he comfortingly said that we still had two engines, and that we would be OK.'

When did she realize the severity of the situation? 'When they called me to the cockpit and I opened the door,' she says. 'The minute I opened that door, it was . . . the only way I've been able to describe it is as if you opened a furnace door, and the heat hitting you would be so enormous. For me, it was what was in the air.

'It wasn't anything they were doing,' she stresses. 'Al and Bill were gripping the yoke, and I could see the strength they were putting into it; Dudley was doing his job. There was total calm. They were all professional and businesslike. But still, the minute that door opened, it hit me. This isn't just a garden-type emergency. This is a crisis.'

It was a colleague of Brown's, another Jan, who found Denny Fitch and passed his message to the cockpit. Meanwhile Brown, in the first instance, was concentrating on two things: what she needed to do in light of what Al Haynes had just told her about the state of the plane, and how her face should be looking. 'I didn't look at anybody: it's like children cover their eyes and think "they can't see me". You can always tell fear by a particular look. And on an airplane, any time there's a bump, people look at you to see if they can read your face to see how serious it is. So I had developed, not a casual look, but an everything's OK look.'

In order to disguise the severity of the situation from the passengers, Brown briefed her flight attendants in small groups. 'I couldn't call them together because it would tip the passengers off that something was wrong.' But it was, of course: very wrong. Brown briefed her team that the captain had told her that all hydraulics had been lost, and that they should secure the cabin and prepare the passengers. There was, at the time, a booklet with precise instructions on the process of readying the cabin, from fastening seat belts to the brace signal and position, and the process of evacuation. Brown felt solid. 'I willed myself. I said: number one, I have to be calm. I've had instances in my past that made me stoic, or taught me stoicism. So I just make up my mind something's going to be that way, and I don't consider there would be any other alternative.'

Years later, a passenger told Brown her hands were shaking when she picked up their tray. She said: 'You must have been one of the first two rows, because I saw that hand and said: Jan, you have to get a grip. Literally, a grip.' She picked up the microphone, on a long coil cord, and prepared herself to address B zone about emergency preparation. 'I thought: your hand will *not* be shaking. That will *not* inspire confidence.'

And, perhaps because of the calmness she and her staff were projecting, there was no panic in the plane. 'For the most part, I know there was underlying prayer, consternation, and maybe a little crying. But I had a great crew, and I give credit to the passengers too. We went around as if it was business as usual.'

Brown had three children at home. But, she says, 'I never gave myself a thought,' and it really doesn't come across as bravado. Given how exceptionally busy they must have been, you can well believe it. 'Even after we had done the emergency prep and the flight attendants had gone through the aisles reassuring people about their seat belts or answering their questions, even when we had rehearsed the brace positions and we were all in our jump seats, I remember thinking: have we covered everything?'

And then she remembered: lap children.

This is the element of *United 232* that would haunt Brown more than anything else. Airline policy for emergencies at that time dictated that children under two without their own seat should be placed on the floor and surrounded by pillows or blankets, not held on the lap of the parent. There were four lap children on the plane.

Earlier she had given those parents a briefing on what to do, so they had time to get their children used to being on the floor. But when it became necessary to tell them to do it, 'I could not believe I was uttering those words. It seemed to be utterly ludicrous to be telling people to take their most prized child and put them on the floor and, in other words, hope for the best.' One flight attendant spotted 'a blanket with a suspicious bump in it' and realized a man had a child belted in with him; she had to convince him the best thing to do was put his infant on the floor. 'It amazes me. To this day.'

She must have trained for it; had it seemed ridiculous then, or only when she had to try it in reality? 'That's exactly it. I remember thinking: in a classroom situation this might sound OK, but right now it's totally absurd. How can we be doing this?'

The cabin was as ready as they could make it: a great achievement given that they had been halfway through a meal service less than forty minutes earlier and they'd had to work in a pitching, tense environment. 'After that,' she says, 'it was just waiting for the brace signal. I remember looking across at a businesswoman in a suit, wondering if she was praying. Her hand was up on her head, in deep thought. I wondered what she was thinking.'

*

Haynes himself doesn't remember precisely what he said to the passengers at any point in the descent. 'Fifteen minutes before we got to Sioux City I got on the phone and said the engine problems had caused some problems to the airplane, so we weren't going to Chicago,' he says. 'So we were going to make a landing in Sioux City, Iowa. I told them: because of the control problems it's going to be a hard landing, harder than anything you've been on, so please listen to what the flight attendants have to say as far as preparing yourselves. Something of that nature.' He looks down. 'They've told me it was enough to alert them, but not to frighten them. There was never any panic back there.'

Jerry Schemmel, a passenger who wrote a book on the experience, recalls an announcement from Haynes saying that there had been damage to the back of the plane and that the crew was having trouble flying it. 'Now the crying seemed to be coming from all around me,' Schemmel wrote. 'There was no widespread panic but a strong sense of impending doom and our own powerlessness.' He thought about Haynes's words, and what might lie behind and between them. 'His strategy, I was convinced, had been to tell us just enough to make us aware that the situation was serious, while also offering reassurances to keep us hopeful and the panic to a minimum.' He, too, noted the stress the flight attendants were under.

The flight attendants completed their briefings. Schemmel, automatically, shifted his watch from Mountain Time to Central Time, for Sioux City. He later accounted for this apparently obscure attention to detail as 'a nervous attempt to fill the frightening emptiness before touchdown'. That done, he reviewed his life's successes and failures in his mind, then wrote a note to tell his wife where the documents for his new life insurance policy were. He then recalls Haynes making one final announcement, reminding people of the 'Brace! Brace! Brace!' instruction that he would give thirty seconds before landing. Schemmel remembers him saying: 'And folks, I'm not gonna kid anybody, this is gonna be rough.'

It was time.

In the cockpit, Fitch took Dvorak's seat in order to keep operating the throttles, while Dvorak moved to the so-called jump seat, which in those days was used for anyone else who was in the cockpit for landing apart from the crew. Fitch would later recall being struck with a realization 'like a thunderclap. Dear God: I have 296 lives literally in my hands.' Which was still an improvement on what he had first thought upon surveying the flight-control panel when he entered the cockpit: 'Dear God, I'm going to die this afternoon. The only question is how long it's going to take Iowa to hit me.'

Haynes, who remembers nothing of the impact or its aftermath, gave the instruction: *Brace, brace, brace.* They had lined up with the runway at Sioux City – albeit not the one they had initially been going for – and though it was a closed runway, cracked and grassy, the ground staff had cleared it. It looked, for a moment, like they might actually make it intact. 'There is a possibility,' Fitch had realized, 'that we can make this survivable.'

An announcement from the cockpit to ground, almost chirpy: 'We have the runway in sight. We'll be with you very shortly. Thanks a lot for your help.'

But it was time for their luck to shift on its fulcrum once again.

The navigation station that would have told them exactly how far they were from the airport was out of service that day – not that it would have made a huge amount of difference, so little control did they have. It had become clear to Fitch that there was an optimum speed that gave the crew as much control as they were ever going to get, but that speed was way above the 150 miles per hour with which a DC-10 would normally approach the runway; they were approaching instead at 250. The speed required a steep descent, the more so since the 330,000-pound plane would have no brakes to stop if it ever landed, so it needed to get down at the very start of the runway, although they were pleased to see a field of corn at the end of it rather than a building.

At 400 feet above the ground Haynes looked at the airspeed indicator, saw 220 knots (253 miles per hour), so fast that the tyres would explode, and said: pull the power off, slow us down. But Fitch knew it couldn't be done without the nose and right wing dipping. All he had time to say was: 'I can't. That's what's holding the wing up.' He knew he had one chance: a moment before landing, to pull all throttles back to idle and hope that the corn at the end of the runway would slow them down. 'Then we're going to open eight doors, slides are going to inflate, 296 are going to slide down, we're going to the nearest saloon and I'm buying.' But it was not to be. Fitch saw a suddenly high rate of descent as the plane entered a new phugoid: 1,800 feet per minute, three times in excess of the structural capability of the landing gear, and so he pushed both the throttles forward to push the nose back up and reduce the impact speed.

'But there just wasn't time.'

*

There is a video, at one stage believed to be the most frequently replayed clip in history, of *United 232*'s last moments, taken from outside the airport perimeter by a news crew who had learned of the plane's distress. You can find it dubbed with the flight recording, and in the moments before impact you hear a voice – it is Bill Records – shouting: Left! Left! Left! Left! *Left! Left! Left!* An alarm goes off: *Whoop whoop, pull up, pull up. Whoop whoop, pull up, pull up.* On the video, the plane vanishes behind a water tower, then appears again, briefly glimpsed between trees and telephone wires. There is a shout:

God, or something like it, the sound of someone in anguish. The next thing you see is flame. The camera, or another camera, shifts to a second vantage point through a wire fence at the edge of the airfield, with a black-on-yellow sign saying *Restricted area: do not go beyond this point*. And behind it, as the right wing touches the ground before the plane, the wing breaks off and cartwheels, and the fuselage flips over. It is unthinkable, seeing the footage, as dense black smoke engulfs the wreckage, that anybody could have survived.

Fitch described the impact as being like a giant hand behind his head shoving his face into the radio. He bounced back off it, he said, like a jack-in-the-box. He recalled looking left and seeing corn stalks go by, and thinking: it's true, they really do grow the corn that tall in Iowa. 'The captain of a DC-10 sits about 22 feet above the ground,' he realized. 'They don't grow it *that* tall.' The impact had taken out the landing gear.

Fitch would remember 'a terrible sound, a tearing of metal, G-loads, yaw to the right. Simultaneous with that change of direction was this sensation that something was drop-kicking you in the backside. You could feel yourself moving up and over, head over heels.' He remembered the windshield going completely green, then brown. It lightened again, then went brown once more. 'The heat, humidity and violence were beyond any words I could ever hope to bring forth.'

Schemmel, in the passenger cabin, would write that 'it felt, for lack of any comparable experience, exactly like you'd expect it to feel if you'd dropped thousands of feet out of the sky and hit the ground'. He felt himself floating in his seat, held back only by his seat belt. Even through his clenched-shut eyes he could tell that the cabin lights had gone out. He heard screams amid the sounds of the impact, reached out to brace again against the seat in front, but found no seat there. He opened his eyes and saw a human body fly past him upside down. Then another, a woman, still strapped in her seat, on the other side of him. He described a storm of debris, the eye of a hurricane, a ball of fire from the front to the back of the cabin. A helpless feeling, he wrote; a sensation of total vulnerability, while time moved in slow, elastic increments. Then the plane flipped, and remained upside down until it settled.

I ask Jan Brown if she remembers the impact.

'Oh yes.'

There is a long pause.

'In my wildest dreams I could never have imagined the impact,' she says. 'It's like trying to describe the terror of being petrified: you're never sure the words are strong enough for the actual feeling. The impact of smashing into Earth? That's close, but it's not quite descriptive enough.

'I remember involuntarily closing my eyes and saying to myself: I cannot believe my body parts are still connected, we hit so hard. I just passed out. And it saved my life.

'I was in a flash fire as we were rolling over, and I went into a deep unconscious state. I thought I was starting to resist it, and then my grey cells realized: you're going wherever this is taking you.

'Then I couldn't hear anything any more. Initially, I was hearing all this screeching metal, and noises I never heard before. But then it was very serene, the state I was in. I realized I was on fire but I didn't feel any pain. The pain was gone. The best way I can describe it is it was the most serene moment of my life. This is how I'm going to go. And as fast as that feeling overcame me, it was gone.'

Because she had lived. 'Within a second or two we stopped. I was amazed: I'm still alive. And then the job just kicks in. Because if I'm still alive, then we're getting out of here.'

What had happened was this. At the moment before landing, the plane had entered another downward phugoid and veered right, leaving no time for the crew to compensate. The right-hand wingtip hit the runway first. Fuel was spilled and ignited. The tail section broke off. The landing gear was ripped from the jet, and the fuselage, after bouncing, bouncing, bouncing on the hard concrete runway, split into several pieces. The right wing came off. The main part of the fuselage rolled, entered a cornfield to the right of the runway, and came to rest upside down.

When the plane stopped, she and everyone around her were upside down, hanging from what used to be the floor of the fuselage but was now the ceiling, amid dense, acrid, toxic smoke. 'I had no sense of being upside down,' she recalls, though she couldn't undo the rotating dial on her harness, which in a flight-attendant seat covered the shoulders as well as the lap. A man helped her, and she must have fallen on him as he undid the clasp, but she can't remember it. 'My first memory is that I opened my eyes, and I was standing up, and it was black. I told him to get out. I didn't recognize anything: it was like waking up on another planet.'

The intense violence of the crash had by now killed most of the people the accident was going to take, but it would also save lives, by ripping gaps in the fuselage that people simply walked out of into the cornfields. 'We were open to where first class had been. There was no first class: the cockpit had separated back by the runway, and we were in a cornfield upside down. I was just looking for light. Light meant an opening.' She thought she saw someone's ankles, trapped, and tried to help by pulling them; behind her, somebody said there was an opening, and she turned and saw it, through a mass of cables and other things hanging down. Next, she was holding all those cables to one side as passengers walked out to safety. 'People were filing by,' she recalls, 'in a manner that I could have been saying: Thank you for flying with us today.'

To her delight she saw an elderly woman who, during the

descent, had told her she thought she was having a heart attack. 'And I found myself unbelievably saying: I'll get back to you. I was on my way to the cockpit.' But as with everything else on that flight, teamwork had been working even under that extraordinary stress. She had told another flight attendant, a qualified nurse, who had gone back and put the woman on oxygen, and now she had survived. 'Everyone was working as such an integral team. It was amazing.'

But it was time to go. The smoke was increasingly intense. 'It was like a tornado, except it was roiling on what had been the ceiling level. That forced me to leave. It was so deadly. I have never seen anything like that. That smoke, that dark black.'

And she emerged, reborn you might say, into the cornfield. 'Actually it never occurred to me that, oh my gosh, I'm in a cornfield. I'm still working.'

*

There were 296 people on board: 111 of them died in the crash, most from impact injuries but thirty-five from smoke inhalation in the middle part of the fuselage, directly above the fuel tanks. Another would die a month later. There was a random distribution of apocalypse. People died from row 1 to row 38. People were unharmed yet had neighbours on either side of them die horribly. There was no safe place to be.

There were fifty-two children on board; it had been a day of United Airlines' Children's Day promotion. Eleven died. The child passengers included four so-called lap children – too small to have their own seat. One died. He was Evan Tsao. And when Brown emerged, she had her second acquaintance with Evan's mother, Sylvia.

The woman had not been able to keep hold of her son: how

could she possibly have done so, in the unthinkable torsions and violence of the impact? She had made it out of the plane, but upon realizing that her boy had not made it out with her, was trying to get back in again. 'I see Sylvia coming towards me,' says Brown, speaking very slowly now. 'And I know she's heading to the wreckage. I blocked her path. She said: I've got to get my son.'

And then, recognizing the flight attendant who had tried to help her, she said: 'You told me I should put him on the floor. You said he would be OK. And now he's gone.'

At this point two things happened to Brown, one physical, one emotional. At this moment, feeling returned to her. She was burned and suddenly started to feel the enormous pain. But, alongside it, something else: 'In my mind, I was saying that this was something I would live with for the rest of my life.' She was right. All she could find to say to Tsao at the time was: 'It was the best thing we could do. It was all we had.'

*

Up front – which was no longer the front, the cockpit having been severed from the rest of the jet – Haynes remembers nothing beyond the landing. 'I was unconscious, and anything after that, I've been told.'

What is the next thing he remembers?

'I woke up in the cockpit, after the crash. Dudley was talking to me, and then I passed out again. Then I remember being taken out of the cockpit on my stomach, and I passed out again. I remember being in the ambulance before we left for the hospital, but I don't remember the ride in. Next thing I know I'm in the emergency room, and the next thing, in the bedroom. That day is fuzzy.'

In fact, all four of the crew in the cockpit had survived, though it took time and suffering for them to be rescued. The cockpit had been compressed to waist height. Rescuers couldn't recognize it, and ignored it. It was more than half an hour after the crash that rescuers found them, and longer still before they figured out a way to get the men out.

By now, an element of good luck was returning as the pendulum pitched again. It so happened that the accident occurred just as a shift change was taking place at a regional trauma centre *and* a regional burns centre in Sioux City. Those who were about to go home stayed, and were ready to treat the injured as soon as they arrived. It also so happened that the Iowa Air National Guard was on duty at Sioux Gateway Airport – 285 of them, almost exactly the same number of personnel as there were people on the plane.

'There were a lot of things,' Haynes says. 'Luck was where we were. We were over relatively flat land, and not over the Pacific or some big city. The weather was nice, and back there there's thunderstorms almost every day. It was daylight. The emergency response crew had had a drill a year before on an airplane crashing at Sioux City on that very same runway. The fact that all the emergency response groups around the state responded. They have a way that everyone is meant to work together, but they didn't pay attention to that: even if they weren't involved in the plan, they went anyway. We had people from 120 miles away responding to that crash. There was a tremendous response from the people on the ground. A very important part of it was luck.'

With the incarceration of the flying crew in their crush-packed tomb, responsibility now turned to the flight attendants and the passengers themselves. There were many examples of heroism. Schemmel left the plane before returning to it after hearing a baby crying; he found her in an overhead baggage locker, which, with the plane inverted, was now on the floor. Michael Matz, who would go on to win a silver Olympic medal in equestrian showjumping in Atlanta seven years later, saved several children.

The flight attendants themselves, some of them badly injured, showed quite incredible bravery and fortitude, and conducted impromptu triage amid the cornfields while they waited for rescuers to find them.

For his part, Haynes considers himself to be remarkably unscathed, and was back at work within three months. 'I had a cut on my ankle, a bruised rib, a bruised sternum, a lot of cuts and bruises, ninety-two stitches to my scalp and my left ear was just about cut off, but I didn't break anything.'

'Everyone else in the cockpit had bad injuries,' he says, apparently without irony. Haynes is not bombastic or pious in the least, instead an engaging and straight-talking man, but he's clearly not the sort to consider ninety-two stitches in the head to be an injury. 'I didn't have any,' he insists. 'Mine was a concussion. My equilibrium was affected and I had to wait until I got that back in balance before I could go back to work. But mentally, I was ready to go back, because I had very good psychological counselling. Five days of two of them: one staff psychologist and one psychiatrist, meeting me twice a day.'

Like Haynes, Brown's injuries could have been far worse. 'I have great guardian angels,' she says. Five days earlier, she had decided to shift from wearing skirts to trousers. 'A skirt is not the thing to be wearing when you're on the floor of a galley trying to release a cart or look for something that's been dropped, or help a passenger find a pen. It was definitely a pant job.' It is hard to calculate just how fortuitous this sartorial decision turned out to be. 'Because of that, my only burns were around my ankles. They were second- or third-degree burns, where my nylons had melted.' Beyond that, not a broken bone. 'When you're unconscious, you are really relaxed.'

*

Today, a crash survivor – particularly an aviation professional – would receive sophisticated counselling, with a keen eye for the symptoms and challenges of post-traumatic stress disorder, or PTSD. Now there is a wealth of knowledge about this condition, from the parts of the brain that are affected to the social complications that follow it and the best methods of managing them. But it's a relatively recent field of study: the term was first coined after the Vietnam War and was only formally recognized as a condition in the United States around 1980.

How sophisticated was psychiatric treatment, and the understanding of post-traumatic stress, in 1989? 'It wasn't near as good as it is now, but they had started to understand PTSD,' Haynes says. United had begun what it called critical incident stress debriefing in Baltimore a few years earlier and had developed a programme of sending peers to talk to people who had experienced stress, 'because too many professionals wouldn't talk to a psychiatrist. They didn't want it on their record. A pilot doesn't want it on their record that they went to a psychiatrist, and neither does a fireman or a policeman.' So pilots would talk to fellow pilots. In Haynes's case, several pilots, someone from the National Guard, and even a passenger came and talked to him. 'I didn't want to talk to him, because I didn't understand critical incident stress debriefing. The first thing the psychologist said to me, he said: we're going to talk about the crash. I said: no, I just killed 112 people, I don't want to talk about it. He said: we're going to talk about it anyway.'

I had wondered if he might have felt this way. *United 232* is odd: it is simultaneously a story of a group of people doing the impossible and saving 184 people, and of a tragedy that killed 112.

'Admittedly,' he says, 'we had done everything that we could do. I still had tremendous feelings of guilt, the guilt of survival, which is a very, very big problem that people are only now beginning to recognize. But there wasn't anything else we could do.'

So did he genuinely feel that he had killed rather than saved people?

'The first thing on your mind is how many died. That's the first thing. In the ambulance, I asked Dudley – I was on my stomach with a towel over my head, I couldn't see anything, I was bleeding so bad – and I asked Dudley if everybody made it. And he said no. And I said: oh my God, I killed people. And somebody else in the ambulance said: no, you didn't, you saved people. So it's that half-full, half-empty glass.

'The first thought in my mind was: I was the captain, I was responsible. I didn't do what I was supposed to do, and that's take the airplane from point A to point B safely.'

It would later become clear just how unreasonably the odds were stacked against Haynes, Fitch, Records and Dvorak. Very soon after the crash, United began putting people into simulators and trying to replicate the exact conditions of *United 232*. 'They said twelve tried it immediately and they didn't come close to the airport,' Haynes says. 'Then they had forty-five others, after they figured out why the plane was rolling. They still never had a successful landing. Whether they got as close as we did, I don't know. But nobody successfully landed it.' In all of the continuing recorded history of aviation, there has still only been one incident to compare with it, when the crew of a DHL cargo plane, an Airbus A300, succeeded in getting their aircraft back on the ground after it was hit by a surface-to-air missile in Baghdad in 2003, causing a loss of hydraulic flight-control systems. It landed following the same techniques as Haynes, Fitch and their colleagues had used in 1989.

Nevertheless, survivor guilt must have been profound in a crash whose victims and survivors were as random as those of *United 232*, and I ask him to explain how the condition manifests itself. He illustrates not with his own experience but through a fellow passenger. 'One of our passengers told me there was a boy sitting in front of him and they were playing peekaboo. There was another one next to him. There was a man next to him and a woman behind. They all died, all four of them. He got a scratch on his ear or his neck.' He and his boss had been going to Chicago, Haynes explains, and the boss had a reservation on an earlier flight while the passenger had been flying standby. 'He couldn't get on, so the boss said: I'll wait and go with you. He said: no, go on and I'll meet you there. But the boss did wait for him, and he didn't survive.'

By now it is clear he is talking about Jerry Schemmel, whose boss and friend, Jay Ramsdell, waited to travel with Schemmel after an earlier flight was cancelled – in fact, *232* was Schemmel's fifth attempt to board a flight that morning. I say so, but Haynes looks embarrassed. 'I didn't want to mention any names. But he felt it was his fault, because the boss waited for him. He made that decision, you didn't make that decision. It's not your fault.'

And how did it affect Haynes himself? 'The psychiatrists helped me a great deal. They gave me that mental attitude to go back to work. But still I felt people died because we weren't able to do what we were supposed to do. I didn't even think about Bill and Dudley feeling the same thing, but they were. We were crew and we all had the same responsibility to get there safely. And we didn't do it. But I was taught that there wasn't anything else we could have done. And it wears off. I've talked myself out of it, I guess.'

It seems remarkable that a man could be back piloting a plane just three months after that crash, but that is what happened. Haynes had to retrain after three months out, but it only involved getting back in the simulator and making three take-offs and landings in order to re-qualify. Records and Dvorak were back in action around the same time, though Fitch, the most severely injured of the four, was out for nearly a year.

As he prepared to fly, Haynes did have some worries. 'I was a little bit concerned, not about flying the airplane, but the landing, those last 500 feet. If you've ever heard the tape, the ground-proximity warning goes off: *whoop whoop, pull up, pull up.* And I thought, that last 500 feet, is that going to bother me?'

So he requested a very experienced co-pilot alongside him and, specifically, an instructor. 'Their job, if they are checking out captains, is they sit in the right seat and the captain does all the flying. They are qualified pilots but they don't actually fly. What they are there for is making sure the pilot is doing things in the right way.' Haynes wanted such a person alongside him because he knew they would immediately intervene if he did something wrong. Once again, Haynes, a captain, was seeking out somebody who would contribute: somebody who would not hesitate to challenge his authority.

An instructor came and talked to him. Haynes told him: 'I think I'm fine, but if you see me do anything wrong, don't wait. Take the airplane away from me and we can discuss it on the ground. I don't want a discussion in the air.' He flew from Seattle to San Francisco, on to Los Angeles, and then to Chicago. He was a little worried about his profile. 'At the time there was this awe about being able to fly with Captain Haynes, and I didn't want any of that stuff, I wanted someone who would speak up.' He found himself with an experienced check pilot.

So you were back?

'Yes. No problems.'

Just like Haynes, Jan Brown was back at work within three months. 'On Friday 13th,' she says. She had done some test runs before resuming actual duty, and had not had the experience she expected. 'I expected anxiety or fear, but instead it was enormous sadness. I could have just cried my eyes out that first trip. I went in coach – in economy – and I came back in first class, so I could absorb everything that happened. I was feeling all of the fear that the passengers went through.' The only thing that was different from these test runs when she did resume duty was sitting in the jump seat. 'And that took some adjustment. Each landing, you're feeling the same anxiety and fear: how are we going to land? I guess it's post-traumatic.'

She, too, received some modest counselling for PTSD, but nothing like the amount or sophistication one would be offered today. 'Was PTSD recognized? I think it was starting to be. Every once in a while you'd hear something about it. But not as much as now, after the wars that we've had. Maybe back then they might have called it a flashback.'

Indeed, flashbacks were how PTSD exhibited itself for Brown. 'People were digging on my street a week or two afterwards. I was getting so nervous – uncharacteristically nervous. Then I realized it was the noise: all that screeching metal noise.' The only thing she has never got over is turbulence. 'That's the one ongoing reaction. That out-of-control feeling. I've got punished for saying: oh, a little turbulence is fine on a smooth trip. I'd settle for boredom right now.'

*

Haynes continued flying for two more years until he reached mandatory retirement age at sixty. When he took his farewell flight from Denver to Seattle, Records and Dvorak flew with him – as passengers – as well as survivor Jerry Schemmel and his wife, and most of the flight attendants, including Brown. When the plane landed, a passenger was taken ill and the plane was met by ambulances. It seemed somehow fitting. 'I told the crew I loved them,' says Brown. 'But I won't fly with them any more, because there is always an emergency.'

Haynes's relationship with the passengers from *232* has always appeared very positive, which was not always the case for other crew. In his *First Person* interview, Fitch narrated an incident when a mother of a nine-year-old girl who had died approached him and said, 'You killed my daughter.' Fitch's reaction? He agreed with her, and told her he would much rather he had died and she had lived.

Nothing like that happened to Haynes? 'No. But I would understand if they felt that way. Usually that is a first reaction,' he says. He turns to Jan Brown's confrontation with Sylvia Tsao. 'Jan knew that this lady didn't mean it but what else were you going to do? You told me to do this, and now he's gone, and it's your fault.' In Brown's case, he says, 'it made her change her life'.

So, after the accident, a return to routine; then, two years later, retirement. So what then? Haynes would always, from now on, be associated with *United 232*. So how to move on?

In Haynes's case, there are two answers: talking about it, and Little League. One stemmed from the other.

When I first contacted Haynes, through Diane Titterington at the Aviation Speakers Bureau, she provided this advice before lining up the interview. 'Many think of Captain Haynes as a hero for *UA232*,' she wrote in an email. 'Those who know him know that he is a hero in so many more ways.' She told me of his unerring commitment as a volunteer umpire for Little League baseball and high-school football, sometimes working on several games per day. 'For the football games, he would not only memorize the names and statistics for the home team, but the visiting team also. This is all volunteer work. Al was a hero long before the flight of *UA232*.'

When I meet him, I tell him of Titterington's remarks, and he chuckles. 'Well, I've been involved in Little League since 1971. I started umpiring my son's games because they didn't have any umpires.' He rose through the ranks of umpiring, up to the Little League's World Series games, until eventually, post-crash, he began to drop out of umpiring and instead announced tournaments. 'I've done just about everything you can do for Little League. Marked the field, dragged the field, cleaned bathrooms, because it's a good programme. The only thing I refuse to do is pass the hat.' He has been similarly devoted to high-school football, ever since his son was eight years old in 1970, starting out on the chain crews which measure whether a team has made the requisite 10 yards for a new first down, or phase of play. When I meet Haynes, he has been announcing a game the previous night, peering through the fog. 'It keeps me busy. Otherwise I'm just retired.'

What does this mean to him? 'It's my contribution back to the game. I never played ball as a kid – I can say this now I've quit flying, but I had asthma as a kid.' He found the game really through his kids and his wife, the biggest sports fan in the family. The involvement in these sports pre-dates the crash by nearly twenty years, but it's clear that maintaining those routines has become increasingly important to him since.

And then came the talks. A while after the crash, a Little League district administrator and fellow umpire asked him to speak to his Lions Club – an Illinois-based secular organization based on helping local communities – in SeaTac, the area around Seattle's airport. There were about fifteen people there; Haynes just went along and told them what had happened. The first district administrator told another, across Seattle's Puget Sound, who pulled together three Lions Clubs for a dinner and asked Haynes to speak there. 'We had maybe seventy-five to a hundred people. So I took my model of the DC-10 over there –' he points to a model United jet up on the bookshelf – 'and I told them what happened.' Next came Rotary, then a district Rotary convention. 'Well, I went down to the convention centre and this room was so big they couldn't even see the plane from the back of the room.' Next, a society of aviation experts invited him to the Midwest and asked if he had any video. He brought what is known as the Alert 3 tape, which covers the interaction between the pilots, controllers and ground staff over the radios prior to the crash, along with interviews with medical and ground people involved that day.

Over time, the talk evolved into something sophisticated and motivational. Illustrated with slides, it focuses on five factors that helped to save nearly two thirds of the people on the plane, and how they can be applied anywhere: luck, communications, preparation, execution and cooperation.

He has now given this talk 1,700 times.

Why do people want to hear it? 'I don't know,' he says, but not dismissively, instead with a sense of contemplation. 'I don't advertise. I don't do audition tapes. Somebody has got to have heard about it. It has turned out to be a generic talk, not just about aviation; the groups are not necessarily associated with aviation when I do talks for them.'

Is there a therapy in this for him?

'Oh, it's all therapy. Every time you talk it's therapy. People say: how can you see that tape again? I say: I've seen it so many times. Each time I end up hoping it will work out different, but it never does.

'You have to talk,' he says, leaning forward to emphasize the point. 'You *have* to talk. That's all part of post-traumatic stress, is talking about it. You can't just lock it up.' He points out of the window. 'A friend of mine lived down the street from us. Her nineteen-year-old son was killed in Vietnam. You could not mention that boy's name. You couldn't talk about him, say anything about him; you weren't allowed to do that. She carried that with her for a couple of years, and my wife finally got her to start talking. She got her out of her shell. Because when you're like that, you affect not just yourself but your family. This denial affects everybody.'

Sadly, Haynes has found himself with plenty more to talk about in the years since *United 232*. His son, Tony, was killed in an accident in 1996. Haynes's wife died in 1999. Then his only surviving child, Laurie, was diagnosed with aplastic anaemia and required a bone-marrow transplant to survive.

'We speak very freely of Tony, my son who was killed,' Haynes tells me, with confronting candour. 'I speak very freely about my wife who died within two months of her illness. Just: bang. Very suddenly. Tony was killed while I was doing a talk and my wife was at Little League. We had to come back home. A motor-cycle crash.'

There is one piece of brighter news: when it became clear that his daughter's insurance would not cover her transplant, Haynes contacted the Air Line Pilots Association, who not only gave money but also brought the situation to public light. Among the many donors of money were several survivors of *United 232*. She got the transplant.

'My daughter was just celebrating the anniversary of the bone-marrow transplant. We talk about it all the time. It could have been fatal. We talk about the good things we did, the funny things Tony did, the stupid things he did as a kid. Because it's all part of it, and you can't change it. That's what I try to tell people: you cannot change what happened. You have to accept it and the only way to accept it is to talk about it.'

*

For Brown, moving on has been all about trying to change things, specifically around child safety. It has been about trying to find a positive in an immense negative; a redemption after a wrong that was clearly no fault of her own.

Her union had her and her colleagues do a press conference about a week after the crash, and that was the first time she spoke out about child safety. A Canadian show called *Marketplace*, rather like the US *60 Minutes*, then interviewed her and she spoke out again. Increasingly, she would only give interviews if she could use it as a platform for child seats. 'For a ten-year period I averaged two programmes a year on the crash, or on something to do with air safety.'

In the 1990s, there were a number of measures before Congress to implement changes to the way infants are transported on planes. One was brought by a congressman from Iowa, where Sioux City is located. But in three consecutive sessions it never got to the floor for a vote. In 1990, she testified before an aviation subcommittee in Washington in favour of child seats, and again in 1996; then, when Bill Clinton and Al Gore set up an aviation safety commission, she testified in front of that as well. But eventually there were no bills in Congress to be discussed. 'After that, I just decided that it was the FAA [Federal Aviation Authority] that was responsible to mandate child seats, so I went to them directly. By now my email address book had really grown, so I would have email campaigns.' In 2004, the National Transportation Safety Board was considering dropping child seats from its 'most wanted' list – a set of advocacy priorities – so she battled to keep it on, successfully, only for it to vanish within a year or so.

So what, precisely, does she want? 'That every passenger on an airplane has a seat and a seat belt.'

Even for small babies, I ask? And, although I can't see her, I picture her taking a deep breath before launching into a well-rehearsed admonishment. 'A lot of people don't make the connection,' she explains patiently. 'When a baby is coming to the airport, they have to be in a seat, with a seat belt, no matter whether they are a day or a year old. And once they're two years old, they have to have their own seat. Why are we discriminating against the most vulnerable, little people? Coming to an airport in a car doing 60 miles an hour, they're in a seat belt. Getting on a metal tube doing 500 miles per hour, they're bouncing them on their lap. If they wouldn't do it in a car, why are they doing it on an airplane?'

'I've spoken to quite a few parents and invariably they say: if they allow it, it must be safe. But to allow it is in essence to say: I don't care.'

'What incenses me is when they've allowed a lot of this tech stuff to be used in flight, they say: you still have to stow your laptop for safety purposes for take-off and landing. And my question is: what about lap children? They're insignificant.'

So what would change it? 'I hope it's not going to take a death. But that is how the FAA operates.' She says that someone in the FAA's test facility in Oklahoma City told her exactly that in 2001. 'I said: what's it going to take? He said: it's going to take death.'

And would a change in the law conclude things for her, and bring her a sense of achievement and relief? 'That's the final piece,' she says. 'It's frustrating it's taken so long. I am not a public person. But I'm not one to shirk a duty.

'I think it's made people more aware; more and more people are bringing car seats. But I won't be satisfied until it's done, a done deal.

'What they are showing on a safety card is just egregious,' she says. 'It shows holding with one arm, when in fact you can't hold a child in two arms.

'People think their love for their child will hold them. And it won't.'

*

Brown stayed in the airlines until retirement in 1998, but the mission for child safety has clearly given her a sense of meaning and direction in her life, as well as perhaps alleviating the guilt of the day when she simply followed instructions, saved lives, but was blamed for the death of a toddler. She saw Sylvia Tsao twice more on the day – once in a clearing in the corn while attempting to conduct triage on the injured, and once in the emergency room – but never again since that day, not once.

'I feel very strongly that when something bad happens then something good must come from it,' she says. 'It's a lesson to be learned. They learned that they couldn't put hydraulic lines together even though they were saying one in a trillion odds of it happening. Well, that was the one.

'What is it about making the same mistakes and expecting a different result? It's quite unbelievable to be still working on a safety issue that involves life. Life that can't protect itself, but looks to us for protection.'

Brown has done other things too. She finally got around to finishing college, fifty years after having dropped out of it to become a flight attendant. 'I left college after two years to be a stewardess. I said: one day I'll finish. And fifty years later, I graduated.' She chuckles. 'Had I stayed in college my graduation date would have been 1962, but life made it 2012.' She gradu- ated in history at a college in Manchester, New Hampshire. 'I had grown up down the hill from it, when it was strictly a boys' college,' she says. 'My mother worked there for the dean of students.' Her mother got a degree there too, and so did her son, as well as a commission in the marines. All in history.

I have the impression that if I was in a tight spot on a plane, I would want Brown to be my flight attendant, and I am reminded of the outrageous range of abilities we expect from these increas- ingly underpaid people, who one minute are supposed to be dealing with our surly complaints about soggy meals and reclining seats, and the next are meant to save our lives. 'Well, I wanted to be a stewardess from the time I was eight or nine years old,' she says. 'I couldn't be a nurse because I couldn't stick anyone with a needle and I wasn't too sure about blood. I was too bashful to be a teacher. I couldn't be a secretary because I couldn't type worth a darn. And, in the late 1950s, those were our choices. An airplane was the only place I was ever comfortable.'

*

Having been caught on television, *United 232* captured enormous worldwide media attention.

The story then ended up on the big and small screen. It was used as the basis for a TV movie in which Haynes was played by Charlton Heston. This story focused more on the ground rescue efforts – and features numerous members of that effort in cameo roles – but pays little attention to what actually happened in the plane. 'The passengers weren't involved in *232* [the movie, actually called *Crash Landing: The Rescue of Flight 232,* and sometimes screened as *A Thousand Heroes*], the flight attendants weren't involved, and if it hadn't been for Heston being involved, the cockpit crew wouldn't have been.' Nobody contacted Haynes in advance, except to ask for pictures. 'The Crew Resource Management wasn't there: Captain Heston made all the decisions and everyone went along with it. That's not the way it was.' That said, lots of the cockpit dialogue was taken straight from the voice recorder. Director Lamont Johnson was nominated for an Emmy, and Haynes wondered if Harve Bennett, the writer, would be too. 'I said: if they nominate you, I'm going to tell on you, because everything that was said came right out of the cockpit voice recorder.'

Then there was *Fearless*, a different matter altogether. Released in 1993, this Peter Weir film was a big-budget event: Jeff Bridges, Isabella Rossellini, Rosie Perez and John Turturro all starred. It depicts a crash of a plane – from San Francisco to Houston in this case – during which a man, portrayed by Bridges, finds himself at peace with the knowledge he is going to die and comforts many fearful passengers. Surviving the crash, he believes himself to be untouchable by death, taking steadily greater risks. He is fearless. He becomes close to fellow survivors, including one who lost her baby son in the crash.

Appearing just four years after *United 232,* it is very clear that the 1989 crash inspired the framework of the movie, if not the behaviour of its characters. The plane crashes in a cornfield and the surviving passengers have to feel their way out back to the runway – a clear reference to *232.* Even the overhead shots of the right-hand arc the wreckage takes from the runway into the field are reminiscent of the aftermath of the United crash.

Some found considerably greater parallels in the movie than they were comfortable with. Jerry Schemmel is convinced that the Jeff Bridges character is based on him and starts his book with a chapter called 'I was never "fearless"'. Some of Schemmel's connections seem tenuous: 'Bridges plays an architect. At the time, I was also a professional, working as a deputy commissioner and legal counsel for the Continental Basketball Association.' But there are a lot of other, truer parallels. Bridges' business partner and best friend died in the crash, as did Schemmel's. A woman sitting near to Bridges on the plane had a two-year-old boy who died in the crash. That, very clearly, is a reference to Sylvia Tsao, whose twenty-two-month-old son Evan died in the crash, and who was indeed sitting very close to Schemmel. Bridges tries to comfort a traumatized youngster in between the explosion and the touchdown. This also chimes with something Schemmel did. And, in particular, Bridges emerges from the wreckage carrying a baby, which is the action Schemmel is most renowned for.

In the years ahead Schemmel would find that friends assumed the rest of the movie, which is fictional, was accurate: he reckons half a dozen people awkwardly told him they had no idea he'd attempted suicide (he hadn't, but Bridges' character did). Some also wondered if he had had an affair with another crash survivor, given Bridges' onscreen relationship with Rosie Perez. 'I began,' Schemmel said, 'to feel just a little exploited.' This gave way to anger and resentment, and, eventually, to contacting a lawyer to ask about suing Warner Brothers. He finally decided against it, but wrote: 'They took my story and exploited it. They caused me a great deal of pain. They made a movie about me and didn't even bother to tell me they were doing it.'

I wonder if Brown has seen *Fearless*, since the Rosie Perez character is very clearly modelled on Sylvia Tsao, and in the film she meets a flight attendant at a group therapy meeting and blames her for her son's death. The attendant, by extension, must be Brown.

'I was sitting in a movie and the previews came on, and of course the first scene was the plane crashed in a cornfield,' she says. 'I was just stunned.' She never watched it in a cinema, but did rent it to watch at home. The scene between the mother and the flight attendant, which she hadn't expected, shocked her. 'I was rather glad that I saw it at home rather than a theatre.' Then again, she seems pragmatic: she also watched *Flight*, a more recent film involving a plane crash, and found herself 'upset about totally different things. How could she not report a pilot who drinks on a plane? I wouldn't have tolerated it for a second.'

And Haynes? 'That movie I objected to too,' he says of *Fearless*. 'It acted like it was telling this story, but it was pure fiction.'

It's possible, though, that it had a subliminal effect on how they all remembered it. Denny Fitch also gave a great many talks about the crash and, like Haynes, had to find ways to lighten them up a little from time to time. 'Denny said facetiously: I always knew the corn was high in Iowa, but I didn't know it was 30 feet high,' says Haynes. 'But if I remember correctly, the cockpit never went through the cornfield.' The cockpit, remember, had separated from the rest of the jet; while Jan Brown and most of the passengers emerged into corn, the cockpit crew did not. 'In the movie it did, but I don't think that happened. But Denny thought so. Whether he said it just to lighten it up, or if he thinks it happened, I don't know. But to him, it happened.'

I suppose, I say, if you are told things after the fact, you come to believe them. 'Yeah, that's true, that's absolutely true. Anything that happened after the crash is what people told me. I just remember bits and pieces.'

*

Have the crewmembers stayed close? 'Oh yeah,' says Haynes. 'We're going back to Germany next month for some awards dinner. Bill and Dudley live here in Seattle.'

Brown is still in touch too – it is Haynes who encourages her to speak with me, angry that flight attendants have never had the recognition they deserve – and she visits a memorial for the flight attendant who died on the crash, Rene LeBeau, who lived in Schaumberg, the same Chicago suburb as Brown. 'As a crew, we get together, on the anniversary,' she says. 'We planted a tree and put up a plaque for Rene.' She lived not far from Denny Fitch, who also lived in Chicago. But, with utter injustice, Fitch died of brain cancer in 2012, aged just sixty-nine. Haynes shakes his head. 'Yeah,' he says. 'That was a real shock.'

It's notable that it took four men to get the plane down, and that one of the key roles – the flight engineer, in this case Dudley

Dvorak – no longer exists. In a flight of a similar duration today, one could expect to have only two people up front. A rare exception is on a cargo flight – and that DHL jet that suffered a missile strike did have a flight engineer, without whom the plane would almost certainly have crashed. Beyond that, 'There are no three-man crews any more,' Haynes says. How does he feel about that?

'The reduction of crews is fine if everything works,' he says. 'If it doesn't work, then you've got to have enough knowledge up there [in the cockpit]. My concern right now with the people they're bringing in is that a lot of them have no stick-and-rudder knowledge: they have all been on computer-flown airplanes. All you have to do is know how to use a computer and you can fly an airplane. But if the computers go out and you've got to fly the airplane, are you used to doing it?'

*

The ground rescue team is a whole other story there isn't room to tell here, except to say that the Sioux City air crash was extraordinary for the sheer range of heroes it created, from pilots to cabin crew, National Guard to the passengers themselves.

Today, when you go to Sioux City, you can find the Flight 232 Memorial, a statue of a man carrying a young child to safety. The man is Lieutenant Colonel Dennis Nielsen, part of the ground rescue team that day with the Iowa Air National Guard, and the boy is Spencer Bailey, who was three years old at the time. The statue re-creates a famous photograph taken by Gary Anderson, then a photographer with the *Sioux City Journal*. Spencer's brother Brandon also survived the crash; their mother, Francie, did not. The statue stands on the Sioux City riverfront.

It is surrounded by columns in a sunken garden next to the

Missouri River, and a line of pink quartzite boulders leads down the path, each embossed with quotations. One says:

Let no one go unmentioned. Yet once again, we say
We're proud of Siouxland and all who helped that day.

8

Apollo 8

Just think about this for a moment.

For the first four and a half billion years of the Earth's existence, nobody had ever seen the world as a whole: as a sphere, a ball, hanging there in space. It took us long enough to figure out that the thing was even round, and it wasn't until well into the twentieth century that we got high enough above it to be able to perceive any curvature in the surface with our own eyes. By 1968 a handful of Americans and Russians had been high enough to make out land masses, continents even, but still the expanse of the Earth would run out of sight in every direction. Imagine, then, being the very first members of our species to see our world in its totality, as it really is: suspended there in the nothing, rotating in the void, a dab of colour in the blackness.

This is what the three-man crew of *Apollo 8* saw in December 1968. They were the first people to fly to the Moon, the first to truly leave Earth, the first to see the dark side of the Moon – which, from their perspective, wasn't dark at all. *Apollo 11* is naturally the most feted of the Apollo missions, since that was the one that put Armstrong and Aldrin on the Moon to take their small steps for (a) man, their giant leap for mankind. But *Apollo 8* has always seemed to me the most visionary, the most pioneering, the most extraordinarily daring flight that humans have ever taken.

I will learn that, in later life, Frank Borman, Jim Lovell and Bill Anders have found themselves bonded by other, less predictable connections than their shared experience on *Apollo 8*. So far as I can tell, this is the only Apollo mission whose three crewmembers' marriages have survived not only the pressures of the space programme – which were manifold – but the subsequent forty-five years too. All three men, and Bill Anders in particular, built successful careers in corporate life afterwards, rather than drifting, as some have done, into a later existence in which nothing else ever quite lived up to what went before. And they are linked by the fact that none of them, despite having seen it so close up, would ever walk on the surface of the Moon, a source of gnawing regret to at least two of them.

Part One: Before
I meet Jim Lovell in his office above the family's restaurant, Lovell's of Lake Forest, about forty minutes north of Chicago, just inland from the western shore of Lake Michigan.

Downstairs in the restaurant lobby, behind the bar and stretching its entire length, is a fabulous mural of leaping horses, heads straining upwards, powering out of a murky backdrop beneath a brilliant cloud-frayed light. Called *Steeds of Apollo,* it was inspired by the emblem for *Apollo 13,* the near-disastrous but ultimately victorious flight that Lovell commanded in 1970.

There's a story behind this painting: it was commissioned to artist Luman Winter in 1969 by the St Regis in New York, and for years hung in the hotel's main lounge. It then appeared to vanish when the hotel was refurbished. It turned up in a collector's auction catalogue one day, whereupon a generous pair of donors bought it and shipped it right back to Lovell as a gift. I had known this part of the story before arriving, but not who the donors were. It turns out to have been Tom Hanks and his wife – Hanks having portrayed Lovell in the film *Apollo 13*.

Apollo 13 is everywhere here. On the restaurant's website there's a tab for *Apollo 13*, but not for *8*. When I tell people I'm interviewing Lovell, *13* is the one they all mention. 'Ask him,' my wife says, 'to say: Houston, we've had a problem, and then tell him that Tom Hanks said it better. He'll love that.'

So when I meet him – a fit and energetic eighty-five-year-old, cheerful and open and strikingly tall, right up against the height limits the space programme used to impose – that's the first thing I ask him. Everyone knows *Apollo 13*, the heroic failure. Everyone's seen the movie. But where's *Apollo 8* here? Wasn't that the triumphant one?

He smiles broadly. '*Apollo 8*, by all means, was the high point of my space career,' he says. 'The first people to leave the Earth for another body; the first to see the back side of the Moon, to orbit it, to look at those craters and then look at the Earth. In that respect, *Apollo 8* was the highlight.'

*

The mission's genesis was odd. Originally, Borman, Lovell and Anders had nothing to do with it. The prime crew of *Apollo 8* consisted of Jim McDivitt, David Scott and Rusty Schweickart, and the mission was to stay in a low Earth orbit and try out the brand-new lunar module, which would eventually be used to put astronauts on the surface of the Moon. Borman and his crew were instead the prime crew for *Apollo 9*, which would follow on from *Apollo 8*'s tests in an elliptical medium orbit and conduct more rigorous tests on the lunar module.

'But two things happened,' says Lovell, 'that changed things significantly.'

By late 1968, it had become clear that Grumman, the contractor for the lunar module, would not be ready in time for the planned flight. 'Second, we had intelligence information that the Soviets were going to put men around the Moon in the late fall of 1968. They were very serious about this – we know a lot more about it now than we did then.' We now know that in September 1968 *Zond 5* flew to the Moon and back carrying, among other things, some (presumably Soviet) turtles, which survived the flight; another unmanned flight, *Zond 6*, also went to the Moon and back in November that year. Lovell believes that leading Soviet cosmonauts, among them Alexei Leonov, wanted to make that latter flight manned, so as to beat the Americans, but were overruled. (Leonov's autobiography makes it clear that he's absolutely right.)

Information on all of this in the US was sketchy in those secretive times, but sufficient to prompt the proposal of an audacious plan. How about *Apollo 8* going up without a lunar module, and instead flying all the way to the Moon? 'We'll change the flight,' Lovell recalls the pitch. 'Take it to the Moon, then orbit it – because that's part of our overall plan to land – and we can test out the communications and the navigation. We'd have a crew that would be within miles of the surface, and they could look at suitable landing spots. We could accomplish this in 1968 and maybe beat the Russians. So that's why we did it.'

McDivitt was wedded to testing out the lunar module – all of his training had been geared towards it – and he didn't want to switch to this strange new mission that wouldn't even take a lunar module aloft. So the crews of *Apollo 8* and *9* swapped missions. Borman, Lovell and Anders would take the flight to the Moon on *8*, while McDivitt and his colleagues would wait for the lunar module's readiness and test it out on *9*.

In fact, Lovell's presence on the flight was even more random than that. He had originally been scheduled to be the command module pilot – the one who flies round the Moon while two other astronauts descend and set foot on it – on *Apollo 11*, which would eventually be the victorious mission that put Armstrong and Aldrin on the Moon. Mike Collins was assigned to *Apollo 8*, with Lovell as his backup. But Collins had started to struggle with an old injury that had been caused during an ejection from an aircraft back in his air-force days before he joined the space programme; it became clear that he needed surgery. So Lovell took Collins's place on *8*, and Collins took Lovell's on *11*. 'It was very fortunate,' says Lovell, which is debatable, but he is clearly a glass half-full kind of a guy. There isn't an injustice he can't put a positive spin on.

The timeframe proposed for *Apollo 8* was extraordinary: there were just four months between the decision on the changed mission and it leaving the ground at Cape Kennedy. And it is hard to convey just what a leap, literal and figurative, would be involved in this shift from orbiting our world to orbiting another. Prior to its flight, the greatest distance ever achieved from Earth was 850 miles. This mission would lift the record to 240,000. Literature of the time tried to express it in terms of a basketball representing the Earth. Prior to *Apollo 8*, the greatest distance ever travelled away from that basketball would be one inch above it. But on the same scale, the Moon would be a baseball 23 feet away. That was where *Apollo 8* would go.

On top of that, it is easy to forget, as we look up at the Moon, that it is actually moving at 2,300 miles per hour, meaning that *Apollo 8* had to aim not at where it was, but where it was going to be. It would then have to navigate itself into the Moon's orbit, 69 miles above the surface – which, returning to our basketball/baseball analogy, was eight one-hundredths of an inch above the baseball. Borman called it 'a quarter of a million mile skeet shoot'.

It was an odd mission in a way, having a three-man crew including a trained lunar-module pilot but no module, and so the responsibilities were divvied out. Lovell had particular experience in navigation, using systems that had been developed by MIT, and made this his key area of expertise for the mission. 'I can recall going up to Boston and sitting on top of the Draper labs,' he says, referring to the MIT laboratories. 'Some of the first portions of the navigation which would be used for doing alignments with the stars were done using the light on the top of the building across the Charles River.'

For his part, space travel was nothing new: by the time of *Apollo 8*, Lovell was the most experienced space traveller alive, having flown twice in the Gemini programme. The first of these flights was *Gemini 7*, surely the ugliest hospital pass of a mission ever assembled, requiring him and Frank Borman to spend two entire weeks in a tiny Gemini capsule that Borman described as being the size of the front seat of a Volkswagen Beetle, and Lovell as being like spending two weeks in a flying toilet. 'Spending two weeks with Borman anywhere is a challenge,' Lovell jokes, and there really must have been an oppressive claustrophobia for one as tall as him in such cramped surroundings for so long, the more so since one of the central requirements of the mission was to conduct endless medical tests on themselves. He then flew again on *Gemini 12*, with Buzz Aldrin.

So when *Apollo 8* came around, one might well ask why he wasn't the mission commander. But that role, instead, went to Borman, a man Lovell knew well. The two men were born within a few days of each other and had attained equivalent rank in the armed forces, with Borman having come through as a fighter pilot with the air force, serving, among others, with Chuck Yeager. The only mission Borman had flown at this stage was the *Gemini 7* flight with Lovell.

Borman lacked Lovell's easy charm and cheer – Borman has since described himself as 'something of a loner', and had a blunt duty-shaped temperament moulded by West Point – but impressed all around him with his bull-headed decisiveness. 'I was the most impatient and outspoken of them all,' he later wrote. 'I had a very simple code: if you can't do your job, get the hell out of the way so I can do mine. I had started being that way when I was at West Point and I never changed. I'll concede I wasn't the most popular astronaut for that very reason, but I didn't give a damn.' Mike Collins, in his wonderful memoir *Carrying the Fire*, would describe him in this pen-portrait: 'Aggressive, capable, makes decisions faster than anyone I have ever met – with an amazingly good batting average, which would be even better if he slowed down a bit.' And Andy Chaikin, in his definitive *A Man on the Moon*, comes up with this: 'His hearing in one ear had been bad ever since he ruptured an eardrum early in his air-force career, but there were times when he seemed not to hear very well with the other one; in meetings he'd listen to a number of views and then make a decision as if no one had spoken.'

Borman was known as a strong leader and manager as well as a pilot and engineer, and for this reason he was the one who had driven the recovery effort after the *Apollo 1* fire in January 1967, which killed Gus Grissom, Ed White and Roger Chaffee. He was the only astronaut chosen to serve on the Accident Review Board that was charged with investigating the causes of the disaster and working out how not to let it happen again. He devoted almost every waking moment for two years to getting Apollo back on track, spending countless hours in the charred cabin and replaying the communications tapes with their unidentified scream of *'Fire in the spacecraft!'* until he heard them in his dreams. He, as much as anyone, was associated with Apollo's return to readiness.

So the simple fact is that *Apollo 8* flew with two people who were amply qualified to be captain. Did it bother Lovell that he didn't get the nod? 'Well, yeah . . . Borman was the commander again. But then I got *13*, so, that was the way it went.' Lovell's irrepressible positivity again. 'Better to go than not to go at all because you're mad because you're not the commander.' And then, again, another positive view. 'As a matter of fact, the idea of being the navigator was much better than I thought. The commander on *8* didn't really do much. The re-entry was all automatic. I did all the navigation, and aligned the platform.'

The two already knew each other probably far more intimately than they would ever have wanted to. And with them would be a third, younger flyer, and less of a known quantity to the two of them: Bill Anders.

*

I have been warned that Bill Anders can be taciturn, abrupt; that he doesn't suffer fools gladly. But in all of the research for this book nobody offers me greater hospitality, generosity and time than he does. I first reach him by phone – he is hiking at the time – and after putting me through my paces a little, he invites me to stay in his home.

Home happens to be in one of the more remote locations in the continental United States. First you go to Seattle; then you drive two hours north to the port of Anacortes; then you hop on a ferry for an hour and a half to the San Juan Islands, where the Canadian border flits and weaves through the sound. He's eschewed the more populous of these beautiful fir-drenched islands and lives on one called Orcas, whose population for most of the year is about 4,500; once there, he's on one of the most remote bits of it too, and that's about as much information about his whereabouts as he'd likely want me to reveal.

The logistics of all this take a little setting up, but when I disembark the ferry at Orcas, I spot a man in jeans and a baseball cap amid the other waiting locals, unremarkable in most respects, except for the fact that he was one of the first three people to slip the surly bonds of Earth orbit and travel to another world. 'Congratulations on swimming this far upstream,' he says, and we drive off in his SUV, stopping for a moment to check on his boat, a spacious cream cruiser whose name I'd better not reveal but which has a pleasingly orbital tone.

This is a ravishing part of the world, largely unspoiled as far as I can see, with the Douglas firs and Western cedars stretching unfettered across the island. And Anders's home is stunning, a beautiful wooden construction looking across the sound, filled with the accumulations of an exceptional life: the Apollo memorabilia, of course, though that is largely confined to an office; a dresser filled with mementos from his time as an ambassador to Norway; and an original Alan Bean painting on the wall. He is, he says, the only astronaut who actually owns one, which is less of a surprise when you know how much they cost.

Anders does not give a lot of interviews. Of all the astronauts, he and Armstrong have been the ones least keen to cash in on the celebrity of Apollo, and, also like Armstrong, he stopped giving autographs a long time ago, recognizing that doing so was simply creating a market for others to profit from. And, while he doesn't judge others for signing things for a fee, recognizing that not everybody came out of NASA with the where-withal to build another career afterwards, he clearly finds the idea distasteful.

He can afford to do so. Of all the Apollo veterans, Anders has surely had the most exceptional post-flight career in public- and private-sector life. He ran the country's main nuclear agency at forty. He rose through the ranks at General Electric alongside the most feted of corporate leaders, Jack Welch. And his turn-around as chief executive of General Dynamics was so swift

252

and dramatic that the Harvard Business Press has used it as a case study on leadership.

It's clear that this is the reason Anders, who is often approached for books and interviews, has agreed to speak with me: he takes greater pride in what came after Apollo than during it. Normally, when I reach people like him, I have read their memoirs and everything else I can find about them, and come equipped with so much background knowledge on their missions that I half feel I know what the answers to questions about Apollo are going to be before I ask them. But with Anders it's different: there is no memoir, and he insists as a condition of the interview that I read only one book – and it's the Harvard one, about General Dynamics, not an Apollo account.

*

Looking back, Anders attributes his later success to an early recognition that he was pretty low on the greasy pole of Apollo greats, and understood early on that there would need to be a life beyond the missions. He was helped in this respect by the hoops he'd had to jump through to get on to Apollo in the first place, being advised that he needed a graduate degree and finding himself assigned to one on nuclear engineering – one which he supplemented by studying a whole other night-school course on aeronautical engineering at Ohio State simultaneously. There had been an earlier degree from the Naval Academy; he was a highly qualified man before he ever got to Apollo.

Apollo literature depicts him as an outsider, bracketed with Walt Cunningham, Rusty Schweickart and Alan Bean as having an intellectual perspective that distanced them from the others in the group and perhaps worked against them in securing missions. I ask him if that's true.

'Yeah, the eggheads,' he says. 'The four of us were pretty

much together trying to psych out what it took to get a flight, and we were all dead wrong. It was just a matter of the clock ticking.' To this day, many astronauts don't understand the reasoning that was applied to the assignment of missions, and the fact that it took his friend Bean, a brilliant test pilot, six years to fly remains a source of bafflement. 'I could never understand why I got a flight before Alan,' Anders says. 'I wouldn't want to say he was naïve. He just wasn't quite as Machiavellian as I was.' Someone had given Anders a copy of Machiavelli's *The Prince*. 'I read it, and I thought: well, that's the way to do it.'

In fact, peers of Anders remember him not as scheming at all, but as serious and hard-working: Frank Borman once described him as a young Frank Borman, which appears to have been meant as a compliment. In the end all of his brainiac friends would get a flight. 'Deke Slayton's criteria, in retrospect, was priority, and top priority was when you showed up. There was no credit given to education.' (And the eggheads are all still in touch. Months later when I call Anders to run through a fact-check, Walt Cunningham calls him on the other line. All I can make out of their conversation is: 'You still owe me half a cheeseburger.')

Whereas Borman and Lovell had come through in the second group of astronauts, the *Mercury 7* being the first, Anders came in the third group of fourteen candidates, an intriguing mix of men whose fates would prove a distillation of the space programme in general. Buzz Aldrin, Alan Bean, Gene Cernan and Dave Scott would go on to walk on the Moon, and Bill Anders, Mike Collins and Dick Gordon to orbit it; Charlie Bassett, Roger Chaffee, Ted Freeman and C. C. Williams would all die in accidents without ever leaving Earth. Eisele, Cunningham and Schweickart would make Earth-orbit flights. But when they first came together, for various reasons, Anders considered himself, Schweickart and Cunningham as being 'at the bottom of the totem pole. Both Rusty and Walt had a habit of pissing other people off. I at least kept my mouth shut a little more.'

When *Apollo 8*'s reshuffled mission came about, Anders was unique among the three crew in not being thrilled by the assignment. That's because of the knock-on consequences it had for him. Anders, like Neil Armstrong, had been focusing on learning to fly the lunar module, or the LLTV vehicle that NASA had devised as a training aid, a contraption so unwieldy that it had become known as the Flying Bedstead. He was good at it. But *Apollo 8*, of course, would have no lunar module. And from what he had learned about the sequence of missions, he was sure that he would not find himself scheduled for a lunar landing mission until well after he expected the programme to have been cancelled anyway (and, in this, he was more prescient than most). In short, despite the excitement of his first mission, it was apparent to him from the outset that the switching round of *Apollo 8* and *9* had cost him the Moon.

'I got screwed, in my view,' he tells me. 'If they hadn't done that, I'd have been out there opening doors and talking about my flight landing on the Moon. I went from being a lunar module guy, having flown in the lunar module, to a command module guy.' Strictly speaking, Anders's role on the flight was still as lunar module pilot, but since there wasn't a lunar module *to* pilot, this didn't make much difference. Anders realized: It's gonna have to be *Apollo 23* before I walk on the Moon. And *Apollo 23*, he knew early on, would never happen; in fact the last one would turn out to be *17*.

In some respects, he says, it was a great assignment. 'Got to see the Moon, take the picture.' But then again, 'Do you remember who the command module guy from *Apollo 15* is? I don't.' [Al Worden, I say. 'Probably. Good for you,' he replies.] 'Those guys were always second-rate citizens afterwards.' He compares the hand he was dealt with the many men who landed on the Moon in their first-ever spaceflight. 'Charlie Duke. He's a nice guy, but he just got flopped on the Moon almost by luck. It wasn't a lottery, but it was not a highly managed selection process. And for me it meant I was clearly cut out of walking on the Moon.'

But surely, I say, this was still a remarkable pioneering mission in so many ways. Alongside the disappointment and the feeling of being screwed, didn't he have a sense of the scale of what was being done on *Apollo 8*?

'I wish,' he says, 'that I could paint a picture of a guy with that big a vision. But I was so mad I wasn't a lunar module pilot with a lunar module. I was focused on walking on the Moon, and it really didn't occur to me at the time that this was a Lindbergh-type flight.'

*

A Lindbergh-type flight indeed it was, and as if to illustrate the fact, the afternoon before *Apollo 8* launched, Charles Lindbergh himself came to the Cape to talk to them. Relaxed in the presence of fellow aviators, Lindbergh told them about the time he had met Robert Goddard, the father of US space rocketry, not long after Lindbergh's famous flight across the Atlantic to Paris. Goddard had told him it was theoretically possible to design a multi-stage rocket capable of reaching the Moon, Lindbergh remembered, 'but that it might cost as much as a million dollars'.

Lindbergh asked how much fuel would be consumed at the launch; the answer was that the astronauts would be climbing into a capsule on top of 531,000 gallons of kerosene and liquid oxygen. Lindbergh began scribbling on a piece of paper. 'In the first second of your flight tomorrow,' he announced, 'you'll burn ten times more fuel than I did all the way to Paris.'

His visit was a touch of aviation royalty, although Anders didn't really note its portent at the time. 'I was so focused on making sure I knew how the control system worked, and the rocket plumbing, that I didn't really fully appreciate the significance of that,' he says. 'Although it was a really great honour. I had read his book. But I wanted to get back to my room and go over the systems diagram one more time.' The significance would not sink in until, some time afterwards, he received a long, sincere, handwritten letter from Lindbergh – a letter which Anders had thought lost but which, coincidentally, his archivist Dydia DeLyser has found on the very day of my arrival. 'After the flight, I was thinking: boy, this is something. This guy sat down and spent a long time writing this letter.'

And then to bed, for a 2.30 a.m. wake-up call.

*

Apollo 8 started with a launch the like of which nobody had ever seen before. The American space programme had used a range of rockets to get its astronauts airborne in the past – the Atlas, the Redstone – but what it was really all building towards was the Saturn V, to this day one of the most extraordinary machines ever built. There had been two unmanned tests before this, but *Apollo 8* was the first time humans had been strapped to the top of this vast, bubbling, seething missile and launched into space upon it.

There is an uneasy history to the Saturn V; it was the brainchild, like so many of the landmarks of propulsion over the previous decade, of Wernher von Braun, whose claim to fame prior to Apollo had been designing the V2 rockets which the Nazis rained down upon London during the Second World War. Everyone involved with Apollo had had to make a certain moral accommodation with von Braun, and accept that the race to the Moon had meant a compromise with a Nazi scientist.

But, beyond doubt, it was an extraordinary machine: still the tallest, heaviest and most powerful rocket ever brought to operational status. It also remains, to this day, the only vehicle to have transported human beings beyond low Earth orbit, and it would take twenty-four of them in total, three of them twice – Lovell being one of them.

The numbers around Saturn V, the fuel loads and the pounds of thrust, are so big they are meaningless: what matters is, the Saturn V never failed, not once.

At 7.51 a.m. on 21 December 1968, the engines fired – so far above them, the astronauts felt strangely removed from their power, although Anders did find himself surprised by it. 'We had simulated everything you can imagine, but we didn't imagine the sideways forces,' he says. He tries to convey the height of the rocket, and the way that the engines at the base would be constantly adjusting to keep it pointed straight up. 'I've always thought of an analogy like an old whip antenna on an automobile. You're just a beetle at the top. I thought we were banging into the launch tower. Borman had the insight to get his hand off the abort handle.' Just as well: had he twisted it accidentally with the motion, the crew would have been launched off on a separate rocket to drift down into the sea off Florida.

'For the first – it seemed like an hour, but it was probably ten seconds – you couldn't hear yourself think,' Anders says. 'It felt like I was in the jaws of a rat or a terrier.'

*

Once aloft, the first problem was that Borman got spacesick. This had not been such an issue on the Mercury and Gemini missions, since there was simply no room to move around in those tiny contraptions. The three-man Apollo service modules, by contrast, were relatively roomy, and that turned out to induce nausea.

'On Gemini it didn't show up too much because we were strapped in, looking forward, and there was no place to go,' says Lovell. 'But on *8*, you got out of the couch, you could float around and do things. I was the first guy out of the couch, and I could feel it right away, that nausea coming on. I was very, very careful of what I had to do, and looked forward. But Borman never quite got over that. So for the first day out, he was more or less a passenger.'

It was, clearly, no fun for Anders and Lovell being around as Borman's vomit, and worse, flew around the capsule, unrestrained by gravity, but Anders did begin to take something of a scientific fascination in it. 'I remember Lovell was sitting on one side, I was on the other. We heard Borman say: I'm sorry, and this greenish blob came up, obviously vomitus.

'I looked at it, and initially I was disgusted. Then I thought: man, that is interesting.' He shapes his hands to illustrate the pulsating movements of the glob. 'Three-dimensional vibration, oscillation. I thought, man!' And then it split in two, with the two parts heading off in opposite directions – 'Newton's law! Conservation of momentum!' – with one of them heading straight for Lovell, cornered in his spacecraft. 'Lovell, I'll never forget his eyeballs. Did he mention this when you met him?' He did not, I report. 'It splatted on his chest like a fried egg.' If Lovell had thought he could get no closer to Borman's bodily functions after *Gemini 7*, he was wrong. 'It was not,' Anders recalls, 'a good experience.'

Though they couldn't feel it at the time, the crewmembers were also undergoing a new and potentially perilous experiment. Between the Earth and the Moon exists space radiation, in quantities that were not entirely clear at the time of the mission.

Earth itself is surrounded by the Van Allen radiation belt, a layer of charged particles held in place around our planet by its magnetic field. They start about 1,000 kilometres above us, so had never threatened any previous mission.

As the nuclear specialist, Anders had the most knowledge of the crew about this, and wasn't concerned. 'I didn't worry about it on our flight. I had a little meter that I had designed to detect heavy doses of radiation from solar flares and it didn't even make a beep.' He does say, though, that there appears to be a link between the long lunar flights and cataracts. He says some astronauts from the Moon missions, notably Aldrin, reported getting flashes in their eyes when they slept. 'This was basically cosmic radiation going through the oculus part of their eye.' Anders didn't see them himself, but then, he barely slept.

The unpleasantness of space vomit and the dangers of cosmic radiation were soon replaced by a moment of true history: the first sighting of the Earth in its entirety.

'The greatest impression,' Lovell says, 'was not the Moon itself, but looking back at the Earth at that distance. It gave you a clear indication of our existence here in the universe. You could see the Earth as a small body, and you could see how it was around the Sun, and that the Sun is merely a normal star on the outer ridge of a galaxy called the Milky Way. The Earth looked completely uninhabited, but you knew there were 5 billion people living there.

'I could hide the Earth with my thumb, and everything I knew disappeared. The historical evolutionary period of the Earth ceased to exist. It was not there. And then you realized, number one, how insignificant we are, and number two, how fortunate we are that we have a body of a proper mass and at a proper distance from the Sun that provides life as we know it today.'

In fact, they barely saw the Moon at all on the way there, and had been told not to look at it in case the brightness gave them snow blindness, due to the lack of a filtering atmosphere. There was a point, just before the moment of the lunar orbit injection burn that would put the craft into orbit round the Moon, when Borman broadcast to Houston: 'As a matter of interest, we have yet to see the Moon.' Houston, in disbelief, responded: '*Apollo 8*, what else are you seeing?' Anders replied: 'Nothing. It's like being on the inside of a submarine.'

One element of the mission that had bothered the astronauts from the outset was that the four-minute burn of the engine to slow the craft down enough to enter lunar orbit would have to happen when they were behind the Moon, and therefore out of radio contact with Earth. In Houston, there was nothing they could do but wait for word when *Apollo 8* came back round the other side. There was a huge amount at stake: if the engine didn't fire, *Apollo 8* would go straight past the Moon, never to return. If it fired for too long, then the craft would not enter lunar orbit but crash into the Moon. If this was pressure for the astronauts, it was nothing compared to the horrors it caused their wives. Marilyn Lovell would later recall realizing: that engine would have to be perfect, or she would never see Jim again, a moment of recognition that caused her to break down and cry. But NASA's projections about when the astronauts would regain radio contact with Earth in the event of a successful burn were so accurate, down to a fraction of a second, that Borman half-accused his Houston colleagues of tricking them

'Honest Injun, we didn't,' CapCom replied.

*

For all three men, the most remarkable moment of the trip came on their fourth orbit when they went round the Moon and caught sight of the Earth once again. 'As we came around from the far side, the Earth rose, just like the Sun and the Moon rise out of the Earth's horizon,' Lovell says. It was *Earthrise*.

The picture that resulted from that moment, known as *Earthrise*, is believed to be the most frequently reproduced image in history; Al Gore says as much when using the picture in his *An Inconvenient Truth* documentary. It's also the image on the front cover of this edition.

There has been some confusion over the years as to who took it: Anders is the short answer, and indeed he was responsible for most of the photographs taken on the trip, including the many taken of the lunar surface. However, in his autobiography, Borman claims to have taken it. Anders's explanation for this is that Borman may well have grabbed a black-and-white camera – there were a few floating around – but that Anders definitely took the colour one. And Lovell? 'Well, I recognized the value of the picture.' He is grinning: he knows what this all means to Anders, and has joked that 'Bill will mention this to you before he says absolutely anything else.' 'I said: give me the camera, and Bill said: no, I got it. But I always tell him now: yeah, you took the picture, but *who directed it?* Who told you to direct it at a certain angle with the composition perfect, huh? Who told you that?'

When I tell Anders, he smiles about it. 'I'm quite willing to share. I mean, look, I'm just a guy, I didn't know what I was doing. Click, click, click. I didn't have a light meter so I machine-gunned the Earth and they picked one.' For those who want to know, the famed photo was on a 70mm lens, F-stop 11, with a 1/250th of a second shutter speed, and was taken on a Hasselblad 500 EL using Ektachrome film developed by Kodak. Still, when I later ask the photographer of the world's most famous image if he actually likes photography, his answer is a resounding 'Nah!' Incidentally, the famed postage stamp in the USA that used the image printed it upside down.

Earthrise is not actually Anders's favourite photo he took of the Earth – 'I've never been able to figure out the continents'. He prefers another, just of the Earth itself, in which the Earth is about the size of a fist at arm's length. 'Beautiful, through a lot of clouds.' Anders is characteristically somewhat mocking of the lack of attribution for the *Apollo 8* photo by Al Gore. 'He thinks he took it right after he invented the Internet.'

It has been said that the photograph set the world's fledgling environmental movement in train. 'Oh yeah!' Anders says. 'Kicked it off. I feel kind of sorry for the old people who were pushing a wet rope trying to get the environmental movement going, but this did kick it off, almost to the point where I kind of regret, because it might be the pendulum swung a little further than it should.

'But it doesn't do the job that I think is even more important, and that is to show the insignificance of the Earth. A bunch of slightly different brands of humans fighting each other, blowing each other up. It reminds me of a bunch of ants on a log floating down a river fighting over whose log it is.'

Anders would later deliver his most famous remark: that they went to the Moon in order to discover the Earth. 'That's what impressed me,' he says now.

*

Then, of course, almost as an afterthought, there was the Moon itself. The three men were the first to see the dark side, as we call it, with their own eyes. How did it measure up to expectations?

'It was rougher than I had expected,' Anders says. 'They still haven't got a good explanation of why. Is that why we're locked into synchronous rotation, so we basically always see the same side of the Moon? Or were we locked in and there was a massive lunar melting and it pulled the molten lava towards the Earth and smoothed things out? To the best of my knowledge it hasn't been fully explained, even today.'

Lovell found it closer to what he'd expected. 'It's all shades of grey. The far side is much more pock-marked with smaller impacts, so there is some relationship to the Earth and how it formed originally, because it looks like the major impacts are on the near side, creating the large basins that we have, and some of the large craters like Tyco.' He leans forward conspiratorially. 'Have you seen the pictures taken with the lunar reconnaissance orbiter satellite? With this camera, you can see the descent engines that were left. You can see the prints of the wheels of the rovers on this thing. It's absolutely amazing what we can see. I have a picture somewhere here –' he looks around his office, which is a little cluttered, with cardboard packaging on the floor – 'of just a quarter of Tyco, where you can see all the interior, the rims, exactly how it was formed.'

This leads us to the question of Mount Marilyn. The movie *Apollo 13* made this famous: in one of the opening scenes, Lovell's wife, Marilyn, looks to the Moon, where Armstrong and Aldrin are standing a quarter of a million miles away, and asks where her mountain is. It was a mountain Lovell had found while looking through the window of *Apollo 8*. I ask him about it.

'I was studying the near side of the lunar map,' he says. 'Of course, ever since the fourteenth or fifteenth century when people started getting telescopes, they started naming craters after famous astronomers, physicists, religious people and so on, so it was all fairly well named on the near side.' *Apollo 8*'s orbit, with a future landing in mind, went over the big, long ago-named craters of Tranquillity and Serenity. Tranquillity would eventually become the first landing site.

'As we looked along our route, on what I likened as the shoreline of Tranquillity, there was a little crater on one of the edges, called Secchi Theta. There were several craters all around it, and I guess the people at the time said: that's secchi, that's secchi alpha, beta, gamma, and here's theta. But there was a triangular mountain, sort of pointed right into the Sea of Tranquillity, and that mountain never had a name. It was at the place where we would be coming around and starting our descent. I saw it and said: if it doesn't have a name, why don't I name it after my wife? I'm going to be gone anyway, and she doesn't like me to be gone, so I'd better bring her back something from it.'

And so he named it Mount Marilyn. It did become a navigational point on the mission of *Apollo 10*, the dress rehearsal for the lunar landings, and was used again on the real deal, *Apollo 11*. It's never yet been formally recognized by the International Astronomical Union, which for some reason has jurisdiction over these things, but nevertheless, for forty years now the name has stuck.

The *Apollo 8* astronauts had craters named after them too, this time officially, although to their profound irritation (or Anders's, anyway), the ones that were selected were within a small sliver of darkness on the far side – the only bit they couldn't actually see. 'I've been mad about that ever since.'

It would be hard to call the Moon beautiful. 'After a while,' says Anders, 'the Moon looked like dirty beach sand. It was just pounded. You could tell very quickly that there was hardly an original feature left.' For Anders, his impressions of the Earth were more resonant than this monochromatic, ruined Moon. 'It was sandblasted. After about four revs,' he confesses, 'it became boring.'

Anders's chief job in orbit had been to photograph the surface of the Moon, with an endless list of requirements: craters, potential landing sites, outcrops. But to his disbelief, after a few rotations Borman informed Houston that he was cancelling all assignments for the foreseeable future and ordered Anders and Lovell to sleep. Borman's view was that the crew, particularly Lovell, were tired and beginning to make mistakes, and that his priority above everything else was to get them safely home. Angry at the time, and not a little tired, Anders has since mellowed about it. 'His theory was: we came here to get around the Moon and go home, and let's not risk anything by taking silly pictures or making geologic observations,' Anders says. And was Borman right? 'In one sense, yeah. I mean, we made it back.'

So the two men went to rest, Anders unsuccessfully, Lovell not so much. 'Lovell's snoring already,' reported Borman, a man who knew plenty about Lovell's snoring from bitter past experience. 'Yeah,' said Mission Control. 'We can hear him from down here.'

After a few more hours, they got up again. It was Christmas Eve, and time to do something unique.

*

The broadcast of the *Apollo 8* crew on Christmas Eve 1968 was one of the most memorable broadcasts in history, watched or heard by as many as a billion people. Something remarkable needed to be conveyed.

Six weeks before launch, Borman had been called by Julian Scheer, in NASA's public affairs division, telling him that one of the television broadcasts would be made from the Moon on Christmas Eve. 'We figure more people will be listening to your voice than that of any man in history,' he was told.

'As we prepared for the flight,' says Lovell, 'we were trying to think what would be appropriate to say around the Moon. We were looking at the trajectory and realized we would be orbiting the Moon on Christmas Eve, but we couldn't think of something. How about changing the words to "A Night Before Christmas", or "Jingle Bells"? Nothing was right.' Borman went to a friend who in turn contacted a former United Press International reporter called Joe Laitin, by now in government. 'So the story goes,' says Lovell, 'late that night, his wife came downstairs and said: what are you doing? And he told her the story and said he had to write something that it would be appropriate for the *Apollo 8* crew to say. And she said: why don't they speak the first ten verses of Genesis from the Old Testament?'

NASA would later be sued for this by an atheist activist called Madalyn Murray O'Hair on the basis that they imposed one religious belief on all listeners (today, Anders recalls, 'What I learned from her is that it's not so much who your friends are, it's who your enemies are that make you famous'), and today Lovell is keen to put the Genesis words in context. 'That was the basis of many of the world's religions: not just Christians but also Hebrew, and Islam.' In any event, the plan was approved, and when they took off they found the ten verses written on the back page of their flight manuals.

On Christmas Eve, Borman began a broadcast, and each of them gave their impressions of the Moon. 'The Moon is a different thing to each of us,' Borman began. He spoke of a vast, lonely, forbidding type of existence, an expanse of nothing. Lovell spoke of two worlds: the 'grand oasis' of Earth, and the lonely Moon he could see. Anders talked about lunar sunrise and sunset. They told viewers about the landmarks beneath them, including the Sea of Tranquillity, where Armstrong and Aldrin would land less than a year later.

Then Anders said, 'We are now approaching lunar sunrise. And for all the people back on Earth, the crew of *Apollo 8* has a message we would like to send to you.'

Anders began. 'In the beginning, God created the heaven and the Earth.' He read a few verses, then Lovell took over, and then Borman. 'And God saw that it was good,' Borman concluded. 'And from the crew of *Apollo 8*, we close with, good night, good luck, a merry Christmas, and God bless all of you, all of you on the good Earth.'

Today, Anders recalls, 'It fit with the solemnity and significance of the flight. Even today I feel like I would think it's a good choice. It caught people's attention and really surprised the hell out of 'em. Although a reporter later said the biggest thing on Apollo was getting Anders, the Catholic, to read from the King James version of the Bible.'

Despite the Christian reverence of the moment, the more religious members of the crew found some of their long-standing views being challenged by the experience. Anders looked at how small the Earth appeared, then considered that even if they travelled 1,000 times further than they just had, they would still not have got to Mars. 'And by then, the Earth is just a dust mote. I would have thought that by now more people would focus on the physical insignificance of our home planet. I think in our lizard-level brain we kind of think that the Earth, and we, are still the centre of things. It didn't help my Catholicism to start thinking about that.'

Anders had, in fact, been quite a devout Catholic prior to the flight, arranging for a priest to visit him the morning before the launch, which for some reason profoundly irritated Borman, who snapped, 'Are you gonna take communion every thirty seconds before the flight?' In my research for this book I had already met a number of people with differing religious inter-pretations of Apollo, most obviously Charlie Duke (religious) and Ed Mitchell (spiritual, but with no faith in conventional religions), and wondered how Anders was affected. He doesn't want to badmouth religion, and asks not to speak on the record about the subject, but it's clear his faith was affected. 'It did change my perspective,' he says.

Borman, who had always been somewhat religious too, had

found himself drifting to something of the opposite conclusion. When he had reached 21,000 miles above the Earth and seen it as a whole, 'dwindling until it became a disk', he recalled: 'We said nothing to each other, but I was sure our thoughts were identical – of our families on that spinning globe. And maybe we shared another thought I had . . . This must be what God sees.'

*

It was time to go home, which meant another burn of the engine, this time for what was called Trans Earth Injection. Every bit as critical as the lunar orbit injection, this once again had to take place while the astronauts were round the far side of the Moon and out of radio contact. Borman would recall thinking of the vital SPS engine that would deliver the burn, 'the reliability of its one hundred moving parts holding our lives hostage'. (This reminds me of Alan Shepard, who was once asked what he was thinking as he waited on top of a Redstone rocket on the launchpad in May 1961, about to become the first American in space. 'The fact that every part of this ship,' he said, 'was built by the lowest bidder.') Once again, Mission Control, and families at home, were in the dark. They just knew that if the engine had worked, then *Apollo 8* would re-emerge from behind the Moon at nineteen minutes past midnight on Christmas Day, Houston time, with the mission clock on eighty-nine hours, twenty-eight minutes and thirty-nine seconds. That time arrived, then passed. And then: 'Houston, *Apollo 8*. Please be informed there is a Santa Claus.' It was Lovell. 'You are the best ones to know,' said Ken Mattingly, on CapCom. *Apollo 8* was coming home.

They landed before dawn in the Pacific Ocean a thousand miles south-west of Hawaii, where the aircraft carrier *Yorktown* was waiting for them. For some reason nobody has ever quite figured out, when it hit the water a wave poured in, all over Borman; the combination of that and the impact stopped him releasing the chutes, and the craft was dragged upside down. Borman threw up. They stayed this way for an hour and a half before it became light enough for them to be retrieved, a somewhat ignominious return for the heroes. When the hatch opened and the sea air flooded in, Borman would describe it as the best moment of the entire mission.

The significance of *Apollo 8* was much greater than it might have appeared to the astronauts at the time. One has to realize just what a disastrously tempestuous state American society was in throughout 1968. Sentiment against the war in Vietnam was intense and turning violent. The Kent State shootings had taken place, and both Bobby Kennedy and Martin Luther King had been assassinated in the course of the year. 'It was a very bad time,' Lovell says, soberly now. 'The Vietnam War was going on; it was very unpopular, and it turned out the young people were right.' This is not a concession that all the men of his era, military almost to a man, willingly make. 'It was not a war to stop communism, it was a national war to integrate Vietnam for the Vietnam people. It took a long time for us to realize that, until long after the war was over.'

It was a war that he, and most of his peers, would have taken part in, were it not for Apollo. 'Exactly. As a matter of fact, we were all military. All my friends in naval aviation who I trained with and had been in squadrons with went over to Vietnam. Of course,' he says, with a slightly embarrassed laugh, 'I flew over it 330 times, but too high: the SAMs couldn't get me.'

Anders recalls that '68 had been so bad that anything would have made it look better.' After the mission, NASA received a letter, now famed: *Thank you*, it said, *for saving 1968*.

'It was one of the things I was truly grateful for,' Lovell recalls.

'At the end of 1968, there were riots here, at the Democratic convention in Chicago. There were shootings on campus by overzealous military-type people. But we were able to bring something . . . to be positive. We could say: we did that. Look what happened here.'

*

The crew of *Apollo 8* returned to an atmosphere of ticker-tape and felicitation. They were the *Time* magazine men of the year. They won an Emmy for their broadcast on Christmas Eve.

There was a parade down Broadway, where the street signs had been changed to Apollo Way, painted in orange and black. They were presented to the UN, given a dinner at the Waldorf-Astoria by New York Governor Nelson Rockefeller. A million people watched their Chicago parade. There was another in Washington, where Borman addressed a joint session of Congress. They all received the Distinguished Service Medal from President Johnson. Borman, in particular, travelled the world, and was sent on a goodwill world tour with his wife by Nixon after he assumed office from Johnson in 1969. They met the Queen and a teenage Princess Anne, Charles de Gaulle, Pope Paul VI.

'Well, I didn't think too much of it,' says Lovell. 'I thought naturally that's what's going to happen, but after this goes over and everyone says good for you, and you get all the accolades and the medals, all this stuff soon disappears.' In their case, it disappeared quickly because attention had turned to *Apollo 11*, upon which Lovell was a member of the backup crew, stopping him from joining Borman in the round-the-world celebrations. 'I didn't participate in all that. I was working hard to get [*Apollo 11*] squared away and making sure Neil was healthy. I was looking to see if he would break a leg and then I would get

271

his spot . . . But I wasn't successful in that.' He does confide, though, that Armstrong told him much later that he wanted him, Lovell, to take Aldrin's place on the flight. 'Buzz was a very intelligent guy, but he is very . . .' I can't quite work out the word on the tape, but I think it's 'contentious'. 'There was a bit of a hullabaloo about who was going to set foot on the lunar surface first. It went almost to the White House.' Many people from Apollo mention this about Aldrin, although he himself has described it as run-of-the-mill jockeying among test pilots.

The adulation, Anders says, 'was quite an experience, but it's like drinking from a fire hose: after a while it got almost too much. I don't know if it makes you cynical but I kept thinking: well, it was OK, but we were just three guys. What about the rest of the help that did it?'

*

Of the three of them, only one would ever fly in space again: Lovell, who should have been the fifth man to set foot on the Moon but instead became far more famous by failing to do so, on *Apollo 13*.

The explosion on that journey, in an oxygen tank, crippling the service module two days into a journey to land on the Moon, impeding everything from power to cabin heat to water to the removal of carbon dioxide and plenty else besides, created challenges for the crew and for NASA that none had expected ever to have to face. But they did, and Gene Kranz, the flight director, famously depicted in the movie by Ed Harris, described it as 'NASA's finest hour'.

'Well, I think Gene's right,' Lovell says. 'You have to look at it this way. In developing these spaceflights we were very careful, and we worked with the idea of four nines of reliability,' or 99.99 per cent. Over a period of years, specialists would look at every possibility, every failure, and work out a procedure that they would have to hand if the problem ever arose. But *Apollo 13* was far beyond anything that those contingencies had ever considered. 'This was something that was completely unexpected, something we had not planned. And it was really . . . well, let me see, there's a word I want to use here, an idea of how people can work together. Dedication. A dedication of working together.

'It was an almost certain catastrophe, which through good leadership and teamwork and initiative and perseverance and motivation of Mission Control working with the flight crew, was turned into a successful recovery. In that respect, I think it stands out alone in our spaceflights to date. And that includes all the ones after Apollo.'

Because of it, I suggest, he is more famous than ten of the twelve men who did set foot on the Moon, with only Armstrong and Aldrin as exceptions.

'Well, you're right, probably I am. But *Apollo 13* is probably more well known to everybody only because they made a movie of it.'

It is interesting to note that both Borman and Anders also had the chance to fly in space again – and Anders says he was originally assigned to *Apollo 13* with Lovell. But Anders, knowing that role would be a command module pilot rather than a Moonwalker, looked elsewhere. 'I'm thinking: I gotta go back and do the same thing as I did before. Did I really want to do that? I had the sense that, once the flag went in the ground, Apollo was really over: we'd beaten the Russians.' Actually, he was a little surprised the space programme was continuing at all. 'I was of the view that we ought to stop the programme before somebody busted their ass,' he says. '*Apollo 13* scared the hell out of Nixon. I'm surprised that they talked him into going past *15*.'

'If I was gonna be on a lunar landing crew, I would have stayed,' says Anders. 'Today, I feel quite satisfied, though given the choice I would rather have landed on the Moon.'

For a talented geologist and nuclear engineer, Anders is under no illusions that science had anything to do with Apollo. 'It was a political programme,' he says. 'It was, as Frank Borman said, another battle in the Cold War. It was not, as NASA liked to say, technology development. They invented Velcro? Bologna. They invented Teflon? Bologna.' (I know what you're thinking, but he definitely doesn't say 'baloney', he says 'Bologna'.) 'And after that [the landing], it was basically a jobs programme for NASA.' Anders served as Aldrin's backup on the historic *Apollo 11* landing, though he continues to feel to this day that he would have been a better option than the man he backed up.

As for Borman, he was in the frame to be the first man to stand on the Moon; Deke Slayton, whose decision it ultimately was, later wrote that Borman was a prime candidate for the first lunar landing, but Borman, who had been away from home for almost two years, had already decided *Apollo 8* would be his last mission.

Had it happened, Anders thinks Borman 'would have been a good choice, though maybe not quite as good a choice as Neil'. (Incidentally, Slayton did say very specifically that his original first choice to set foot on the Moon was Gus Grissom, but he died in the *Apollo 1* launchpad fire. By the time he needed to announce the crew for the landing, Armstrong was one of five people Slayton had confidence in as the historic mission commander, the others being Borman, McDivitt, Pete Conrad and Tom Stafford. In the end, Armstrong's moment in history came simply because of the existing crew rotation. His number just came up. 'They couldn't have made a better choice than Neil,' says Anders, 'but you know what? I don't think it was a choice. I think it was just, "OK, next", and up popped Armstrong.')

After *13*, Lovell stayed for another three years before leaving NASA in 1973. His remaining time in the space agency was spent running the scientific room, 'trying to coordinate all the scientists and examiners and experimenters for flights that were on the lunar surface'. One scientist would be working hard for time to be spent on his project – likely his life's work – while another would be arguing equally hard for his own. 'I was the moderator, the referee.' With his 1973 departure, all three crew members of *Apollo 8* had left NASA.

Part Two: After
So then what? How does one move on from having seen such rare spectacles, from broadcasting to a billion, from travelling to another world?

'This country,' says Lovell, 'is an entrepreneurial country,' as a freight train whistle sounds appropriately in the background. 'It's not like in some countries where if you do something great they put you on a pedestal and make you a baron or a count, or they give you a subsistence to live on and a chateau. This is a country that says: that was great, but what can you do for me now?'

Since almost all Apollo men had come out of the military, that represented a natural place to go next, but none of the *Apollo 8* crew took that route. In Lovell's case, this was partly because of a sense of embarrassment. When he had joined NASA from the navy, it was presented as a three-year short-duty station, in order that his military career would not suffer. This arrangement was continued for a further eleven years. Along the way – and this was the case with most of the military men in the space corps – he was promoted frequently, and by the time of his departure from NASA had become a four-stripe captain, 'which was very early, very unusual, and in some respects not very good,' Lovell says. 'President Johnson had this thing where when people made a flight they got promoted by one.' And Lovell, of course, made four flights.

Consequently, by the time he looked to go back to the service, the next step was admiral. 'And I looked at Lovell with his eleven years of NASA, and then I looked at this guy over here that had two tours of Vietnam and all sorts of school training, armed forces experience and so on – who would I pick?' says Lovell, recalling his attempts to be objective about his own achievements. 'I'd pick the guy with all the military training, not Mr Lovell. So I decided to retire.' This, too, was in 1973.

'So then the question is: what do you do? This is a free country. Thank you very much for your space programme, but what are you going to do next? So I looked around, and finally I got a job.'

This was with the Bay-Houston Towing Company, the largest of two tugboat operations in the port of Houston, which was then the third largest seaport in the USA. It was a family business and the man who ran it was getting old, and though he had ambitions of passing it to his son, that was not yet practical. 'He could entertain shipboard captains to three-martini lunches, but that was it.' Lovell, as a naval officer, knew about ships, and some mutual friends put them together.

'So I was hired to do that job. A good job: I was there five years.' Lovell became CEO of the company in 1975. 'But it was a family company, and I knew there wasn't really any advancement. They had a grandson coming up who was quite intelligent and being groomed to take over. So I looked around for what to do.'

The next step turned out to be telecommunications. 'Around this time, one of the last monopolies in this country was coming to an end: the Bell system, and AT&T.' At this stage, everyone in America who had a telephone had to lease their system through AT&T or one of the other monopoly companies around the country, but by the late 1970s a Supreme Court decision on selling equipment connected to the long lines, the interconti- nental systems of the telephone industry, signalled 'the beginning of the end of the monopoly'.

Seeing things changing, Lovell joined Fisk Telephone Systems, a small company built around computer digital equipment, unlike the analogue systems employed by AT&T. This was perhaps Lovell's greatest business success, and he served as president from 1977 to 1981, at which point the business was sold to Centel, which was one of the other big telephone companies in the USA at the time.

Having sold the company, Lovell stayed with it, working there until 1991 and retiring as an executive vice president and board member. One of the lasting impacts of that time was it provided him with his secretary, Mary Weeks, whom he inherited when he sold Fisk to Centel; she continues to work with him today, and has now done so for thirty-two years.

It was at this point that Lovell finally found himself with time to write the book he'd been talking about for several decades. He was trying to work out how to start it when he received a letter from Jeffrey Kluger, who at the time was a staff writer for *Discover* magazine, wanting to write about *Apollo 13*. Lovell liked Kluger's writing style so they got together, set a fifty–fifty split of earnings, got an agent and wrote a proposal, with an outline showing the proposed structure of the book. Houghton Mifflin took it up, gave them an advance and told them to write it within a year.

'Then, about a month or two later, when I was just starting to do the interviews and flesh out the chapters, I got a call from my agent. He said: are you sitting down? We've just sold your book to the movies.

'I said: but we haven't written it yet. Isn't that illegal?'

What had happened is a useful illustration of just how many lives were touched by Apollo. Their agent had sent the outline round to a few movie production companies, one of which was owned by the director Ron Howard. On his staff was a young man called Michael Bostick, whose job it was to look through the volumes of screenplays, books, proposals and so on to see if anything was worth a closer look. Michael's attention was caught by *Apollo 13* for a singular reason: his father, Jerry, had been a flight controller on the *Apollo 13* mission itself, working at Johnson Space Center in Houston. Michael, knowing the story well, took the pitch to Ron Howard.

'Now Howard wasn't really a guy who was interested in the space programme,' Lovell says. 'He was Opie on a little TV thing, then was in . . . er . . .'

'*Happy Days!*' comes a disembodied voice, Mary, from the hallway. (It's as well she's listening: Lovell these days struggles for a name or a date, and the interview is punctuated with the occasional bellow of '*Mary!* Do you remember that guy's name! That guy! You know, the . . . never mind.')

Howard was convinced to buy an option, so Lovell and Kluger went to talk to him in California while he was directing the Michael Keaton film *The Paper*. 'We went out for what I thought was a two-hour session. It ended up being five. He got more and more interested, and the last thing he asked me was: if we do this movie, who do you want to play your part?'

Lovell's call was not Tom Hanks, but Kevin Costner, who did have a certain resemblance to what Lovell looked like in the 1970s. He was, unfortunately, tied up with *Waterworld*; if you've seen it, you'll know this is unfortunate in more ways than one. 'It was,' Lovell says, trying to be diplomatic, but not all that hard, 'a bomb.'

Lovell was nevertheless impressed by Hanks. 'He did a super job. He was younger than I was, but he portrayed it very nicely.

The whole crew was very dedicated to that movie. We hear a lot of stories about movies and prima donnas; not this crew.'

The film itself is widely liked in the astronaut community, and Tom Hanks is seen as a good friend of the space programme. Most of the film was scrupulously accurate, with dialogue taken directly from the mission transcripts, with just a few concessions to dramatic narrative, such as Ken Mattingly being the only one working for a solution in the simulator when in fact a great many astronauts were involved. I know Lovell provided an audio commentary for the film; I take it he liked it? 'Oh yeah. It was fine for the Lovell family, fine for NASA, fine for education, fine for the country. A win–win situation.'

He recalls only one major piece of inaccuracy. 'There's one scene in the movie where Ron Howard has Jack Swigert talking to Fred Haise about who threw the switch, and there's an argument back and forth.' The movie crew noticed this hadn't appeared in the transcripts. Howard called Lovell. 'I said, no, it wasn't there, we didn't have any argument. But Howard said: listen, I've got to put it in because I can't show anxiety or stress or being foggy or sleepy with perspiration and a close-up of some guy's face. I've got to have an oral confrontation. I said: if that makes the movie, put it in.'

He also remembers how critics of the movie complained about a scene in which his wife, Marilyn, loses her wedding ring down the drain of the shower in a bad omen on the day of the launch. Several reviewers considered the scene unrealistic, and an over-the-top mawkishness. 'But it was a true story,' says Lovell. 'What they didn't show, of course, was about two hours later the plumber coming to pull out the trap and get it back.'

After the corporate life, the book and the movie, there was still more time to fill. Lovell had retired to Chicago, 'and tried to figure out what to do'. He had made some money-making speeches, but then another opportunity came along via his son, who had gone through a culinary school in Chicago and had worked at the nearby Deer Path Inn Hotel. 'One day he came to dinner and he noticed that I had had too much wine. About my third glass,' Lovell recalls. 'And he figures this is a good time to hit me. So he says: Dad, why don't we go into business together? Let's start a restaurant.

'I thought,' he says wryly, 'he meant a little bistro. A hamburger place, or a deli. We ended up with this 15,000-square-foot fine dining restaurant we've had since 1999.'

And how has it all compared to the wonders that went before? 'There are two parts to this thing,' he says. 'In military life it is quite disciplined. You know who you report to and who reports to you. In some respects, that's kind of nice: you know how to go along, you know what the odds are, you know what to do.' NASA, clearly, was like this too.

'In corporate life,' he says, 'it's not quite that easy. You can be very lucky, be well thought of, be promoted over some guy who is very dedicated; in that respect, corporate life is difficult.

'I think,' he says, 'that being your own entrepreneur is the ultimate way to go. You're responsible for your own actions, your own livelihood, your own success. And in this restaurant, that's the way it is.'

Lovell is simply great company. Not all astronauts like one another, something I realize more and more as I meet them, but you won't find anyone with a bad word to say about Lovell. His skill as an aviator was matched by an easy-going nature that would prove to be extremely important several times over, first on his maiden flight, the flying-toilet mission with Borman on *Gemini 7*. And on *13*, of course, calmness was everything.

Today, he laughs frequently, a big-hearted guffaw. After our interview I drive to the Adler Planetarium in Chicago, where there is a whole exhibition dedicated in theory to the space programme but in reality to Lovell; the very first thing you see in the lobby, just to the right of the doors, is a larger-than-lifesize bronze statue of Lovell in his astronaut uniform, looking to the distance somewhat in the manner of those iconic Russian monuments to a striding and earnest Lenin, but in Lovell's case, what he's looking at is a distant Earth, which he is obscuring from his own view with his thumb, as he did on *Apollo 8*. The exhibition has a mock-up of Lovell's schoolboy bedroom, of the home-made rocket he made as a kid after shyly asking a Chicago industrial chemical store for ingredients, and the *Gemini 12* capsule he flew in with Buzz Aldrin, a tiny contraption whose grim grey interior for some reason puts me in mind of the 1970s dashboard of a Ford Cortina. A few miles further down the road at the Chicago Museum of Science and Technology, I find his *Apollo 8* command module, fished out of the Pacific Ocean after its return to Earth in 1971. Lovell is the home-town hero, even though he actually grew up in Milwaukee. He is very much loved.

*

The finest corporate career of all of the astronauts belongs to Bill Anders, and it stems, in some sense, from that very early recognition of where he stood in the astronaut pecking order. It was clear to him from the outset that there would need to be a life after Apollo. 'I knew, having been less of a designated rock star than the rest of them, that likely I would have to work for a living. Then the opportunities [after that] were just the choices I made. It all stemmed from those little decisions.'

He didn't want to be a door opener, as others chose to do. 'It's kind of sad, but they were getting, we thought, big money, $25,000 a year to be an investor relations officer of the company. I decided that likely that wouldn't happen with me, and if it did, it wouldn't last. That was the key decision which frankly a lot of the guys missed. They thought it would last, and it doesn't.'

After *Apollo 8*, Anders would sometimes state his views on the future of the Apollo programme – which, almost uniquely, he thought should stop doing lunar landings and 'be a bit more Earth-like'– to NASA administrator Tom Paine. Clearly his opinions made an impression, because Paine asked him to come to Washington to help plan NASA's post-Apollo programmes through a vehicle called the National Aeronautics and Space Council. 'And I thought: you know, do I really wanna go around the Moon again on *Apollo 13*, or might I go and start doing something where I thought I could be useful to the Nixon administration? This,' he adds, with a wry raise of the eyebrows, 'is before Agnew and Nixon got their you-know-what in the wringer. I was a naïve guy about that stuff.'

Anders agreed provided he had the option of coming back to NASA – 'I used the phrase "keep my union card current"' – and persuaded an administrator to write a letter saying he could continue to fly NASA aircraft so long as he worked for the government. This would, later, lead to the curious arrangement of America's ambassador to Norway flying T-38 jets.

While in his new job, Anders was involved in selling the idea of the Space Shuttle, 'which in retrospect was a big mistake. One of the most serious national policy errors ever made, because it ate NASA hollow – I'm reminded of those little wasps that lay their eggs inside the caterpillar, and the baby wasps eat the caterpillar hollow – and didn't really accomplish much.' He sees me raising my eyebrows at this and presses the point. 'It made a lot of noise, looked good, but it was a cuckoo in the nest – it shoved out other good programmes. I did a pretty good job getting it sold,' he laughs, 'even though it was the wrong thing to do. I didn't realize it was a jobs grab for NASA and a vote grab for Nixon.

'I didn't realize because I believed NASA that it would reduce the cost of orbit by a factor of ten. It doesn't take much research to find out that not only did it not reduce the cost of orbit by a factor of ten, it increased it by a factor of ten.' (He takes a similar view of the International Space Station. 'Can you name one thing the space station's done for you? I don't know either. Hardly anybody knows. I know that goldfish will float both ways. And ants. It vibrates so the microgravity people don't want it. It lets off gases so the deep-observation telescope people don't want it. It's mainly there to give the shuttle a place to go, and now we got no shuttle, so it's gonna be selling rides to tourists.')

The shuttle also meant the end of the Saturn V, against Wernher von Braun's recommendations. 'Wernher was suffering from prostate cancer and dying, and wanted to do Saturn V über alles,' Anders says. 'But the manned-flight guys didn't like Wernher because when he was a Nazi most of them were World War Two vets, and he was getting a lot more attention than they thought he needed even though he did a great job. So he didn't get too much of a hearing. In retrospect, it's too bad, because that's what we should have done.'

With that done, Anders recommended that the council he had been appointed to should be closed. While this might have torpedoed his career, he was hopeful that his employers would be impressed enough to put him on to something else – not that the Nixon administration was in much of a state by then. 'By this time Agnew had pissed in his mess kit and Nixon was getting the Watergate thing, and I was kind of sour with the administration.'

But another job did come up. A new commissioner was needed for the Atomic Energy Commission, a political appointee, and this was something Anders actually knew a great deal about. Way back when he was sent to graduate school by the air force, he was pushed into an advanced degree in nuclear engineering, somewhat against his will and for reasons he couldn't quite fathom. 'They would never give me a straight answer: oh, well, you had good math grades. Nah, nah, nah.' He would later realize it was because of a new air-force programme called Airborne Nuclear Propulsion, which involved putting nuclear reactors in B-36 bombers and flying them around.

In any event, the nuclear degree had led him to a position in the nuclear weapons lab looking at space radiation shielding, and when he applied to NASA, he turned this to his advantage, knowing that NASA was worried about the impact of space radiation on astronauts. 'They were more worried than they should have been, but I didn't tell them that. I said: I'm the only guy that can save your ass. To my amazement they hired me, and I indeed was responsible for the Geiger counters and whatnot.'

All this experience, real and invented, was recalled when the Atomic Energy Commission came up. There was only one nuclear engineer on the five-member commission, and he turned out to be the one Anders was replacing. Anders found himself put in charge of all nuclear-power development in the United States.

Nuclear, really, is the only word to describe the rise that Anders had undertaken. 'I go from un-flown astronaut, to low man on the totem pole in *Apollo 8*, to working for the likes of Spiro Agnew. Now I'm forty years old and in charge of all nuclear power.' He even had oversight of Hyman Rickover, a four-star admiral known as the Father of the Nuclear Navy, who directed the development of naval nuclear propulsion and ran it for three decades. 'He was nicknamed the "Kindly Old Gentleman",' Anders recalls. 'He was old. He wasn't kindly. He would probably tell you from his grave that I was a bit of a pain in the ass.'

From time to time his path would cross with other former astronauts, and on one occasion he found himself having to testify in front of John Glenn, the first American to orbit the Moon and by now a Senator. 'John called me,' Anders laughs, 'and says: psst, Bill, what do I ask you? I wrote the questions down, and we did great. He was smart enough to do that. John's a good guy.'

In time, the commission was split up to resolve a conflict between nuclear developers and the people who regulate them, and so Anders ended up as a chief nuclear judge. At one stage he shut down ten General Electric reactors. There was a perverse and inevitable humour to the fact that Anders's entry to the private sector would start with him being hired by none other than General Electric.

But there was one curious step between these two jobs, between regulating nuclear power and building it in the private sector: he became ambassador to Norway. How? Why?

'Well, that was a fluke,' he says. 'I had miscalculated my government pension.' He could give that up now and never notice it, he acknowledges, but with his finances as they were then, it was crucial at the time.

'We didn't have any money,' Anders says. 'NASA doesn't pay worth a damn.' He remembers Valerie joining a sewing group in Washington whose members were all political presidential appointees' partners, and were therefore broke. Dottie Blackmun – whose husband, Justice Harry Blackmun, would achieve national fame in legal circles as the author of the court's opinion in the landmark abortion test case *Roe* v. *Wade* – taught Valerie how to sew. 'Valerie's clothes were all handmade. I'd pick up a nickel in those days.'

So Anders couldn't give up that pension, yet had insisted on only a one-year term at the Nuclear Regulatory Commission, which had now expired. Fortunately, a number of ambassadorships were coming up, and Anders had made sufficient friends in government to be offered some of them by then-President

Gerald Ford. He was offered Czechoslovakia, and Australia; Valerie, however, had her eye on Norway after being on an enjoyable state-department trip a few years previously (the ambassador's residence had washed a trunkload of dirty kids' clothes for her, and it seemed to make an impression). The existing Norwegian Ambassador got sent to Prague, and the Anders family found themselves in Oslo.

It was a curious existence. 'It wasn't a very hard job. I figured it was one third of the day being ambassador, a third of the day being the F-16 programme manager, and a third of the day learning how to cross-country ski.' He tried to make himself useful, particularly bringing his fighter-pilot experience to bear in assisting the Norwegian air force in its use of American jets, but there was clearly a certain amount of ceremonial hobnobbing, going fishing with princes and dining with the king. He remembers it all fondly. 'We made a lot of friends. Our daughter met a nice guy. Everything was great.' To this day, when one dines with the Anders family, Bill commences and ends the meal with a Norwegian tradition of toasts and speeches, all conducted with a smile.

Upon his return to America in 1977, Anders reached twenty-five years in public service of one form or another, so he submitted his retirement and had it approved by the state department. Many former astronauts were now making their money from advertising, and Anders considered it. 'I'd been asked to do a couple of product statements, like I always buy Ajax batteries, and I love Palmolive soap,' he says. 'I was asked to do Casio, which had a watch with a built-in computer with little buttons on it. I got a call: we'd like to take a picture of you with that watch on and have you say something nice about it. Well, when you don't have any money, it's not quite as easy as it is now to turn that down, even though I thought it was a little unseemly.'

Anders called the lawyer who had represented all the astronauts in their exclusive contract with Time-Life during the Gemini and Apollo years. The lawyer got Casio up to $30,000. Anders said, 'You know what, if I'm going to sell my virginity it's gonna be more than $30,000.' So he didn't do it. Shortly afterwards, he was going through Chicago O'Hare Airport and ran into the Mercury veteran Wally Schirra. 'Look at this watch!' Schirra said. 'I'm gonna be in *Fortune* magazine next week wearing it.' Anders asked how much Schirra was being paid to wear this watch, which he recognized as the one he had been offered $30,000 to model. Schirra proudly responded, '$20,000!' Anders chuckles. 'I didn't have the guts to tell him.'

Still, Anders was in no position to be turning this sort of money away, and it was around this time that the private sector came calling.

At General Electric, Anders was put in charge of the nuclear-energy products division in San Jose. 'I sort of brag about the fact that two of our products were Fukushima 1 and 2. But they worked as they were designed.' He remains of the view that 'nuclear is still the only answer. The problems have been, I think, massively overstated. They made a big deal out of Three Mile Island,' the partial nuclear meltdown in a Pennsylvania reactor in 1979. 'But if you stood on the bridge downwind of the plant and breathed deeply the whole time, you'd get less of a dose than you would if you flew from Baltimore to Denver twice. I mean, the whole issue of radiation dosage is massively misunderstood.' In his view, 'we're going to get constipated over here in fuel,' and he has his doubts about many alternatives, leaving nuclear a vital long-term option. 'But we're not going to pull our socks up until people are freezing in the dark.'

He talks for a while about oil pricing, about fracking, and 'probably the biggest crooks in the world, the Saudis – and you can quote me on that – who are screwing us every time we turn around at the gas pump'. He remembers going to Harvard on a leadership course with General Electric and finding himself in the same can – a pair of rooms sharing a living room and bathroom – as Ali Al-Naimi, who at the time was with Aramco, the Saudi oil behemoth, and has since become the Saudi Arabian Minister of Petroleum and Mineral Resources. 'I asked him one time: how do you set your pricing on something that is almost free to you guys? He said: oh, we price it just below what we think the Americans can tolerate before they go off and do nuclear power.'

The move was transformative financially for a family with six kids to put through college. It was an interesting time to be at General Electric too, since it coincided with the rising through the ranks of Jack Welch, who would go on to become perhaps the most famed and well-regarded CEO in the corporate world. 'It was clear that Jack was a favoured son, whereas I was a newcomer,' Anders recalls now. 'We weren't buddies, but we were friends.' It went well: Anders rose through swift promotions until he was in charge of everything related to aircraft except the engines themselves, plus a radar division.

Next came a big offer from a company called Textron, which he remembers less well. 'I was brought in,' he says. 'I was discovered not to be a golfer. That was a real mark against me. Plus the fact that I started applying General Electric management techniques. That went over like a lead balloon in Textron.' The main criteria for performance at Textron, and the basis of bonuses and ultimately retirement packages, was return on investment, but it was a flawed plan because, rather than trying to boost returns, managers could do equally well by just reducing investment. Anders tried to point this out to the CEO and made little headway. 'I basically said: well, there's no sense in pissing into the wind.'

This was, though, the job that made Anders properly wealthy, thanks to an incentive scheme built by their finance director involving deferred compensation upon which the company would pay heavy interest. 'I became the biggest contributor. They still owe me millions of dollars.'

Anders, now wealthy, considered retiring at this stage, but then came the job that would represent his greatest success post-NASA: General Dynamics.

*

The interviews have been running for several hours now, and we break for the evening. As the fireplace crackles with wood from the surrounding forest, warming their elegant home, Bill's wife Valerie serves a beautiful three-course meal with a main course of halibut and salmon that Anders has just caught on a fishing trip to Alaska, and I can't help but think: your life is good.

At dinner Anders brings out two rocks and asks me to guess which is from Australia (knowing that I have Australian citizenship as well as British, he has latched on to this) and which is oldest. One, a nondescript dark rock you could never possibly notice without instruction, is from a meteorite that landed in Allende, Mexico, during the Apollo programme; it is, he says, older than the solar system, over 5 billion years. The other, he says proudly, comes from the Jack Ridge in Australia, and is the oldest exposed crystal on Earth. Apollo, it is clear, made him a geology nut: he befriended Harrison (Jack) Schmitt, who would later fly on the final Apollo mission, *17*, in 1972, the sole geologist ever to set foot on the Moon. In those early days Schmitt was several groups behind Anders in the Apollo waiting list, and Anders sought him out for personal instruction on how to understand the Moon rocks he would find when he got there. It's unlikely that either man thought at the time that Anders would never set foot on the Moon and that Schmidt would; it's equally clear that Anders's presence on a Moon walk would have been valuable. 'I was a rock guy,' he says wistfully.

Sitting at the table with Anders and Valerie, I am reminded of the strength of the *Apollo 8* marriages, which apparently thrive to this day.

Anders's wife, Valerie, was just sixteen when the two met and nineteen when they married, and, like so many Apollo wives, there's no question she made a great many sacrifices on the altar of her husband's career, raising six kids through their peripatetic military and NASA existence. Meeting her now, though, it's clear that she is a strong force in her own right. She's on one of the boards of the Smithsonian, has just stepped down as chair of a programme that brings top classical musicians to the island – something she has run for fifteen years – and is probably the driving force of reunions among the wives, though they have become less frequent as everyone gets older. Across the dinner table, Anders says proudly just how much he has been helped by having the stability afforded by a wife who is independently successful (notwithstanding the fact that, when in earshot, she corrects the details of his anecdotes mercilessly). She is funny too: conversations at dinner are of course off record, but I don't think she would object to me retelling the story of how, during Anders's ambassadorship to Norway, she opened the door and found King Olaf standing there. Unsure as to the king's appearance, she also thought it might be the butler, but decided to curtsey on the off-chance – 'better to curtsey to a butler than not curtsey to a king' – which turned out to be just as well.

The Anders marriage is not the only healthy one among the crewmates. Then there are the Lovells. Through *Apollo 13*, many people are familiar with Lovell's wife, Marilyn, portrayed as a loyal but tough beauty by Kathleen Quinlan in the film. When I meet him, he is excited because a lunar satellite is going to take the best image ever recorded of Mount Marilyn, which he will then blow up and give to his wife. (When I contact him to catch up later, I ask him how it looks. 'Great,' he reports.)

Lovell, I have learned at the restaurant, is not only close to his four children but in business with some of them. In the fine dining restaurant the family owns in Lake Forest, son Jay is the owner, and daughter Susan, whom I briefly meet, runs the books. An avid photographer, she admires my many-pocketed camera and lens vest, which is a refreshing change, since my friends mock it cruelly. How is it working with family? I ask Lovell Senior.

'Family can be very difficult,' he says, though, as always, he's grinning when he says it. 'So my son leases the restaurant from himself and his three siblings, so he pays rent to himself and three other people. Dad here has to be the monitor of the whole thing.' He and Marilyn own 1 per cent apiece, the kids 24 per cent each. It's clearly had its moments. 'We're looking at divesting ourselves of this place. He [Jay]'s getting older. I'm certainly getting older.'

As for Borman, he wrote candidly about the pressures his career, both at NASA and at Eastern, put on his wife. 'When Susan married me, she also married a man who may have been the most competitive brand-new second lieutenant in the whole United States Air Force,' he wrote.

She accepted this unquestioningly, absorbing his intensity, supporting her husband in his successes. Early in their marriage somebody gave her a copy of *The Army Wife* and she pored over every word, from dress code to officers' wives' events, to deferring to the spouses of officers senior to her husband. 'Susan absorbed it all as holy scripture,' Borman said.

He was absent, constantly, first on the revisions to Apollo after the 1967 fire, then on *Apollo 8*, and then again in later corporate life, and one day in August 1973 Susan was hospitalized with a nervous breakdown. When she was released he spoke to the psychiatrist and outlined his sense of guilt at the way his and Susan's lives had been. He recalled taking Susan's picture with him on both *Gemini 7* and *Apollo 8* and never bothering to look at it on either mission.

One time, the psychiatrist asked him, 'Have you been asking yourself lately if the missions were worth it?'

'Many times.'

'And what was your answer?'

'They were.'

Despite this, he describes himself as a family man, and his marriage to Susan has lasted more than half a century. The two still live together on their ranch in Montana.

*

Morning on Orcas Island: jetlagged, I'm up at four in the immaculate wooden guesthouse they keep for visitors a little further up the slope from the main house, transcribing tapes until the sunlight illuminates the trees and the water. It is a radiant place.

After breakfast, Anders and I sit in a ground-floor room to talk about the era that appears to give him greatest pride. When the Harvard Business Review Press author William Thorndike was looking for candidates for its book *The Outsiders*, which examines successful CEOs who did not fit the usual corporate mould, Bill Anders and General Dynamics were given their own chapter: 'The Turnaround'.

The American defence industry was in a mess in the aftermath of the end of the Cold War. 'In 1989,' wrote Thorndike, 'after nearly thirty years as the international symbol of Cold War tension and anxiety, the Berlin Wall came down, and with its fall, the US defence industry's long-time business model also crumbled.'

General Dynamics was arguably in the worst condition of all defence companies. Historically a lynchpin of American defence innovation, it is associated with names like the B-29 bomber and the F-16 fighter jet, as well as leading submarines and tanks. But it was not set up for a changing world. When Stan Pace stepped down as CEO in 1991, the company had $600 million of debt, negative cashflow, and was being talked about as a candidate for bankruptcy. Goldman Sachs analyst Judy Bollinger called it 'the lowest of the low', the worst company in a bad industry.

Perhaps the key to Anders's success was that he was allowed to spend a year as vice chairman, getting to know the company in St Louis under Pace before replacing him. That year, in retrospect, 'was a phenomenal gift'.

Anders spent much of it travelling around the various General Dynamics plants, 'and I couldn't believe what we had. Wonderful engineers: they invented almost all of the tactical missiles, the Tomahawk, the Stinger, the advanced cruise missile, nuke and non-nuke version.' But alongside the stalwarts like the F-16 warplanes, submarines and tanks, 'they had a bunch of businesses that most of the board didn't even know about. They were building race-car carburettors.' He took a product list to the board and found that most of them didn't even know some of the more obscure things the company was making.

At General Electric, Anders knew that if you didn't have your inventory under control, you were history. The General Electric way required that inventory was reported monthly, in a figure divided by the sales, 'and the number better be small'. Payroll, too, was closely monitored. 'You always paid at absolutely the last minute. *Just in time* was the buzzword in those days.'

General Dynamics was nothing like that. 'I went to the F-16 plant, and if you were an artist, it would be a great perspective class. The building was so long. It was one mile and one foot long.' Anders asked what their inventory terms were, and the managers didn't know what that meant. 'There was this huge pile of canopies. It reached to the ceiling. And they were building two a month.' The inventory issue was symptomatic of a rather fuzzy approach to the details of management.

By the time he stepped up to the top job he had formed a strategy to fix the company. The first part was straight out of the Jack Welch approach: the company should only be in businesses where it was the best or number two. The other was that it would exit other businesses, and also low-return commodity businesses.

At the same time – and again General Electric had clearly been an influence here – he set about emphasizing shareholder value and return on equity. And to do this, he replaced almost everybody in management. He promoted Jim Mellor, who had run the shipbuilding business, to president and chief operating officer; the two of them ousted twenty-one out of the top twenty-five employees in the company in the first half of 1991. And that woman analyst who had described General Dynamics as the lowest of the low? He asked her to come and talk to his management team.

The results were not just extraordinary, but extraordinarily fast. Anders was only CEO for three years. Over that time, the company, which had been overleveraged and had negative cash-flow, would generate $5 billion of cash.

This came about primarily because of an intense focus on costs, such as the inventory issue Anders had found in the F-16 plant. 'In the first two years of their regime,' writes Thorndike, 'Anders and Mellor reduced overall head count by nearly 60 per cent (and corporate staff by 80 per cent), relocated corporate headquarters from St Louis to Northern Virginia, instituted a formal capital approval process, and dramatically reduced investment in working capital.' Indeed, for the first couple of years they didn't really need to spend anything, such was the scale of the accumulated inventory.

But it also happened because Anders was ready to sell absolutely anything that wasn't core – and, subsequently, even something that was. There were many buyers around. 'Lucky for me, the growth mentality was still alive and well with my colleagues,' he says. 'It was amazing to me that when I'd offer something to sell, there was somebody that would buy it at a high price.' And nothing was sacred. 'I said: for the right price, I'll throw Valerie in. If these guys would pay us what we evaluated at 1 and they'd pay us 1.5, I thought it was unfair to the shareholders to keep it. If necessary, we'd sell the whole goddamn company.'

He damn near did. Anders sold not just a few businesses, but the majority of them: the Cessna light aircraft business, the missiles and electronics businesses among them. But then came a real test of Anders's sell-anything philosophy.

Anders had remained a reservist while at General Dynamics, flying the company's F-16s; he wasn't paid for it, since he was both a supplier and a customer and wanted to avoid conflict. 'I worked hard,' he says, 'not to get my tit in the conflict-of-interest wringer.' But he clearly enjoyed owning that business, and saw the chance to fly fighter jets as a perk of the job. It was also the company's signature product, and an immense source of pride to its staff.

Since fighter jets were a core product, and since General Dynamics now had a ton of cash from divestments, Anders went to see Lockheed and offered to buy that company's fighter-plane division, informally known as Skunk Works, an iconic business that over the years has been responsible for aircraft as famous as the U-2 and the SR-71 Blackbird. 'I was lusting after it,' Anders says. 'If you own the Skunk Works, your you-know-what grew in that industry. I wasn't totally immune to bigger is better.' At the end of his pitch, the Lockheed chairman,

Daniel Tellup, said, 'Bill, that was a hell of a good idea. We gotta do that. We'll accept, with one little exception.' What's that, Anders asked? 'I won't sell, but I'll buy you.' Anders recalls, 'I thought: shit.'

If he was to be true to his word, Anders had to consider selling the fighter-jet division. He asked the experts on his staff about the true value of the division. Then he took the number, multiplied it by 1.5, and gave it to Lockheed. 'He took it.'

He sold this business for $1.5 billion, and it is this step, more than any other, that has fascinated analysts who study the behaviour of top executives. 'What he did is very revealing,' Thorndike says. 'He agreed to sell the business on the spot without hesitation, although not without some regret. Anders made the rational business decision, the one which was consistent with growing per share value, even though it shrank his company to less than half its former size and robbed him of his favourite perk as CEO: the opportunity to fly the company's cutting-edge jets.'

It must have stung for a fighter pilot, I say. 'Oh, it did, yeah.' It was controversial, too, in the defence industry and in the Pentagon. Some air-force top brass took Anders to task for not consulting with them first. One, a four-star general who was running combat command, 'got mad at me. We've never really made up. But I figured we had to do it.' Fortunately, since Anders was by now a major general himself, he did have some credibility in Washington.

By this time only tanks and submarines remained in the company, and by now Anders had the reputation among some people of being nothing more than a liquidator.

Still, he had some friends: the shareholders, who were watching the share price go through the roof. Along the way, and just before the fighter-jet sale, the company and Anders had caught the attention of one investor in particular: Warren Buffett, the man behind Berkshire Hathaway, and perhaps the world's most famous and celebrated investor. The Crown family, which had a major stake in the company, was selling down its stake, and Buffett came in.

Buffett is known for seeing the world simply. I met him once, at a press conference when he was buying a small private-jet business in Europe, and I always remember him describing his investment philosophy to me in light of his ownership of Gillette, the razor company: 'I sleep soundly every night knowing that hair is growing on millions of men's faces and women's legs.' That, in a nutshell, was Buffett: businesses he could under-stand with stable markets. Once interested, he rarely changed anything, instead trusting the management who had attracted him in the first place.

Putting these attitudes into practice, Buffett confounded the Crown family, who controlled General Dynamics, by declining their offer of two seats on the board and instead giving all of his proxies to Anders. Such was Buffett's shareholding by this stage, he had effectively given Anders complete control of the company. 'I didn't flaunt it, but there were a couple of times, particularly when we came to selling the F-16 division,' Anders says. 'Crown was against it. That was our signature product. I said: we're gonna sell it, Lester [Crown], and if it comes down to a proxy fight, you're gonna lose. He looked at me and said: OK. He never really liked me since.' Buffett certainly liked the idea. 'I made Buffett multibillions.'

The two got on well: once, without announcing he was going to do so, he got Buffett to turn up at the last minute at an analyst meeting. 'You could have heard a pin drop. That didn't hurt.' Another time, Anders remembers asking Buffett why he had bought See's Candies, a well-known California-based choc-olate manufacturer. 'I got a new marketing strategy,' Buffett said. 'We're passing the word that See's Candy is a great aphrodisiac.' It became an in-joke, and Buffett took to sending the Anders family See's Candy for Christmas every year. After two years, Anders wrote him a thank-you card. 'Warren. Thanks for the nice box of See's Candy. But with regard to your marketing strategy, I gotta tell ya, my sex life hasn't improved and Valerie's gained 150 pounds.'

Shareholders other than Buffett had plenty of reason to like him too. Having accrued billions of dollars of cash, Anders had a choice: use it to buy other things, or return it to shareholders. Aided by lawyer and accountant Harvey Kapnick, who had been chairman of Arthur Andersen, he chose option two. He did so through three special dividends, equivalent to almost half of the company's entire equity value, tax free. Having done so, they then announced a $1 billion tender to re-purchase 30 per cent of the company's shares. 'My theory was, why should we invest into businesses we don't know, like sewing machines? Let's give it back to the shareholders and let them diversify.' On a similar principle – and doing nothing to improve his reputation as a cold-hearted liquidator – he stopped giving money to charities, a major shift from his predecessor Stan Pace's approach. He did this, remembering something Buffett had once said: 'It's easy to give other people's money away. Give it back and let the shareholders decide.'

Also, Anders had put in an incentive programme by rewarding management and, if they wanted, regular employees with stock. This, like all the other measures, started to push the share price back up again. 'Then,' Anders says, 'it became a runaway.'

From January 1991, when Anders became CEO, to his departure three years later, every dollar of stock had increased sixfold (my own calculations put it at even more than that, but six is the number Anders's records show). That, says Anders, 'is what made me famous, or infamous, depending on what side of the deal you got.' And it is clearly a source of immense pride, perhaps greater than Apollo: alongside the many props of spaceflight in his home are just as many celebrations of business life, featuring on the cover of trade magazines, and throughout the financial press.

Whether you rate Anders's performance probably largely depends on whether you were a shareholder. His tenure also saw a lot of people put out of work, a considerable shrinkage of the company, and a great deal of capital that could have gone on R&D sent back to enrich shareholders instead. But that argument misses the point that, without the restructure, General Dynamics might well have gone to the wall anyway – in which case everyone would have lost their jobs.

Anders's tenure certainly put his predecessor Pace's in the shade, and this clearly became a source of friction. 'It made him look so bad,' Anders says. 'Without me trying to make him look bad. What can you say? For whatever reason, he was dealt a bad hand, and he didn't play a bad hand well. He's never spoken to me since.'

This can no longer be ignored. Listening to Anders's accounts of business life, there are a striking number of anecdotes that involve people who have never spoken to him again. Does it bother him, falling out with people?

Answering this, he first defends the plant closures, in particular one in San Diego. 'I've had employees from San Diego come to me and say: I really hated what you were doing but you made my retirement possible.' He also argues that many competitors who once considered him nothing more than a cynical liquidator ended up doing similar things. 'They all realized that there's a limit to growth in the defence industry. They kinda hate to admit it that this boy upstart, a fighter pilot, got ahead of them. But there's not really a lot of guys who aren't talking to me.'

Instead, he depicts some of his relationships with rival business leaders in something of a frat-humour light, such as with Norm Augustine, the former president and CEO of Lockheed Martin with whom he had something of a battle of words, at one point saying publicly that a cage of marmosets does not equal one gorilla, comparing General Dynamics to Lockheed. Augustine sent him a stuffed gorilla. Anders, with some effort, found a stuffed marmoset – 'it's hard to find a stuffed marmoset' – and sent it to him. Augustine sent another gorilla. At this point Anders heard Augustine was going to the South Pole with Rusty Schweickart, Anders's old friend from Apollo. 'Rusty,' he said, 'I have a classified mission for you.' He gave him a stuffed gorilla and told him to put it at the barber pole marking the South Pole so that Augustine would find it when he got there.

*

The vast improvement in the General Dynamics share price, coupled with Anders's model of remunerating management in stock, had vastly enriched him, and he retired from General Dynamics after just three years. (As a footnote, he also resigned as a board director of Enron in 1992, having become wary of the company's growing interest in derivatives. 'By this time the walnut shells were whizzing around, and I thought: there's not a bean under any one of those walnut shells.' Enron went bankrupt in the aftermath of an accounting fraud in 2001.)

As he looks back now, he thinks leaving NASA turned out for the best. 'If I had stayed, I don't think that would have resulted in our being able to start a museum and a foundation. Valerie's a big wheel on the Smithsonian Institute National Board, and why? Because we can write big cheques. I have to admit it. Both of us will.' But he's also big enough to say that his trajectory has not been by design. 'I wish I could say I laid all that out. Fighter pilots are good: oh shit, here comes a rocket. They gotta make snap decisions, and I made a lot of decisions that had a tremendous effect on both our lives and the family and not thinking about it more than five minutes.'

The money has allowed him to do a lot of other things. Harvey Kapnick had recommended that Anders set up a family foundation. Through it, the family then donated a million dollars to the Smithsonian, which in turn put Valerie on that board. Anders is a little cynical about the title. 'That's a very artful name. It's a board with absolutely no authority. The only responsibility is to get money.' But, recognizing that, he and Valerie clearly enjoy the engagement with one of the world's most extraordinary repositories of learning and history. 'I'm not above using our donations to make a point here and there,' Anders says. 'I'm interested in geology, and the current director of the Smithsonian is a geologist. I make sure that our gift goes to buying him a new super-duper X-ray something or other to measure the ratio of these rocks for ageing, so I can guarantee that my old rock is, indeed, the oldest rock in the world.'

Outside of the Smithsonian, Valerie is emeritus chair of a charity in Olympic Park, and they have founded a museum that recently moved from Billingham to Skagit Regional (Bayview) Airport, on the mainland near the Canadian border, devoted to old aircraft. A little like Lovell's restaurant, this is something of a family business. 'Of our six kids, four of them could care less about the museum. But we have two sons who are definitely interested in aviation, and then maybe their kids would follow on and it would become a long-time family thing.' Most of the planes are still perfectly capable of flight, and Anders himself flies all of them that are maintained to flightworthiness.

What's his favourite? He leans back in his chair to contemplate. 'It's kinda like good-looking women, whether it's blonde or brunette. I like 'em all. Whichever one I'm in. But the Mustang,' he says, 'is the sexiest.'

*

Borman is the one I don't reach. I'm told he and his wife, getting older now, don't venture much from their Montana ranch these days, and when I don't hear back from my interview requests, I don't push it.

Borman's post-Apollo life was another success story, although it involved a lot more suffering than Anders's did. He tells his life story in the book *Countdown*. He worked in the Nixon administration for a while, was sent on goodwill missions to the Soviet Union (successfully, leading to the joint Apollo-Soyuz mission in July 1975) and worldwide in support of POWs in Vietnam (unsuccessfully, receiving a 'vitriolic tongue-lashing that left me shaking' from Indira Gandhi), and joined Eastern Airlines, a stricken airline which he revived with enormous success before eventually being brought low by deregulation and union battles. He approached corporate life with the bull-headed determination that had characterized his NASA years, with similarly polarized outcomes.

*

The very last thing I ask Anders about is the Reno air races, which I have heard he competed in right into his seventies. The Reno races are a legendarily lethal and lawless set of contests between gathered air racers in Nevada. 'If there's not a good crash, people feel cheated,' Anders says. He did compete several times, he tells me, but stopped around 2006. 'About half of those guys are really not very good pilots. All it takes is money to enter, and a pilot's licence.'

When someone crashed a Mustang into the crowd in 2011, killing himself and ten spectators, 'I wasn't surprised. This was just inevitable. I had a couple of guys damn near kill me because they were just crappy pilots doing dumb things.'

'I just did it for fun,' he says, 'and to be able to say I did it.

I probably should have quit sooner.' Knowing how to quit when ahead, to change direction and do something else, appears to have been a vital life skill for Anders.

As my fourth hour of interview draws to a close, he shows me around some of the minutiae of his possessions, the accumulations of an extraordinary life. Here is the Emmy he got for his broadcast from the Moon – 'ridiculous', he says. Here are the lamps in the guest bedroom, one made out of a nuclear fuel rod, the other from Gatling guns. And here on the shelf is the Pete Conrad memorial bottle of wine, with a picture of the gap-toothed third man on the Moon in his mirror shades. There are photos of Anders with numerous presidents over the years: Johnson, Nixon, Carter. Apparently there's also one of him with George W. Bush, but he keeps that over a toilet in his museum.

He touches upon his decision never to sign autographs any more. 'It's kinda sad the way a lot of these guys have been left like fish out of water flopping about, having to sell autographs,' he says. 'I don't blame them for doing it. I just think it's sad that they have to.' As a consequence of his decision, an Anders signature has become one of the most valuable items of Apollo memorabilia you can get.

As I leave, he hands me a photograph of *Earthrise*. It is signed.

9

John McCarthy

The popular imagination recalls John McCarthy blindfolded and chained to a wall of some filthy underground cell in Lebanon, or emerging, beaming, from a VC-10 at RAF Lyneham, but I meet him instead at a Starbucks on Teddington High Street. An exceptionally pleasant human being, he strides over to me with a broad smile and apologizes for being late (he is, at the absolute outside, 25 seconds behind our scheduled meeting time). We talk about the traffic, the high-street shops, and the weather, with the Thames in flood at the bottom of the road. It is possibly the most English introduction ever.

And McCarthy is English – by which I don't mean the obvious fact of his place of birth, nor the affluent middle-class manner we tend to associate with this articulate, well-spoken alumnus of Haileybury School, the Home Counties incarnate. What I mean is that he *belongs* to the English, in that his life and captivity and relationships were appropriated by the nation in a way I can't ever remember seeing before or since.

When John McCarthy was taken captive by Islamic Jihad on the way to Beirut Airport, about to fly home, in April 1986 as a handsome and fresh-faced twenty-nine-year-old, neither he nor anyone else could have expected the brutal duration and

304

manner of his captivity. He would be held, mainly in chains, for five and a half years, denied any communication with the outside world, even when his mother was dying in cruel unawareness of her son's fate. He was beaten, deprived of everything, transported between cells in horrific circumstances, tied and taped and mummified in a scalding metal box beneath a truck for hours at a time. He had a gun held to his head, was threatened frequently with execution, and given false hope of release time and again.

At the time, none of us in the outside world knew this; for several years, the British government and media were privately saying that he and other hostages had been killed shortly after their capture. But as a proxy instead we had Jill Morrell, the pretty and shy but immensely driven young Yorkshirewoman, his girlfriend and sort-of fiancée (one of the many challenges she would face for five years was the fact that they had never formalized any intention to marry, leaving her uncertain of the terms of their relationship and how she should narrate them, particularly once he had been absent for longer than they had ever been together in the first place). Morrell and McCarthy's friends campaigned tirelessly, endlessly, building in the Friends of John McCarthy something so much bigger than a campaign group: a collective of tens of thousands of people fighting for someone they had never met and didn't even know to be alive.

Britain loved the story of the woman left behind and soon they got another love story, too, when the Irishman Brian Keenan was released, having been held in the same cell as McCarthy for almost four years. Intense, intellectual, angry and poetic, Keenan brought with him evocative descriptions of their lives in Lebanon, the support they had drawn from one another, and the agony he had felt in being released first. 'How much freedom can there be for a man,' he said, 'when he leaves one half of himself chained to the wall?' And now, knowing that McCarthy was alive and that people could emerge from this hell intact, the campaign grew louder and wider, even though it was still not clear to whom the appeals should be addressed. A nation wanted to show that it remembered this man, whom almost none of its people had even heard of before his disappearance; and it wanted its fairy-tale ending, with John and Jill reunited. Royal weddings have been less keenly expected.

Five and a half years. The local and world events alone give a sense of the missing, frozen time: the fall of the Berlin Wall, the reunification of Germany, the release of Nelson Mandela, the wedding of Prince Andrew and Sarah Ferguson, the disasters at Zeebrugge, Hungerford, King's Cross, Hillsborough, the arrival in popular consciousness of AIDS, the privatization of British Gas – 'If you see Sid, tell him' –, Eddie the Eagle at the 1988 Winter Olympics, the poll-tax riots, Mad Cow Disease, Teenage Mutant Ninja Turtles, Maradona's Hand of God goal in one World Cup and Gazza's tears at the next one, Ben Johnson's drug-busted 100 metres final at the Seoul Olympics, the Chernobyl disaster, *Robocop, Dead Poet's Society, Ferris Bueller's Day Off, Home Alone, Ghost,* Rick Astley, Kylie and Jason. And, of course, there was the capture of Terry Waite, who was in Lebanon trying to negotiate McCarthy's release. I was fourteen and at school on Merseyside when McCarthy was taken, nineteen and working a summer job in South Carolina when he was released; just pondering the life milestones that happened for me within the intervening years puts in stark relief how long he was gone for, the vast majority of it without any knowledge of what was happening in the world.

And then his release in August 1991, to extraordinary public love but microscopic media scrutiny, which Morrell might have seen coming but which McCarthy, a relative nobody when he vanished, was overwhelmed by. As a nation, all of whom had invested ourselves in his ordeal and release, we felt we owned him. For a while he was a prisoner again, and whether for that or other reasons, the fairy tale failed to reach its commissioned happy ending, and he and Morrell parted company in 1994. It took years, but eventually they both returned to normal life, to the drudgery and routine of getting along.

And this is what fascinates me, and my reason for asking him to speak with me today. When you have spent five and a half years chained to a wall dreaming of freedom, with no way of knowing when, or even if, it ever might happen, how does the reality of it all measure up, when the elation has passed and you are waiting for payday or cleaning the toilet or trying to find a parking space on the school run? Does freedom bring with it a duty to make every day exceptional, something that becomes a burden?

*

McCarthy is still a good-looking man. I realize this is a rather inexact barometer of physical attraction, but he's the only one of my male interviewees whom my neighbour Louise claims to have had a crush on, and several of my female friends agree: the combination of looks and a vulnerable decency seem to have been very appealing to women. With more than twenty-two years having passed since his release, though, he is no longer constantly recognized. We are untroubled as he pulls up a chair next to me, projecting boundless energy, enthusiasm and generosity.

I tell him I don't want to dwell on his captivity itself, because it has been so comprehensively explored by a whole canon of hostage literature: his and Morrell's *Some Other Rainbow*, published with a sense of cathartic cleansing two years after his release in 1993, Brian Keenan's extraordinary *An Evil Cradling*, Terry Waite's *Taken On Trust* and a host of other memoirs from the

Americans with whom they were held. The one thing I do wonder about that time is just how he pictured freedom, and what he thought he would do with it when it came.

'I suppose the obvious thought of freedom was the ability to stand up and walk out of a room,' he says. He never had this in his five and a half years, not once; no prison yard for daily exercise, nor any of the other relative luxuries afforded to Western prisoners, not least a trial or even a crime to warrant having one in the first place. 'But in terms of what I was going to do, the main thing was getting back to my life, and hoping I could pick it up.

'I had no idea what had happened to my then-girlfriend Jill Morrell. And what about going back to work? In the last year of captivity we had a radio, and I heard about the internet. Particularly in our world as journalists –' McCarthy was a producer for the news agency WTN and had been a stand-in head of the Beirut bureau for a month when he was taken – 'communications and satellite television had moved into a totally different orbit. And I thought: I'm going to be so far behind I won't be able to catch up, and they won't be able to employ me.' That concerned him, but his chief ambition was nothing more than normality. 'The main thing was to ignore the last five years and pick up where I left off: doing quite well at work, engaged to a beautiful woman, everything happy, lovely mum and dad and brother at home.'

From his own perspective, he felt he was weathering his captivity quite well, and could even perceive advantages in it. 'I had obviously changed, because I had experienced the terror of being captive and chained up and kept underground in various places and being physically abused, but that had probably changed me for the good in terms of being a journalist,' he says. 'I had experienced rather more than I had as a happy middle-class boy from the Home Counties. I had suddenly seen how other people live, or those in Lebanon, and Palestinians in refugee camps [because of a month reporting on the ground before his kidnapping]; suddenly it made sense. It meant I could approach what their life was like rather than just thinking: that looks terrible. I felt an empathy with them.'

So the big question was how the rest of the world would receive him. And when freedom did come, how realistic was it for him to pick up where he had left off?

'When I came out, I thought, right: I've dealt with the hostage thing. And, to a large degree, I suppose I had. I had become, not used to it, but able to cope with it, and in a strange sense there was an advantage to being held longer, because one had to fight one's battles with oneself, and also with the people holding us. Having found the strength from within, and with in particular Brian Keenan the strength to stand up to the guards – occasionally going on hunger strike, those sorts of things – put one in a different realm of experience. I could still be terri-fied in those experiences, but I felt I had dealt with it: dealt with myself, dealt with the environment and all the people in it.

'But coming out . . . It obviously wasn't that simple.'

*

By the time of his release, McCarthy had learned about his mother's death; the American hostages Terry Anderson and Tom Sutherland had had access to a radio and heard about it, and when the two Americans were later put in the same cell as McCarthy, they broke the news to him more than a year after it had happened. He had processed that as best he could. The challenges, instead, were not within his family but the broader population of his homeland.

'There was this thing about being so famous,' he says. 'Which I got a hint of, because we had a radio, so I knew about the campaign Jill was running with other friends; I knew this was a nationwide thing, that people were marching in Trafalgar Square on the anniversary of my kidnapping. And I thought: fucking hell, that's amazing, who are all these thousands of people?

'My friends,' he says, 'I could think: well, that's lovely. But there were tens of thousands of people around the country and I still couldn't translate that into meaning, that therefore when I walk down Teddington High Street everyone would be going: good lord, it's John McCarthy. I'd never been famous at all before, I'd never done anything to be famous, and suddenly it was quite a shock. That was slightly unnerving.'

Public attention was one thing, but it gained its clearest expression through the focus of the media, and most acutely the tabloid press. The *Sun*, in particular, had embraced McCarthy's cause late in his incarceration, and to a degree every other media outlet had too. So there was a sense of owing, and a headlong pursuit of the human-interest story, specifically he and Jill being reunited.

'The focus of the media shifted from respecting Jill as a campaigner to seeing her as just the pretty girlfriend, and treating me as this weirdo – well, not a weirdo, more of a hero person – and her as the beautiful woman who had been waiting.' He encountered the paparazzi for the first time, and combined with the oddity of being returned to life in the first place, this made for a doubled burden.

'I was getting better in terms of being able to put the hostage experience behind me, but steadily, not immediately,' he says. 'It took years, probably, for it to leach out of the system where I could talk about it without it . . . not upsetting me, but without it just being there. It took that long until I was absolutely living in the present again without a hangover.'

Some of the challenges of release were practical and physical. I have read that he lost his depth perception through having never looked at anything further away than a cell wall for more than half a decade, and I ask him about this.

'Yeah, that was very weird. I remember just after being released, the moment after, I was handed over by the kidnappers to Syrian military intelligence in Beirut. And I was then driven to Damascus to be publicly liberated. But driving through the Bekaa Valley, which I had never been to . . .' He stops, and laughs. 'Well, I had been there, but in the back of a truck. Or in the bottom of a truck.' He is smiling broadly, which if you have ever read his or Keenan's descriptions of the ordeal of being entombed in these truck-slung boxes, 'made to endure slow and crippling death in this tight heart darkness' as Keenan put it, is quite incredible. 'We were driving through, and I was thinking: this is beautiful, but how weird. The cliffs were like this four-storey building across the road –' he points across the street at a high Victorian shop front – 'and they were just going up for a thousand feet. I thought: that's quite odd, these cliffs they've got here. I had lost the sense of perspective.'

He couldn't make sense of it for a little while. 'It wasn't until two or three weeks later when me, Jill and Chris [Pearson, another friend] were in Wales, and I was looking across this valley and thinking: how weird that some of those cows are big, but some are really small. I wonder what special breed of cows they've got to make them really small? And then something in my brain went: no no no, they're just further away! They're not all on this cliff in front of you. Some are 300 yards away and some are half a mile away. And I realized that must have been what it was in that valley in Lebanon.

'It was, I suppose, like getting back on a bike. As soon as my brain clicked on that it was like going through the hard drive until you find it.'

And as he understood this, he came to another realization. 'Christ! I've been driving a fucking car.'

311

Indeed, his friends had been somewhat apprehensive of letting him have the wheel. 'I remember driving down the M4 on that Wales trip and saying something like: it's quite weird looking at cars through the rear-view mirror. And Chris saying: yeah. But don't. Look through the windscreen.'

Other physical adjustments were troubling, and poignant. Very soon after his release, while staying with his father and brother in some other borrowed place far from the media, he met the fiancée of Terry Anderson, the longest held of the hostages. Madeleine had been pregnant with Anderson's baby when he was taken; Anderson would not meet his daughter, Sulome, until she was almost seven, having kept his photo under her pillow and kissed it every night before she went to sleep. (Perhaps remarkably, Sulome now works as a journalist in Beirut.) When McCarthy met Madeleine and Sulome, Anderson was still inside. 'And I was left with this terrible but wonderful responsibility of meeting the families.'

'Happily,' he says, 'with those I had been held with, I could genuinely say they're in good shape. But I was very conscious that they were looking at me thinking: what's our boy going to be like? So I was desperately trying to appear compos mentis.' Madeleine and Sulome had brought with them a series of photos of Anderson, most of which had been released by Islamic Jihad over the years alongside demands for the release of prisoners in Kuwait, and they asked McCarthy which of the pictures Anderson today most resembled. He pointed to one, and they were delighted: the picture had been taken just before Anderson was kidnapped.

Pleased to be of help, McCarthy decided to spend some time alone with little Sulome. 'I was completely useless with kids at that stage: I'd never had any, no nephews, no nieces. I'm still quite freaked out generally. So when she said, let's go and look at these ponies in the paddock, I was grateful.' But there was a problem: walking to the paddock meant crossing a patch of modestly undulating pasture. It was the first uneven ground he had walked on since 1986. 'I was suddenly thinking: this isn't flat. What's all this about? All I had done was walk on concrete.' He reaches down and taps the floor of the Starbucks. 'That's all I'd been used to. And now I'm here wearing shoes, which I also hadn't done for five years, and I was terrified I was going to fall over. It was like walking on the Moon.' Knowing that if he fell he would frighten Sulome about the condition her father would return in, he managed to keep it together.

It's remarkable, I say, what the human mind and body can be conditioned to accepting. 'Yes, and I think it's fascinating. I suppose one's conscious that it happens to caged animals, and to people who are held longer than I have been, particularly in solitary confinement, pacing up and down. Luckily, that was one of those things where I just had to practise, and it was there again. But it was a weird moment.'

*

What strikes me about McCarthy's return, as distinct from that of the other hostages, was the extraordinary pressure on his relationship with Morrell. Keenan had been single when captured, and his case was largely advanced by his sisters in his absence; Anderson's fiancée, with the child, clearly represented a relationship one would expect to be resumed, even if they hadn't formally married; Sutherland and Waite were married and their wives were waiting for their release. Only McCarthy and Morrell had the sense of a story at mid-point, with such high hopes of a public resolution. They did end up together again, lasting the better part of three years, and even that seems miraculous. How on earth, I ask him, does a couple deal with such an intense level of national engagement in your relationship, no matter how well-intentioned?

'I think we did recognize that it was absolutely well-intentioned, by everybody,' he says. 'We also realized that from the tabloid media point of view, it was just a good story for them. Therefore they got quite agitated that we didn't give them the fairy-tale ending immediately, and therefore their readers thought it was slightly out of order that we weren't doing the decent thing.' He laughs; although McCarthy has long since moved on, marrying the photographer and book editor Anna Ottewill in 1999, he appears comfortable talking about Morrell. 'The snappers were after us, until we did a press conference after a few weeks and they sort of backed off. But, for me, it felt like I was being hunted again. There were photographers everywhere and I felt uncomfortable about it. There was a background sense that I will feel safe when I get back home, off the streets. Not a sense of being in danger, just somewhat vulnerable.'

Yet he doesn't blame that scrutiny and intrusion for the fact that they didn't last the course. 'As time went by they were no longer interested in us, so it did get easier. But it didn't actually put any pressure on us to make a decision. I don't think we felt: well, we'd better make our mind up. We were mature enough to think: well, let's see how this goes, and we're not going to talk to anybody about it.

'We lived together for another two or three years and then ended it amicably, but that became normal, because we were back in the real world, rather than as a celebrity couple,' he says. 'Actually, whether it's because of what happened or because, like lots of relationships, they just don't work out over the years, I don't know. But we ended up going our separate ways and remained friendly.' Are they still in touch? 'Yeah. I don't see her that often, once or twice a year, but yes, we are still very close friends, and always will be, I hope. From my point of view,

I still love her as a friend.' One has to feel sad for Morrell: she never settled or had children, having spent five important years of her late twenties and early thirties in limbo. The two wrote their book together – it takes the format of McCarthy writing a section, then Morrell writing a section, each covering their own experiences during a particular timeframe – and did not feel able to read each other's halves until some time later. 'When I did, I just thought: what an extraordinary achievement. I realized how much she sacrificed for me, particularly half the time when she couldn't be sure I was alive. Eternal respect, and eternal love and gratitude.'

Even amid the intrusion, there were moments of dry humour. One time the press tracked him down to a house somewhere, where Terry Anderson and his other daughter from a previous marriage, Gabrielle, happened to be staying with him. 'Terry answered the door, and being gung-ho and American, he said: what on Earth are you guys doing? Why don't you fuck off and leave him alone?' The journalists, failing completely to recognize the longest-held of all the Lebanon hostages, asked Anderson if he was McCarthy's agent, thus missing out on a perfectly good story.

*

In the manner of mid-morning Starbucks worldwide, a troop of mums with pre-school children has moved into the seats next to ours, and their number seems to multiply for the next hour. At one stage a girl of no more than two, a dummy in her mouth, totters round and stares at McCarthy with the wide-eyed and unabashed gaze of a toddler. The thought occurs: McCarthy must not have seen a child for five and a half years.

I ask him about what came next after the book, and how he returned to work.

'Because of the celebrity, people started out saying: would you like to be interviewed? And then: would you like to do interviews?' Although he was a journalist, this was new to him: his background was as a producer, not a reporter, and his job had been to fix local crews and arrange satellite transmission. But people were enormously supportive, training him on the job, and steadily a number of great opportunities came his way. One of his closest friends is Nick Toksvig, whose sister, Sandi, is a famous entertainer; in 1995, she and McCarthy sailed round the coast of Britain and wrote a book about the experience, making a TV series along the way. He was hired to present BBC World Service programmes such as *Outlook*, and gained wide acclaim in radio.

He knew where the work was being driven from. 'All of those things came about on the back of my experience largely, but certainly on the back of the celebrity thing.' Equally, though, he was good at it, and worked hard until he wasn't getting gigs as an ex-hostage but as an accomplished broadcaster. 'I learned the skills, so more work came in, TV and more and more radio. I began to think that, although I fully accept I am always going to be a former Beirut hostage even though I'm however many years older, the work would be completely unrelated to it. More and more over the years I believe I haven't got this job because I'm famous or because as a hostage I'm a good peg for a story, but because they think I'm good at the job in hand. And that feels good. Great, in fact.

'I know being a hostage is what people will always remember me for, and that's fine. No matter how much older I am, it's no problem.'

He's also written several books. Aside from *Some Other Rainbow* and the sailing book with Toksvig, McCarthy wrote *Between Extremes* with Brian Keenan, a much-loved account of a trip the two former hostages took to travel the length of Chile, realizing a dream they had outlined when given access to an incomplete set of the *Encyclopaedia Americana* in their Beirut cell after their conditions dramatically improved in 1990. The plan in its entirety had involved setting up 'Paddygonia Enterprises' in Chilean Patagonia to corner the world market in yak products. There was a less well-received book about his Irish ancestry, *A Ghost Upon Your Path*, and then, in 2012, a new one, called *You Can't Hide The Sun*.

This last book is fascinating on a number of levels. To start with, it's his most ambitious attempt at producing something important that is not about himself, but instead is concerned with adding to the available knowledge about the Middle East. Tightly focused, it tells the story of Palestinians in Israel – that is, not those in the West Bank or Gaza, but Arabic people who live (and have always lived) within what today is Israel proper. They make up 20 per cent of the national population, though are little talked about in the them-versus-them popular narrative of Israel against the Palestinian Territories. A work of study and journalism, it tells the story through detailed interviews with Israeli Palestinians who have lived through considerable traumas and indignities over the last sixty years. In his earliest books, McCarthy wrote about wanting to prove himself as a journalist, and one imagines a study like this is exactly what he aspired to.

But what's more interesting to me is how heavily McCarthy takes the Palestinian, Arab position in this book – when he was imprisoned by Arabs, and probably in some cases Palestinians, in a period of intense personal suffering. There are few people in the world who would be more justified in having appalling things to say about the Arabic Middle East, yet he takes their side with considerable zeal.

The book enters our conversation because I had it out on the table to give him a clue who I was if I couldn't recognize him. He points at it now. 'That book was me feeling I could write a story that I was very interested in and very concerned to tell, having worked out a way of telling it.' Enthused and in his element, he is talking about 200 words per minute now, gesturing, focused, which is just as well, because the tribe of pre-school kids behind him is swelling in number and volume by the second. 'Using that, and then painting the scene to make it approachable: that's what I'm trying to do with my radio and my writing. It's not academic, it's about getting ordinary people to talk.'

I mention the surprise of seeing him so strongly present the Palestinian view despite his own background.

'I think it was because, although the situation of being held hostage was extremely abusive – total denial of my human rights, total illegitimate removal of me, removal from my loved ones of their real freedom because I was banged up – I did come to realize that things were not straightforward. I was very lucky to be held with Brian Keenan in particular: he had interesting insights, having grown up in Northern Ireland, particularly Belfast, during the Troubles as a very politically minded young man, and a sensitive, intellectual guy. So we came to realize that whilst we hated one or two of these guards because they were vicious bastards, it was only one or two. And while they were all responsible for putting a chain on me, for putting a gun to my head, for making us wear blindfolds when they were in the cell, let's step back from that. I'm interested that most of these guys are not abusing us.'

Given almost infinite time to consider their position, the two hostages came to try to think of the guards' perspective and motivations, particularly those who were, within the absurd parameters of the situation, behaving with a moderate amount of humanity. 'On a psychological level, these guys are behaving as we would understand to be their norm. So what's their story? We have arrived here in Lebanon ten years into their civil war. These guys are about twenty. So since they've been ten, their experience has been chaos, horrible chaos, brutal, brutal lunacy, civil war that you and I will never understand, where suddenly your dads will shoot each other because of political reasons or because your dad's a Christian and his dad's a Muslim. Most people would think of [the guards] as monsters, and certainly the outside world would depict them as Islamic terrorists. But we would think: that's not really true, is it? They're just young men who bizarrely seem to have, for the most part, some sense of human decency.'

This seems an exceptionally generous appraisal of people who served his food on the floor, caused him to have to take a shit on a bit of newspaper in front of another man, tuned a radio to static and hung it outside his cell door on full volume for weeks at a time, and countless other unnecessary torments. But, even so, the recollection of some remaining humanity in his captors informed his career choices ever after.

'It became more clear to me as I returned to the Middle East, and I thought it was really important to recognize, as it is in any conflict,' he says. He realized, too, that the Lebanese who had been holding him were the underdogs in Lebanese society up to the civil war, and the sense of an underdog came to have some resonance for him. He recalled, too, in the brief month in Lebanon before his capture, that he had visited Palestinian refugee camps. 'I recall feeling almost like a voyeur, and then realizing: home, home, home,' he says. 'You were asking me what I was thinking about in captivity, and it was home. What must it be like, when you've grown up and your parents and your grandparents are talking about home as somewhere else, somewhere you can't go, someone bombing you, where the country doesn't welcome you? Bloody hell, that's an extraordinary state of affairs. All I've got to do is survive this place and get on a plane and fly back to little old England, to Essex where my parents were then, or Camden Town where Jill was, and

I will be safe and sound. Nobody's going to get me in my homeland.'

Israeli Palestinians, then, were the ultimate underdogs, and so their story appealed to him. He talks about their background and treatment, the way that people in the West Bank call them the '48ers', in reference to the year of Israel's foundation. To my great surprise, he tells me he has read an article I wrote while in Palestine several years earlier, and recalls my comments about the then-rising wall between Israel and the West Bank, making frequent incursions into Palestinian territory. 'Tragically, it hasn't changed, except that the wall is right across the street now.' McCarthy is such a pleasant and genial man, with such immaculate diction, that I am briefly put in mind of that internet trope about English national security levels being raised from 'miffed' to 'peeved' or even 'a bit cross'. But now he describes the wall as 'disgusting', and absolutely hisses the word, the most passionate expression of the interview. It is very clear what the situation means to him.

Could he have written this book, or have wanted to do so, without his experience?

'Obviously one's life experiences affect everything. You know that as a journalist: it affects the way one conducts an interview, an ability to empathize. But I think the book was driven by the undertow with having experienced injustice and wanting to try to understand where that was coming from. Coming home and being celebrated as someone who had survived that adversity, the assumption was that I would be anti-Arab, but I think without that background experience I would not have been so drawn to write about it. I would hope that it will encourage a few thousand to read this book and have a better understanding.' It didn't go down terribly well in Israel – one blogger in Tel Aviv said that 'maybe this guy should have been left chained to a radiator' – but he says that in readings to Jewish groups in London, the response has been largely positive, with just a few walk-outs and claims of anti-Semitism, but far more people grateful for a balanced work on a complicated subject.

*

McCarthy's understanding of the Middle East is now clearly both nuanced and passionate, but I wonder just how long it took him to figure out who exactly had taken him, and who behind the scenes had finally secured his release.

'Ah. Now that's another story that I was very slow to come to terms with, embarrassingly so.' Behind him, a toy car flies through the air inches behind his head and hits a window, where it sticks, anchored by a porridge of considerable adhesive tenacity. 'When I was first taken, I couldn't imagine who I could have been taken by. I didn't know much about the Middle East, and I thought: who could hate Britain enough to take me? It must have been the Palestinians, that would make sense, rather than the shadowy Islamic groups like Islamic Jihad who were taking Americans.' That theory was scuppered when they found themselves in the same underground prison as the Americans. But it wasn't until he came home that it became clear that the real captors were probably Hezbollah, the Shia militant group in Lebanon, more powerful by far than the national army.

Of more lasting concern to McCarthy is his belated recognition of the man who was probably most instrumental in getting him out. His book, *Some Other Rainbow,* makes no mention of an Italian man called Giandomenico Picco, who was undersecretary general at the UN under Javier Perez de Cuellar during McCarthy's captivity. 'It is a tragic, criminal omission. I didn't realize he brokered the deal that put everything in place so that we did come out.'

Picco's UN life, lived largely behind the scenes, was extraordinary.

He is credited with brokering the peace that ended the Iran–Iraq War, and from that experience decided that the key to the release of the hostages was to start in Tehran. He shuttled between there, Jerusalem, Tel Aviv, Washington, London, Damascus, Beirut and countless other places besides, attempting to bring the great many interested parties to some sort of common ground. This was tortuous.

'But what I didn't realize was the day I was handed over, the day I was looking at those cliffs in the Bekaa Valley, he was walking out at night on to the streets of West Beirut. He walked out of the Iranian Embassy, turned left, and turned right, as per prior agreement – to be kidnapped. The gang that had held me picked him up and took him and quizzed him.' He would do this every time a hostage was released, in order to discuss with them the next steps: right, McCarthy's out, what's the next thing? 'And every time, he was completely alone. He never saw them. Sometimes they'd make him wear a blindfold, or they would wear ski masks, or sit behind a screen. He put himself at enormous risk, again and again.' He did it nine times, achieving the release of eleven Western hostages and dozens of Lebanese who had been detained by Israelis in southern Lebanon. And he had a young boy at home, and knew that if any of these meetings ended in captivity, his son would suffer just as much as he would, maybe more.

Picco's book on this time, *Man Without a Gun*, is exhausting enough to read, so the idea of actually living his life is unthinkable. It depicts an endless morass of flights, no sleep, negotiations going round in circles, intractable positions, blindfolds, of being shoved face first into the floors of speeding cars, of top diplomacy and day trips to Libya and midnight rendezvous with Israeli agents at checkpoints in the Golan Heights. If there's a second volume of this book, I'll seek him out, if only to discuss a line in one of the closing chapters, just after the last hostage,

Terry Anderson, has been released and told him: 'My God, I really want to kiss you.' This is the line: 'Life usually goes in one direction after such an emotional climax, and that's downhill.'

McCarthy later met Picco while filming a documentary on hostage negotiators, and learned a great deal more about him. The two men came to share a view that most parties in even the most apparently atrocious behaviour are, at heart, human. Picco told him about the last time he was driven around Beirut, and put his hand on the arm of the man next to him, who he believed (he couldn't see) was Imad Mughniyeh, the military mastermind of Hezbollah who would later die in a 2008 car bomb. 'He said the guy was shaking like a leaf. He said he recognized this guy's actions were deplorable, but he wasn't doing them for personal gain. He was – Giandomenico had a great expression for it – a misguided patriot. This guy wasn't really full of bravado; he thought he was doing the right thing and this was the way to do it.'

This chimed with McCarthy. 'I was really struck by that. It so echoed the thing I had about these guys: terrible, terrible stuff, but within the context of the world they had grown up in, this is what they thought. Nobody was good in this, inside or outside.'

*

As McCarthy's acclaim as a broadcaster grew in the years after his release, and as he focused more and more on the Middle East, he occasionally found himself back in the orbit of the people who must have been at some level responsible for his captivity. He went back to Lebanon in 2004, partly for a sense of moving on, and partly for an assignment on Shia Muslims. While there, he interviewed Hassan Nasrallah, the leader of Hezbollah.

'He always denies responsibility,' McCarthy says. 'But when I interviewed Nasrallah, I asked him: what about the hostage situation? He said: Hezbollah was always working very hard to ensure the release.'

He laughs wryly, as a child shrieks behind him at a pitch that, no word of a lie, causes a faint ripple in my coffee. Having pitied McCarthy earlier for not seeing a child for five years, I'm beginning to think he got the better end of the deal. 'It was very clever wording. He didn't say we did do it, but he didn't say we didn't do it. It's like saying: of course a kidnapper also wants to negotiate the release of hostages, that's why they took them in the first place.'

During the same trip, McCarthy was with a local journalist in Baalbek, a Shia-dominated town famed for its Roman ruins in the Bekaa Valley, where McCarthy was very likely held for at least a part of his captivity. While there, he was walking round a pretty park in the centre of town, and noticed a fleet of cars going round them at the edge of the park: three jeeps, a couple of Mercedes. He asked the journalist: what are those cars doing? And he said, 'It's your friends. They've come to take a look at you.'

The inference appeared to be that they were his old guards. He felt safe, he said, knowing that his meetings with Hezbollah had been approved to the very highest level, and was assured by his fixer that the people in the cars would not try anything, nor even risk attempting to speak with him. Emboldened, and seeing one car had a window down, McCarthy bent down as they passed and gave a cheery wave. 'And the convoy raced off.'

There is a part of me that thinks this might be the most British behaviour in human history.

He enjoyed his return to Lebanon. 'That experience of feeling the chill again in the southern summers of Beirut, going to Baalbek, seeing this beautiful country more than I had ever seen it, obviously. I could go into the Christian heartlands now, which I couldn't do in those days. And now I was seeing it as a free man, with a sense that: they're not interested in me, except as a bloke who was once here. I'm allowed to come here.'

It is possible to forgive his captors?

'I still remain angry that they never let my mother know about me. They knew my dad was appealing for news when she was dying. I didn't know that, I was completely incommunicado at that point, but subsequently I learned because the Americans had a radio. They knew she was ill. All they had to do was come in, click, and release a statement from me with a photograph holding the *Daily Star* [a Lebanese paper] with a date on it. Then she could have died knowing I was alive. And I don't know why they didn't do that. I don't think they were monstrous, so I cannot understand. I would like to ask that question. Why would somebody not do that? It was a completely unnecessary cruelty on top of the fact that they had taken her son away.'

It is deeply moving to hear this, but he looks very calm as he says it; it's clear that twenty years have allowed him to process a great deal of emotion and to deal with it. Sadly, he has had more to recover from since his release, as both his father and brother died young. His father passed of cancer in 1994, barely three years after John's release, half the time he'd been captive. Brother Terence, frequently mentioned in his memoirs, followed. It seems a further injustice, as if there hadn't been enough already, that he's had to bear these losses so early.

'But in terms of forgiving them? Forgiveness is an important part of many people's faiths, and the Christian tradition I grew up with, but I don't feel I have a need to forgive. People used to say: don't you feel terribly bitter? I said I feel angry, yes, but the world has changed for me and I've been lucky with the way it panned out. Work is good, I've moved on, I'm married with a little girl, and I'm not going to say my life was ruined by it. It was blighted, for a little while, and perhaps towards the end my mother's life was ruined by it, but everyone else has come through it all right. If I'm bitter, I'm still a hostage to them.'

I ask the question that fascinates me most: after dreaming of freedom for so long, is there a pressure that every day has to be exceptional?

'No, I think the ordinary McCarthy returned, who is still someone who is a terrible procrastinator.' He smiles. 'I'm getting better. I mean, this morning, I thought: oh, I'm going to meet Chris. A year or two ago, this would have been the day's event, then I'd better go home and think. Whereas this morning I was emailing some radio clips to put a voice reel together, was in touch with my producer about a trip to Kurdistan for a radio documentary, I took Lydia [his daughter] to school. The procrastinator is still tempted, though.

'I don't think I ever really felt that pressure. I keep thinking, what have I done in all those years since? I vowed when I was locked up that I would read more books so that if, horribly, I should get caught up again, I'll have something more to occupy my mind. I've been able to travel a lot more and learned more about the world, but I haven't read all that I would have liked to have done, or watched all the movies.'

Still, being able to relax is not to be overlooked; it's an achievement, in fact, given that there must be so many other temptations for someone released from ordeal, not least the allure of alcohol. 'Initially it was much easier to go and have too many drinks,' he says. 'I think that is probably quite common. And it carried on for quite a long time. But at the same time, I was beginning to work again. That gradual process of relaxing into my life and thinking I can do what I wanted to do wasn't really restricted by captivity. I wasn't that confident or ambitious in my own right before either.'

*

I ask if he's still in touch with the other hostages, and he speaks of them with great affection. Keenan is the one he's most closely linked to, and he says they are still very close; Keenan now lives in Dublin with his wife and two boys. Of Terry Waite, McCarthy says, 'I've got great affection and enormous respect for him, on two counts: first of all he put himself into that position for me, and also for his honesty in recognizing that he got in a muddle and was foolhardy about it. Unbelievable respect for the man to survive four years in solitary confinement. Four months would send me insane.' McCarthy is also in regular contact with Terry Anderson. 'With these three in particular, we understood each other best in captivity. The understanding we had and the responsibility we took for each other, and a sense of humour that we really shared – we had to teach the American the sense of humour, obviously, but once he got it, he could understand that I was hilariously funny – I suppose it was an emotional, intellectual thing which for me happened quite naturally.'

One thing the public have always liked in the McCarthy–Keenan relationship – what these days would no doubt be labelled a bromance – is the way they were unfathomably rude to one another as an anchor to their friendship. McCarthy still relishes the thought today. 'Anderson was intrigued by Brian and me: Brian's intellect, a poetic soul, a background in the Troubles of Northern Ireland; and how we got on, Brian a man with Republican national leanings in terms of the Irish political situation, and me a Home Counties public schoolboy. We were so rude to each other but thought it was hilarious. And the Americans used to think: Brian's going to go bonkers, he's going to start hitting him! Did you hear what he just called him! The Englishman's gone mad! And then Brian would look at me and roar with laughter. They couldn't understand it at all.'

Do you still speak to each other that way now? 'Yes!' He sounds triumphant. 'Yes, we do. It's great.' But last time they met, when Keenan was over in England with his wife, Audrey, they all went out for dinner and nobody mentioned Lebanon once. 'There was so much else to talk about.'

He was less close with other hostages. He says he 'lost touch fairly quickly' with Sutherland, and he was known to be upset that Sutherland had participated in a controversial Granada TV dramatization of the hostages' ordeal so soon after their release. Frank Reed, apparently troubled with the worst demons of all the hostages, has since died.

Along the way, McCarthy has been absorbed into the zeitgeist of British culture and society. Stiff Little Fingers wrote a song about him. Linus Roache played him in a film. So did Colin Firth. The Hull University student union bar is named after him. And, perhaps the ultimate badge of honour, David Brent refers to him in *The Office* while lobbying his agent for a spot on *Parkinson*. 'He had that guy in Lebanon who spent years chained to a radiator, what did he do?' moans Brent to his agent. 'Nothing! He was chained to a radiator!'

When I mention this, McCarthy leans back in his chair and laughs. 'I think that's brilliant. Funnily enough, I was invited on Michael Parkinson's radio programme after that, and referred to the fact that this mad Ricky Gervais character had said all I'd done was be chained to a radiator for five years, and he [Parkinson] hadn't heard it. That was quite fun. Friends were saying, did you know you're in *The Office*? How cool is that?'

Better still, he says, is a scene in *Father Ted* in which the priests have pet hamsters in a cage, and ponder what to call them. Noting their captivity, they settle on Keenan and McCarthy. 'That's brilliant!' McCarthy says, with what looks like real delight. 'Forever, we are a real footnote.'

Since he's mentioned *Father Ted*, I tell him about a scene I had been reminded of earlier when McCarthy was talking about losing his depth perception while staring at cows. There is a scene in a caravan while Ted tries to explain exactly this problem to moronic Father Dougal, pointing in turn to some small plastic cows, then a herd of real cows outside the window. 'OK, one last time,' he says. 'These are small. But the ones out there are far away. Small. Far away.' Dougal can't get it. Hearing that his own experience of sensory incompetence has been mirrored in an Irish sitcom seems to sit well with McCarthy. 'Brilliant. That's brilliant.'

*

The interesting thing about the Friends of John McCarthy was the fact that the vast majority of them had never met him. Their devotion towards his cause was admirable, and said something about British society at the time. But I've often wondered how he must have felt upon his release, encountering all of these strangers who lobbied for him without him having asked. Does it become challenging to feel you owe something to people you don't even know?

'When I first heard of the Friends of John McCarthy, I assumed it was just . . . my friends,' he says. So when, in the late stages of his captivity, he had access to a radio and heard a World Service broadcast, in which a correspondent said the Friends of John McCarthy were altering British policy, he was perplexed. 'I thought: what's that all about? I heard of the campaign with thousands of people marching. And I thought: what have my friends been telling the rest of these people about me? Who do they think I am? I was humbled, but also slightly wary of it.

'Then coming home and being treated with so much respect and adulation, as a hero character, I did find odd. But I don't remember anyone ever giving me the impression that I should be saying thank you.' He remembers one old university friend telling him that, alongside all the effort, they had a lot of fun too, socially. 'It wasn't all doom and gloom. That was a huge relief. So I never did feel overburdened by all that. I did feel confused by it, but gradually that went away.'

He recalls speaking to Keenan, who had got out a year earlier than him and had already dealt with all these strange events. McCarthy asked him: what is it, who do people think I am? Keenan told him, 'We have been somewhere nobody could imagine: terrifying, chained up by Middle East terrorists, in this alien environment, terrified, abused physically. Nobody knows what that's like. But we're normal blokes. Ordinary little blokes. And we've survived. So people look at us and think: that's my mate. That's my boyfriend, or my son, or my uncle, or my colleague. So we're everyman, which we are, because we're ordinary people. It's sort of like they're looking at you and they think they know you, and they think: we could have got through that. I can understand that.'

McCarthy is, after Nadia Comaneci, the second-youngest person to be interviewed in this book; he is fifty-seven when we meet and has such boundless energy that it is clear he has a great deal more to do. He is about to head to Kurdistan, after which he will do the Dubai literary festival, and has just been in Budapest, and speaking on a Cunard cruise. What are his ambitions now?

'Still to see more of the world,' he says, and then talks about his eight-year-old daughter and his ambitions to encourage her to see the world too, 'and to understand that people are different, and weird things happen'. That includes, he says, helping her to understand that the people who held him hostage 'are bad men on one level, but it's not quite so simple'. He is delighted to have become a parent, which he did in his fiftieth year. 'I'm so glad we did. It's utterly, utterly . . .' Uncharacteristically, he tails off. 'When we talked about perspective earlier, I realize that the ultimate perspective has come from watching a young person develop, grow up, and to see within that person me as a young person, learning stuff.

'Oh, and my other ambition is to read some of those bloody books I still haven't quite got to.'

He asks me about my book, about work travel, about my family, and seems genuinely interested. We have been going for almost an hour longer than the time he had committed to – so long that the pre-schoolers have gone, leaving a trail of debris behind them that McCarthy, when he finally turns and glimpses it, describes ashen-faced as 'utter carnage' – and it is time to wrap up. 'Right m'darlin', time to go,' he says, and rises to his feet.

As we leave he reiterates one point that he has clearly been able to believe after twenty years of thought and reflection. 'Ultimately,' he says, 'I think I found a better perspective because of that experience than if I had caught that plane home from Beirut in the spring of '86.'

10

Ray Wilson

You will have seen the famous picture, now a statue too. Wembley Stadium, 30 July 1966, and England has just won the World Cup. There's Bobby Moore, all proud and blond and handsome, raised on the shoulders of his teammates, the Jules Rimet trophy held easily aloft in his right hand. To one side there's West Ham's Martin Peters, the ahead-of-his-time complete midfielder who had scored England's second in the victory. Taking some of Bobby's weight is Geoff Hurst, the hero, the hat-trick man. And the shorter guy on the right of the picture, the one bearing most of Bobby's weight, his shoulder up the great man's left arse cheek? That's Ray Wilson.

You don't remember Ray? That's no surprise. The average football fan would get through the whole of that historic side before recalling him. Aside from Moore, Hurst and Peters, they'd remember brilliant Bobby Charlton, and his granite-stock defender brother Jack; small and squeaky Alan Ball, who had the game of his life, or gap-toothed gurning Nobby Stiles, apparently the antithesis of a skilful athlete but in fact peerless in his position; the genius goalkeeper Gordon Banks and the record-breaking Liverpool forward Roger Hunt; and Wilson's fellow full-back George Cohen. They'd likely remember Jimmy

Greaves, who was dropped for the game, and Alf Ramsey, the manager who dropped him, first.

If you don't remember Wilson, there's a reason for that. While most of the others stayed in some way connected with the game, either as managers or club directors or just wheeled out for ceremonial occasions with the everlasting glow of a national treasure, Wilson more than any of them turned his back on football. He became, instead, an undertaker, and a good and successful one, in Huddersfield, West Yorkshire, and eventually retired nearby. He went from inspiring people to burying them. When I heard that, I decided he was the footballer I wanted to have in the book.

England's World Cup victory, it seems to me, has a role in the English psyche similar to that of the lunar landings in the American, in that the more time elapses since it happened, the more improbable it seems that it ever actually occurred in the first place. To anyone who isn't English, that will sound ridiculous, but anyone who actually lives here knows that the prospect of ever winning the World Cup again is such a tantalizing yet distant dream that the feat of having won it in 1966 is progressively magnified by every successive failure. The truth is, the heroes of 1966 (as they have latterly come to be seen) were never really properly rewarded for what they did; in particular Bobby Moore, our charismatic captain, died young in financial trouble, and the adulation with which he is now remembered in England seems to have been largely posthumous. Now? They're venerated, sainted, awarded, a reminder that we once excelled at the game we brought to the world before spending half a century being knocked out of major tournaments by Germans and Portuguese on penalties.

So, with a moment like that behind you, what next? And what makes you turn your back so completely on the game to spend the next three decades embalming people? There's surely no greater anonymity, no bigger distance from celebrity, than spending your time with people with whom your only relationship is to commit them to the furnace or the soil.

*

Reaching Ray Wilson proves to be harder than almost anyone else in the book, since he has not sought fame, and in any case retired from the undertaking business more than fifteen years ago. But, eventually, inquiries through Huddersfield Town lead to a former player who has Ray's number.

I call and get his wife, Pat, but when I explain the book to her, she is not keen. Ray's memory is not what it was, and she is worried he will be embarrassed if he can't recall the events I'm asking about. 'Shall we leave it then?' she asks gently, though it's not really a question.

I get off the phone deeply saddened: part of the reason for writing the book was to tell people's stories while they are still able to tell them, and I feel like I've left it too late. But then a thought occurs, and a month later I call her back, asking how she'd feel about an interview with both of them together, so she can help him out along the way: after all, she was seventeen and he twenty when they met, so she's been along for the whole adventure. After some thought, she agrees, and invites me to Yorkshire to visit them.

Ray and Pat live in the Pennine village of Slaithwaite not far from Huddersfield, a town accessed through roads with names like Thick Hollins and Netherthong Road and Ned Lane. It is classic Yorkshire Pennines, with everything that your hopeful mental picture of such a place would include: a stone viaduct, precipitous hills with rain-stained terraces tumbling down them, a slow-moving river with ducks on it, a restored canal, a chimney stack of black brick, a pub called the Shoulder of Mutton, a café where the full English breakfast is not complete without both black *and* white pudding. It is a gorgeous day in early March when I arrive and the place looks idyllic.

Pat Wilson, a friendly and generous woman with a sense of unflappable steadiness about her, meets me at the gate of her house perched on one of the many hills around the town. She ushers me inside, introduces me to their exuberant dog Joe, and Ray emerges from the kitchen.

From pictures of him over the years, I wasn't sure what to expect: the rugged hard man he appears to be in club photos from his Huddersfield, Everton and England days perhaps? Simon Hattenstone, the *Guardian* journalist who tried to track down the surviving members of the 1966 team eight years before my visit, described him thus: 'Cross the Ancient Mariner with Compo from *The Last of the Summer Wine* and you've got Ray Wilson.' But in person, white-bearded, the word that springs to mind is mischievous: twinkle-eyed and winking, all cheeky asides and one-liners in a voice that mixes Yorkshire with a bit of the mid-sentence plunges of the Midlands (he grew up in Shirebrook, an old mining town on the Derbyshire and Nottinghamshire border).

'This isn't going to be easy, you know,' says Pat, with warmth, but in fact he is spritely and alert and apparently in very good humour. He has a chuckle at my literal pronunciation of Slaithwaite ('Slowit, that's how they say it round here,' he corrects) and upon hearing of my northern background mocks my accent for having turned southern. Pat, in turn, tells me I sound Australian, which prompts Ray to make a truly preposterous attempt at an Australian accent himself. 'You ought to talk like me!' he says. Ice suitably broken, with him nestled in a sofa in a comfortable living room with paintings of Yorkshire scenery on the walls, we begin.

The first thing I'm keen to get a sense of is the difference in the life of a professional footballer from then to now. It is telling that, in shifting from his job doing shift work on the railways, he took a significant pay cut to join Huddersfield Town in 1952. This is not atypical: most of the boys of '66 would have been in an industrial job if they had not excelled at football, and Jack Charlton, for example, briefly worked down a coalpit. Was work on the railways tough? 'No, that weren't as tough as wagon repairing,' he says. 'I had that job before the railways. Shoving the coal on, and whathaveyou.' He can't have been older than fifteen.

He was earning £15 a week on the railways, which was decent for his young age and the work involved. 'When I went to Huddersfield, I signed for £5 a week,' he says. 'I paid £2.75 for me digs. I could afford a bus one day, but then I had to walk the next two days because I couldn't afford it again.' That was a few miles each way. He even had to buy his own football boots.

Pat looks across at him. 'We've been poor, haven't we?' I ask how she remembers the time. 'Well, we were broke, absolutely stony broke, when we first married. We'd nothing. We could just about afford to survive and that was it.' When they married, their accommodation changed from the digs Ray had shared with four or five friends. 'In those days there weren't any mortgage to pay because we paid £1 a week rent to stay in a club house. But for a year or two . . .' She shakes her head. 'When I worked, before I gave up, I was earning more than Ray.' Doing what? 'I worked in the mill. I was a mender.'

The mill mender supporting the professional footballer. We are speaking in a week when Wayne Rooney has signed a new deal worth £300,000 a week.

It's not unusual, though, for young footballers to struggle, and the lower leagues today are full of people barely staying afloat, or running other jobs to get by. But what is striking about

336

Wilson's experience – which was wholly representative of the time – is that it stayed pretty much the same even when he was a full international. At the pinnacle of his abilities, he would later sign for Everton, who then as now were among the finest and richest football clubs in Britain, but even so, they paid him only £50 a week.

Still, in the classic Yorkshire way, this description of near-poverty is not told for sympathy so much as with a sense of pride of getting by. 'We've lived a decent life,' says Pat. 'But we've never been big spenders, have we, Ray?'

'Well, I'm not,' he shoots back. Pat groans: he will spend the interview winding up his wife and then winking at me, while Pat shoots him looks of infinite contempt and long-suffering tolerance. They're a fantastic double act, grounded and enormously likeable.

When Wilson joined Huddersfield Town, then in the second division (what in England today is called the Championship), he came in on the ground staff, and then had to battle his way into the first team. Before having much of a chance to do so, he was called up for national service. 'When I signed the form to say where would you like to go to do your national service, I put Great Britain, England, Scotland, Ireland. So they sent me to Egypt. Serve you bloody right.'

Did he still play while there? 'Oh, yeah. I played inside left. We had some really good wins out there: we beat Egypt a couple of times, and we beat Cyprus, a decent team at that time.' On what pitches? 'In the serious areas there were grass pitches, like in the cities and whathaveyou, but we played out on the sand really.' He was twenty when he came back.

Once he did so, it was back to Huddersfield – which is no doubt what he wanted, but then again, he would have had no choice. 'Once you signed in them days, that was it,' he says. 'You signed for that team for life. You couldn't do like it is now, where after a couple of years with one team you can disappear to another team. Which is fair enough, when you think about it: when you're working, you can leave work and go and work with somebody else. But they wouldn't let you do that in football. You might say: I'd like to move away from here. Well, right, bugger off, you're not playing for anybody else. You were tied to them until they wanted to get rid of you.'

Still, once he cracked the first team, Wilson thrived there. He quickly became an international – it wasn't so unusual for a second division player to reach national honours because there wasn't the freedom of movement that would concentrate ability among a handful of teams as is the case today. More than that, he became a new kind of player.

'I started as an inside left as a kid, then played outside left, then I played left half, then left back. Then me next move were left out.' He's being self-deprecating, but actually the transition he describes – basically a winger to a full-back, in modern parlance – was quite significant for the game, and would become especially so in 1966.

'Full-backs in them days were 6 foot 2 and 15 stone and it took 'em ten minutes to turn round,' he says. 'Whereas the wingers they were playing against were 5 foot 5 and were straight past 'em.' He makes a whooshing noise and motions with his hands. 'So it seemed to me a good idea for full-backs to be the same as wingers: to be quick. That were start of it.'

If you watch a recording of, for example, the 1966 final, Wilson at left back and George Cohen at right back would not look out of place in a twenty-first-century premiership side. They are everywhere: forging forward, getting almost to the opposition goal line and putting crosses in before tracking back to try to keep pace with opposing wingers. They are not just defenders but a source of attack, overlapping with their own players, particularly since manager Alf Ramsey had abandoned his own wingers earlier in the tournament. This was revolutionary stuff in the 1960s, and Wilson has been described as England's first modern full-back. 'It were new. It were just about the start of that.'

Other elements of the game, though, were less progressive, not least the ball. If you go to the excellent Museum of Football in Manchester, you can see the match ball from 1966, which, aside from being a surprisingly vivid orange, shows every bit of its half-century-old vintage: it is battered, made of interlocking leather panels, and looks (and presumably is) very heavy. Still, it looks in considerably better shape than another ball in the same cabinet, with which England were hammered 7–1 by Hungary in 1954. That one looks like a deflated leather vegetable, some sort of lethal alien potato that has been drenched, cooked, battered and buried.

'The ball was pretty heavy, and especially when it were raining and the water were getting inside the ball,' he says now. 'And of course it had laces on. So when you headed that . . .' He makes a noise like a cartoon, as if Tom were being smacked about by Jerry with a frying pan. 'It hurt.' When he recorded an interview for the Everton Former Players Foundation in 2008, he said, perhaps in jest, that heading such a ball is the reason he now needs to take tablets to fend off senility, and whether he meant that or not, there are plenty who do believe balls like that have caused mild brain damage in players. It was absolutely routine at the time to see centre-backs coming off the field bleeding. Today, Wilson jokes about it. 'I were that good I used to wait to see the ball turn round and headed it then,' to avoid the laces.

Wilson made it to the 1962 World Cup in Chile while still plying his trade at second division Huddersfield. He says his time in national service meant he wasn't overawed by the novelty of the place. England acquitted themselves well, losing in a quarter final to the Brazil side that would win that year's World Cup. Through this and later tournaments, he would play against some of the greatest people in the history of the game: Pele, Puskas, Eusebio, Beckenbauer, though he still rates Stanley Matthews as the greatest he ever played against. 'The referees used to look after him,' he adds. 'I had my name taken for farting in front of him.'

'No, you didn't!' objects Pat. 'Stop it! That's a joke.' I know it is because, incredibly for a defender, Ray was booked only once in his entire career, and not for a foul, but for dissent (and presumably not for farting in front of Stanley Matthews). You were a clean player, I say.

'I was. I'm a clean husband as well.'

Is that true, Pat?

'Shut up.'

And, while Huddersfield may not have the cachet of other teams in football history, some great names did pass through: Bill Shankly, who would later become truly legendary at Liverpool, was instrumental in bringing Wilson through to the first team, and also gave a debut to Denis Law. Of Shankly, he recalls, 'He was a good manager, an excellent manager. He were football mad.' He has previously described being slightly saddened for Shankly, for apparently having nothing else in his life. 'But if you're going to be good at anything, you've got to have that sort of feeling, haven't you.'

Despite an injury-hit first season, Wilson was a success at Everton, thriving at the top table of English football at the time. Just a couple of months before the 1966 World Cup, he was part of the team that won the FA Cup. By then, he was a trusted and experienced international, thirty-one years old and a senior member of the national side.

Did he used to get recognized?

'Oh, one or two ladies did.' A wink; a further pitying glower from Pat.

And then the World Cup came home.

*

Whether you like football or not, it is well worth finding the BBC's broadcast of the 1966 World Cup final, if only as a reminder of just how much time has passed, and how much has changed, since England lifted that trophy on their home ground. England beat West Germany 4–2 after extra time, but the game itself, though filled with controversial moments, was not a classic; the appeal of watching the tape today is how magnificently dated it all is.

Kenneth Wolstenholme, a man who had flown more than a hundred hazardous flights over occupied Europe and had bombed Germany barely twenty years earlier, was the principal commentator; his impeccably enunciated words narrate the broadcast. 'Those rival supporters having a chanting, shouting and singing contest with each other.' 'Let's hope Nobby Stiles doesn't have problems with his boots all afternoon.' 'That was the wrong foot for Mr Emmerich!' 'English hearts have slumped.' 'Well done, Gordon Banks!' 'Charlton didn't altogether agree with that decision.' 'Yes! Peters has his name taken by Mr Dienst!'

One consistency between then and now is the monarch: Queen Elizabeth was on the throne, and was present in the royal box. She looks young, and beautiful. Prince Philip, on the other hand, looks more or less identical to today, scowling through the national anthem with the right-hand side of his mouth open in a sort of tongue-poked sneer. Harold Wilson, the nation's first Labour prime minister, is in the box too.

Later, the camera cuts back to them all; someone is smoking, and stubs out their fag on the royal box's floor.

A strong breeze flutters the British and West German flags on the twin towers of the old Wembley stadium, though, in black and white, the German flag could be anything. The players come out, Bobby Moore impeccable, Bobby Charlton already largely bald. The marching band – Her Majesty's Royal Marines, Portsmouth Group – leave the arena. There are people in suits in the crowd. Simple white-on-black script fills the screen with the names of the players ('Charlton J. Charlton R.') in a loose approximation of their playing positions. It all just looks so incredibly long ago.

*

On the morning of the final, Wilson was rooming with Bobby Charlton, as he had done for some time. 'Alf Ramsey roomed me with Bobby,' he says. 'I were one of them to just let time go by before the match. Bobby always had to kill time by doing shopping, buying this, buying that, and of course he took me with him.

'Before I started rooming with him I just stayed in bed as long as I could, and tried to kill it that way. Killing time by trying to keep it nice and easy. But Bobby would wake up about four in't morning: come on, Ray! Get up!'

When out with Bobby, Ray would find himself largely anonymous. 'Everywhere we went, everybody was saying: Bobby! Bobby Charlton! Look! And who's that little bugger with him?'

Still, on the weekend of the final, Ray had something else to occupy him: Pat had blown up the car.

'I drove down on the Friday with Norma Charlton,' says Pat, Norma being Bobby's wife. Halfway down the motorway, the exhaust went on her Ford Zephyr. 'Oh, it did! What a noise it made, as well. Oh, my God.' It is fair to say Pat is more emotive about the explosion of her Ford Zephyr's exhaust than she is about the World Cup final itself. 'So I dropped the car off where they were staying, and I said: he'll have to get that sorted in the morning.'

It was, perhaps, a useful way to kill any nerves, spending the morning of our nation's most significant sporting moment getting an exhaust fixed. But, in truth, Ray was little affected by nervousness. 'If you thought that were going to bother you, you wouldn't have been on anyway,' he says, when asked about the atmosphere within Wembley when he entered the stadium. Pat, who was watching with all the other wives, felt differently. 'I was very nervous. I hardly watched the match. I certainly didn't watch the extra time.'

On the TV footage, Wilson looks tough and stocky, with cropped thin hair; he has the look of a short but powerful TV hard man. He had had a terrific tournament, but his World Cup final did not start well. After twelve minutes, he planted a weak header right in front of Helmut Haller, who scored. But from then on, he had an excellent game, frequently forward, never slumping despite extra time that took the total playing time to two hours, in an era when no substitutes were allowed.

What sort of game does he think he had now? 'I played a reasonable game,' he says. 'I made a bit of a mess with the first goal for the Germans, I have to say that. But I say to them: well, I set you going, because when we were one–nil down, we started playing then.' He is chuckling: the error has clearly never caused him demons.

The game itself is forever remembered for a few key moments: Germany's last-minute equalizer in normal time, when England were literally seconds from winning; Geoff Hurst's endlessly disputed goal in extra time which bounced on the line (if you're German) or slightly over the line (if you're English), a moment that made a lifetime celebrity of Azerbaijani linesman Tofik Bakhramov; and the very last kick of the game, as Hurst raced forward once again. Surely most of England can recite Wolstenholme's commentary. 'Some people are on the pitch. They think it's all over.' Hurst unleashes a vicious shot into the German net. 'It is now!' It is still the only hat-trick ever scored in a World Cup final.

And then there's Bobby Moore, politely wiping the sweat from his palms before taking the trophy and lifting it with a smile as Bobby Charlton, behind him, bursts into tears. *God Save the Queen* is observed, the Queen herself, in a furry hat, still looking so youthful. (Philip, meanwhile, still looks miserable.) There's Nobby Stiles, gappy and bounding, and there's Bobby Moore on his teammate's shoulders.

'Oh yeah!' shouts Ray, reminded of the photo and statue (which, incidentally, stands on a junction in East London near West Ham's ground). 'Who's the fellow with him?'

'Geoff Hurst,' says Pat. 'Don't swear.' He hasn't sworn.

'He's about 6 to 8 inches taller than me, so Bobby's just off his shoulder. He's only on mine.' When sculptor Philip Jackson conceived the sculpture, he gave Wilson an expression of solid, dependable strength, which was entirely fitting for his performance through the game as a whole, but is not quite historically accurate: if you look at the pictures the sculpture was modelled on, Wilson is clearly grimacing under Bobby Moore's weight.

I ask them what they did after the game. Pat says, 'Well, there was a banquet, if you like, with everyone else and their wives there, but we wives [i.e. the players' wives] weren't invited. After that, we did go out. Can't remember where.'

'Did we go dancing?'

'No . . . I know we went to a club somewhere, but I can't remember where . . .'

'We'd have had a pint or two, din't we?'

'Oh, I'd imagine so.'

I try to imagine what the players and WAGS would get up to if England won the World Cup today.

*

After the World Cup, Wilson lasted another couple of years at Everton, playing in their FA Cup final defeat in 1968 but, at thirty-three, he was starting to get on. He went to Oldham Athletic on a free transfer in 1969 and retired in 1971. He spent a short while as caretaker manager at Bradford City, just for ten games in late 1971, but that was the end of his involvement in the game. He has really never looked back in more than forty years.

Wilson wasn't alone in moving on from the game. You could only really say two of the team of '66 made a successful career out of management: Alan Ball, who spent fifteen years as a manager, including time at Portsmouth, Southampton and (disastrously) Manchester City; and Jackie Charlton, who had great success at Middlesbrough and the Republic of Ireland, whom he took to a World Cup quarter final in 1990. You could make a case for Geoff Hurst, too, who worked in the England set-up for a while, was briefly manager at Chelsea before being sacked in 1981, and spent a few years managing in Kuwait before entering the insurance industry.

Others tried management, but didn't really succeed and so moved on almost by default. Gordon Banks, whose top-flight career had been cut short by the loss of his sight in one eye after a car crash, became a coach at Port Vale, but was demoted, then managed part-time club Telford United, where he was sacked, and ended up accepting a position as raffle-ticket seller before leaving the game completely, somewhat broken-hearted, in 1980. Bobby Moore tried it too, briefly managing Oxford City, Southend United and a team in Hong Kong, but after that ended up unsuccessfully trying to build businesses before dying obscenely young of bowel and liver cancer aged just fifty-one. Nobby Stiles lasted a week as manager of Preston North End (resigning in support of his predecessor, Bobby Charlton, who in turn had resigned in protest at a transfer and never really managed again) and later coached the Vancouver Whitecaps and West Bromwich Albion, though he did have greater success as a youth team coach at Manchester United.

Some others stayed close to the game in other ways. Bobby Charlton has been a member of the Manchester United board for thirty years at the time of writing, and remains one today. Martin Peters was on the board at Spurs, though most of his post-football life was spent in the insurance industry. Roger Hunt, though he moved into a family business in haulage, kept a peripheral involvement in football by becoming a sitting member of the pools panel, who used to predict the results of games that had been washed out by bad weather for the national football pools prizes, in 1975. And George Cohen, who was dogged with ill health and fought a successful battle against bowel cancer, coached the Fulham youth team and England's under-twenty-threes for a while.

But nobody changed direction quite so dramatically as Ray Wilson. Why wasn't a life in football for him? 'I just hadn't got the commitment for it,' he says. 'It just . . . wasn't anything to do with me. It's a certain thing in players. Like, Bobby Charlton tried a bit as manager, at . . .'

'Preston North End,' chimes in Pat.

'Preston. He hadn't got the ability to be a manager. Whereas Jack Charlton . . .' He growls in imitation of the big man. 'Different altogether. And you've got to have that to be manager, got to be able to control, and make these people look up to you. Bobby would have no chance at all.'

'And neither had you,' says Pat.

'No, I hadn't, no doubt about that.' He looks at his wife. 'I manage you, though.'

'Oh, aye. That's true.' It is clearly anything but true.

One problem Ray had found during his playing days was that the money, not great at the best of times, dropped off considerably during the summer, so in order to make ends meet he would help out at Pat's father's undertakers' business. Ray's retirement coincided with Pat's father wanting to step back, so he decided to take the business on. 'I think it were just a simple matter that Pat's father wasn't doing that and I was happy to give it a go,' he says. 'Got on all right, didn't we?'

He did. Although the business never grew beyond him and Pat, it ran successfully around the Huddersfield and Halifax area for the best part of thirty years. What does it take to be a good undertaker?

Pat begins. 'What you have to have is the ability to meet people and –'

Ray cuts in. 'Well, it's like everything else. You've got to realize that these things happen, that people do die and so on, and the people you've got to see are going to be upset.'

Pat: 'You're meeting people at their lowest time, aren't you?'

Ray: 'And if you can cope with that, you're all right.'

Pat: 'As far as I can make out, he were quite good at that.'

It occurs to me that this engagement with people is the greatest possible reversal from a life in football. As a professional for Huddersfield, or Everton, or England, he was associated with great joy, escapism, exuberance. We go to football in part to forget the mundanity of everyday life, and to be engaged collectively in support of something, to be elevated or heartbroken or frustrated or ecstatic, but generally to feel *something*, even though (or maybe because) it's based on conditions we can't control. Being among a crowd of 30,000 people cheering a goal or a victory is a feeling without equivalent: a great, shared, communal happiness, fleeting but briefly majestic.

Yet being an undertaker is as far from that as it is possible to be. As an undertaker, the only reason you meet someone is because they are in a miserable, unfixable state of grief. They are, as Pat says, at their lowest when you meet them. The only other people you meet in the job are corpses.

Ray doesn't dwell on this. 'I don't think that people tied the soccer in with the business. I think they just looked on me and were hoping I was a decent funeral man.'

Pat says: 'You never got used to children, did you? That was the worst thing. But he was good at his job.'

Entering undertaking meant going back to school at forty. Ray had left school without qualifications and he needed to gain maths and English, and then embalming exams. 'He came out with a distinction in his embalming exam,' says Pat, with some pride. In those days, there weren't many embalmers around, but a man called a trade embalmer, who would go to different funeral homes in different towns, took Ray under his wing and helped him to learn the trade.

'It was a small family business, we couldn't afford to employ anybody,' says Pat. 'But it was successful just for Ray and I.' The logistics, stated in bleak practicalities, were that an average of one and a half deaths a week were sufficient to support a decent living, Pat says.

'She don't mean that there were only half a body,' says Ray.

He retired in 1997. In retirement, he has walked a lot: from the top of Scotland to the bottom of England ('not in one day, mind'), across the Pennines, coast to coast, all over Wales, and up just about every fell in the Lake District, by Pat's estimation. Every question I ask about retirement brings a further answer about walking. He still goes out with the dog most days. Here in the hills is where he has always felt at home: even when at

Everton, he couldn't wait to move back. 'He loved it,' says Pat, remembering it's roughly where I'm from, 'but, you know, it's flat, in't it?' They have never moved from this corner of Yorkshire since. He still goes and watches Huddersfield Town occasionally, and his sons took him to Goodison Park to watch Everton last year. He has two boys, Russell and Neil, in their fifties now, and five grandchildren.

The '66 team have an annual reunion, though it's been a couple of years since he's made it to one. 'When they meet, it's as though they've seen each other yesterday,' Pat says. 'It's that sort of friendship.' But, like many of his teammates, he's had to sell the World Cup winner's medal (in 2002 in his case, though Pat has said it was just because they didn't know which son to leave it to).

What does he think when he looks at football and its riches today?

'I'd be delighted,' he says. 'It'd be nice to play now.' Both of them say they don't begrudge modern players their money – 'if they're going to offer it, you'd take it,' Pat says – but they must look at the Rooneys of this world and think: what if. 'It's pointless, it can't be changed,' says Ray. 'But I wouldn't mind being born like another fifty year on. The money would be nice.'

I don't imagine he'd like the celebrity, though. 'He wouldn't,' Pat says. And how about you, Pat? Would you have liked the Posh Spice existence? 'That's not my life,' she says. 'I admire her, I admire them both. But that's not my style.'

Ray chips in with an impish beam: 'She loves spending money.'

He's blown it this time.

'No, Ray! You're being very naughty there! I don't spend any money at all, except on food.'

Ray, the mischievous expression dimmed by just a touch of sheer terror, shoots me another aside. 'She's getting angry.'

'I do get angry, because you're saying things that aren't true, and it makes me cross.' Never accuse a septuagenarian woman from Yorkshire of being a spendthrift: there is no graver accusation that can be made. Pat is, I think, proud of a fulfilled life achieved on modest means.

I move on by making a graver mistake still by admitting that I am a Liverpool fan. Pat, who is halfway across the room with a cup of tea, stops in her tracks. 'You kept that quiet! If I'd known that, you wouldn't have got in the door!' Ray chuckles away and I try to make amends by telling him about one of the favourite photos I have seen, when he, at Everton, and Roger Hunt, at Liverpool, carried the World Cup trophy on to the pitch together at Goodison Park before the 1966 Charity Shield. It strikes a chord.

'Oh!' says Pat. 'He's a lovely man.'

'Do you mean me?' asks Ray, with one more wink.

'No,' she says witheringly. 'I mean Roger.' And Ray smiles with victorious delight.

11

Russ Ewin, The Sandakan Survivor

Russ Ewin is watching the sun set into the South China Sea from the window of a Borneo hotel. 'They always have great sunsets here,' he says, as a wash of orange light floods the bay. 'Of course, I saw three and a half years of them.'

The remark does not come with obvious bitterness, and that is remarkable, for the three and a half years he refers to were spent as a prisoner of war in two Japanese internment camps. Much of that time was spent in the camp with the lowest survival rate of them all, at the very bottom of a league table of atrocity that includes Changi, Sonkrai and Kanchanaburi. On the day that I meet him in 2010, he and his fellow Australian and great friend Leslie 'Bunny' Glover are thought to be the only remaining able-bodied men with first-hand experience of perhaps the most notorious POW camp of them all: Sandakan.

They are here to take part in a memorial, held on 15 August every year, to commemorate the most desperate sadness in Australian military history: the Sandakan death marches. Russ and Bunny are, remarkably, the lucky ones, part of a group of officers who were transferred out of the Sandakan camp in October 1943 to another near Kuching, also in what today is the Malaysian part of Borneo. They were removed as a punishment – the Japanese wanted to reduce the senior ranks in the camp so as to undermine leadership – but it was a penalty that saved their lives. After they went, remaining inmates were forced on terrible marches through the jungle after which even the survivors were executed. At the start of 1945 there were 2,434 Australian and British soldiers in Sandakan. Six would survive the war.

Six. That's one in every 300 Australian troops, and none at all of the 641 British, who were slaughtered to every last man. It is a rate of murder so complete that many people still don't know the marches ever happened, as there is nobody left to talk about them.

I originally meet Russ for a magazine article, and not for this book. But then one day, thinking about candidates who have moved on from some seminal event in relative youth, it strikes me very clearly: he should be in it. Because in all of my life, I don't believe I've ever had an experience as humbling as listening to Russ Ewin tell me about how he survived internment, and even, extraordinarily, found positives in the experience that enriched his ample later life. He is ninety-three when I meet him; he was twenty-nine when freed from captivity. No more worlds to conquer? Not a bit of it.

*

When *The Australian Way*, the in-flight magazine of Qantas, asks me to fly to Sandakan to cover the annual memorial in 2010, I must confess I have not heard of the death marches. Like many British people I have a direct family connection to people incarcerated during the Second World War; my grandad's brother, Joe, was on the Burma Railway, also commonly known in Britain as the Death Railway, immortalized in the book and movie *The*

Bridge on the River Kwai. It is thought that 90,000 Asian labourers and 12,399 Allied prisoners of war died on the railway, and since more than 6,000 of them were British, this is the one that is remembered in my home country when one talks of Japanese POW abuse in the Second World War.

Although more than 600 British died in Sandakan, I find fewer people know it. And while more Australians are familiar with it, I find that not nearly as many are aware as one would expect, given that it involved a near total obliteration of thousands of its troops. It does not, for example, have anything like the same touchstone resonance as more noted Australian military tragedies such as Gallipoli or the Fromelles. It brings home to me why this is the case: there was almost nobody left to talk about what they saw.

The *Australian Way* commission puts me in touch with Gwenda Zappala, a Queensland-based representative of the Sabah Tourist Board, Sabah being the Malaysian province where Sandakan resides today. In the manner typical of freelancers, I am keen to wangle as many stories from the trip as I can; in the manner typical of the tourist board publicist, she is keen to help; and in the manner typical of the freelance who is also supposed to be a stay-home dad and primary carer, I am keen to wedge it all into as small a trip as possible. So it is that, on the day when I first meet the survivors, I awake at 2 a.m. at the Laban Rata guesthouse two thirds of the way up Mount Kinabalu, the 4,095-metre granite-crowned peak that dominates and defines Sabah, which Russ will later tell me he saw with delight from a Japanese hell-ship on his way to the Sandakan camp in 1942, and which I am also writing an article about. I haul myself step by step to the summit by sunrise, where the jungle gives way to the starlit exposure of open rock, then descend about 3,000 metres down the mountain, slipping and bruising in the rain and mist, and at the bottom catch a jeep to Kota Kinabalu, during which journey my legs seize up. Arriving at the Hyatt, where I have been kindly accommodated by the tourist board so I can meet the veterans, I stagger upstairs in boots that have literally fallen apart, run a bath, and am about to climb into it when the phone goes.

It's Gwenda. 'The boys —' they're ninety-three and eighty-nine but, to her, they're still the boys — 'are up in the top-floor lounge and are keen to meet you. Come on up.' There follows a very swift bath, sort of a rigor mortis lunge into the water, and a change of clothes before I limp up and meet them. There, I find myself in a position of mortified bathos as two men with a combined age of 182, who have survived years of the worst that warfare can throw at a human being, comfort me with genuine concern about the state of my seized-up legs. For the next two days, even while I'm interviewing people about their experience of bestial cruelty, torture, starvation and neglect, they keep asking how my legs are feeling.

The two men are very different: Russ Ewin quiet, introspective and considered; Bunny Glover the life and soul of the party, happy to grab a girl and pull her on to a dance floor even now he's pushing ninety. Russ is tall and a little hunched, with a dignified sadness in his eyes and jowls, while Bunny is all stocky spark and solid-chinned grin. The intention is for me to interview both after the memorial in Sandakan a couple of days from now, but in the end Bunny feels unwell and it is Russ who I will spend the most time with, and he will be the man through whom I just begin to understand what Sandakan is all about.

This evening is only a quick hello with no interviews, but when Russ looks out at that sunset and remembers the years of them he witnessed from the Borneo camps, it's already clear to me I am dealing with an extraordinary man.

Next day we all fly to Sandakan, and as the veterans rest up ahead of the following day's memorial, I see some of the other things Sandakan is famous for beyond its miserable history:

some of the world's greatest wildlife and nature reserves, and in particular the Sepilok orang-utan sanctuary. It's a remarkable place, the more so for the incredible devotion of the staff: they work with these beautiful apes for as long as a decade apiece in order to help them rehabilitate into a natural jungle life and, when it is time to say goodbye, they weep as if they are saying farewell to a child they have raised, which, in many respects, they are. Just miles from the site of the Sandakan camp, it's a reminder of the far extremes of what human behaviour is capable of.

I'm also taken to a church, St Michael's and All Angels, designed by a New Zealander back in the nineteenth century but today associated with the memory of the war. Many prisoners spent the night here before being marched to captivity, and in almost all cases death, at the POW camp. There are several beautiful stained-glass windows in the transepts, many of them gifts from the Australians and British, and in some cases from family members of prisoners who passed through the church.

There is a book of remembrance here with the names of the 2,428 Allied servicemen who died at Sandakan, on the marches or at their destination in the mountain jungle at Ranau. On the day I visit, the book is turned to the A page or, more specifically, An–As. It takes a whole page to get from Anderson (there are five of them on the page) to Ashby. It is a very thick book.

*

Before meeting Russ, naturally, I have been reading up. The experience of doing so has been an education of the most appalling sort, horror combined with a cloying guilt of never having heard of these events before. Not everything below happened to Russ, but it did happen, and he is now one of the few focal points through which we can begin to visualize the men who endured it and, in almost all cases, died in doing so.

So this is what happened.

In February 1942, Singapore fell to the Japanese. The then-British island was supposed to be a fortress: Churchill was aghast at its loss, and called it the 'largest capitulation' in his country's military history. There, 80,000 British, Indian and Australian troops became prisoners of war in the largest surrender of British-led personnel on record; believing themselves to be facing a far bigger force, they surrendered to an invading army of just 30,000, who had perhaps one more day's worth of ammunition.

The surrender, coupled with the capture of 50,000 other Allied prisoners in Malaya, dramatically increased the number of people the Japanese had to house, and prisoners began arriving in Sandakan on the north-east coast of Borneo later that year, with a contingent of 1,500 Australians arriving from Singapore in July. In April 1943, they were followed by 776 British POWs, and another 500 Australians shortly afterwards.

Their roles originally were similar to those in other camps: forced labour to build infrastructure for the Japanese forces, in this case two military airstrips and the related service roads. On the scale of inhumanity found elsewhere and later in the war, life was at first reasonably bearable: workers left the camp at 7.30 a.m., cleared scrub, filled in swamps, dug gravel and pushed it in trucks along a light railway. They marched back to camp at 5.30 p.m. This was prisoner-of-war life as we like to imagine it from the chirpy and spirited POW movies that appeared in the first twenty years after the war: sufficient food, cigarettes, even a payment of ten cents per day and a canteen within which to spend it on bananas and turtle eggs. There were concerts. An Australian bombardier, Dick Braithwaite, was allowed to send a postcard home, although the words upon it were vetted or even chosen by his guards. 'We are well. We are happy. We are well fed. We are working for pay.'

It didn't last.

New, brutal Formosan guards arrived in April 1943. Beatings became commonplace. They made frequent use of a new form of punishment known as the cage, a small barred wooden structure high enough to sit in. POWs within it would have to sit at attention throughout the sapping heat of the day and would have no bedding or mosquito netting at night. They would receive no food during their first week in the cage, and would be beaten twice daily. One of the six march survivors (though now long dead), Keith Botterill – from whose accounts we know so much about life in Sandakan – recalled being in there once for forty days. 'There were seventeen of us in there,' he said in a statement he later gave. 'No water for the first three days. On the third night they'd force you to drink till you were sick. For the first seven days you got no food. On the seventh day they started feeding you half camp rations.' He was dressed in just a G-string, and could not wash. He was beaten every evening.

When released, he and his follow prisoners fought starving dogs for the swill that had been poured into a trough from the kitchen. 'We'd all hit together, the dogs and us, and we'd fight the dogs for the scraps. If you've ever tried to pull a bone out of a starving dog's mouth you'll know what it was like. The dog would fasten on to your wrist to take the bone off you, and you'd still be putting the bone into your mouth. And you'd finish up the better.'

Maltreatment like this became commonplace. In July 1943, an intelligence network that had been built up between the camp, local civilian prisoners and guerrilla units in the jungles and mountains was betrayed to the Japanese. Its organizer, Captain Lionel Matthews, was arrested, tortured and later executed. So were eight locals. It was in the aftermath of this that officers like Russ and Bunny – Russ, in particular, having been involved in the underground movement through developing radio transmission – were removed from the camp.

From then on, everything bad multiplied, and everything good diminished. Beatings became daily, regardless of whether there was any perceived misdemeanour to punish. Workloads increased, rations decreased. Illness swept the camp. By late 1944, Allied warplanes began bombing Sandakan and the airfield, making it useless by the end of that year. This was a mixed blessing for the prisoners: since they no longer had any use, a steadily lesser effort was expended on keeping them in any state of health. Although rice was in sufficient supply, daily rations were cut again and again, and, in January 1945, stopped altogether. All that was left was an 85 gram per day allocation from stores that the prisoners of war had built up in fear of exactly this moment.

By now it was clear that the Japanese were losing the war, and they knew that when the Allies came the invasion would start at the coast. So the Japanese made plans to move the POWs into the mountains, to Ranau, 260 kilometres to the west. On 26 January, the prisoners were told that 455 Australian and British prisoners were to leave Sandakan for another place where, it was said, there would be plenty of food. They were divided into nine groups and left the camp at intervals between 28 January and 6 February. They were all malnourished. Many had beri-beri or other debilitating diseases. Most had no shoes. They had rations for four days only. They had to carry rice, ammunition and other equipment on their backs. And in this condition they marched into swamp, jungle and mountains.

Botterill, whose statement we have to thank for telling us of the conditions, was in the third group. For the first three days they had a little rice and six cucumbers between forty of them: just enough to keep them alive, and no more. It took them seventeen days to reach Ranau, which thirty-seven of their original fifty did, the others having died of exhaustion or been shot or beaten to death when they were unable to go on. Botterill recalled five being shot in a single day when they had to climb a mountain outside Ranau, and he knew the same had happened in the two groups that had gone ahead of his: he could smell the dead bodies as he passed.

Botterill's group actually had one of the better averages. In the first five groups to set off, seventy out of 265 died on the march. Groups six to nine stopped at the village of Paginatan, because there was no room for them at Ranau, and within a month there were only sixty-eight left of the 138 who started out. At the end of March the survivors of those latter groups were marched on to Ranau, forty-six of them making it alive. When they met up with the first groups, another eighty-nine had already died at the camp and another twenty-one on rice-carrying details between Ranau and Paginatan.

'No effort whatsoever was made to bury the men,' Botterill would report. 'They would just pull them 5 to 15 yards off the track and bayonet them or shoot them.' And there was a clear policy that nobody incapacitated should survive: after the last of the groups came a killing squad with the job of finding any POWs who had fallen out from earlier groups but were still alive. They were all bayoneted. 'Once you stopped,' said another of the six escapees, William Dick Moxham, 'you stopped for good.'

Ranau was unspeakable misery. The men were put in crowded, insanitary huts where dysentery was rife. Death came at night, burial in the morning. Botterill testified, 'You'd wake up of a morning and you'd look to your right to see if the chap next to you was still alive. If he was dead you'd just roll him over a little bit and see if he had any belongings that would suit you; if not, you'd just leave him there.' And then he would turn to the other neighbour to repeat the process. They would tie dead comrades at the wrist and ankle, put a bamboo pole through the knots and carry them like dead tigers. They put them in 6-inch graves, the ground too hard to dig any deeper. 'We'd lay the body in and the only mark of respect they got, we'd spit on the body, then cover them up.' By 26 June, there were six left alive at Ranau of the more than 450 who set out.

Meanwhile, back in Sandakan, things were scarcely any better. Between February and May 1945, 885 POWs died at the camp. There was enough food and medicine at the camp to have saved all of them. In May, after a heavy bombing of Sandakan, the camp was evacuated and burned. Despite the misery they had suffered within, one survivor would later remember an enormous sense of loss as he looked at the flames: the little pieces of wood they had fashioned into possessions had become like the family jewels, he said.

Around 530 of them were gathered into eleven groups for a second march to Ranau. Shortly afterwards, seventy-five more who could walk were sent on a third march to Ranau. The numbers around these marches are even more appalling than the first. In group two of the second march, for example, twelve of the fifty marchers died in the first day. Another two of the eventual survivors who later testified, Nelson Short and Dick Braithwaite, were on this march. Short said, 'If blokes just couldn't go on, we shook hands with them, and said, you know, hope everything's all right. But they knew what was going to happen. There was nothing you could do. You just had to keep yourself going. More or less survival of the fittest.' Short ate snails. He ate tree ferns. There wasn't anything else.

This second march took twenty-six days; 183 of the 530 lived. And not one single person survived the third march.

Despite their desperate condition the survivors were still put to work in Ranau, cutting bamboo, collecting wood and carrying food and water for the Japanese officers. The prisoners themselves were by now receiving a small cup of rice water per day with about an inch of rice in the bottom. No sanitation.

As for the POWs left at Sandakan who were too ill even to be marched, they thinned out, dying at a rate of about a dozen a day. They either starved, died of disease or were shot, every last one. A Chinese worker called Wong Hiong witnessed the last of them die. 'His legs were covered with ulcers. He was a tall, thin, dark man with a long face and was naked apart from a loin cloth.' He was taken to a trench. 'Fifteen Japs were already at the spot. Morjumi [sergeant major Hisao Murozumi] made the man kneel down and tied a black cloth over his eyes. He did not say anything or make any protest. Morjumi cut his head off with one sword stroke.' It was the day of the Japanese surrender, the supposed end of the Second World War.

And at Ranau too, as the war came to an end, it was clear that not one prisoner was to be allowed to survive. According to the outstanding but heartbreaking account produced by the Australian Commonwealth Department of Veterans' Affairs, *Laden, Fevered, Starved*, from which much of this section is drawn, 'strong evidence suggests that the last POW survivors at Ranau were not killed until 27 August, twelve days after the official Japanese surrender'.

But six had got away.

*

The penalties for attempted escape had been sickening even in the context of the treatment of the men in general. Just one story, provided by Australia's Department of Veteran's Affairs, suffices to convey the cruelty of it. Gunner Albert Cleary's treatment was, as the DVA puts it, 'of a special horror'.

He would have been twenty-five when he tried to escape from Ranau in March 1945. By this time he had already survived the first march, and it must have become clear to him that the only way to get out alive was to escape, which he tried to do with a colleague, Gunner Wally Crease. They lasted four days, then were recaptured.

Cleary had already been beaten up before he returned to the camp. When he got there, his arms were tied high up behind his back and he was made to kneel with a log tied between his knees. He was kicked and punched all over by two guards. Sometimes his head was held while his throat was punched, and he was terrorized with bayonets. His guards would jump on the log tied between his legs. Every half-hour he was made to stand on his feet, sending the blood back to his lower legs and ending any hope of desensitization. He was hit with rifle butts and sticks. On the first day this went on for three and a half hours.

Next morning, it started again. Botterill, from whose admittedly emotional and, as we will learn, slightly questionable testimony we know this, went away from the camp on a work party. When he got back, the guards were still beating Cleary. He could be heard begging constantly for mercy. There was none. The beating continued all night. The guards were changed; the new ones, refreshed, were worse than the first.

Botterill was sent from the camp again, this time for four days, and upon his return found to his shock that Cleary was still alive, in a filthy loincloth, tied by the neck to a tree. He was covered in blood and excrement, and was suffering from dysentery. He suffered the heat of the day and the mountain cold of the nights unprotected. Day after day, he was still beaten, with fists and rifles. It took him twelve days to die.

The guards told the other prisoners, 'If you escape, the same thing will happen to you.'

But what else to do, but try?

Owen Campbell escaped from the second death march along with four others, all of whom died. Separately, Dick Braithwaite

362

also escaped from the second march. Keith Botterill, Nelson Short, William Moxham and Bill Sticpewich all escaped from Ranau. All six, to varying degrees, were aided and ultimately saved by local people, who ran a truly extraordinary risk that not only they, but their families and even their entire villages would be destroyed if they were found to be helping the Australians.

The six would be the only survivors of the almost 2,500 Allied POWs who had been alive at Sandakan at the start of 1945. Their testimony is the only reason we know anything accurate about prisoner experience after the officers like Russ were moved out of the camp in 1943.

But all of them were immensely damaged by their experiences, both physically and mentally. The attitude of the time seemed to be not to talk about their experiences; one could legitimately call it a cover-up in Australian society. Moxham, having survived all this, committed suicide in 1961. Sticpewich, having had the strength to cope with three years of animalistic cruelty, was knocked down and killed while crossing a Melbourne road in 1977. Braithwaite died of cancer in 1986, Short of a heart attack in 1995, Botterill of emphysema in 1997 and Campbell, the last of them and a recluse at the end of his life, in 2003.

Since the survivors are no longer around, I speak instead with an Australian historian called Lynette Silver, who has spent more than twenty years writing on Sandakan with a truly forensic eye for detail. Her research, a lifetime's effort, has at times helped to find the identities of previously unknown dead in uncommemorated graves, and helped long-grieving families find where their relatives' remains are. She's the person behind the stained-glass windows project in the church. At other times, the extent of her research has unearthed uncomfortable truths: in 2012 she found herself arguing against a mooted award of the Victoria Cross to Gunner Cleary, whose tortured death we discussed earlier. Over the years she had earned the trust and friendship of the survivors and in particular Keith Botterill, upon whose testimony three prison guards were hanged for murdering Cleary; on his deathbed, Botterill confessed to Silver that parts of his account had been falsified in order to ensure that the guards were put to death. Nevertheless, whatever embellishments Botterill made – probably around whether Cleary eventually succumbed to the elements or was outright murdered – surely pale into insignificance amid the broader, unquestioned misery.

Silver is as close to the Sandakan atrocity as anyone, and I catch up with her and her husband at a business centre in one of the town's hotels. Passionate and fast-talking, and armed with a photographic memory for detail, she is the author of *Sandakan – A Conspiracy of Silence,* a definitive 1998 account of the atrocities, and when I meet her she is proudly presenting her new book *Blood Brothers,* which tells the Sandakan story from the local point of view.

Silver is interesting to talk to about the relative anonymity of the Sandakan atrocities. 'When you have six people come out alive out of 2,434, and every Brit is wiped out, those six people are very traumatized,' she says. 'They have seen people murdered in cold blood. They have seen the most terrible atrocities. They come back to Australia, they don't particularly know each other, and they're told the best thing they can do is go home and get on with their life.' The six barely interacted with one another at all until decades after the war. 'So they are in isolation, they are having nightmares every night about what has happened, there's nobody who survived to talk about it with, the government has decided not to tell the relatives about it, and it would have been hard to find out anything about it even if you wanted to before 1975 because of secrecy laws.'

There was something of a paternalistic approach by the

Australian government after the war, no doubt well-intentioned, but with lasting consequences. It was an attitude of: it's better that you don't know. This was an era in which, if a child died at birth, a mother would not be allowed to see its body, lest it be an upsetting sight. It was not a time of open discussion, of the resolution of demons by confronting them and talking them into inexistence, but that was how it worked: the facts of Sandakan were actively supressed for thirty years out of fear that Australia simply could not cope with the reality of it.

In the aftermath of this silent claustrophobia, Silver came to know three of the six survivors and ended up feeling enormously sorry for them. She remembers Botterill being interviewed – it took place at her house – and being asked to distil all of his suffering into a three-minute grab for an idiot interviewer whose first question was 'Where's Borneo?' Seeing him desperately ill with emphysema at the time, she thought, 'You poor old thing, if a few more had got out alive you wouldn't have this huge responsibility.' She still feels that way. 'I've said to people who've lost their relatives: you'll find this hard to believe but your relative was one of the lucky ones, because the unlucky ones were those who survived.'

Botterill was probably the one she was closest to – he told her more and more as he neared death, having been haunted by his memories every day of his life – and she knew Short, whose memory was failing, and Campbell, who didn't want to talk at all. She met the family of Moxham, who committed suicide. He had come home violent, living every day as his last, and having bought a property in remote western New South Wales, he then named it Ranau, as if to force himself to remember his suffering. Once he pulled a gun on his wife and children. 'Eventually his wife took their three children away for their safety. One day he rented a seedy motel room in Haymarket and shot himself in the head because the demons had got so bad.'

Now the only ones who remember Sandakan are Russ and Bunny, the officers who were moved from it to Kuching in 1943. Every other memory has been extinguished.

*

Early, on 15 August, I head with a Channel Seven camera crew to the Sandakan memorial to attend the ceremony. The heat and humidity, even at seven in the morning, are oppressive. Every time I take a lens cap off my camera, the lens fogs instantly with condensation and becomes unusable.

At the memorial, about 11 kilometres outside Sandakan, you walk through a pleasantly landscaped park, with rusting remains of a camp generator and boiler along a path to a commemorative pavilion where stoic words are carved on shining marble, so polished it reflects the dense trees around the clearing. Today, the path is lined by young Malaysians in white, blue and green uniforms for the three armed forces. Allied veterans of the Borneo campaign, many of them people who flew in and liberated POW camps such as Kuching, walk proudly, though many of them now are supported by younger helpers. There are medals, many medals. Australia's Governor General, Quentin Bryce, arrives in a sober burgundy hat, her features arranged in steely contemplation. A troop of the Malay Army, in a blue and white camouflage stripe which must make some counterintuitive sense in green jungle, file past the memorial and the Malaysian national anthem plays. And then a catafalque party, a group of Australian soldiers in khaki short sleeves, make a slow march to take position round the marble monument.

The Governor General is the first of the Australians to speak. She invites a moment of silence for an Australian soldier killed in Afghanistan the previous day, then speaks movingly about the suffering of the prisoners, and the devotion of local people. 'You risked your lives and your livelihoods for our men, those who lived and those who died. Thank you. On behalf of all Australians, I thank you again.' As people do in memorial, she tries to find something positive to hold on to. 'During this time of appalling adversity and shameful human conduct, Sabahans and Australians dug deep to rise above it. Together they vanquished fear and loathing and all their manifestations and in their place chose generosity and love.' She talks of 'a way of living that embodies humanity among peoples and upholds the dignity and work of every individual. These are the lessons of Sandakan and of the death marches.'

And then she steps down and embraces a woman. I recognize her from a function the previous evening: her name is Jenny Smith.

Major Harold Andrews, a Borneo veteran, steps up to read from Revelations 7. 'Never again will they hunger; never again will they thirst.' I had met Andrews the previous day when looking at the Peace Window in the church, and we had talked for a while. In a pattern I had encountered repeatedly in talking to the veterans, he hadn't particularly wanted to talk about the war, or Borneo. Instead he had wanted to tell me all about his wife, who had recently died. And why not: the war took four or five years from some of these men's lives, but their shared existence with their wives lasted half a century or more.

Then the veterans speak. Russ goes first, at ninety-three standing tall in the intense heat. There is a written reminiscence in a printed programme that has been prepared for the day, explaining his experience and his thanks, but he diverts from it almost instantly and speaks without notes. 'The heart and mind become full of such mixed emotions it is hard to say what is uppermost in your mind,' he says. 'Ultimately it settles down and all that is left is an overwhelming feeling of sadness at the futility of it all.'

He talks about the mothers of the soldiers 'who brought their children into the world, and in later years suffered not knowing what had happened to them, wondering if they would ever be returned to them'. He praises the local people of Sandakan. And he recalls 'the care and concern for a mate that was as ennobling as this place was degrading. In the tenderness and love the slightly fitter showed for the weaker, we glimpsed the spirit that lifts us above the horror of this place.'

It is an exceptional speech, and I feel for Bunny having to follow it. But again, they are so different, and it isn't a problem. Bunny is unreconstructed, peppering his speech with references to the Japs, determined to show strength and resilience sixty-five years on. He is even darkly funny. 'A Jap guard bashed me behind the head with a pick handle and fractured three verte-brae in my neck,' he says. 'He thought I wasn't working hard enough. Which was true.' He thanks local citizens who passed medical supplies to the camp hospital, when it existed, and he remembers the Funk family, whose descendants now live near him on the Gold Coast in Queensland; three of the brothers were tortured and imprisoned during the war for aiding the POWs, and some were executed. But he, like Russ, found some-thing to cherish in the adversity. 'We all have families: parents, siblings, who we love. But sharing the frightful life in POW camps with fellow POWs, facing starvation, bad sickness and punishments, creates a very close bond of brotherhood, even closer than family.'

Wreaths are laid. Someone – whether Russ or Gwenda, I never find out who – has prepared one for me and I am called forward in the ceremony to lay it at the memorial on behalf of Australia's media, a gesture I appreciate enormously. In the background, a song, 'Goin' home', is sung:

Nothin' lost, all's gain,
No more fret nor pain,
No more stumblin' on the way,
No more longin' for the day,
Going to roam no more.

The 'Ode of Remembrance' is read, the 'Last Post' is played, and the Australian and British national anthems follow. The slow-stepping catafalque party marches away. The memorial is over, for another year.

*

There is a colonial-style English tea house above Sandakan, where scones and clotted cream are served amid teak antiques, and where one enters by crossing a croquet pitch laid upon immaculate trimmed grass. It is an echo of how things must once have been in this part of the world before the British departed.

Here, after the ceremony, we meet for lunch: the veterans, their families, the Australian members of the tourist board, and a few others linked to the event. The mood is light: there is relief, I sense, that it is over for another year, and I wonder if Russ is still going to want to sit down one-on-one for the interview. He looks tired and I wouldn't have held it against him had he chosen to cancel and lie down. But as the dishes are collected and we disperse, he rises and walks over to me.

'You ready?' he says.

We sit down beneath an idly circling rattan ceiling fan, and I ask him about his life before the war.

'I was born in the country,' he says; in Summer Hill, New South Wales, in November 1916, halfway through the First World War. 'My father, during the Depression, kept a large family going, and finally moved to the city so the children could have a better education.' Russ was an achiever: he won a scholarship at a business school, then moved to work in the New South Wales taxation office in 1933. 'A profession that's attracted much derogatory comment, but I was very interested.'

There was a woman called Joyce he had met and then separated from. By the late 1930s, he wanted her back. 'I continued to pursue her,' he says. 'I tried every subterfuge to see her.' He waited on the railway platform on the way to work in hope of seeing her and took to the streets around her workplace at lunchtime, just in case. 'None of my ploys advanced my cause.' But persistence and decency paid off: eventually they got back together, and were engaged in February 1941.

He had served in the militia beforehand through one of his courses before the war, and promotions had come swiftly once hostilities broke out: sergeant in January 1940, lieutenant in February, captain within a year. He had applied to join the new 6th Division Signals that was being formed and was rejected on the grounds of an earlier hernia operation, to his considerable annoyance. The standards of medical exclusion wouldn't remain this robust for long.

In July 1941, officers were sought to reinforce the 8th Division Signals in Malaya. Russ volunteered, accepting a demotion back to lieutenant because there were no vacancies for captain and failing to mention his earlier rejection, and was accepted. One gets a sense of the scale of the removal of an entire nation's youth by his army serial number. He had been rejected for the 6th Signals as applicant number NX 12589; now, barely a year later, he joined as NX 76171.

Then he went to break the news to Joyce. Seizing the moment, she set up a wedding in two days. On Saturday, 19 July 1941, she walked down the aisle of the Wesley Chapel in Pitt Street, Sydney, and they celebrated at nearby Cahills Restaurant afterwards. 'We departed in a small hired car on a honeymoon of uncertain

370

duration,' he says. They headed to the Blue Mountains on the edge of Sydney, built a snowman on Mt Canobolas – the first snow that Joyce had seen – and came back to Sydney, where Russ found orders, wedged under the doormat, to leave on the troopship SS *Johan van Oldenbarnevelt* on the twenty-ninth. They had been married ten days.

Russ is a master of refined understatement, and he says of his wartime service, 'We had an unsuccessful campaign in Malaya.' By January 1942 the Japanese were advancing down the Malay peninsula towards Singapore. As they closed in he remembers trying his first cigarette; he wouldn't get another until released from POW camp in 1945. Being in signals, scuttling around the jungle by motorbike and maintaining telephone lines, he could see the communications as they came through and knew the end was close.

He was injured twice in his brief time in service, once in a motorbike accident while attempting to destroy cable to prevent the Japanese using it, and once with a shrapnel wound following an aerial bombing attack that killed three fellow members of his signals section; the shrapnel is still in his back, occasionally playing havoc with airport scanners. He was admitted to hospital in Singapore, then discharged and sent to a unit in the city's Botanic Gardens. That's where he was on Sunday, 15 February, when surrender negotiations began and the war ended for him. The following day his unit, still in the Botanic Gardens, was marched 17 miles to Changi.

His brother, Les, was captured too, and they met briefly in the camp. Les, aged eighteen at enlistment, had understated his date of birth by two years in order to get in. They discussed the idea of claiming, a system through which a father and son, or brothers, could claim to be placed in the same unit, which would mean that when transported elsewhere from Singapore they would probably be kept together. They decided they would have better odds of one surviving the war if they remained separate. It would prove a wise choice.

'I spent about five months in Changi,' Russ says, 'which is generally regarded among POWs as one of the best camps. Though the general population seems to think that's where all the brutalities occurred, they were mainly on the railway and Sandakan.' In June came the last chance of a postcard home, barring a pre-printed card from Sandakan in 1943. He still has it, in neat and ordered block capitals.

DEAREST JOYCE. I AM VERY WELL AND NOT WOUNDED. WE ARE WELL CARED FOR AND I AM QUITE HAPPY. LOVE TO FAMILY. LESLIE ALSO WELL. FONDEST LOVE. RUSS, 20 JUNE.

On 8 July, he was one of 1,500 people in what was called a second working party – it came to be known as B Force – to be shipped from Singapore to some unrevealed destination. 'It seemed to be the promise of a land of milk and honey, so I was not disappointed when allocated to it.' He set sail on the *Ubi Maru* and arrived on 17 July. His unit history calculates they had about two and a half square feet each. 'The voyage was a nightmare, possibly the worst experience of my time in captivity,' he says. 'The air was foul enough on the first night, and then became worse as men became sick.' Diarrhoea and dysentery hit, and the most ill could not make it up the steel ladders to the perfunctory toilets. There was no water for washing and little food. Russ arrived with large circles of ringworm on his back and stomach, and dermatitis on most of his body, but was in better shape than many. He slept in a church that first night, then marched 8 miles to the camp, 'confident that this could be a good place. The beauty of the plants and flowers, the sheer size of the trees and the immensity of the jungle were appealing.'

A good place it was not but, in the early days, he found it tolerable, and was put to work digging out part of the slope on one side of the aerodrome site. Little acts of revenge would bring a tiny happiness: each party had to send a few men to the aerodrome cookhouse to bring food and tea for themselves and the Japanese. Those carrying the tea for the guards could pause out of sight, have a cuppa, and urinate into the tea bucket to refill it. When ordered to build a bamboo building for the Japanese, the prisoners spent days collecting bedbugs in match-boxes and then released them into the new building on their final day of work.

Before long Russ set about whatever greater rebellion could be achieved. 'In the camp I became involved in quite a lot of the underground movement,' he says. 'Intelligence operations in the camp were planned from the time we left Singapore, and in the civilian community there was an underground movement mainly through the police. They became amalgamated, and material such as medical supplies and cash and parts for the wireless were moved into the camp. We built the radio and sent the news out.

'Then that was betrayed.' In the interview he starts to tell me that two people had a personal argument and one denounced the other, but then decides not to revisit that. 'Ultimately it became too big. They arrested about twenty of us and 120 of the natives.' (Fastidiously accurate, he later contacts me to say an alternative account suggests 230 Asian civilians and police were arrested.) One of the arrested soldiers was Lionel Matthews, who was later executed; Russ subsequently created a detailed statutory declaration in support of a recommendation for a George Cross for him. 'I fortunately wasn't arrested: the testimony of another of the officers protected me. I was very fortunate to survive that.'

In fact, he would not learn just how fortunate until well after the war. Another man, Rod Wells, had worked with him on the intelligence network, and they happened to have consecutive identification numbers in the camp: Russ 666, Rod 667. Rod Wells was tortured during his interrogation and asked about other people involved. His captors told him, 'We know there was another. His number was 666.' Rod said 666 was his old number before they were changed. Out of character, the *kempeitai* – the terrifying military police – believed this, and in fact could not cross-check it, since the records had been lost. The man had suffered appallingly yet protected his friend, and this very likely saved Russ's life. One account has it that Wells, who was tried with Matthews, was sentenced to death and saved because of a typo in correspondence with Japanese command in Saigon. Instead, he was sentenced to ten years in the notorious Outram Road Gaol in Singapore, a terrible and brutal incarceration that eventually lasted twenty-one months until Singapore's liberation in August 1945, but which saved his life by sparing him the Sandakan marches. He survived the war, albeit permanently injured; among his tortures by the *kempeitai* was a terrible moment when his interrogator hammered a wooden skewer into his left ear, right through the drum. He was never able to hear with it again.

In the aftermath of the arrests, on 15 October 1943, all the officers working outside the camp were ordered to return and were given one hour to pack and assemble on the parade ground. All but seven of the officers were taken to a small coastal steamer called the *Tiensten Maru* and sailed for a week to Kuching. 'We were sent away, and that was a saving grace,' Russ says. 'When we got there, they said: you officers have been very naughty. You are not going to be allowed out of the camp. You are not going to be allowed to work. So the rations start to subside very substantially, as we didn't have to expend our energy on working.'

Despite the lack of food, the punishment, if that is truly what it was intended to be, that stopped them from working probably saved a lot of lives. Boredom was more of an enemy, but they turned that to their advantage. And this is when Russ says something that stays with me today. 'We set up quite a good educational programme, and learned to know each other and meet people of other professions,' he says.

'I found it very rewarding for my character, and I think most of the others did.'

This floors me, and I come back to it. What does he mean? Did it make you a better man? 'Absolutely. It was a big development in my character.' It was the range of abilities of the people around him that inspired him. There were barristers, doctors, labourers. 'A well-known doctor from Sydney, a leading obstetrician, took lessons in chook farming from a farmer. I talked to a Catholic priest, because he didn't have a business background and he wanted to know how to run a parish. That interchange of information had a cultural effect on us: we all became more understanding, more tolerant of each other. Soldiers often say the bond of prisoners of war is greater than among other humans. That's some of the saving grace.'

Kuching, it would later become clear, was a far better place to be than Sandakan, but generally they had no news of their former campmates. One reminder came in March 1944 when Lieutenant-Colonel Suga, who ran Kuching, announced there would be a funeral of an Australian officer, and that six officers could attend. Russ was one of them, and as the weak Australian pallbearers came into view struggling with a coffin, he knew instinctively it was Lionel Matthews. 'Blood was pouring from the rear of the plain timber coffin. I have never remembered the rest of the service.'

Rations diminished still further from March 1944 and although the Kuching officer prisoners were not suffering forced marches or beatings as severe as those in Sandakan, malnutrition and even starvation were becoming a real threat. Vitamin deficiencies set in, as did dysentery, which Russ contracted. A tall man, he says he was 7 stone 10 at the end of his time in captivity, a figure that was so far in excess of the average that he picked up the nickname 'fat boy'. 'Most of us were very thin, but we were in nowhere near as bad a condition as the British ORs,' he says. 'They died so often. They played the "Last Post" at every funeral, and it would be ten or twelve times a day sometimes.' He attributed this to them being accepted into the British Army at a lower level of fitness than was the case for the Australians. 'The demands on the people of England were such that even those who were quite unfit were called in.' He wondered, too, if there was a difference in the willingness to accept death. 'Some people say: I'm going to die. And did die. Australians would say: bugger him, you're not going to kill us.'

Leaflets began to be dropped in 1945 about Japanese surrender, and then food and medical supplies were dropped from RAAF Catalinas circling over the camp. Then it was a question of waiting for troops to arrive, which they did on 13 September. 'It surprised most of us, I think, to realize that all thoughts of revenge had passed from our minds. It seemed to be beneath our dignity to hand out the kind of treatment we had endured and merely ignoring our former captors seemed to be enough. Punishment could be left to the appropriate authorities.'

It would later become clear that they might never have had the chance to await that justice. The Allies found orders in Suga's office ordering that all prisoners were to be marched to Dahan for elimination. There are mixed accounts of what happened: some consider Suga a hero who refused to follow orders and thus saved a great many lives. Others believe he postponed instructions for the march because it was convenient to do so, and that the war simply ended before the orders could be carried out.

'As it emerged, we were going to suffer the same fate on the same day,' says Russ, referring to the Sandakan marches. 'Lieutenant-Colonel Suga, it has been established only fairly recently, did receive orders, and he put them aside for ten days or so, and that was the vital ten days before the end of the war.' Bunny has previously taken the generous view of Suga, and Russ says, 'I agree with Bunny, he probably was a humane man thrown into an army.

'Although we knew the war had ended, we were not told even that there had been surrender in Europe. They kept the news from us for ten months. When [Suga] did tell us, he broke down and cried, and he talked about an atomic bomb, and it turns out his wife and two children were killed.' Russ is quiet for a moment, then resumes. 'It doesn't matter whose side you are on, it's not right. War is never right. Each side is human I think, and soldiers have to follow what their leaders tell them.'

*

Freedom brought challenges. On 13 September they were taken in small craft to an Australian Hospital Ship off the coast. Only now did news begin to filter through, and the first inklings of what had gone on at Sandakan after they had left the camp. 'We still didn't know how many had died. When we got home the story was suppressed by the government.' Frantically, in this age before easy communication, soldiers tried to get word home, while their families, in agonies of uncertainty, waited for news. 'My mother had two of us away at just about the same time. My brother was underage: when I joined the army, he put his age up and signed up too. For two years she didn't know if we were dead or alive.'

On 15 September the ship touched in at Labuan. He received letters for the first time in years. One of them brought dreadful news: his brother, Leslie, was dead. He had been put to forced labour on the Burma Railway, then moved to Singapore, and was being transported on the ship *Rakuyo Maru*, which was sunk by two torpedoes from the American submarine *Sealion* near Hainan Island in September 1944. Leslie did not survive. Russ has researched the ship's fate exhaustively: how the hold full of prisoners was evacuated calmly as the water poured in; how the ship stayed afloat for twelve hours; how the Japanese crew were picked up by their navy's destroyers and how the abandoned prisoners took over the remaining liferafts; how 141 survivors were picked up by Australians and 136 instead by Japanese; how the last survivor was pulled from the sea five long days after the ship was torpedoed, yet so many were never seen again. He has wondered about the circumstances and extent of his brother's suffering ever since.

Alive but now grieving, Russ watched the first of his colleagues disembark at Brisbane; many of them fell on hands and knees to kiss the Australian soil. On 13 October they sailed into Sydney Harbour. Taken in an ambulance to the Australian General Hospital at Concord, when he arrived he walked through to reception. 'I saw Joyce rushing towards me, arms outstretched, to make it perhaps the most splendid day of my life.' A few days later he was discharged. On his first night home with his wife he woke screaming, believing a Japanese guard was taking his money, and threw himself across her to look under the mattress for it. She would get used to it.

Not everyone came back to domestic bliss. 'I think it was in lots of cases difficult,' Russ says. 'Quite a few came back and found their wives were no longer living with them; they had found someone else, got divorces, found sweethearts. While most settled down reasonably well, there were lots of mental problems. There were four suicides within the years I came home.'

But Joyce had waited. 'She carried on her normal working life. She said there were times that she was losing the memory. But she hung on.' And at this, his voice cracks, and he starts to cry. 'I had a very good wife. She died last year. We had a very happy life together.'

He takes a moment, and then talks about the fact that, for all the increased attention on Sandakan, ignorance is still widespread. 'Today you can still go to people in the street and say "Sandakan" and they give you a blank look. I had a tradesman in the house the other day. I said I was in the war. He said: was that the Boer War? He was serious. He didn't have any idea of when the wars had occurred.'

Is forgiveness possible?

He thinks awhile. 'It's hard to distinguish between forgiving and forgetting,' he says. 'I suppose you could forget, then you wouldn't have anything left to forgive.'

It is clear he has thought this through in great detail, decades of reflection. 'What do you do when you forgive?' he asks. 'Say I no longer hate you because of your actions? I never hated the Japanese, I recognize that wars have gone on like that, we all have our dark moments, every nation. I am not religious but I always recall the saying: don't visit the sins of the fathers upon the sons. I have no feelings against the generations that have come since.'

He's more interested in ensuring that it doesn't happen again. 'They say the price of liberty is eternal vigilance. If there are warning signs, do something about it. But I'm afraid my belief in human nature is such that I don't think it's going to happen.'

There is perhaps a nervousness that Sandakan could, as other tragic wartime sites have sometimes done, attract a mawkish voyeurism, a box to tick rather than deferent recognition, but for the moment servicemen seem pleased that people are becoming more engaged, and enraged, with what happened. 'The tragic events are known by many people,' says Russ, 'but not enough people.'

*

As society returned to normal, Russ returned to tax. He built a successful career there but, ever practical, decided his military experience was better suited to supervision and then administration, and so set his path in that direction. He was Assistant Deputy Commissioner of the New South Wales tax office by the time he retired in 1976. 'I always enjoyed my work,' he says. Retirement, in practice, meant a further decade spent lecturing on taxation across Australia's capital cities and the bigger towns of New South Wales. 'We made each occasion a holiday,' he says.

In the time-honoured Australian way, he built a home in 1947, at Castlecrag, by Sydney's beautiful Middle Harbour. He spent his whole remaining life in Sydney, enjoying being close to family. Daughter Jacqui was born in 1949 and, by the time I last contacted him in late 2014, he had two granddaughters and five great-grandchildren, the eldest of them six years old.

Even when the time came to move to a retirement village in 1986, he put his skills to use, spending years as the chairman of the body corporate: '228 living units,' he says, with characteristic exactness. It was here that Joyce developed Alzheimer's, suffering from it for seven years before her death in 2009. Russ was able to care for her for all but the last three months. He's still there, in the retirement village, capable and organized, with no intention of moving.

Throughout his later life, the military, and Sandakan in particular, would be regular fixtures. He became a member of the 8th Division Signals Association in New South Wales. 'Large and very active,' he says. 'Held every office until it closed down due to diminishing membership.' Diminishing membership? He means, of course, that they are dying out. The same applies, he says, to the Taxation Office sub-branch of the Returned Soldiers League, although he says that's still managing to hang on through the Australian veterans of the Korean and Vietnam wars. The Old Sandakian Association lives on, and through it he has dealt with many enquiries about people who died there over the years, while also talking to children from Western Australia to Sabah itself. 'Wonderful working with the children,' he says. Time and again he has returned for Sandakan memorials or other commemorations across Borneo.

When I reach Russ in late 2014, he is about to take a trip to Japan with three other ex-prisoners of war and their carers at the invitation of the Japanese government, as part of something called the Japanese/POW Friendship Programme. He sends me the itinerary. It would be demanding for a thirty-year-old, never mind a man of ninety-seven. It reads:

October 24
05.50: depart hotel.
06.37: depart Shinagawa Station.
10.31: Arrive Hiroshima.
11.35–12.05: Exchange Programme with students of Noborichou Primary School.

And so on, through a week of travel and briefings and commemorations, from Tokyo to Hiroshima to Kyoto to Osaka, via ministries, war memorials, NGOs and schools.

He returns unwell, with a lung infection, but tells me he feels the sentiments of contrition expressed to him in Japan were heartfelt. 'These seemed to me to be genuine expressions,' he writes. 'Certainly, the people we met, the citizens of Japan were most friendly and helpful, no signs of animosity, and a wish for world peace.' Japanese treatment of prisoners 'is not to be forgotten', and should be taught not just to Australians but to Japanese,' he says, but this is 'history from which lessons should be learned and applied today. Both our nations share responsibility with the rest of the world to work toward greater cooperation in shedding the poverty, degradation, war and terrorism that still abounds.'

His role in Japan has been important but has clearly worn him down; when he sits down to write to me he is amid a third course of strong antibiotics. His doctor has told him he is doing too much and he has accepted this may be the case. 'I will be trying to eliminate some features from my life (can't get rid of old age), which will include withdrawing from some of the constantly recurring ex-POW activities,' he writes. 'I just can't handle them at present.'

This makes me think of what Lynette Silver said about the march survivors she met: about the burden they all faced in having to tell people about what they had suffered, to represent it endlessly to an ignorant population. As so many other veterans have passed, something similar is happening to Russ, called upon far too often to relive and remember the painful events of seventy years ago.

It has been a full existence. But the important point is not so much the minutiae of later life, the advancement through the tax office and the association memberships and the retirement village and the rest. The importance is that life went on at all despite the privations he and so many others had endured.

Russ is in this book because his capacity to look back on such atrocity, to compartmentalize it, to process and analyse and learn from it, is overwhelmingly powerful. He will always be known as a former Borneo POW; that is what he will be remembered for, the defining event of his life, and as a society we seem more intent upon burdening him with this role the older he becomes. But, for me, I will always recall him talking with such sad gratitude about his wife, and it tells me that the life they built together would not be defined by the small slice of it he spent incarcerated and emaciated in the Borneo heat.

*

There is one other thing Russ says that prompts a little more research: a diversion from Russ's story, perhaps, but something he is absolutely insistent that I include in the chapter if he himself is to be in any way celebrated.

Lynette Silver had spoken to me about the disproportionate attention given to Australians compared to the many equally heroic local people who lost everything.

'For the Australians who came here, it is a tragic story, obviously it is, but they were soldiers,' she said. 'When they enlisted, there was the possibility that they might not survive. But the people here were civilians, already defeated and under occupation. Their courage was of the highest and rarest order, inspired not by the prospect of victory but the reality of defeat and oppression. The courage they exhibited under the circumstances exceeds any person who has won a Victoria Cross. It's a different sort of courage: this is long-term stuff, month after month, knowing that if you are caught the best thing that can happen to you is execution, and the stuff that goes beforehand doesn't bear thinking about.'

In her research she met numerous people who had lost four or five members of the same family, and heard of countless others that had been wiped out entirely. She began to feel uncomfortable about the importance placed upon the Australian losses. 'All nationalities do it, and selfishly we concentrate on our own little patch, but it was getting to the point of embarrassment here for me, cringe factor,' she said. 'It is insulting for us to come here constantly and talk about the Australian story and perhaps only a passing mention of local people.'

Putting this idea of greater recognition of local suffering to Russ, I find him in absolute agreement. 'I've always done that. Other people haven't and I've always been conscious of it. We all come over to another country and talk about our dead, but not the dead of your country. I've never been comfortable with it. Never.'

To respect Russ's wishes – insistence, really – that locals be reflected in this chapter, I seek out a man called Phillip Mairon Bahaja who embodies the spirit of local people that the veterans are now keen to recognize.

In 1943, Phillip was fourteen years old, living in a Borneo town called Penampang. Keen for work, he and his friends went to the nearest major town, Jesselton, and were recruited by the Japanese for manpower. He said goodbye to his father, not knowing he would never see him again, and was put on a timber boat for four days to Sandakan. Far from being treated as employees, they were worked as slave labour and beaten with rifle butts, much like the POWs. After being repeatedly threatened with beheading, he escaped into a rubber plantation and then the jungle, where he was sheltered by a local tribesman, staying there and living in traditional tribal ways. When the Japanese then arrested that tribesman, he set out to try to find a British and Australian camp in the jungle; having done so, he joined with the Australians as a teenager guerrilla warrior for the rest of the war.

When I meet him, he is a man with cropped grey hair wearing a great many medals, an Australia badge, a sharp dark suit with a grey tie, and a creased-eye smile of the most enormous pride. He is here with his family, lots of his family: looking now at the picture I took of them all, there are sixteen people in the frame. I have arranged our meeting in advance and he has prepared for it, presenting me with a commemorative flag adorned with his wartime picture, the Malay and Australian ensigns, and a proud dedication beginning: 'My Adventure'.

Our interview takes place in broken English, so it is better to quote from a personal history he has written that somebody has translated into English. He remembers the officer in charge, Captain Russell, who offered him and his friends a choice of weapons: Bren gun, Awan or Austin? 'I chose the Austin gun because the bullets will come out non-stop from the barrel like heavy rain and enemies will not have a chance to shoot back.' Like so many involved in the war, he was clearly still a child. He was trained for a week and then deployed. 'We were given an instruction to proceed operation with our own tactic to fight the Japs.'

If Bunny has not forgotten or forgiven the atrocities of the war, that's nothing compared to this generation of locals. 'We had to fight to the end to defeat the Japanese because they killed people as they liked, and raped women,' Phillip says. 'I saw with my own eyes, the Japanese bayonetted a baby, beheaded a local and raped a local girl.'

He soon had his first chance for revenge, setting an ambush and killing three soldiers. As he stepped out of hiding to check his work, another group of soldiers came and shot at him, hitting his leg. 'This gives me a souvenir mark which remains until today.' He escaped, believing he did so because of an amulet the tribal leader had given him.

With about 500 other locals, he continued in this vein for the remainder of the war. 'Without much experience and skill in war, we were suddenly in the jungle fighting. But we were high in spirit and we were proud to wear the Australian Army's uniform to fight the Japs.'

One day in 1945, he was called to headquarters at Kaniogan and told the guerrilla operation was at an end as the Japanese had surrendered. They gathered to celebrate and prepared to go back to their villages. Before he left, Captain Russell gave him a handwritten letter. Phillip couldn't read it: he was illiterate. But he knew it expressed appreciation.

Heading home he passed through Sandakan and found dead bodies to the sides of the road, the town destroyed by bombs, ships sunken in the harbour. With nothing else to do, he thought he might as well join the army, and was introduced to an Australian, Captain York. 'I can still remember he was wearing a uniform the colour of green jungle.' But he was rejected, because of his height – he was shorter than a rifle – and his age: this veteran of the war was, at the most, sixteen.

Phillip was devastated by the news: he had no money, no family nearby, no way of buying food. But then he remembered the letter from Russell, and showed it to York. York read it and said to a colleague: 'Mess boy.' And that is what he became. 'I jumped for joy,' he says. 'I didn't care what job was given me as long as I worked in the military, had salary and food to eat. That same day, I was given a uniform which I received proudly. I clutched the uniform to my heart.'

Phillip's account is filled with gratitude: towards Captain Russell, towards Captain York, towards all Australians, to the military itself. But it is obvious just how much thanks should be flooding in quite the opposite direction, at this child who missed his youth in order to chase invaders around the jungle with a bayonet.

Peace was not lasting, not in this part of the world, and the subsequent years brought more problems for North Borneo: pirate attacks, the Brunei Rebellion, confrontation with Indonesia and eventually separation from the British. During the pirate attacks – and there were many, fifty-four recorded between November 1958 and October 1959 alone – Phillip was attached to the warship HMS *Barossa* as an interpreter. Other times he accompanied Gurkhas as a native pilot, and he still has a kukri, the curved Nepalese knife used as both a tool and a weapon by the Gurkhas, as a herald of his service with the Royal Gurkha Rifles, considered one of the elite fighting forces in modern history. By 1962 he had become an officer. He retired from the military and police in 1974 after thirty years of service – aged forty-five.

'My age now,' he tells me with a smile, 'is eighty-two. Whisky, Johnnie Walker! Still going strong.' His family wrote to tell me that he died on 12 December 2012.

*

Russ unfolds his long frame and stands with a slight stoop. He shakes my hand and tells me he has enjoyed meeting me; tongue-tied, I try to tell him that my time with him has been a great privilege, but I doubt it comes out right. So much sadness here, but so much dignity; and the repercussions and echoes won't die with people like Russ.

Also at the lunch is Jenny Smith, the woman the Governor General had embraced after her speech.

I know of her because I have read a poem written for her in the name of her father, Thomas Ebzery, a Narooma butcher who went to war in 1941 and was imprisoned in Sandakan when Jenny was a small child. It's a poem that could speak for so many of those cruelly treated men, and the impact of their loss on every later generation.

'My little girl,' it begins. 'If I could but have held your hand for just a little while.'

It talks about his wishes to have spent time with his family;

his love of his wife; the sorry circumstances of his existence in the camp, as friends fall away. And then:

'My sadness is, my little one, I may never see this through.'

He did not.

12

Chuck Yeager

Edwards Air Force Base sits amid a desolate, flat, windswept wilderness in Southern California, just south of the drone and rumble of the Mojave–Barstow Highway. It is built around the Rogers Lake Bed, a desert salt pan whose tough, flat surface creates a natural extension to the base's asphalt runways. When you stand at the edge of it, it is blinding bright and limitless, heat radiating from its cracked surface, a spirit-level-flat nothingness right up to the Air Force Flight Test Center entrance sign that says, in a strident italic: *Warriors supporting Warriors. Testing the Future Today . . . Toward the Unexplored.*

You wouldn't think it from the bitter, dusty crosswinds, strong enough to blow your car door out to its hinges when you open it by an inch, but this is an outstanding place for aviation. It remains one of the nation's pre-eminent locations for military flight testing, and was often in the public eye as the landing runway for the Space Shuttle programme, but its finest moment came back in 1947 when the place was called Muroc Army Airfield. On 14 October that year, Captain Charles Elwood Yeager climbed out of the belly of an airborne B-29 Superfortress into an experimental aircraft suspended beneath it called the Bell X-1, severed the connection between

389

the two, fired the X-1's rocket and broke the sound barrier – the invisible, impenetrable wall scientists used to believe existed at the speed of sound – for the first time in the history of aviation.

Today, I am sitting directly behind Chuck Yeager in a chunky MPV being driven around Edwards by a captain from the Air Force Test Pilot School, looking for the wreckage of Yeager's old house on the perimeter of the base. We approach a sign warning of live ammunition being fired ahead. 'Don't worry about it,' he tells the driver. 'It'll be fine.' Beside me is Victoria, his second wife, much younger than him, and somewhat as tough. She is the person one has to get through in order to secure an interview with the man, although you don't really know whom you're corresponding with until you finally meet her. In my case, this has taken six months to arrange.

He is craggy and granite-featured, but then again, from the photographs I've seen, he was craggy and granite-featured in 1947, and probably as a baby too. He wears a Glamorous Glennis baseball cap – *Glamorous Glennis* being the name he gave to the X-1 he broke the sound barrier in, Glennis being his first wife, who died of cancer in 1990 – and a black windcheater with *Cal-Ore Lite Flight* written on it, over a blue shirt. He has a particular grin that makes his eyes crease inwards. It gives the impression of a lizard about to deliver a punchline.

It seems our interview will take place on the move, and Victoria gestures to my recorder and urges me to get started. So I lean forward and, in the manner of these things, start with an easy lay-up question to make things comfortable. Earlier, I have driven along Yeager Boulevard, one of several thoroughfares at Edwards named after legendary aviators, the difference being that normally they wait for the aviator in question to die in a plane crash before bestowing the honour. Yeager, uniquely in this honoured crew, is still alive.

'General Yeager,' I begin, ready to ask about his connections with Edwards. But I don't get far.

'Is that an English accent?'

'Yes.'

A pause.

'I gotta tell you, I hated the English even more than I hated the Germans in World War Two. The meanest people I have ever seen, and we were supposed to be *saving* your goddamn asses.'

And so we begin.

*

Calling Chuck Yeager tough is like saying the *Titanic* had a bit of a scrape on its maiden voyage. Yeager isn't tough, he's indestructible, and represents the kind of epic, heroic American that simply can't exist any more in this cynical age. He became a Second World War flying ace (that is, five kills – shooting down five aircraft) aged twenty-one, not in a year or a week of flying but in a *single mission*. He amputated a shot colleague's leg with a penknife before carrying him up a snowbound Pyrenean mountain to save his life. He once parachuted from a plane and was hit in the face by his own ejector seat, causing his head and hand to catch fire; upon landing he calmly asked a passer-by for a knife with which he cut off two of his own charred fingertips. When Tom Wolfe wrote *The Right Stuff*, the definitive account of post-war test-pilot bravado and skill, the term was really coined for Yeager himself. 'The most righteous of all the possessors of the right stuff,' Wolfe said.

A case in point is the record-breaking flight itself. Everyone knows Yeager broke the sound barrier. But that's not the best bit of the story. To understand Yeager, you need the rest of it.

Two nights before the flight, he decided to go horse-riding

in the dark in the middle of California's Mojave Desert. Galloping between the Joshua trees on a moonless night, he failed to see a closed gate and was thrown over it, breaking two ribs. He refused to tell anyone in command in case they grounded him, and instead got his ribs taped up by a veterinarian. 'He said: don't do nothin' strenuous,' Yeager says. 'Like break the sound barrier,' Victoria retorts.

But he had a problem: though he could fly his X-1 jet with broken ribs, he couldn't seal the hatch. So he got his trusted flight engineer, Jack Ridley, to saw the end off a broomstick, fashioned it into a lever, and used that instead. Then, wounded and with a broom handle wedging the lock, he went off and broke the speed of sound for the first time in human history.

It's clear that one of the things that shaped Yeager was his background in poverty in Hamlin, West Virginia. At the time the state topped the nation in unemployment, and he was from the poorest parish within it, Lincoln County. 'It wasn't really tough. It was just a variety of experiences,' he tells me today as we bounce around the scrubby desert on the edges of Edwards. But it's not a childhood a lot of us would recognize: by the time he was six he knew how to shoot a .22 rifle and hunted squirrels and rabbit, skinning them before school and leaving them in a bucket of water for his mum to cook for supper. He slopped hogs, milked cows, weeded gardens and stole watermelons from farmers who kept shotguns loaded with rock salt 'to sting the butts of kids like us'.

But Yeager has written that West Virginia made him the pilot he was. I ask him what that means. 'What is the secret to combat?' he asks me. 'Deflection shooting.' That means shooting at where something is going to be, not where it is now. 'What do the kids in the hills do? They hunt. They shoot at animals that are running. And that makes them experts at deflection shooting.' More to the point, his background and lack of education made him a

Chuck Yeager

fighter, stubborn, saying what he thought and meaning what he said. 'I was impulsive or headstrong. Something is either right or wrong.' This would constantly help him as he rose through the ranks, overtaking more qualified and experienced people along the way.

Another vital part of the Yeager legend was his vision, rated 20/10, or exceptionally sharp; this was at the heart of his success as a fighter pilot in the Second World War since he could see German planes further away than anyone. Also, lacking education – and self-conscious about it – he benefited instead from an endless fascination with the most minute detail of an aircraft, making him an engineer as much as a pilot.

Yeager got started in flying after joining the Army Air Corps, the predecessor of the air force, in 1941, aged eighteen, shortly before America's engagement in the Second World War. He started out in Tonopah, Nevada, where he was one of thirty fledgling pilots who underwent intensive training to join a combat fighter squadron, the 363rd. He took to it like a duck to water, logging 100 hours of flying in his first month, and never looked back. They were a gung-ho lot. One fellow pilot, apparently doomed as he glided in with engine failure, bounced off the roof of a passing truck in order to get enough altitude to clear the airport fence. But even among this balls-out fraternity, Yeager stood out.

The training was truly brutal: thirteen pilots died in six months, mostly through individual error. But already, so young, Yeager seemed immune to it. 'A gruesome weeding-out process was taking place,' he wrote in his viciously invigorating autobiography, *Yeager.* 'I turned my back on lousy fliers as if their mistakes were catching. When one of them became a grease spot on the tarmac, I almost felt relieved: it was better to bury a weak sister in training than in combat, where he might not only bust his ass, but do something that would bust two or three asses in addition to his own.' He speaks of 'getting mad at the dead', not just for losing their lives so young but 'for destroying expensive government property as stupidly as if they had driven a Cadillac off a bridge'. It sounds almost obscenely lacking in empathy, but that's what fighter pilots had to do. 'Anger was my defence mechanism . . . either you become calloused or you crack.' And 'Those who couldn't put a lid on their grief couldn't hack combat.'

The legend got rolling before Yeager even went to war. A friend with a ranch had mentioned he wanted to get rid of a tree; Yeager flew by and topped it with his wingtip, before trying to explain to a maintenance officer why there were hunks of wood rammed into the wing. He buzzed the main street of his home town of Hamlin, West Virginia. He herded antelope from his P-39, shot them and barbecued them for his training squadron.

That was nothing compared to wartime. It didn't start well for him: on one of his earliest missions, aged twenty-one, he was shot down. He was protected by the French Resistance, who eventually sent him on foot over the Pyrenees with another airman. Resting in a woodshack, they were discovered by German troops who fired at them, so they leapt down a logslide at the back of the shack, several hundred metres down into a creek. The other airman had been shot in the knee in the escape, with only a tendon remaining intact; Yeager cut off his lower leg with a penknife, then dragged him up the side of a snowbound mountain to the border. Again, there's a sense of bullheadedness driving his actions rather than empathy for another man. 'I don't know why I keep hold of him and struggle to climb,' Yeager wrote. 'It's the challenge, I guess, and a stubborn pride knowing that most guys would've let go of Pat before now, and before he stopped breathing.' Yeager pulled them both into Spain, leaving the airman by a road where he was picked up and saved, returning home – minus half a leg – six weeks later.

Having escaped, Yeager had a problem; nobody who had been assisted in escape by the French Resistance was allowed to fly again, because if they did so and were captured a second time, they could reveal crucial information to the Germans about the Resistance activities. This was supposed to be a hard and fast rule, but Yeager, feeling cheated out of a war, was having none of it: he fought his case all the way up to General Eisenhower, later the US president, who eventually took his side. After that, Yeager excelled, spotting enemy aircraft early and taking advantage of the extra time his sight gave him. The day when he shot down five aircraft in a single mission was the first, and perhaps the only, incident of a US Air Force pilot ever having done so; many acclaimed aviators didn't achieve five kills in the entire war.

Sometimes his enthusiasm for the fight was alarming. Writing about an incident when his squadron encountered about 150 Luftwaffe, he recalls, 'We couldn't believe our luck.' He has called dogfighting 'a clean contest of skill, stamina and courage, one on one. There is no joy in killing someone, but real satisfaction when you outflew a guy and destroyed his machine. For me, combat remains the ultimate flying experience.'

The Second World War is where his contempt for the English stems from. I don't take it personally. As he gradually decodes my accent and recognizes I have done some research, he warms up a little, and four times he apologizes to me for being rude about the English. But he can't help himself: each time he follows up by being even ruder about them. 'All our missions ran about eight hours, 36,000 feet, no pressurization, freezing cold with people shooting at you, and when you came home from an eight-hour mission you would take a bicycle out on the country roads to unwind,' he explains. 'And then a goddamn farmer with a pitchfork would come out and say: get off my road, you damned Yankee. I hated the British more than the

Germans.' He gives me that classic Yeager lizard-punchline smile, a combination of a grin and a sneer. 'Ain't your fault. I don't hold it against you.'

When he came home, luck was on his side. After a short and miserable spell training in Texas, he moved to Wright Field, Ohio, in order to bring his newly pregnant wife, Glennis, closer to family support in West Virginia. In doing so he fluked the right place at the right time, because Wright Field was to become the centre of what Yeager calls 'the greatest adventure in aviation since the Wright brothers – the conversion from propeller airplanes to supersonic jets and rocket-propelled aircraft'. In 1945 he flew for the first time in a Lockheed P-80 Shooting Star, the first operational American jet fighter – 'like being a pebble fired from a slingshot,' he recalls – and felt like he was truly flying for the first time. In August that year he travelled to Muroc, accompanying Colonel Albert Boyd, head of the flight test division and the man who would trust Yeager more than any other to deliver the pioneering spirit of the jet age. Muroc was where history would be made: the first flight through the sound barrier.

*

Driving around Edwards today, in the relentless sandblasting wind of the Mojave Desert, Yeager recalls the process of beating the sound barrier with a mixture of pride and bitterness. The first place he takes me to is the remnant of a shack way out in the middle of the desert just outside the modern edges of the base. Angular cacti dot the flat landscape for miles around amid the dull yellows and light greens of the tinder-dry scrub. There's not much left now: a few stumps, flat concrete slabs dotted with fragments of brick, the top of the well they drew their water from, the frame of a swimming pool he built out of cement. ('Where'd you get the cement?' asks a test pilot who is escorting us around the base. 'Stole it,' Yeager replies.) Rattlesnakes, scorpions and coyotes were rife here in the 1940s, and probably still are. Here, he lived with his wife and infant children, because the base would not allow his wife on to it, since he was there on temporary assignment from Ohio. 'No housing. No nothing. So we rented a little shack, and that's where we set. My wife was not allowed to use the hospital, commissary, nothing. I'm a pretty bitter guy.'

He has not a word of sympathy for the people who ran Muroc at that time. 'Muroc was staffed by the dregs of the air force. They were useless.' I want to make sure he knows I'm recording him and that he will be quoted, so show him the tape recorder. He stares right at me and speaks into it: 'I cannot over-emphasize, this base had the most sorry-ass people on it, the most useless people I have ever seen.' Yeager isn't someone you have to worry about retracting his quotes.

Still, as he says, 'I was bitter, but on the other hand I was a very happy guy because no pilots ever got this opportunity again.' He is referring to the X-1 programme, the very first time the air force had been permitted to do research flying, and which was given a mandate to work out how to beat the sound barrier.

Back in the 1940s, there was a widespread belief that it was impossible to fly faster than the speed of sound without breaking the plane apart, because the closer one got to it, the more shock waves smashed against the fuselage. A famous British test pilot, Geoffrey de Haviland Jr, had died when his own experimental aircraft, *The Swallow*, disintegrated at Mach 0.94 (that is, 0.94 times the speed of sound) in early 1947. The US had long wanted to go supersonic, and initially their star man was a civilian called Chalmers 'Slick' Goodlin, who had been piloting a new test jet called the X-1, manufactured by Bell. But Goodlin had demanded a renegotiated contract and $150,000 in pay to go beyond Mach 1, paid in instalments to beat taxes; the air corps lost patience, took over the project from Bell, and that's where Yeager came in. He charged $283 a month – his regular army captain's pay.

Despite his record, Yeager was not an obvious choice for Colonel Boyd to make as the pioneering test pilot. But Boyd was, in essence, an older version of Yeager himself. 'Think of the toughest person you've ever known, then multiply by ten, and you're close to the kind of guy that the old man was,' Yeager recalls. 'He also came up the hard way. And what he saw in me was I knew maintenance. My dad was a natural gas driller and I worked with him and used to overhaul all his engines. As a twelve-year-old kid I could disassemble dome regulators, and that was the heart of the X-1.' Boyd himself, who died in 1976, said shortly before his death, 'Above all, I wanted a pilot who was rock-solid in stability. Yeager came up number one.'

Nevertheless, there was plenty of fuel for Yeager's sense of educational inferiority. 'It wasn't easy. When you're a maintenance officer and you're assigned to the prime research programme, and you've got twenty prime test pilots looking down at this maintenance officer flying something they'd give their limbs to fly, it wasn't easy.' Not that it bothered him all that much. 'Test pilots couldn't fly worth a shit.'

Preparing for test flights on the X-1 was hellish, as scientists experimented with the effect of high altitude and extreme G-force on them. He and wingman Bob Hoover wore the first high-altitude pressure suits. Flights began in August 1947; the X-1 was carried up attached to the belly of a B-29 bomber, which would climb to 25,000 feet, then dive to pick up speed. Yeager takes me to a curious cross-shaped bay set into a concrete apron, now on the edge of a boneyard of retired planes; this was where the X-1 would be placed before the B-29 positioned itself above it and the two were attached, with barely centi-metres of clearance between the X-1 and the concrete. There's a plaque here now, commemorating his flight; in fact, Edwards is chock-full of tributes to Yeager, including a statue.

'Good memories?' I try. 'Nah. I don't live in the past. See these arrows? That shows where the nose wheel of the B-29 went. There, that's where it did a 90-degree turn.'

Once airborne in the B-29, Yeager would climb down a ladder from the mother ship to the test jet, and then the bomber would release him. On the first flights they carried no fuel, gliding down to the lakebed. The cockpit was pressurized with pure nitrogen so as to be inflammable; there was no backup oxygen system beyond what he was breathing. Lacking a proper hard-hat helmet, he made his own by cutting the top out of a Second World War tank helmet as a protective dome, and put his own leather helmet over the top of it.

The first powered flight came on 29 August, by which time Yeager had established, if not a closeness with the plane, then at least an understanding with it. You can still see the X-1, or a perfect replica, hanging from the ceiling of the base's museum, and the first impression apart from its garish orange colour is that it barely looks large enough to fly or carry fuel to power its hidden four-chamber rocket engine. Bell designed the thing to look like a Browning .50-calibre machine-gun bullet with wings, reasoning that nothing was more stable in flight than a bullet.

Dick Frost, a project engineer, once said it was 'a beautiful airplane to fly, but at least half the aviation engineers I had talked to thought it was doomed'. I remind Yeager that he once wrote there were a dozen ways the X-1 could kill you. 'Nah,' he says. 'There were at least a hundred. You had no way of getting out of the X-1. You could open the door and roll out, but you'd be sliced in two by a razor-sharp wing.' But he was confident in the jet's ability to pass the speed of sound without disintegrating? He looks at me with eighty-nine years' worth of contempt. 'Obviously. Or I wouldn't have flown it.'

Dropped from the B-29 on the first powered flight, he lit the rocket chambers, leaving diamond-shaped shock waves in his exhaust, then promptly ignored the flight plan to jettison fuel and land, instead doing a slow roll and then rattling the base. Subsequent missions steadily increased the speed, working out what happened the closer they got to the sound barrier. At .94 they ran into trouble as he lost pitch control, and for a while this looked like the end of the line, until engineer Jack Ridley – a true hero of the programme, who Yeager speaks of with absolute reverence and considers 'the brains of the operation' – came up with a fix. 'We modified the airplane with a jackscrew that would change the angle of the horizontal stabilizer, making a flying tail,' Yeager explains. 'That was the answer to the whole X-1 programme: if you're gonna fly supersonic, you gotta have a flying tail. It took the British, the French and the Soviet Union five years to figure out that little trick.' At the next flight, .96, the windscreen frosted, forcing him to land blind, guided verbally by another pilot. And, finally, on 14 October – after breaking his ribs in that horse-riding escapade – his X-1 created the first sonic boom ever heard on Earth.

Going supersonic turned out to be a whole lot easier than being nearly supersonic. While nearing the sound barrier the shock waves caused great disruption to a plane's handling, beyond it was 'smooth as a baby's bottom', Yeager wrote. 'Grandma could be sitting up there sipping lemonade. After all the anxiety, breaking the sound barrier turned out to be a perfectly paved speedway.' It was, he recalls today, an anticlimax. 'When we were successful, I suppose I was let down a little bit that it didn't blow all to hell.' Unsurprisingly, having fallen off a horse before this perfect flight, he then crashed a motorbike that night.

Oddly, the air force kept the flight secret for months, perhaps to allow production of supersonic jets to get under way before the Russians became aware of what the Americans had achieved. 'That gave us a hell of a quantum leap over the rest of the world's air forces for five years, that's the reason it was classified,' he says today. This created an odd situation for Yeager: first a sense that nothing had happened ('Thunder with no reverberation,' as Wolfe put it), then an intense heroism and a speaking circuit that he was deeply uncomfortable with. It is odd to think of that forced anonymity today, now that Yeager is a true American icon, made famous by Wolfe's book and portrayed by Sam Shepard on film. But at no stage did the flight or its acclaim bring any money. He told his superiors he wanted to buy his long-suffering wife Glennis – still raising several kids in a shack in the middle of the desert and drawing water from a windmill pump – a fur coat, but was refused. 'We lived no better than a damned sheepherder – maybe worse.'

Making twenty speeches a month while still test-piloting, before long he was on the cover of *Time* magazine, but the fame didn't help him, particularly within the armed forces. He hated the public speaking. 'Some goddamn friend of a senator would be head of the Rotary Club and would say: hey, can you get Yeager to make a speech for us?' The air force, seeing an opportunity, would tell him to do it. 'I'm not a talker. I'm a flyer,' he would say. But to no avail. He recalls one early assignment. 'So I crawl into a goddamn P80 in Muroc, roll up my uniform, stick it in the nose at 60 below zero, fly to Lansing, Michigan, land on the goddamn runway, shake the damn ice off me, and go to the hotel.' Nobody knows who he is and two minutes before his speech the head of the club asks him: what are you famous for? 'I almost got up and walked out.' Also, the reputation didn't help him within the air force, creating a lot of jealousy and enemies wanting to knock him down.

Soon, his career began to mesh with the space race. On the public-speaking circuit he often crossed paths with John Glenn, the first American to orbit the Earth, and before long the astronauts started coming to Edwards. In the 1950s it became the place where most of the prototype supersonic jets in the air force came for testing. This was a time of extraordinary technological achievement and endeavour, with attendant risk; at one stage a test pilot reached Mach 2 in his fighter, outraced the shells he had just fired from his cannons, and shot himself down.

Yeager was not a fan of the first round of NASA (then NACA) astronauts, considering them arrogant and unwilling to take advice. 'In the old days I rated them about as high as my shoelaces,' he says. He has zero sympathy for Scott Crossfield, a golden boy of NACA's early days who would later be the first man to pass Mach 2, but who put a prototype Super Sabre jet through the wall of an aircraft hangar in 1954. 'He was a proficient pilot, but also among the most arrogant I've met. Scotty just knew it all, which is why he ran a Super Sabre through a hangar,' he says. Yeager is no more reverent about Neil Armstrong. 'Armstrong may have been the first astronaut on the Moon, but he was the last guy at Edwards to take any advice from a military pilot.' Yeager never quite got over the time when Armstrong, against Yeager's advice, attempted to touch their plane down in a lakebed and got it stuck, marooning the pair of them. (Recalling the incident today, Yeager has mellowed, calling Armstrong 'a good guy'; Victoria interjects that the two get along fine now. Armstrong died shortly after our interview.)

In the early days of the Mercury programme that made household names of Alan Shepard, John Glenn and the rest, Yeager took great delight in pointing out that there was no flying involved and that the first flights were conducted by chimps (which was true). Many years on, Yeager still thinks very little of the space programme, Apollo included. 'What did we learn other than bringing back a few pieces of rocks from the Moon? The whole space mission programme in my opinion was a waste of a lot of money. What did we get out of it? Nothing. Sent up a bunch of people, go round the goddamn Moon.' Even Apollo? 'No. What did they do?'

Part of his contempt stems from the fact that during the Mercury, Gemini and Apollo programmes – which enriched astronauts – real flying innovation was taking place, largely un-noticed, in the air force, for no reward. This is the theme that underpins Wolfe's *The Right Stuff* and the film that followed. 'The film really laid it on the line,' Yeager says. 'What you saw was air-force test pilots killing themselves to support the space programme. And very few people knew it.'

His attitude is slightly odd because he later came back to Edwards to run an astronaut training programme that subse-quently put twenty-six people into space, mainly on the Space Shuttle; also his alumni from earlier test-pilot days included leading Apollo astronauts like Moonwalker Dave Scott, commander of *Apollo 15*, who he remembers fondly and with great admiration. (The feeling is mutual. One week earlier I had met Scott in Tucson and asked him what he thought I should ask Yeager. 'Just ask him about hunting,' he'd said. 'Then he'll talk all day.') So was Yeager's training school also a waste of money? 'No. We trained them here, then sent them over to NASA. NASA's the ones who wasted the money.'

Yeager himself was excluded from consideration for the space programme through lack of a college degree, but doesn't appear to regret it. 'I'm not for sending a dumb pilot who can't fly into combat, that's a bad choice. The same applies for going into space: you'd better get some smart guys.'

*

Yeager's name peppers the early history of jet flight and the space age. In fact, researching the book, it sometimes feels like half of my interviewees, and pretty much all the astronauts, have crossed paths with Yeager: Charlie Duke, Ed Mitchell, Bill Anders, Frank Borman. They remember him with a wide range of emotions from affection to contempt.

Borman, who is almost as unlikely to suffer fools gladly as Yeager himself, wrote of his time answering to Yeager: 'He spent an awful lot of time hunting and fishing but he was an excellent boss, completely supportive and very likeable in his own gruff way. He also happened to be one pilot who lived up to his press clippings.' Borman called him 'absolutely fearless, with a streak of the daredevil in him, an admirable trait in a test pilot but also a trait that on one unhappy occasion undid all the work we had put into our F-104 rocket planes.' The resulting crash is covered below, but its impact on Borman, who had worked to develop the plane, was unhelpful. He writes:

> The Air Force figured that if the world's greatest test pilot had nearly bought the farm in our bird, it must be inherently unsafe, and it was scrubbed from the Edwards training program. I had to blame Yeager for it. I thought he'd pulled a showboat stunt with an airplane designed for a specific purpose, and setting altitude records wasn't on its agenda. What Chuck had done was wipe out the most cost-effective vehicle ever developed for preliminary space training.

Still, Borman's conclusion on the man was mostly positive, which is more than can be said for Borman's *Apollo 8* crewman, Bill Anders. Sitting by a log fire at his home on Orcas Island in the far north-west of Washington State, Anders recalls how he had applied to Yeager's test-pilot school in order to get the requisite experience to enter NASA as an astronaut, only for NASA to change their own criteria, meaning Anders was eligible whether he got into Yeager's school or not. Anders was driving home from work at Albuquerque in a little Volkswagen when the radio broadcast the changed stance from NASA, and he pulled over to the side of the road to write down the details, wrote up a letter of application and got his wife, Valerie, to type it up. 'We had to do it four times, cos we had carbon paper in those days,' he recalls. He sent it in, got through round after round of interviews, and eventually received a call from Deke Slayton, head of astronaut selection and the man in charge of the crews for the Gemini and Apollo programmes, telling him he'd got in.

Shortly afterwards he received a call from Yeager, saying, 'Well, Anders, you didn't make it.' Anders replied, 'Well, Colonel, I got a better offer.' There was silence. When Anders explained, he says, Yeager said it wasn't possible because he, Yeager, had been chairman of the Air Force Selection Board, had screened all the applications and thrown out everybody who wasn't a test pilot, despite NASA no longer making that a criterion for selection. Anders, irritated by now, said it must have been down to the letter he'd sent. 'You went around channels,' Yeager told Anders. 'I'm gonna have you kicked out.' And, Anders said, he really did try. 'You bet he did. He was livid,' Anders says.

Slayton was pretty much as tough as Yeager was, and Yeager's attempts to remove Anders from NASA were unsuccessful, but Anders himself never forgot it, and was delighted to find in later life that he had finally come to outrank the legendary aviator. 'Years later, he retired as a brigadier general, and I retired as a major general,' Anders says. 'I usually try to play that down, but one time I pulled rank on him.' One time at an air show, Anders says, Yeager had claimed he'd been asked to fly the Space Shuttle, 'But I told 'em not until they cleaned out the banana peels and the monkey shit,' a reference to his familiar goading that astronauts' jobs could be done by apes. Then, later, Anders found himself at some event honouring Yeager, and put up his hand. 'Gentlemen,' he said, 'General Yeager has really had a fine career, though there is quite a bit of evidence that he wasn't the first guy to break the sound barrier. But in the sense of full disclosure, I really ought to tell you about a disturbing experience I had just last night regarding Brigadier General Yeager's red pickup truck, with the licence plate Bell X-1.' This was widely known to be Yeager's truck. 'I looked inside, and I'm sad to report it was full of banana peels and monkey shit.'

Anders tells the story as a good-natured bit of ribbing between old military men, but his distaste for the man – 'a piece of work', he calls him, and 'a sad man' – is pretty clear.

*

In the context of this book's central question – what next – Yeager is probably the one who, more than anyone else, just kept on doing exactly the same thing. In particular, he flew. He flew everything that could fly, and a few things that turned out not to be able to fly. Also, he crashed. He crashed planes before the sound barrier flights; he crashed planes afterwards.

Consider this extraordinary litany of near death, with commentary from his book.

1943: In a P-39 at 400 miles per hour over Wyoming, 'there was an explosion in the back. Fire came out from under my seat and the airplane flew apart in different directions. I jettisoned the door and stuck my head out, and the prop wash seemed to stretch my neck three feet. I jumped for it. When the chute opened, I was knocked unconscious. A sheepherder found me in the hills and tossed me across his burro, face down.' He ended up in hospital with a fractured back.

1944: Shot down over occupied France. 'The world exploded.

I ducked to protect my face with my hands, and when I looked a second later, my engine was on fire, and there was a gaping hole in my wingtip. The airplane began to spin. It happened so fast, there was no time to panic. I knew I was going down; I was barely able to unfasten my safety belt and crawl over my seat before my burning P-51 began to snap and roll, heading for the ground. I just fell out of the cockpit when the plane turned upside down – my canopy was shot away.' He escaped with shrapnel punctures in his feet and hands. This was the flight that led to his underground-protected escape from France.

1946: In a T-6 prop trainer with an instructor, the master rod blew apart in the engine over rural Ohio. Yeager aimed for two fields and landed in between them in the path of a farm-house, going through a chicken house and ending alongside the farmer's wife's kitchen window. 'She was at the sink, looking out, and I was looking her right in the eye through a swirl of dust and feathers. I opened the canopy and managed a small smile. "Morning, ma'am," I said. "Can I use your telephone?"'

1947: One month after breaking the sound barrier, Yeager's next flight in the X-1 went wrong when the plane was dropped from the mother ship and had no electrical power at all. Yeager, without radio, couldn't tell anyone. 'The ship is dead and I'm dropping like a bomb, loaded with five thousand pounds of volatile fuel, certain to blow a giant crater into the desert floor 20,000 feet below.' He managed to vent enough fuel to glide down at high speed and make a landing. Numerous later flights experienced smoke in the cockpit.

1950: Assigned by the air force to fly for the John Wayne and Janet Leigh film *Jet Pilot*, Yeager was asked to dive into a cloud inverted at 12,000 feet, then pull out near the ground. When he tried to pull out, the elevator ripped off his tail, taking about a third of the horizontal stabilizer with it. Too late to eject, he managed to land, but his wingman had assumed he had crashed and broadcast as much to the ground. Two days later the turbine wheel engine came out of his plane, 'leaving me sitting at 2,000 feet with no engine. I was feeling good that day.' He landed the plane without an engine.

1953: Now flying the new X-1A, Yeager aimed to reclaim the world speed record recently set by Scott Crossfield at Mach 2. He hit 2.4 but, having gone too high and fast, lost control. 'We started going in four different directions at once, careening all over the sky, snapping and rolling and spinning, in what pilots call going divergent on all three axes. I called it hell.' His visor fogged and he had no ejector seat. His helmet hit the canopy so hard it left a dent. After falling about 51,000 feet in fifty-one seconds, the plane entered a spin, which he corrected, successfully landing the plane. His wife Glennis would say this was the most shaken she ever saw him. Boyd (by now a general) said, 'I don't know of another pilot who could have walked away from that one.' Boyd would occasionally play the tape of Yeager's communication with the tower during this incident to new recruits as an example of dealing with intense stress.

1963: Yeager took a test flight in a Lockheed F-104 Starfighter, the first Mach 2 fighter aircraft, aiming to encounter zero G conditions and set a new altitude record. He reached 104,000 feet, but on descent the thrusters designed to keep the nose down didn't work. The engine locked and hydraulic pressure was lost. The plane made fourteen flat spins; Yeager stayed through thirteen, then ejected. Unfortunately his ejector seat, still spewing the rocket charge used in the ejection, became caught in his chute lines, hit him in the face, penetrated his helmet and ignited the rubber seal around it, which erupted in the pure oxygen environment. His head caught fire and his hand too as he tried to scoop in air to breathe. When he hit the ground a driver who had seen him descend came and offered to help. Yeager – his face like charred meat – requested a knife, cut off his glove, and parts of two of his burned fingers came off with it. 'The guy got sick,' Yeager recalls.

For all its bravado, this was the crash that enraged Frank Borman.

1965: Not flying this time, he and colleagues were at Rocky Basin Lakes in the high Sierra Nevada mountains and climbed into a Huey helicopter. It took off, climbed 80 feet, and descended upside down into the middle of the icy lake. He made it to the side of the lake, whereupon his colleague – a general – told him he could see Yeager's brains through a head wound. Undeterred, Yeager walked 9 miles to an airstrip, received 138 stitches, and made it home for a dinner party (which his wife shrewdly cancelled the moment he walked through the door).

*

At the time of writing, having flown 361 different aircraft, he has reached the age of ninety-one, and this seems as unlikely as Keith Richards still being alive.

After his near-death experience in the X-1A in 1953, Yeager began to consider life after test-flying. He asked his engineer, Jack Ridley, to calculate how long he could keep doing this before the law of averages suggested he should be dead. Ridley got his slide rule out and came to the conclusion that, statistically, Yeager had died three years ago. But in Okinawa, in 1954, he found himself in arguably the most dangerous test assignment yet: flying a Russian-built MiG-15 gained from a defecting North Korean.

Later assignments would take him to roles in Germany and Pakistan, service in Vietnam, and finally the rank of brigadier general. He never stopped flying. Commanding a tactical fighter wing in the Philippines for service in Vietnam in 1966, he accrued another 127 missions, this time mainly in a light bomber. He was, after all his early brushes with authority, his fear of intellectual inferiority and his feeling of being an outsider, a consummate air-force man, and could have stayed longer. In the end he retired in 1975 on curious terms that showed where his priorities really lay: he would be a consulting test pilot for the air force for no pay, on the condition he could fly all he wanted at Edwards.

Dave Scott, the astronaut and a devoted former student of Yeager, was the man who brokered the deal. 'I wonder if you would consider consulting with us on an official basis, including chase flights with the F-104s?' he recalls asking Yeager, in his autobiography. 'With our limited budget I must explain that we would only be able to afford to pay you a dollar a year, but you would be welcome to come fly whenever you like.' Yeager, he says, accepted instantly.

By 1979 Wolfe's book was out and, by 1983, the film, and only then did he really find himself truly famous outside of the aviation community. Life since then has involved a great deal of public appearance, consultancy, and his great loves in life: flying, and hunting.

He was called upon for years for public positions, although they didn't all go smoothly. He was put on the panel to investigate the explosion of the Space Shuttle *Challenger* in 1985, and recalls the accident. 'If you remember, they cancelled the launch the first day, then cancelled the second day, the PR guys are getting itchy because the press is leaving: we've got to get this thing in the air so we can get coverage. Well, they got it in the air, and they got coverage.' His lack of tact, while probably useful, drew criticism. 'I was one of the twelve accident board members. They showed us film of the fire coming out between the O-ring seal and squirting into the hydrogen tank. There it is, what do you need to do, look at it again? We could see what caused it, we all agreed. I left, and I was criticized because I didn't stay there and spend a month of Uncle Sam's money staying in a plush hotel doing nothing.'

In the years since Edwards, a considerable cult of personality has grown up around Yeager, partly to do with his extraordinary achievements in aircraft, partly about his uncompromising toughness, partly even around the way he talks.

Though it has mellowed today, Yeager was once renowned for the strength of his West Virginia accent; his first wife, when she met him, reckoned she could make out about one word in three. Major General Fred J Ascani, who was the executive officer in flight test in 1947, would later recall: 'He barely spoke English. I'm not referring to his West Virginia drawl; I mean grammar and syntax. He could barely construct a recognizable sentence.' This was something of an issue knowing that Yeager would, as a record-breaking hero, become a very public face. '[Colonel] Boyd fretted about the Air Corps' image if its hero didn't know a verb from a noun.'

But Tom Wolfe would argue in *The Right Stuff* that Yeager's accent had somehow permeated its way into the speech patterns of commercial aviation pilots across America. 'I agree with Tom Wolfe, a lot of people pick up your accent, and my accent used to be a hell of a lot worse than it is now,' he says today. 'It was obviously a lot of guys wanting to be me. But I didn't get to be me by hanging around a bar patting some gal on the butt. You had to work on it.'

An interview with Yeager is not the smoothest experience. Sitting in a lecture theatre in the test-flight school now, an exchange runs like this:

Question: Is there really such a thing as the right stuff?
Yeager: Nah. It sells books. It was Tom Wolfe trying to explain what does the right stuff mean; it's rather futile.

Question: Then what makes a great pilot?

Yeager: My answer would be: nobody ever told me what to do. My opinion is, the guys who do it on their own are the best. It's a simple statement but it is so true. If you have to run around and say how can I be the best, they'll wipe you off the slate.

Question: How did the MiG-15 fly?

Yeager: I was the first American to fly one. It was quite obvious when I walked up and looked at the airplane with its goddamn fixed stabilizers – they went out with the goddamn balloons. When I flew it I knew exactly how it was going to fly. At .94 Mach you're going to lose control, and I did.

Question: Deke Slayton said you should never ask a pilot who the best ever pilot is; you should ask who the second-best is, since the pilot is bound to think he's the best. Who's the second-best you flew with?

Yeager: If he's alive, he's a good pilot. It's that simple. It's not the best; some pilots have different capabilities, whether it's combat, test pilot or carrier pilot.

Question: When you were burned ejecting from the F-104 in a flat spin, was that the worst accident you had, the scariest?

Yeager: Probably, I reckon. I got a few holes in me during the war, but what the hell, it didn't kill me.

Question: When did you last fly a jet?

Yeager: October. Here. An F16. It's no problem. Hell, airplanes don't change, like the steering wheel on your car: you turn right, it turns right. I'm just lucky, I've been flying air-force planes for seventy-two years.

Question: Will you fly one again?

Yeager: I don't know. If I do I will, if I don't I won't. I don't live to do things like that.

Suffice to say I never got him on to any kind of introspection about moving on from a moment in history, or the oddity of having your most famous hour so young; he was having none of it. But at no stage did I ever feel there was a sense of false bravado about Yeager, or that he was being anything other than himself. He genuinely, in all honesty, in a way that is true of so very few people, does not appear to give a flying fuck what anybody thinks of him.

Yeager's toughness is at times alarming. When he was four and a half, his six-year-old brother was playing with his father's 12-gauge shotgun, found some shells, and accidentally shot and killed their baby sister. This unthinkably traumatic incident and its aftermath occupy seventeen lines of a 400-page autobiography, perhaps because it's a private matter, but also one suspects because he thinks there's nothing else to say. He never discussed it and nor did his parents. 'That's just the Yeager way; we keep our hurts to ourselves.'

And hurts there have been. Its is heartbreaking to read Yeager's 1985 autobiography when he notes, with triumph, that Glennis has beaten cancer; reading it today, we know that in fact she had just five years left to live before succumbing. And his second marriage has brought great friction with his children, three of whom sued them in 2004, leading in turn to Chuck Yeager suing his own children for diverting his pension fund in 2006; it all ended up in the California Court of Appeal in 2008, which ruled for Yeager. (Litigation appears, if anything, to be increasing with age. More recently, in early 2014, he and Victoria were being sued by a Sacramento homeowners' association about unpaid dues. And when I contact the Yeagers for

413

a fact check in March 2014, Victoria takes the opportunity to ask me to support Veterans Amicus, 'In defense of Brig Gen Chuck Yeager's name'; a related website reveals that Yeager has filed petitions with the California and United States Supreme Courts in order to keep control of his own name, whatever that means.) I decide not to ask him about the issues with his children, but they did receive widespread coverage with bitter quotes from all sides in US newspaper reports at the time, and none of them make for edifying reading. The only time I ask about his kids is when we are at the wreckage of the shack where they were raised, and he shuts it down quickly. 'Shit, they got their own damn lives,' he says.

There's no question he can harbour a grudge. Back at the remnants of his shack outside the base perimeter, he is still recalling the injustices meted out to him and his family as he made history for the air force on a pittance. 'Glennis got sick with our first daughter, really, really bad, and we had to take her to hospital in San Francisco. What do you do?' He looks again at the wreckage of his former home. 'The fucking people out here . . . it's hard, you're replacing a $150,000 pilot, $260 a month was my pay, and they wouldn't let me in the fucking base.'

A pause, before he turns to me. 'In your limited mental capacity, have you got what you need? Let's get out of this goddamn wind.'

Still, for all his angry resentments, his goddamns and sumbitches and a few more goddamns, he appears to be happy enough in life today, still getting out into the Sierra Nevada mountains to hunt. This explains the unlikely location where he and Victoria live: Nevada County, California, in pure suburbia but also near the foothills of the Sierra Nevada.

As our interview concludes, Victoria is cheerful. 'Hey, Charlie,' she says – she doesn't call him Chuck. 'I think we might have found an Englishman we like!' Yeager stands – he needs no help from anyone, bar the hearing aids made necessary from years behind thundering Mustang engines – and shakes my hand firmly. 'Well,' he says with that half-grin again. '*Maybe.*'

Epilogue

I could have gone on finding these people indefinitely. It's such a rich source of possibility: one can apply it to almost any walk of life within which people are celebrated for a clear high point. I really wanted Valentina Tereshkova, the first woman in space, but couldn't pin her down to an interview. In fact, I could give you a whole book's worth of women I'd like to interview in this vein: Cathy Freeman, Gillian Anderson, Khaleda Zia, Arundhati Roy. Perhaps that's the next book.

But I was already 50,000 words over the agreed total length and it was time to stop. Over the course of 2014 I set about contacting my earlier interviewees afresh to check facts and generally inquire on their welfare.

It was encouraging to find that, for the most part, none of them had shown any sign of settling into sedate restraint after a lifetime of exceptional existence. Don Walsh, who started me off on the whole adventure, was the first I contacted, and he was a case in point.

I had been in touch with Walsh from time to time over the subsequent years. Once, I interviewed him about the state of the *Titanic* wreck for the hundredth anniversary of the ship's sinking, since he's seen it up close from a submersible. When I reached him again in 2014, I asked what he was up to.

'Still travelling and consulting,' he wrote. 'Have done 100,000 air miles per year for the last four years.' Having told me, aged seventy-eight, that he was getting too old to be tripping over penguins, he now told me, aged eighty-two, that he was planning his fifth trip to the North Pole provided Russian–US tensions didn't get in the way. In 2013, he said, he did 140,000 miles and visited twenty countries. I never really thought he was going to calm down and it appears he did absolutely nothing of the sort.

We spoke again in early 2015 when I was researching an article on ocean exploration and the sea floor, a subject he discussed with passion and intensity for an hour and a half. Along the way, he mentioned a mooted expedition to dive on the wreck of Ernest Shackleton's *Endurance*, somewhere deep beneath the Antarctic ice. Would he want to go on such an expedition, I asked? 'Does Pinocchio have wooden nuts?'

Only one thing had changed, in fact: the proposed title of his still-unwritten 'unauthorized autobiography'. By now, he had decided to call it something else: 'Jockey on a One Trick Pony'.

*

Given their advancing years, I was worried that some interviewees might have fallen into ill health, and the one who concerned me most was Russ Ewin, the Second World War veteran I had last seen on a colonial verandah in Sandakan, Malaysia, since he was the oldest interviewee in the whole book. I didn't hear from him for some months from the email address he had given me, and began to fear the worst; he was the very last one I had not received a reply from.

But when I finally tracked him down again, through Gwenda

Zappala at the Sabah Tourism Board in October 2014, it became clear that I needn't have worried. Aged ninety-seven, Russ was not only in rude health but preparing to fly to Japan. He had been chosen as one of four POW representatives from Australia to receive a formal apology from Japan's Emperor; he was travelling there with Dick Braithwaite, the son of one of the six survivors of the death marches. 'Russ is a mighty man to be admired by all,' Gwenda wrote.

I'd simply misread his writing and put an 'l' where an 'i' should have been in his email address. Apparently happy to hear from me, though 'quite appalled' (his words) at being bracketed with such illustrious company, he set about dealing with my queries with his customary accountancy-honed efficiency and formal style. I forwarded his email to my wife. 'Oh, that we might both be that articulate at ninety-seven! He gives me hope,' she wrote. And he does give me hope, in all sorts of different ways.

In October 2014, Joe Kittinger was pushed just a little further into the history books when Alan Eustace, a Google executive, jumped from 130,000 feet, beating Felix Baumgartner's 2012 record. It was impressive, for sure, and Eustace is to be congratulated. But it won't dim my mental picture of Kittinger plunging into the nothing in 1960. Nothing can diminish the fearless style of that moment.

Astronauts, hostages, gymnasts, mountaineers, pilots, footballers, singers; gradually they all confirmed spellings and dates and all manner of other minutiae. I'm certain, in telling sixteen life stories, I will have made some errors, but I hope the gist of their lives is correct.

What did I learn from all this? Partly, what I expected to: that there is a fundamental richness to life that stops it ever truly being defined by a moment or ordeal, and that the best of us don't dwell on those moments any more than is healthy, but instead look to move forward, and to find new things to be inspired and affected by. Also, I came to understand the diversity of ways in which famous people achieve that: through big business like Anders or museums like Messner, through religion like Duke or advanced consciousness like Mitchell, through talking like Haynes or through being a Yorkshire undertaker like Wilson. There are the cheery and sanguine like Lovell and McCarthy, or the permanently contrary like Yeager. The difference, in fact, was the most gratifying part of researching the whole book.

When I look at them all now in the aggregate, I realize what a privilege it is to have spent time with such an exceptional group of people. I would have been disappointed to find them resting on their laurels, wanting only to talk about the past as if the job was done in a single day in their thirties or twenties or even their teens. But that wasn't the case, not once.

They'll all die eventually; of course they will. Neil Armstrong's passing was a sober reminder of the mortality of that whole era, as of all people. And when they're gone, they'll be remembered just as they already are: the first to the bottom of the sea, to the Moon, to break the sound barrier. Nobody will notice what they did next or think that as much as three-quarters of their lives came after their keystone events. But from having had the pleasure of spending time with so many of them, it's comforting to report that they didn't spend those long suffixed years just looking backwards.

Acknowledgements

A great many people assisted in the creation this book. Firstly and most obviously, I would like to thank the interviewees for their generosity in speaking with me despite there being no obvious benefit in it for them. Nobody was paid for an interview, although one did ask for a donation to a charity of his choice, which I was happy to make. So thanks once again to Don Walsh, Nadia Comaneci, Alan Bean, Charlie Duke, Edgar Mitchell, Reinhold Messner, Joe Kittinger, Gloria Gaynor, Al Haynes, Jan Brown, Jim Lovell, Bill Anders, Ray Wilson, John McCarthy, Russ Ewin and Chuck Yeager. Thanks also to other interviewees within these chapters: Les 'Bunny' Glover, Phillip Mairon Bahaja, Lynette Silver, Duane Ross, Alan Lipkin, Frank Kimbler and Mark Briscoe. My thanks too to Tun Dr Mahathir Mohamad, former Prime Minister of Malaysia, who generously agreed to an interview in Kuala Lumpur but whose interview regrettably did not make it into this volume.

Bill Anders also generously allowed me to use his iconic, wonderful *Earthrise* image on the front cover of this edition.

Thanks to the various agents, representatives, friends and spouses who were involved in arranging these interviews, or putting in a good word to help me secure them. These included

Acknowledgements

Peter Batson at Deep Ocean Expeditions; Paul Ziert and Bart Conner in Norman, Oklahoma; Nicole Cloutier and Gayle Frere at NASA; Kim and Sally Poor at Spacefest; Cathy Beals, EA to Ed Mitchell; Sherry Kittinger; Maddy Zeringue and Alexandra Schoen at Red Bull; Stephanie Gold, agent to Gloria Gaynor; Diane Titterington at Aviation Speakers; Maznah Bahari and Datuk Badariah Arshad in Putrajaya, Malaysia; Dydia DeLyser, archivist to Bill Anders; Mary Weeks, assistant to Jim Lovell; Room 54 Ltd; Gwenda Zappala at the Sabah Tourist Board; Jenny Smith; the Australian Commonwealth Department of Veterans' Affairs; Dan Nelson and Andy Booth at Huddersfield Town Football Club; Pat Wilson; Victoria Yeager; and Jo Burgess and Captain Jeremy Vanderhal at Edwards Air Force Base, California. Special thanks to Valerie Anders for her hospitality.

Scott Pack at The Friday Project was the first person in the publishing industry to believe in this idea and give it a chance, so immense thanks to him. The editor at The Friday Project, Rachel Faulkner, also provided great advice. Late in the day, the book was switched to another arm of HarperCollins, and I am enormously grateful to Martin Redfern for not only taking the book on at short notice, but keeping it on its original publishing schedule too. Doing so required the hard work of several wonderful William Collins staff: Morwenna Loughman, who coordinated the book and kept it on track with enriching good humour and calm; Helen Gray, who provided a thorough and intelligent copy edit and prevented me from spelling JRR Tolkien's name wrong; Louise Tucker, the proof reader; and another Chris Wright – no relation – in production. At the time of writing I was about to start working with Katherine Josselyn in PR and Candice Carty-Williams on marketing for the book, so thanks in advance to them too.

Many of these chapters draw on material of mine that was first published in magazines and newspapers, and I could not have funded the travel involved without the commissions from these editors. In particular I would like to thank Luke Clark and his predecessor Jeremy Torr at *Discovery Channel Magazine*, and Susan Skelly at *The Australian Way*. Without Luke in particular I'm just not sure this book would exist.

Many friends also helped with ideas, read-throughs, points of contact, or even translation (particularly when trying to track down cosmonauts or work out how good Gloria Gaynor's Arabic is). I would like to thank David Prosser, Antony Currie, Rahul Singh (who also kindly took my photo for the price of a pint of pale ale), Clive Horwood, Lisa Wells Evans, Ben Owen-Browne, Darya Kuznetsova, Irina Davenport, Maha Lozi, Sarah and Rachel Bridge, Inés Noé, Elliot Wilson and Colm Cronin. No less important were friends who helped with the kids while I was jetting off to see people, so thanks to Satini Marteraja – our much-loved friend and helper in Singapore who made all sorts of things possible – Louise Tughan, Sonia Delgado Sanchez and Monica Alvarado Gibson. I'm very sorry if I forgot anybody.

My mum and dad, Pat and Jim Wright, were a vital source of support for the same reason, frequently getting the train down from Liverpool at the drop of a hat to help out when I had a sudden interview overseas. It is thanks to them, too, that I have had the confidence and opportunity to write for a living. They have been tirelessly supportive throughout my whole life.

Finally, the greatest thanks to my wife Kathryn and our children Chyna Rose and Quinn, for endless support and love. I have been very lucky to marry someone with the same sense of adventure as me, and equally lucky to end up with kids who have tolerated being dragged around in pursuit of that sense of adventure. None of this would have been possible without them, and it wouldn't mean anything without them either. Love you all.

Bibliography

Apollo
The All-American Boys, Walter Cunningham, 1977
A Man on the Moon, Andrew Chaikin, 1994
Apollo 8: The NASA Mission Reports, ed. Robert Godwin, 1999
Carrying the Fire, Michael Collins, 1974
Countdown, Frank Borman with Robert J. Serling, 1988
Deke!, Donald K. Slayton with Michael Cassutt, 1994
Forever Young, John W. Young with James R. Hansen, 2012
The Last Man on the Moon, Eugene Cernan and Don Davis, 1999
Lost Moon, Jim Lovell and Jeffrey Kluger, 1994
Magnificent Desolation, Buzz Aldrin with Ken Abraham, 2009
Moondust: In Search of the Men Who Fell to Earth, Andrew Smith, 2005
Moonwalker, Charlie and Dotty Duke, 1990
The Outsiders: Eight Unconventional CEOs and their Radically Rational Blueprint for Success, William N. Thorndike, Jr, 2012 (specifically chapter 3, 'The Turnaround: Bill Anders and General Dynamics')
Riding Rockets, Mike Mullane, 2006
The Right Stuff, Tom Wolfe, 1979
Two Sides of the Moon, David Scott and Alexei Leonov, 2004

The Way of the Explorer, Dr Edgar Mitchell with Dwight Williams, 2008 edition

Nadia Comaneci
Letters to a Young Gymnast, Nadia Comaneci, 2004
My Story: The Autobiography of Olga Korbut, Olga Korbut with Ellen Emerson-White, 1992

Gloria Gaynor
Disco, Johnny Morgan, 2011
Soul Survivor, Gloria Gaynor with Liz Barr, 1995
Turn the Beat Around: The Secret History of Disco, Peter Shapiro, 2005
We Will Survive, Gloria Gaynor and Sue Carswell, 2013

Joe Kittinger
Come Up and Get Me, Joe Kittinger and Craig Ryan, 2010

John McCarthy and Lebanon Hostages
An Evil Cradling, Brian Keenan, 1993
Between Extremes, Brian Keenan and John McCarthy, 1999
Man Without a Gun, Giandomenico Picco, 1999
Some Other Rainbow, John McCarthy and Jill Morrell, 1993
Taken on Trust, Terry Waite, 1994
You Can't Hide the Sun, John McCarthy, 2012

Reinhold Messner
All 14 Eight-Thousanders, Reinhold Messner, 1999
The Naked Mountain, Reinhold Messner, translated by Tim Carruthers, 2005

Sandakan
Laden, Fevered, Starved. The POWs of Sandakan North Borneo, 1945. Richard Reid, Commonwealth Department of Veterans'

Affairs, 1999. Can be accessed at: www.dva.gov.au/aboutDVA/
publications/commemorative/sandakan/Documents/
sandakan_book.pdf
Personal history of Lieutenant Russell W. Ewin, NX76171 8th Division Signals. Can be accessed at: http://www.pows-of-japan.net/
booksetc/Composite%20Lt%20Russ%20Ewin.pdf

United 232
Air Crash Investigations: Drama in Sioux City, The Crash of United Airlines Flight 232, ed. Igor Korovin, 2011
Chosen to Live, Jerry Schemmel, 1996

Ray Wilson and 1966
The Best of Times, Simon Hattenstone, 2006

Chuck Yeager
Yeager, Chuck Yeager and Leo Janos, 1985